TRADITION AND THE FORMATION OF THE TALMUD

TRADITION AND THE
FORMATION OF THE TALMUD

Moulie Vidas

PRINCETON UNIVERSITY PRESS

Princeton and Oxford

Copyright © 2014 by Princeton University Press
Published by Princeton University Press, 41 William Street, Princeton, New Jersey 08540
In the United Kingdom: Princeton University Press, 6 Oxford Street, Woodstock,
    Oxfordshire OX20 1TW

press.princeton.edu

Jacket art: Giovanni Paolo Pannini, *Ancient Rome*, 1757. The Metropolitan Museum of Art,
Gwynne Andrews Fund, 1952 (52.63.1). Image © The Metropolitan Museum of Art.
Image source: Art Resource, NY.

Library of Congress Cataloging-in-Publication Data

Vidas, Moulie, 1983– author.
Tradition and the formation of the Talmud / Moulie Vidas.
    pages cm
Based on a thesis (Ph. D) Princeton University, 2009.
Includes bibliographical references and index.
ISBN 978-0-691-15486-2 (hardcover : alk. paper) 1. Talmud—History. 2. Jewish law—
    Interpretation and construction. I. Title.
BM501.V53 2014
296.1′25066—dc23
                    2013027785

British Library Cataloging-in-Publication Data is available

This book has been composed in Charis SIL, Adobe Hebrew, and Estrangello Edessa

Printed on acid-free paper. ∞

Printed in the United States of America

10 9 8 7 6 5 4 3 2 1

Contents

————

A Note on Style Conventions   vii

Introduction   1

PART I   21

CHAPTER ONE
The Alterity of Tradition   23

CHAPTER TWO
The Division into Layers   45

CHAPTER THREE
Composition as Critique   81

PART II   113

CHAPTER FOUR
Scholars, Transmitters, and the Making of *talmud*   115

CHAPTER FIVE
The Debate about Recitation   150

CHAPTER SIX
Tradition and Vision   167

Conclusion   203

Acknowledgments   215

Bibliography   217

Source Index   233

Subject Index   237

A Note on Style Conventions

Biblical verses are quoted from the New Revised Standard Version, sometimes with modifications that clarify the rabbinic reading of the verses. Biblical book references are in standard abbreviated form (*Chicago Manual of Style*). Translations from other Hebrew and Aramaic sources are mine unless otherwise noted, but are often adapted from standard translations. Talmudic references appear in abbreviated form according to the *SBL Handbook of Style*. I used Chanoch Albeck's revision and expansion of traditional rabbinic chronology to identify rabbis by generation (*Introduction to the Talmud, Babli and Yerushalmi*). Talmudic manuscripts were consulted through the Sol and Evelyn Henkind Talmudic Text Databank of the Saul Lieberman Institute of Talmudic Research; references to manuscripts rely on versions and identifications in that database.

TRADITION AND THE FORMATION OF THE TALMUD

INTRODUCTION

The Babylonian Talmud (or Bavli), which was produced in the Jewish academies of sixth- and seventh-century Mesopotamia, is a composite document that proceeds by reproducing earlier literary traditions and placing them within anonymous discursive frameworks.[1] This book concerns the relationship between the creators of the Talmud and these traditions.

For a long time, the Talmud was seen as a conservative storehouse of its traditions, but in the past few decades scholars have recognized the creativity that went into its compilation. Still, even recent accounts of the Talmud's formation understand this creativity in terms of continuity with tradition. The scholars who shaped the Talmud, according to these accounts, creatively revised or interpreted traditions to fit new ideas and contexts, but they did so precisely because they made no distinctions between themselves and the material they received; alternatively, these scholars were aware that their interpretation of tradition was innovative, but saw in it the restoration or recovery of lost meaning. In contrast with these accounts, this book argues that a discontinuity with tradition and the past is central to the Talmud's literary design and to the self-conception of its creators.

The "tradition" in the title of this book refers to the body of received literary material—dicta, teachings, exegetical comments, etc.—which is

---

1 On the dating of the Talmud, see Richard Kalmin, "The Formation and Character of the Babylonian Talmud," in *The Cambridge History of Judaism IV: The Late Roman-Rabbinic Period* (ed. S. T. Katz; Cambridge: Cambridge University Press, 2006), 840–76 (840). On the last stages of the development, see in particular Yaacov Sussmann, "Veshuv li-yerushalmi neziqin," in *Talmudic Studies I* (ed. Y. Sussmann and D. Rosenthal; Jerusalem: Magnes, 1990), 55–134 (101–3 and 106–11). On the academic context, see David Goodblatt, "The History of the Babylonian Academies," in *The Cambridge History of Judaism IV: The Late Roman-Rabbinic Period*, 821–39; Jeffrey Rubenstein, "The Rise of the Babylonian Rabbinic Academy: A Reexamination of the Talmudic Evidence," *Jewish Studies: an Internet Journal* 1 (2002), 55–68.

identified and represented in the Talmud as received material. There are, to be sure, other ways in which we can speak of tradition in the Talmud: in its literary practice, the Talmud continues a tradition of composition that is evident in earlier rabbinic documents; the Talmud's imagery and ideas are drawn from a broad Jewish tradition that goes back many centuries; some traditional textual material—especially terms, formulations, and structures—had a considerable role in shaping the Talmud, but the Talmud's creators embed this material in their composition rather than quote it, not marking it as received from other sources. One cannot speak of the Talmud's literary formation without touching on these matters, but they are not the subject of this book.

My discussion of tradition here centers on the ways in which the designation of something as "traditional" can be used to invoke discontinuity. We can say, for example, of a certain style that it is "traditional" in order to contrast it with "contemporary," and whether we use this contrast to praise or condemn, we indicate with it that the "traditional" style is no longer "contemporary," that there is a difference between that which belongs strictly to the present and that which we received from the past. A similar function of marking something as "traditional" occurs in some religious, legal, and philosophical traditions that distinguish between different kinds of justifications and commitments: in some Talmudic passages, for example, justification that appeals to tradition is distinguished from justification that appeals to reason or logical deduction. This use of "tradition" contrasts what our own reason guides us to do or think with what tradition guides us to do or think. In both of these contrasts, the one between the past and the present and the one between reason and tradition, we posit a gap between us and what is termed "tradition": this is "traditional" rather than "contemporary" because our style has changed; this is based on "tradition" and not on "reason" because we would have acted differently if it were not for tradition.

The first part of this book proposes that this alterity of tradition is central to the Bavli's literary design. The Talmud's creators employ a variety of compositional techniques to create a distance between themselves and the traditions they quote, highlight the contrast between themselves and these traditions, and present these traditions as the product of personal motives of past authorities. While they remain authoritative and binding, these traditions' claim to enduring validity is significantly undermined; they are fossilized and contained in the past, estranged from the Talmud's audience. The second part of the book argues that the Talmud's creators defined themselves in opposition to those who focused on the transmission of tradition, and that the opposition and hierarchy they created between scholars and transmitters allows us both to understand better the way they conceived of their project as well as to see this project as part of a debate about sacred texts within the Jewish community and more broadly in late ancient Mesopotamia.

THE CURRENT VIEW OF THE TALMUD'S AUTHORSHIP AND ITS INTELLECTUAL ORIGINS[2]

Scholarship from the second half of the twentieth century on has concentrated on the literary artifice of the Talmud's redactors or creators, replacing the model by which the Talmud was seen as a thesaurus faithfully conserving the traditions of the Tannaitic and Amoraic periods.[3] A variety of formative literary activities was now attributed to the sages living toward the end of what we call the Talmudic period, whether scholars chose to identify these sages with the last generations of the Amoraic period,[4] with the enigmatic savora'im known from traditional rabbinic chronologies,[5] or with the modern construct Stammaim ("those of the

2 I focus here only on developments in recent decades, without an attempt to offer a comprehensive history of critical scholarship; earlier theories are mentioned occasionally, especially in the footnotes. For doxographies of earlier studies on the Talmud's formation, see Mordechai Tenenblatt, *The Formation of the Babylonian Talmud* (Heb.; Tel Aviv: Dvir, 1972), and Jacob Neusner (ed.), *The Formation of the Babylonian Talmud: Studies in the Achievements of Late Nineteenth and Twentieth Century Historical and Literary-Critical Research* (Leiden: Brill, 1970).

3 Earlier studies that were particularly determinative of this development include Nehemia Brüll, "Die Entstehungsgeschichte des Babylonischen Talmud als Schriftwerkes," in idem, *Jahrbücher für Jüdische Geschichte und Literatur II* (Frankfurt: W. Erras, 1876), 1–123 (see, e.g., the famous line on p. 20, "R. Abina hat . . . die Tradition in Literatur verwandelte"); Israel Lewy's introduction to his *Interpretation des I.–VI. Abschnittes des pälast. Talmud-Traktats Nesikin* (Heb. and Ger.; Breslau, 1895–1914; repr. Jerusalem: Kedem, 1970), 1–23; Julius Kaplan, *The Redaction of the Babylonian Talmud* (New York: Bloch, 1933); and Abraham Weiss's works, e.g., *The Talmud in its Development* (Heb.; New York: Feldheim, 1954).

4 In early studies that did focus on literary activity, that was the prevailing view. See, e.g., Brüll, "Entstehungsgeschichte"; in contemporary scholarship, see Robert Brody, "The Anonymous Talmud and the Words of the Amoraim" (Heb.), in *Iggud: Selected Essays in Jewish Studies: Volume 1* (Heb.; ed. B. J. Schwartz, A. Shemesh, and A. Melamed; Jerusalem: Magnes, 2009), 213–32 (226–27).

5 See, e.g., Kaplan, *Redaction*; for later studies, see Richard Kalmin, *The Redaction of the Babylonian Talmud: Amoraic or Saboraic* (Cincinnati: Hebrew Union College Press, 1989), though "Saboraic" there seems to mean mostly "post-Amoraic." The main reason *not* to identify the redaction of the Talmud with these sages is that the activities attributed to them in Geonic-period literature are mostly additions to what seems to be an already crystallized text, whereas the creators of the Talmud as we know them now have done much more than that; see, e.g., David Halivni, *Sources and Traditions: A Source Critical Commentary on the Talmud: Tractate Baba Bathra* (Heb.; Jerusalem: Magnes, 2007), 10–11. One wonders, however, whether the Geonim saw it that way.

anonymous voice" or "anonymous ones"), or use generic terms such as *aharonim* ("later ones").[6]

The literary activities that scholars now attribute to these later sages include the composition of the *stam*—the anonymous, discursive, interpretive layer of the Talmud; the shaping of the *sugyot* (sing. *sugya*)—the "discourses" or "essays" that constitute the Talmud; the adaptation and transformation of various Tannaitic and Amoraic sources embedded in the Talmud; and, in some cases, the composition of Talmudic stories.

While the image of the Talmud's creators that emerged from these studies was of great innovators of striking originality, scholars have explained this creativity in terms of continuity with tradition. According to David Weiss Halivni, the Talmud's authors, or Stammaim (as he calls them), received their traditions in "apodictic" form, without reasoning or justification. They then reproduced what they received faithfully, and composed the anonymous layer in order to justify these traditions. Their enterprise is thus innovative in the sense that for the first time the reasoning of tradition was put into literary form, but it is essentially a reconstructive enterprise, whereby the later generation recovers lost meaning and justifies its heritage.[7]

Shamma Friedman sees the Bavli's authors as "creative transmitters": they do not reproduce the earlier traditions verbatim, but rather constantly adapt, appropriate, and reformulate these traditions in order to "improve" them (Friedman's term) and harmonize them with new literary, legal, and ideological contexts.[8] Here the Bavli's creators are inno-

---

6 See, e.g., Sussmann, "Yerushalmi," 109 n. 204.

7 Halivni developed his theory of the Talmud's formation in the introductions to the volumes of his *Sources and Traditions*; the most recent account is in *MM BB*, 1–148. A much shorter version of this introduction appeared in English as "Aspects of the Formation of the Talmud" (trans. and ed. J. Rubenstein), in *Creation and Composition* (ed. J. Rubenstein; Tübingen: Mohr Siebeck, 2005), 339–60. While this introduction is comprehensive, it is naturally more concerned with new developments in Halivni's approach as well as responses to various criticisms; for a more general account of his theory, see David Halivni, *Midrash, Mishnah and Gemara: The Jewish Predilection for Justified Law* (Cambridge, MA: Harvard University Press, 1986), 76–92.

8 Friedman's classical statement on the Talmud's formation is "A Critical Study of Yevamot X with a Methodological Introduction" (Heb.), in *Texts and Studies: Analecta Judaica I* (Heb.; ed. H. Z. Dimitrovsky; New York: Jewish Theological Seminary of America, 1977), 275–441 (especially 283–301). He developed his notion of "creative transmission" to explain variation in the manuscripts of the Talmud (see idem, "On the Formation of Textual Variation in the Bavli" [Heb.], *Sidra* 7 [1991], 67–102), and then subsequently applied it to rabbinic literary production in general, and to the Bavli's treatment of its sources in particular; see idem, "Ha-baraitot ba-talmud ha-bavli ve-yahasan le-maqbiloteihen sheba-tosefta," in *Atara L'haim: Studies in the Talmud and Medieval Rabbinic Literature in Honor of Professor Haim Zalman Dimitrovsky* (Heb.; ed. D. Boyarin et al.; Jerusalem: Magnes, 2000), 163–201 (191–92). This note refers to the original publications for

vating through the changes that they introduce to tradition, but the continuity between them and their sources is even more pronounced than it is in Halivni's model. These creators express their voice through the modification of their sources, by retrojecting their words or opinions into traditions attributed to past authorities, often unconsciously. They sense such a continuity between themselves and their literary heritage that they simply reconstruct it in their own image.

Yaakov Sussmann similarly presents the post-Amoraic stage as the stage in which the Talmud became the Talmud, attributing the structuring, final formulation, and organization of *sugyot* to the later generations. But Sussmann, too, presents this composition as an unconscious process that blurs the lines between tradition and interpretation, between early and late, between the Talmud and the traditions it utilizes.[9]

Jacob Neusner's account differs from those of Halivni, Friedman, and Sussmann in the consciousness, purpose, and confidence that he attributes to what he terms "the Bavli's authorship," but his model also posits a continuity with tradition. Neusner argues that through a process of selection, reformulation, and systematization, the Bavli's creators form a single, unified voice with a coherent message to which tradition is subjugated or adapted.[10]

These studies, then, locate Talmudic creativity in the attribution of new concepts, ideas, and interpretations to earlier sources, through either the composition of commentary on earlier traditions, the revision of these traditions, or the composition of new traditions that are then attributed to earlier sages. These activities themselves are often construed as unconscious (thus Sussmann and Friedman—as well as Jeffrey Rubenstein and Daniel Boyarin),[11] and even when consciousness exists, it is described in terms of restoration and recovery (Halivni), of a sense of continuity that allows for creative transmission (Friedman), or of a homogenizing authorship that constructs a unified system from received

---

historical purpose; references from here on are to the versions reprinted in Friedman's collected studies.

9   Sussmann, "Yerushalmi"; see especially 108–11 and nn. as well as 105 and n. 196.

10   See Neusner's summary of his studies on the Bavli in Jacob Neusner, *The Bavli's One Voice: Types and Forms of Analytical Discourse and their Fixed Order of Appearance* (Atlanta: Scholars Press, 1991), xvii–xxix. For a more recent recapitulation and conclusion of his ideas on the Bavli, see idem, *The Reader's Guide to the Talmud* (Leiden: Brill, 2001), especially 3–29 and 259–93.

11   Jeffrey Rubenstein, *The Culture of The Babylonian Talmud* (Baltimore: Johns Hopkins University Press, 2003), 6–7; Daniel Boyarin, *Border Lines: The Partition of Judaeo-Christianity* (Philadelphia: University of Pennsylvania Press, 2004), 66 and 154; idem, "Hellenism in Jewish Babylonia," in *The Cambridge Companion to the Talmud and Rabbinic Literature* (ed. C. E. Fonrobert and M. S. Jaffee; Cambridge: Cambridge University Press, 2007), 336-63 (342).

material (Neusner). The Talmud's creators, in these images, do not claim an identity or voice of their own, distinct from that of their traditions.

This image of Talmudic creativity is tied with specific images of tradition and authorship that derive in part from the rabbinic texts themselves and in part from modern theories of religion and literature. Rabbinic texts sometimes portray their own creativity as part of an almost timeless continuum that begins with the revelation at Mount Sinai and then unfolds through the ages; one famous teaching asserts that "Scripture, Mishnah, Talmud, Aggadah, and even what an advanced disciple will teach in the future before his teacher was already said to Moses on Sinai" (y. Pe'ah 2:6 17a and parallels).

One of the most influential modern accounts of this view is Gershom Scholem's essay, "Revelation and Tradition as Religious Categories in Judaism." Scholem not only explicates this idea but also connects it with the nature of rabbinic literary production:

> What this claim amounted to was that all this [rabbinic teaching] was somehow part of revelation itself—and more: not only was it given along with revelation, but it was given in a special, *timeless* sphere of revelation in which all generations were gathered together. . . . The achievement of every generation, its contribution to tradition, was projected back into the *eternal present* of the revelation at Sinai. . . . The exploring scholar . . . develops and explains that which was transmitted on Sinai, no matter whether it was always known or whether it was forgotten and had to be discovered. The effort of the seeker after truth consists not in having new ideas but rather in *subordinating himself to the continuity of tradition* of the divine word and in laying open what he receives from it in the context of his time. . . . *this is a most important principle indeed for the kind of productivity we encounter in Jewish literature.*[12]

This passage illustrates well the various accounts of Talmudic composition surveyed above: the Bavli's creators freely mold the traditions they received in their own image, attribute to the earlier sages their own ideas or even compositions, or see in their activity the rediscovery or recovery of lost, eternal meaning.[13]

---

12 Gershom Scholem, "Revelation and Tradition as Religious Categories in Judaism" (trans. H. Schwarzschild and M. A. Meyer), in idem, *The Messianic Idea in Judaism* (New York: Schocken, 1971), 282–303 (288–89); emphases added.

13 A connection between statements like the one in y. Pe'ah and the act of the Talmud's composition is made in Sacha Stern, "Attribution and Authorship in the Babylonian Talmud," *JJS* 45 (1994), 28–51 (49–50), and idem, "The Concept of Authorship in the Babylonian Talmud," *JJS* 46 (1995), 183–95 (193–95). Stern recognizes that the Bavli also includes statements of the opposite kind—see "Attribution," 50, and especially

This focus on traditional continuity extends beyond the study of Judaism and it can be illustrated with two modern developments in the study of society and literature. The first development, common in sociologies and histories of religion, is suspicious of this sort of continuity claim and understands tradition as a form of power legitimation. Max Weber, for example, views tradition as a type of authority and understands claims to tradition as attempts to legitimize control over habits and practices by tracing this control, as well as a desired form of these habits and practices, to "the eternal yesterday."[14]

The other development, celebratory rather than suspicious of traditional continuity, is evident in a variety of theories of interpretation, specifically Hans-Georg Gadamer's. For Gadamer, the continuity of tradition functions not as a legitimation of domination but as a necessary, always-present condition for certain or even all kinds of interpretation: "the horizon of the present cannot be formed without the past . . . understanding is always the fusion of these horizons . . . in a tradition this process of fusion is continually going on, for there old and new are always combining into something of living value, without either being explicitly foregrounded from the other."[15]

Modern accounts of tradition in rabbinic literature do not derive directly from these theories and do not follow them in their specific details,[16] but both kinds of explanations for tradition—either as a form of legitimation or as a characteristic of interpretation—appear in Scholem's essay as well as in accounts of Talmudic composition. The Talmud's retrojection of new ideas, institutions, and interpretations to the past is explained as an ideologically driven way to legitimize them; the attribution of new literary creation to previous generations is explained as an exercise of claiming more authority for new literary material, similar to the

---

"Concept," 186–89 and 195, where he discusses the "Bavli's dialectical oscillation between creativity and tradition, individual authorship and collective anonymity," but when he discusses the compositional practice itself, he only appeals to "tradition" and "collective anonymity."

14 The classical division of types of authority appears in Max Weber, *Economy and Society: An Outline of Interpretive Sociology* (ed. G. Roth and C. Wittich; 2 vols.; Berkeley: University of California Press, 1968), 1.215. Weber uses the expression "the authority of 'the eternal yesterday' " in another account of this division in his essay "Politics as a Vocation"; see *From Max Weber: Essays in Sociology* [2nd ed.] (ed. and trans. H. H. Gerth and C. Wright Mills; London: Routledge, 1991), 78–79.

15 Hans-Georg Gadamer, *Truth and Method* [2nd ed.] (trans. J. Weinsheimer and D. G. Marshall; London: Continuum, 2004), 305.

16 Gadamer's hermeneutic theory was applied to the analysis of rabbinic sources, though not to the process of composition but rather to their practices of biblical exegesis. See Moshe Halbertal, *Values in Interpretation* (Heb.; Jerusalem: Magnes, 1998), 193–95.

practice of pseudepigraphy in the Second Temple period.[17] Often at the same time, the Talmud's creative transmission of legal traditions and its retelling of narratives are described as the "fusion" that occurs in the process of traditional interpretation.

The emphasis in current models of Talmudic composition on revision and adaptation as the locus of literary creativity was determined in part by a turn away, in the study of rabbinic literature, from the traditional Western notion of authorship. This development is grounded in the observation of central features of rabbinic literature as well as explicit rabbinic statements: all classical rabbinic texts, including the Talmud, are anonymous; their transmitters, in some cases up until the advent of print, approached them as open texts to one degree or another, and they were subject to changes first by oral performers and then by scribes;[18] many rabbinic texts are inconsistent and betray multiple authors with multiple concerns and styles; some rabbinic statements, such as the statement we have seen earlier from *y. Pe'ah*, devalue individual creativity and understand it in continuous, collective terms. Scholars have also used the work of Roland Barthes and Michel Foucault, which emphasized the historical particularity of our notion of authorship, to argue for the inapplicability of this notion to the analysis of rabbinic literature.[19] The rising recognition in the second half of the twentieth century that many rabbinic texts, including the Talmud, were composed and transmitted orally, also contributed to this development, and rabbinic literary creativity in late antiquity was now seen as the performative, fluid inflection of tradition typical of oral cultures.[20]

While these images of tradition, authorship, and literary production were often developed with the entirety of the classical rabbinic corpus in mind, here we are only concerned with their applicability to the Babylo-

---

17   The connection is made explicitly in Shamma Friedman, *Talmudic Studies: Investigating the Sugya, Variant Readings and Aggada* (Heb.; New York and Jerusalem: Jewish Theological Seminary, 2010), 61.

18   See Peter Schäfer, "Research into Rabbinic Literature: An Attempt to Define the *Status Quaestionis*," *JJS* 37 (1986), 139–52, and on the Bavli in particular, Friedman, *Talmudic Studies*, 163–64.

19   For a recent formulation of this view of rabbinic authorship in general, see Martin Jaffee, "Rabbinic Authorship as a Collective Enterprise," in *The Cambridge Companion to the Talmud* (ed. C. E. Fonrobert and M. S. Jaffee; Cambridge: Cambridge University Press, 2007), 17–37 (and the discussion of literary theory, 19–20 and 35 n. 2); see also Stern, "Attribution" (and the discussion of Barthes, 48–59) and "Concept," though by "authorship in the Bavli" Stern does not mean the self-conception and practices of the Bavli's creators but rather the way the document portrays the literary activity of the rabbis cited in it.

20   See, e.g., Sussmann, "Yerushalmi," 110 and n. 207, 108 n. 203; Boyarin, *Border Lines*, 66 and 154; Jaffee, "Rabbinic Authorship," 33–34.

nian Talmud; and with respect to this Talmud, I argue, these views offer only a partial picture.

THE TALMUDIC VEIL

We will have the chance in the next couple of chapters to rehearse in more detail some of the theories of the Talmud's formation. Here, I would like to discuss briefly how the purpose of the studies in which these theories were developed influenced their image of Talmudic literary creativity. As we have seen, one of the most common images of Talmudic authorship in these studies is the adaptation and modification of tradition, the retrojection of later words and ideas into received material through reformulation and contextualization. The choice to focus on these acts of composition rather than others derives, in part, from the interest of earlier scholarship not in the Talmud itself, but in the earlier Tannaitic and Amoraic traditions that it preserves, and more generally in its reliability as a witness for the periods prior to its composition.

This interest can be observed in several of the foundational documents of Talmudic scholarship in the past decades, which often portray the literary structure created by the Talmud's authors as a layer from which we have to excavate the Amoraic material that is really worthy of investigation. Friedman identifies the purpose of his method of Talmudic study in a key paragraph in the essay that has shaped the consensus among American scholars:

> The collation of Amoraic formulations *apart from* the words of the anonymous layer of the Talmud shall place before scholars of Talmudic law, Jewish history and rabbinic language a *reliable corpus* of traditions, as opposed to the anonymous layer of the Talmud, in which many of the formulations, being the "give and take," are necessarily rejections and conjectures.[21]

E. S. Rosenthal, one of the most influential Israeli scholars, dedicated much of his research to the reconstruction of a *"genuine* Amoraic Talmud,"[22] and opened his much-cited study of *b. Pesaḥim* with an impressive reconstruction of such an "early Talmud": an arrangement of Tannaitic and Amoraic traditions not yet embedded in the dialectical

---

21 Friedman, *Talmudic Studies*, 30. These words, published in 1977, were somewhat retracted in an article published in 2010—see ibid., 60.

22 The expression itself appears in Eliezer S. Rosenthal, "Rav ben aḥi rabbi ḥiyyah gam ben aḥoto?" in *Henoch Yalon: Jubilee Volume* (Heb.; ed. S. Lieberman et al.; Jerusalem: Kiryat Sepher, 1963), 281–337 (322 n. 94); emphasis added.

construction that would characterize the developed *sugya*.[23] Sussmann concludes his influential essay on *Yerushalmi Neziqin* with the statement that the "essence" of the critical study of the Bavli is "the separation of the Amoraic nucleus and its various components from the late Babylonian *sugya*."[24] It is significant that in this programmatic statement, Sussmann does not make the additional distinction between the words of the Talmud's creators and even later interpretations, interpolations, and formulations, a distinction that he does make elsewhere:[25] when he thinks of the "essence" of Talmudic scholarship, the study of all post-Amoraic developments is ancillary. Halivni writes in his recent work about the purpose of his lifetime project: "we have dedicated much study to the time and enterprise of the Stammaim not because of their historical importance *per se*, but mostly because of their contribution to the contrived questions and the forced solutions in the Talmud."[26] Even the study most dedicated to the Talmud's authors sees in their enterprise a contrived interpretive layer that needs to be removed if we are to appreciate correctly the traditions it presents. As Halivni writes elsewhere: "between us and the Amoraim stand the Stammaim."[27]

This exclusive focus on the Amoraic period was driven by a variety of concerns, some of which have their roots in the medieval and early modern commentary tradition.[28] In the studies noted above, the anonymous layer was portrayed as mere literary artifice of contrived objections and solutions, as opposed to "reliable tradition," a contrast that was given different meanings when used in a traditional context (we want to know the law, we have no interest in the rhetorical structure)[29] or a historical context (we want to know the Amoraic opinion, not some later interpretation of unknown origin).[30] To this was added a modern aesthetic sensibility that preferred the succinct Amoraic dicta over the "tralatitious" and "meandering" *sugyot*.[31]

Contemporary scholarship has increasingly focused on the Talmud as an object of study in its own right. To give just two pioneering examples,

---

23   Eliezer S. Rosenthal, "Le-'arikhat masekhet pesaḥ rishon: bavli" (Ph.D. dissertation, Hebrew University of Jerusalem, 1959), 1–5.

24   Sussmann, "Yerushalmi," 113.

25   Sussmann, "Yerushalmi," 109 n. 205.

26   Halivni, *MM BB*, 1.

27   Halivni, *Midrash*, 77.

28   See Friedman, *Talmudic Studies*, 12–15, and see more in the Conclusion of this book.

29   On this approach in medieval literature, see Yedidya Dinari, "The Attitude to the Talmudic 'shinuya' in the Rabbinical Literature" (Heb.), *Bar Ilan* 12 (1974), 108–17.

30   See, e.g., the statements by Sussmann and Friedman cited above.

31   See Rosenthal's description of Babylonian literary development in "Redaction," 6.

Rubenstein's *Culture of the Babylonian Talmud* reconstructs the cultural values of the Bavli's creators,[32] while Leib Moscovitz's *Talmudic Reasoning* gives these creators the same attention it gives Tannaitic and Amoraic sages, and reveals their determinative contribution to the history of legal abstraction in rabbinic literature.[33] Still, the former interest in the Amoraic material has shaped our rules of attention in a way that is evident even today. We have gotten so used to approaching the enterprise of the Talmud's creators as the veil through which we must look in order to see the real objects of our interest that even as we turn to that enterprise itself we continue to focus on its veiling functions, only now the veil itself has become our interest. The focus in so much of contemporary scholarship on adaptation, reformulation, and retrojection is thus continuous with the interests and methods developed by scholars who were not interested in the Talmud itself.

This focus has certainly produced great results for the study of the Bavli, and it is impossible to analyze a Babylonian *sugya* without encountering activities such as reformulation, adaptation, and interpolation. When this focus is exclusive, however, it can create a misleading image of the self-consciousness and purpose of the Bavli's creators. If we think of the Talmud's creators mostly as introducing unconscious modifications, as hiding themselves behind their traditions and retrojecting their own words and ideas into them,[34] as adapting tradition to new contexts and "improving" it,[35] it is because we have focused on these specific activities and not others. The Bavli's creators themselves are not hiding: they are there in almost every *sugya*, structuring the discussion and leading the reader (or listener) through the sources, expressing their voice in the anonymous discussion that organizes most of the Talmud. While their choice of anonymity in itself might be seen as an act of deference toward their predecessors, their literary practice betrays a different set of priorities. As Rosenthal writes, perhaps resentfully, of the dialectical move that characterizes the late, developed *sugya*:

> This dialectical "move" overshadows the sources themselves (Mishnaic traditions, external traditions, Amoraic traditions), which are cited only, as it were, to be used as weapons in the war of Torah: a point of departure and "a proposition" to be disputed; a counter-proof; a supporting proof. *And the war is principal, and the weapon is merely auxiliary.*[36]

32 Rubenstein, *Culture*.
33 Leib Moscovitz, *Talmudic Reasoning: From Casuistics to Conceptualization* (Tübingen: Mohr Siebeck, 2002); see especially the conclusion, 350–51.
34 Boyarin, "Hellenism," 342.
35 Friedman, "Baraitot," 191.
36 Rosenthal, "Redaction," 5; emphasis added.

Jacob Neusner's image of the Bavli's relationship with its traditions might also derive from his early interest in the reliability of the Bavli as a source for historical reconstruction; but more important is the fact that Neusner developed his account of the Bavli as part of a broader effort to establish his "Documentary Hypothesis." The "hypothesis" can be roughly summarized as suggesting that rabbinic texts (or "documents") present a coherent, systematic program, that each of them is to be read as a whole, that they subject each of their sources to a revision that imposes coherency, that they are not "compilations of this and that."[37]

For Neusner, the Bavli is the jewel in the "documentary" crown: the Bavli "is not the product of a servility to the past . . . but of an exceptionally critical, autonomous rationalism."[38] It is the most documentary of documents, in that its authors created an absolutely systematic, homogenous text: "when reason governs, it reigns supreme and alone, revising the received materials and, through its powerful and rigorous logic, restating into a compelling statement the entirety of the prior heritage of information and thought."[39]

Neusner's approach has been subjected to systematic criticism by a number of scholars;[40] the critical argument most relevant to our purposes here is that the Bavli, in the end, is far from a homogenous document: not only does it contain many redactional layers that contradict one another or respond to one another,[41] but it also contains many sources that seem not to have been revised and do not conform to the rhetorical plan, message, or even idiom of the Bavli's creators.[42] Some scholars have taken these unrevised sources as evidence for the absence of a guiding, deliberative authorial hand, not to mention Neusner's "autonomous rationalism."[43] In my discussions of Talmudic passages, I hope to show that it is precisely in the lack of revision that a critical authorship may be

---

37   Neusner summarizes his general position in Jacob Neusner, *Are the Talmuds Interchangeable?* (Atlanta: Scholars Press, 1995), ix–xiii.

38   Jacob Neusner, *Extra- and Non-Documentary Writing in the Canon of Formative Judaism: Volume 3: Peripatetic Parallels* (Binghamton: Binghamton University Global Publications, 2001), 44.

39   Neusner, *Reader's Guide*, 260.

40   See Schäfer, "Research," 146–50, and Robert Goldenberg, "Is 'The Talmud' a Document?" in *The Synoptic Problem in Rabbinic Literature* (ed. S. J. D. Cohen; Providence: Brown Judaic Studies, 2000), 3–12; see also the other articles in that volume by Christine Hayes, Richard Kalmin, and Hans-Jürgen Becker, as well as Cohen's introduction.

41   On the various kinds of layering that one can find within the redactional layer, see, e.g., David Rosenthal, "'Arikhot qedumot ha-meshuqa'ot ba-talmud ha-bavli," in *Talmudic Studies I* (ed. Y. Sussmann and D. Rosenthal; Jerusalem: Magnes, 1990), 155–204; Halivni, *MM BB*, 29–33 and 56-64; Friedman, *Talmudic Studies*, 55.

42   See Kalmin, "Formation," 844–45.

43   See, e.g., Jaffee, "Rabbinic Authorship," 31–32.

found; but it is the kind of critical authorship that transcends Neusner's dichotomy between "servility to the past" and "exceptional criticism."

OVERVIEW

This book examines compositional practices, historical developments, and passages revealing of the way the Talmud's creators conceived themselves in order to draw a different portrait of them. This portrait adds a different set of characteristics to those already recognized by current models. It complements the continuous creative revision with a freezing of tradition and its containment in a way that produces discontinuity; it complements the fusing of horizons with a literary design that *does* foreground one horizon from another; it shows that we find in the Talmud not only appeals to the "eternal present" or "eternal yesterday" but also pervasive literary techniques that thrive on the dialectic and distinction between the present and the past. While Talmudic composition certainly lacks some of the determinative features of Greco-Roman or modern authorial practice, it does, it will be argued, use an "author's voice," and it can distinguish this voice from that of its sources.

Part I of this book explores the Talmud's literary practice through a close analysis of selected passages, or *sugyot*.[44] My claim is not that these *sugyot* are more representative of Talmudic composition than the *sugyot* that have informed previous theories, or that the strategies observed in them are closer to some conjectured essence of this composition. Rather, my analyses of these *sugyot* seek to modify the way we see other Talmudic texts and compositional practices in two ways. First, since the literary strategies observed here expand our thesaurus of what the Talmud *can* do, they problematize accounts that explain the other types of practices by appeal to innate or universal characteristics; they warn us against assumptions about the textual practices of rabbinic, oral, pre-modern, or religious cultures. Second, and more important, these *sugyot* make explicit and visible aspects and potentialities of certain features of Talmudic composition that are less discernible, but still present, in other texts. These features include the division between the anonymous layer and the

---

44   On the *sugyot* and their development as the literary unit constituting the Talmud, see Abraham Weiss, *Studies in the Literature of the Amoraim* (Heb.; New York: Horeb Yeshiva University Press, 1972), 1–23; see also Louis Jacobs, "The Talmudic *Sugya* as a Literary Unit," *JJS* 24 (1974), 119–26. For an alternative account of the *sugya* that prefers "organic development" to "literary creation," see Robert Brody, "Sifrut ha-ge'onim vehateqst ha-talmudi," in *Talmudic Studies I* (ed. Y. Sussmann and D. Rosenthal; Jerusalem: Magnes, 1990), 237–303 (252–55).

traditions it cites, as well as juxtaposition, sequence, attribution, and narration.

Chapter 1 centers on a *sugya* which, it will be argued, is designed to emphasize the distance between the approach expressed by the *stam* (the creators' anonymous layer) and the approach expressed by the Amoraic dictum that it cites. The creators of the Talmud do not revise the tradition to fit their own agenda or even reinterpret it; nor is the tradition justified: on the contrary, its validation in the conclusion of the *sugya* is presented as arbitrary and explicitly contrasted with the Talmud's own long, exhaustive, and theoretically sophisticated reasoning. Far from "hiding" themselves behind tradition or voicing their agenda through it, the authors of the *stam* become a presence in their own creation.

Chapter 2 addresses the historical development of the anonymous layer. It aims to complicate the notion that the division in style and function between the *stam* and the traditions reflects a difference in provenance between two corpora, instead arguing that the Bavli's creators produced both the anonymous layer and the cited traditions, or better, the division between them. This division is not simply a reflection of the different dating of these elements; it was, rather, constructed and imposed by the Bavli on earlier structures and sources. Following a brief discussion of theories about the *stam*'s date, the discussion goes on to compare a *sugya* preserved in the Palestinian Talmud as well as in the Babylonian Talmud. In the earlier, Palestinian version, attributed traditions are employed both for interpretive, narrating functions and for apodictic rulings and brief exegetical comments. The Bavli reorganizes the *sugya* to create a distinction in function, dividing the material between two layers: a narrating, interpretive, discursive anonymous layer, and a layer of brief, non-discursive, attributed rulings.

It is this reorganization that *transforms the traditions into quotations*, that distinguishes between the Talmud's own voice and the voice of the sources it cites. The gap that we observe in almost every Talmudic *sugya* is, then, not just the result of the passage of time between the production of Tannaitic and Amoraic traditions and the production of the Talmud: this gap, as we observe it in texts like the one studied in Chapter 1, is itself a compositional strategy of the Talmud's creators.

One of the most compelling accounts of this ability of quotation to signify a break rather than continuity, alienation rather than identification, is Giorgio Agamben's exposition of Walter Benjamin's notion of quotation. Agamben writes:

> The particular power of quotations arises, according to Benjamin, not from their ability to transmit that past and allow the reader to relive it but, on the contrary, from their capacity . . . to destroy. Alienating by force a fragment

of the past from its historical context, the quotation at once makes it lose its character of authentic testimony and invests it with an alienating power that constitutes its unmistakable aggressive force.[45]

The emphasis in Agamben's passage on the original context of the material that is quoted is less applicable for the function of quotation in the Talmud: we do not know the nature of the literary context in which rabbinic traditions circulated, and at least in the example examined in Chapter 2, the quotation is achieved not by reproducing a tradition from one context in another, but by revising the original context of the tradition, the earlier *sugya*.[46] The important element that Agamben emphasizes in his discussion of quotation as well as of art collection is the capacity of these activities to create a dialectical, objectifying relation to the past; quotation is "destructive" and "aggressive" in the sense that it destroys continuity. Applied to the Talmud, the transformation of tradition into quotation disrupts the chain of tradition.

The *stam*, I argue, is where this problem of the past found its solution. By rendering traditions archaic, fixed Hebrew "quotations" and "artifacts" subordinated to a live, all-knowing Aramaic narrating layer, it enabled the scholars who presented *sugyot* in the academy to create a space for their own self-expression and to justify their necessity. The division between the layers answered what Walter Ong has identified as a challenge particular to oral culture: the distinction between the transmitter and the transmitted.[47] It was an expression of, and a solution to, an "anxiety of influence." We will see this anxiety expressed in one of the *sugyot* studied in Chapter 4, in which members of the Jewish community criticize the rabbis' traditionality, asking, "of what use are the rabbis for us?"

Chapter 3 argues that a similar distanciation is at work even where the anonymous voice is relatively silent. It focuses on a thematic series of *sugyot* that concern the genealogical division of the Jewish people, and argues that the Bavli trains its audience to view the production of genealogical knowledge, and the traditions in which it is transmitted, as manipulated and personally motivated—in other words, that the Talmud

45 Giorgio Agamben, *The Man Without Content* (trans. Georgia Albert; Stanford, CA: Stanford University Press, 1999), 104.

46 Alexander Samely, *Forms of Rabbinic Literature and Thought: An Introduction* (Oxford: Oxford University Press, 2007), 169–71, argues that the quotation of *memrot* and *baraitot* outside of their original literary context effectively "Scripturalizes" the Mishnah; but Samely himself acknowledges that *sugyot* often treat Mishnaic quotations in the same way, and we still do not know whether all *sugyot* were initially intended as commentaries on the Mishnah.

47 Walter Ong, *Orality and Literacy: The Technologizing of the Word* (London and New York: Routledge, 1989), 45–46.

situates and historicizes these traditions. When genealogical traditions are then reproduced and juxtaposed with stories or laws that tell us of such manipulation, we are highly suspicious of these traditions, even though they are not explicitly contested or revised by the Talmud. The Talmud's creators thus achieve a critical distance without relying on the division between the layers, but merely through juxtaposition and arrangement.

These *sugyot* challenge us to go beyond the common dichotomy between an uncritical compilation that does not revise or select tradition and the critical authorship that only produces traditions it agrees with and revises all the sources it produces according to its own agenda. The lack of revision or appropriation, as well as the lack of "redaction" in the sense of omitting sources that stand in clear tension with the Talmud's creators' agenda, can play a role in a critique. Revision and selection are, in a sense, measures of identification; the withdrawal from revision and the production of sources that stand in tension with the values of the Talmud's creators are measures of distanciation.

In the sense that our *sugyot* combine a commitment to tradition with an effort to distance it, on some level, they confront the same problem confronted by rabbinic biblical interpretation: the difference between the values of the interpreter and the values expressed in the text to which the interpreter is committed.[48] In biblical interpretation, the rabbis' most common solution was to interpret Scripture according to their values, a solution that is in part premised on the divine authorship of Scripture: since God is the author of the text, the text can never be wrong, and must therefore reflect the worldview of the interpreter.[49] The *sugyot* discussed in Chapter 3 present a solution that is based on the humanity of rabbinic traditions. Instead of endowing the canonical texts with new meaning generated by new values, the representation of these traditions as contingent on human interests allows the Talmud's creators to maintain their commitment to these traditions without endorsing the values encoded in them.

Part II of this book turns from the Talmud's creators' compositional practices to their rhetoric of self-presentation and self-definition. Building on the work of Ginzberg, Rosenthal, Boyarin, and Rubenstein, who demonstrated that the Bavli places a high value on dialectic and analysis at the expense of tradition and memorization, Chapter 4 analyzes three passages to demonstrate the centrality of this preference to the self-

---

48   On this problem in rabbinic biblical interpretation, see Halbertal, *Values in Interpretation*, passim.

49   For an analysis of this position, see Moshe Halbertal, *People of the Book: Canon, Meaning, and Authority* (Cambridge, MA: Harvard University Press, 1997), 23–33.

perception of the Talmud's creators as well as situate it within a polemical conversation among Jews in late ancient Mesopotamia.

These passages are all premised on a dichotomy between the "received" knowledge of Scripture and oral tradition, on the one hand, and the innovative, creative aspects of study on the other. The first passage, I argue, is designed to claim rabbinic identity for these creative aspects of study, depriving of rabbinic identity those who occupy themselves with Scripture or with oral tradition; the latter, in particular, are presented as enemies of the rabbis. The second passage condemns members of the Jewish community who criticize the rabbis for being too conservative and occupying themselves only with received knowledge, Scripture, and tradition; while it is difficult to know whether there were really Jews outside rabbinic circles who held these views, compositional elements of the *sugya* indicate that the Talmud shares the values on which this criticism is premised.

The third *sugya* concerns the *tanna'im* (sing. *tanna*)—the "repeaters" or "reciters" of tradition—known from other sources as those entrusted with the memorization, transmission, and recitation of rabbinic traditions. The *sugya* includes these reciters in the list of the rabbis' classical opponents; it warns its audience not to "intermingle" with them, and says that they act as the destroyers of the world when they offer legal instruction, an activity reserved for the sages themselves. The rabbis are exhorted not to cross the social borderline between themselves and the reciters, while the reciters are condemned for crossing this line.

The Talmud's insistence on this boundary suggests that in reality it was not that sharp: rabbis did intermingle with reciters, reciters did give legal instruction. This is further corroborated by the occasional references to interpretive, scholarly activities of reciters scattered throughout the Bavli itself. The Talmud's attack on these scholars—whether the reciters or those who intermingle with them—includes two elements that cohere with the other passages studied in this chapter: it constructs a sharp distinction between scholarship and transmission, and it creates a clear hierarchy that values the former and devalues the latter.

These passages, I argue, allow us to posit a contrast between two approaches to tradition. Those targeted in these passages saw memorization, retention, and recitation as primary ways for approaching rabbinic tradition; they saw scholarship as continuous with, but not necessarily central to, these activities. This approach stands in contrast with the Bavli's compositional practices studied in Part I of this book. If the Talmud externalizes and distances tradition, recitation internalizes and embodies tradition; it interprets and revises texts through identification with them. More important, recitation might not have been simply an aid to scholarship but a ritual on its own. The Bavli's portrayal of the reciters correlates with its treatment of tradition itself: just as it fossilizes tradition in non-discursive dicta, it divorces recitation from scholarship and portrays the reciters—in this *sugya* and other passages—as "mindless" performers.

In their effort to construct borderlines and shape rabbinic identity in a particular way, these passages show us that the Bavli's approach cannot be understood as representative of Babylonian Jewry or even the rabbinic academy: both the reciters and the rabbis who "intermingle" with them were, at least in some sense, members of the academic community, and the latter were part of the Bavli's own audience. This complicates previous accounts of the Bavli's vision of Jewish intellectual life, which have identified this vision with academicization or understood it in terms of the contrast between Babylonian and Palestinian Jewish culture. The worldview we see in these passages was one voice in a conversation that took place within rabbinic culture in Babylonia about the appropriate way to approach Torah.

This conversation extends beyond Judaism. In one of the passages on the reciters, the Talmud quotes a comparison between the Jewish reciter and the Zoroastrian magus: both recite and do not understand what they are reciting. Chapter 5 takes this statement as a point of departure to examine discourses about recitation in Zoroastrian and Christian literature. The first section explores a Zoroastrian distinction similar to the one the Talmud makes between the reciter and the scholar. The second section looks at a Christian author who is also using a negative portrayal of Zoroastrian recitation, and argues that in both the Talmud and the Christian text the representation of Zoroastrian practice is used to promote particular visions of Judaism and Christianity and dehabilitate others. Both texts contrast the performative, embodying practice of recitation with the scholarly approach that they promote, and by associating that recitation with Zoroastrian ritual they seek to mark it as foreign, as non-Jewish or non-Christian.

The recitation of sacred text was an important element in the Western cultures from which the Jewish and Christian cultures of the Sasanian Empire developed; but, I suggest here, it is possible that the encounter with Zoroastrian culture, in which recitation took a central role as a main component of ritual and as the exclusive interface to sanctified traditions, increased the importance of recitation for some Mesopotamian Jews and Christians. In this context, the Jewish and Christian polemic against recitation can be seen as an attempt both to fortify the boundaries of Jewish and Christian identities as well as to claim these identities for the particular vision of the two "scholastic" groups of these cultures—the East-Syrian school movement and the leadership of the rabbinic academy.

The problem with reconstructing the conversation that is evident in the Bavli's polemical passage is that we usually only have the Talmud's side of such debates. Chapter 6 argues that the opposing side might be found in a few texts preserved in the tradition of Hekhalot literature. This chapter argues that the *Sar ha-Torah* narrative presents a parody of the ethos of the Babylonian academies and an effort to shift the gravity of Jewish culture away from the kind of Torah study practiced in these academies toward an engagement with Torah that emphasizes retention and recitation. Other Hekhalot traditions present memorization as a type of visionary experience and recitation as a transformative ritual. The chapter proceeds to suggest, based on the fact that the Hekhalot texts enter Jewish history as texts transmitted by Babylonian reciters, as well as on other connections between these *tanna'im* and Hekhalot texts, that the Babylonian reciters took active part in the shaping of Hekhalot traditions. If that is correct, then the Hekhalot texts analyzed in this chapter preserve a response to the Babylonian polemic discussed in the previous chapters.

The period that saw the formation of the Babylonian Talmud was also a period in which the traditions of the rabbis gained unprecedented prestige and following. It saw transformations in the religious life of the Jews that led to the introduction of these traditions to larger, more diverse publics, and it saw the rise of the rabbinic academy, which offered an unprecedented institutional setting for the study of these traditions.[50] Rabbinic traditions were no longer encountered by students and scholars in the intimate circles of Tannaitic and Amoraic Palestine and Babylonia, but in contexts increasingly removed from the ones in which they were produced: in lectures both academic and public, in inscriptions, and even in weekly readings in the synagogue. This process—the creation, in Agamben's words, of "the gap between the act of transmission and the thing to be transmitted," contributed both to the increased ritualization of rabbinic tradition in the mouths of the *tanna'im* and to the objectification and distanciation of this tradition in Talmudic *sugyot*. In this sense, this process offered tradition a renewed vitality; "contrary to what one might think at first, the breaking of tradition does not at all mean the loss or devaluation of the past: it is, rather, likely that only now the past can reveal itself with a weight and an influence it never had before."[51]

50   Seth Schwartz, "Rabbinization in the Sixth Century," in *The Talmud Yerushalmi and Graeco-Roman Culture III* (ed. P. Schäfer; Tübingen: Mohr Siebeck, 2002), 55–69.

51   Agamben, *The Man Without Content*, 107–8.

PART I

Chapter One

THE ALTERITY OF TRADITION

Readers of the Talmud from the medieval period on have observed that it can be divided into discrete elements. This division has become central to the work of modern scholars, who divide the Talmud into two: on the one hand are the attributed elements, the *baraitot* and *memrot,* sources ascribed to the Tannaitic and Amoraic periods respectively; on the other is the anonymous layer, or *stam,* which frames the Talmudic discussion. The first two chapters of this book offer a new perspective on the relationship between these elements and of the function of the anonymous layer, and, consequently, of the nature of Talmudic literary creativity.

The most ambitious and influential account of the function of the anonymous layer is David Weiss Halivni's. Halivni begins by observing the stylistic contrast between the brief, apodictic form of the cited, attributed traditions and the argumentative, dialectical, and often long form of the anonymous literary frameworks. He then offers a diachronic explanation for this difference. The traditions, attributed to sages of the Amoraic period (the second era of classical rabbinic teaching, third to fifth centuries), were produced in an age when rabbinic literary production consisted exclusively of legal rulings and opinions; the rabbis of that period chose not to preserve the reasoning that led to these rulings or opinions, nor did they see fit to preserve and transmit the debates they had among themselves. In the post-Amoraic period the authors of the *stam* undertook to reconstruct the rational and argumentative processes that produced Amoraic teachings. The literary result of this undertaking, the Talmud, embeds rulings in theoretical discussions that seek to justify these rulings, manifesting the "predilection for justified law" that Halivni sees as an inherent characteristic of Jewish culture.[1]

---

1 David Halivni, *Sources and Traditions: A Source Critical Commentary on the Talmud: Tractate Baba Bathra* (Heb.; Jerusalem: Magnes, 2007), 5–148. The principles surveyed

Shamma Friedman, like Halivni, puts at the center of his account of the Talmud's literary nature the distinction between the *stam* and the cited, attributed traditions; he, too, believes that the composition of the *stam* was later than the production of Amoraic traditions.[2] Friedman, however, is concerned less with the function of the *stam* as supplying a literary framework to the traditions it has inherited. His work focuses on how the Talmud's creators use the *stam* to interpret and adapt these traditions. It documents instances of interpolation, expansion, and other strategies of reworking, which, according to Friedman, were employed by the creators in order to give their received traditions new forms appropriate to new legal, literary, and historical contexts.[3]

Halivni, Friedman, and their followers differ in the degree and kind of creative consciousness they assign to the creators of the Talmud, but they all describe this consciousness in terms of continuity. According to Halivni, the authors of the *stam* were aware that, by putting dialectical reasoning into literary form for the first time, they were introducing a great innovation to rabbinic tradition. He insists, however, that they saw this innovation as an accurate restoration of their predecessors' reasoning, and surmises that they connected the necessity of this restoration with what they perceived as the spiritual impoverishment of their own generation.[4] The terms with which Halivni understands the relation of the Talmud's creators to their predecessors are deference, piety, and a humility that borders on self-deprecation: it was out of their piety toward their predecessors that the Talmud's creators faithfully transmitted the traditions they received unchanged; out of their deference that they sought only to restore and justify the reasoning behind these traditions rather than create new traditions or new reasoning; out of humility that they chose to stay anonymous and mention only the names of their predecessors.[5]

Friedman's focus on the creators' adaptation of earlier sources is premised on an understanding of Talmudic literary activity as continuous in nature. The innovation of the Talmud's creators is a result of their sense of identity and continuity with their literary heritage. They therefore interpolate their own ideas and terms into older material, "correcting" it

---

here appear on pp. 5–6. See also idem, *Midrash, Mishnah and Gemara: The Jewish Predilection for Justified Law* (Cambridge, MA: Harvard University Press, 1986), 76–92.

2 Shamma Friedman, *Talmudic Studies: Investigating the Sugya, Variant Readings and Aggada* (Heb.; New York and Jerusalem: Jewish Theological Seminary, 2010), 8–22.

3 See Friedman, *Talmudic Studies*, 22–27, 37–44.

4 David Halivni, *Sources and Traditions: A Source Critical Commentary on the Talmud: Tractate Baba Kama* (Heb.; Jerusalem: Magnes, 1993), 9–10.

5 David Halivni, *Sources and Traditions: A Source Critical Commentary on the Talmud: Tractate Baba Metzia* (Heb.; Jerusalem: Magnes, 2003), 22–23; *MM BQ*, 9–10; *MM BB*, 8–9.

and "improving" it, participating in the "natural development" of rabbinic tradition.[6] Similarly, Jeffrey Rubenstein's work, which applies Friedman's method to the non-legal parts of the Talmud, focuses on how the creators cast the narratives they retell in their own image.[7] Building on this work, Daniel Boyarin describes the creators as "hiding" themselves while projecting their realities back to previous historical periods.[8] Finally, this emphasis on adaptation allows Friedman and his followers to trace even those developments that did not necessarily involve authorial agency; in Rubenstein's words, "many changes occurred unintentionally or subconsciously as transmitters replaced outmoded ideas with those more familiar to them."[9]

As we have seen in the Introduction, underlying these accounts are particular images of tradition and composition, as well as the turn away from modern notions of authorship and the turn toward orality in scholarship on rabbinic literature in general. These images and these developments have shaped and were shaped by the view of the Bavli's creators as the camouflaging transmitters whose creativity is expressed, without consciousness of discontinuity or originality, through the modification and elaboration of open texts. These models capture important aspects of Talmudic literary creation, but I think they miss other aspects, equally important. The first part of this book analyzes a number of *sugyot* to offer a very different image of the Talmud's creators.

This chapter centers on the famous opening *sugya* of tractate *Bava Qamma* to show how the Talmud's creators could use an ambitious literary design to highlight the gap between their own words and an Amoraic tradition. This *sugya* has been used before as an example of the strategies the Talmud's creators employed seamlessly to incorporate tradition to the literary and logical structures they constructed. The analysis here suggests the opposite. The scholars who shaped the *sugya* offered their own systematic approach to the matter at hand, but they did not harmonize the tradition they used with this approach. On the contrary: the structure of the *sugya* emphasizes the contrast between this tradition and this approach. The Talmud maintains the tradition at the end of the

6   Shamma Friedman, "Ha-baraitot ba-talmud ha-bavli ve-yaḥasan le-maqbiloteihen sheba-tosefta," in *Atara L'haim: Studies in the Talmud and Medieval Rabbinic Literature in Honor of Professor Haim Zalman Dimitrovsky* (Heb.; ed. D. Boyarin et al.; Jerusalem: Magnes, 2000), 163–201 (165).

7   Jeffrey Rubenstein, *The Culture of The Babylonian Talmud* (Baltimore: Johns Hopkins University Press, 2003), 6–7.

8   Daniel Boyarin, "Hellenism in Jewish Babylonia," in *The Cambridge Companion to the Talmud and Rabbinic Literature* (ed. C. E. Fonrobert and M. S. Jaffee; Cambridge: Cambridge University Press, 2007), 336–63 (342).

9   Rubenstein, *Culture*, 6.

sugya, but far from justifying the tradition with dialectical reasoning it presents it as arbitrary and divorced from this reasoning.

BAVA QAMMA 2A–3B: OVERVIEW

The Mishnah opens its *Tractate of Damages* with a list of four "Fathers of damages" (*avot neziqin*; *m. B. Q.* 1:1). These Fathers are four causes of damages that are derived from the cases discussed in the Hebrew Bible, primarily in Exodus 21–22: goring oxen, dangerous pits, grazing beasts, conflagration. They are called Fathers because they are used as archetypal or primary cases from which judgment can be drawn on other cases that are not mentioned in biblical law.[10] The Father "Pit," for example, is used by some rabbis to derive all cases of damages caused by stationary property (e.g., I left my knife lying in the street and it injured someone's ox).

The question the Talmud poses in its first *sugya* on this *mishnah* is whether there is any difference in legal consequence between the primary cases themselves and the cases we derive from them, which the Talmud calls "Offspring." First, the Talmud demonstrates that the Mishnah's use of the term "Fathers" is ambiguous: in its discussion of Shabbat laws, the Mishnah uses the term where there is no difference in consequence between the primary cases and derivative cases; in its discussion of impurity laws, the Mishnah applies the same term where there is a difference in consequences between primary and derivative sources of impurity.

The Talmud then cites a tradition from Rav Papa, who argues that here, in the case of damages laws, both senses apply: some derivative cases carry consequences identical to those of the primary cases from which they were derived, whereas other derivative cases carry consequences which are different from those of their primary cases. From this point, the Talmud embarks on a lengthy inquiry to identify which derivative cases belong to the first category Rav Papa mentions (those of identi-

10   On this *mishnah* and its use of the term "Fathers," see David Daube, "The Civil Law of the Mishnah: The Arrangement of the Three Gates," in *The Collected Works of David Daube I: Talmudic Law* (ed. C. M. Carmichael; Berkeley: University of California Press, 1992), 257–304; Halivni, *MM BQ*, 1–7; Jeffrey Rubenstein, "On Some Abstract Concepts in Rabbinic Literature," *JSQ* 4 (1997), 33–73 (67–69); Leib Moscovitz, *Talmudic Reasoning: From Casuistics to Conceptualization* (Tübingen: Mohr Siebeck, 2002), 107–8; Noam Zohar, "Scripture, Mishnah and Thought: Redaction and Meaning at the Beginning of Tractate Neziqin" (Heb.), in *By the Well: Studies in Jewish Philosophy and Halakhic Thought Presented to Gerald J. Blidstein* (Heb.; ed. U. Ehrlich, H. Kreisel, and D. J. Lasker; Beer Sheva: Ben Gurion University Press, 2008), 195–208 (195–97).

cal consequences), and which derivative cases belong to the second (with dissimilar consequences); it goes through each of the primary cases, lists their derivative cases, and examines whether the derivatives carry identical or dissimilar legal consequences. The same conclusion is reached with respect to each of the primary cases: all Offspring turn out to carry legal consequences identical to the consequences carried by their respective Fathers. The question returns again and again: what, then, are the derivatives of dissimilar consequences that Rav Papa mentions?

Finally, after the list of primary cases has been exhausted, the Talmud returns to one of the primary cases, "Foot" (which is included in the Father Ox), and mentions its derivative case of pebbles that shot out under the feet of an animal as it was walking, causing damage to nearby property. Tradition teaches us that the owner of the damaging animal is required to pay in this case only for half of the damage. Since in the primary case of Foot the damaging party is required to pay for the full damage, the case of pebbles, with its reduced restitution, is an Offspring that carries consequences dissimilar from those of its Father; we have found the case to which Rav Papa referred.

THE PURPOSE OF THE DESIGN

In a study that was revolutionary for its time, Louis Jacobs argued that the structure of our *sugya* indicates that it is the product of literary artistry rather than a record of debates held in the rabbinic academies: "In a real debate, it is impossible to imagine that each of the *'avot* [Fathers] would have been examined in detail without yielding any results until someone came up fortuitously with the example of *tzerurot* [pebbles]. Clearly, the editors knew of the *tzerurot* case right from the beginning but consciously kept it in storage." Their purpose in delaying the presentation of this case, Jacobs explained, was to create a persuasive rhetorical effect (to "clinch" the argument).[11]

Jacobs's description of the purpose of the *sugya*'s design fits well with Halivni's account of the *stam*'s purpose outlined in the beginning of this chapter. Rav Papa's teaching itself does not identify which derivatives carry identical consequences and which do not, nor does it give theoretical or scriptural justification to his assertion that both kinds (identical and dissimilar) exist in the case of tort laws. The purpose of the *stam*'s theoretical and scriptural inquiry is then to retrieve Rav Papa's intention

---

11 Louis Jacobs, "The Talmudic Sugya as a Literary Unit," *JJS* 24 (1974), 119–26 (123). A revised, longer version of this article appears in idem, *Studies in Talmudic Logic and Methodology* (London and Portland: Vallentine Mitchell, 2006), 132–51.

by identifying the referents of his teaching and by explaining his rationale, embedding the apodictic teaching in an argumentative essay that
aims to secure a justified sense for a rabbinic tradition.

That Rav Papa's teaching is the object of the *sugya* is evident in the
transformation the Talmud's narrative undergoes in one of its early
stages. Immediately after it presents Rav Papa's teaching the inquiry aims
not at the initial desideratum (a definition of the relationship between
Fathers and Offspring in the laws of damages) but at the referents of Rav
Papa's teaching. The recurring formula that structures the discussion is:
"Hence, an Offspring of (a certain Father) is identical to (that Father) and
what Rav Papa said was about the Offspring (of a different Father)." Our
sugya is not designed to explain a certain legal issue or even to interpret
the Mishnah, but rather to explicate an Amoraic tradition.[12]

In my analysis of the *sugya*, I follow Jacobs in looking at the *sugya* as a
carefully planned literary construct, and I apply Halivni's general theory
to this *sugya* by positing Rav Papa's teaching as the primary object of the
Talmud's inquiry. I would like to suggest, however, that the creators of
the Talmud operate with an intention that is precisely the opposite of the
one Jacobs and Halivni ascribe to them.

The Talmud compels its readers to expect an explanation and a justification of Rav Papa's teaching, only to frustrate this expectation altogether. The dissonance between the non-theoretical ("apodictic," in
Halivni's language) nature of Rav Papa's teaching and the theoretical
nature of the *stam*'s inquiry is never harmonized by the *sugya*. On the
contrary: the Talmud's creators employ a series of compositional moves
to spell out this dissonance to their audience, calling attention, in the
conclusion, to their own voice and narrative.

HOW TO DERIVE AN OFFSPRING

The Talmud begins to answer its question on the relationship between
Fathers and Offspring by laying out two possible meanings the term "Father" can have in the Mishnah:

---

12 While this is true with respect to the frame and thrust of the *sugya* as it stands
now, Abraham Weiss (*Studies in the Law of the Talmud on Damages* [Heb.; Jerusalem and
New York: Philipp Feldheim, 1966], 49–54) demonstrated that the creators of our *sugya*
had incorporated a different *sugya*, which concerned the list of "Fathers," rather than Rav
Papa's teaching, into their own. Yehonatan Ets-Hayim argued that another process of in-
corporating discrete *sugyot* may be detected in our *sugya* in the discussion of the *baraita*
beginning at the end of 2b; Yehonatan Ets-Hayim, *Sugyot muḥlafot be-masekhet neziqin*
(Heb.; Lod: Haberman, 2000). Again, while this may be the case, this originally discrete
material is now incorporated into a relatively smooth master narrative.

1. Since the Mishnah says "Fathers," the implication is that there are Offspring. Are the Offspring like or not like their Fathers?
2. Concerning Shabbat, we learn in the Mishnah: "The Fathers of [forbidden] labors are forty minus one" (*m. Shabb.* 7:2). "Fathers"—the implication is that there are Offspring. Their Offspring are like them. There is no difference between [a labor that is] a Father and [one that is] an Offspring concerning an offering of unintentional sin; and there is no difference between [a labor that is] a Father and [one that is] an Offspring concerning stoning. . . .
3. Concerning impurity, we learn in the Mishnah: "The Fathers of impurity are creeping things, semen, and those rendered impure by proximity to a corpse" (*m. Kel.* 1:1). Their Offspring are not like them; for while [an impurity that is] a Father renders impure people and vessels, [impurities that are] Offspring render food and drink impure, but not people and vessels.
4. What is [the case] here [in the laws of damages]?
5. Rav Papa said, "Some of them [the Offspring] are like them [the Fathers], and some are not like them." (*b. B. Q.* 2a–b)

In the laws of Shabbat, the term "Fathers" is used to describe the thirty-nine archetypal labors that are forbidden for Jews on Shabbat; other forbidden labors, termed "Offspring," are derived from these thirty-nine labors by abstraction and expansion. The Talmud tells us that these Offspring are identical in consequences to their Fathers: an unintentional transgression of either will lead to offering of the same sacrifice of unintentional sin; and intentional transgression of either will lead to execution by stoning.[13]

In the laws of impurity, the Talmud shows us, the term "Fathers" is used to describe animals, liquids, or persons that can impart impurity on contact with them; the "Offspring," in this case, are objects or people that became impure on contact with the Fathers, receiving their state of impurity. These Offspring, the Talmud continues, do not carry the same consequences as their Fathers: vessels and people coming in contact with one of the Fathers (e.g., semen) will become impure, but vessels and people coming in contact with one of the Offspring (e.g., with a vessel that had come in contact with one of the Fathers) will not become impure—for Offspring can only render food or drink impure, not vessels or people.

As Isaac Reines noted, in each of these two cases the terms "Fathers" and "Offspring" have a different meaning and it is this difference in

---

13 On the Mishnah in Shabbat and its use of the term "Fathers," see Yitzhaq Gilat, "The Thirty-Nine Classes of Work Forbidden on the Sabbath" (Heb.), *Tarbiz* 33 (1960), 20–27; Rubenstein, "Abstract Concepts," 61–67.

meaning that leads to the difference in legal consequences.[14] In the case
of Shabbat laws, the Offspring are connected to the Fathers by logical
derivation. Since we derive the Offspring from their Fathers on the basis
of identical characteristics, there is no reason to treat them differently
than the cases from which they are derived. In the case of impurity laws,
the relationship between Offspring and Fathers is physical rather than
logical. The Offspring received their derivative impurity from the Fathers
through contact, not logical derivation, which is why we understand
their impurity to be diminished and capable of rendering fewer things
impure.

Following the discussion of the two different uses of "Fathers" in the
Mishnah, the Talmud reiterates its original question: are the Offspring in
the laws of damages like or not like their Fathers? At this stage, however, there is something surprising, even puzzling about this question.
Surely the Mishnah's use of "Fathers" in damages implies a logical, not
physical, connection to their Offspring. The Fathers here, like the Fathers in Shabbat, are archetypical cases from which further cases are
derived on the basis of common characteristics, and the Talmud just
showed us that this use of "Fathers" means that the Offspring will have
identical legal consequences.

Rav Papa's teaching is puzzling for the same reason. Abraham Weiss
addressed this problem by suggesting that this teaching is misconstrued
by the Bavli. According to Weiss, Rav Papa did not mean to say that both
kinds of Fathers and Offspring exist in the laws of damages. Rather, Rav
Papa observes, as the Bavli does, that both kinds exist in the Mishnah
generally: "Some of them"—in the laws of Shabbat—"are like them, and
some"—in the laws of impurity—"are not like them."[15] Weiss's suggestion is compelling; it is indeed only the setting in which the Bavli places
Rav Papa's teaching that prevents us from reading it as referring to all
instances of "Fathers" in the Mishnah—but it is impossible to verify.

Whatever its original intention may have been, Rav Papa's teaching
puzzles us because the Talmud places it immediately after its discussion
of the passages from *Shabbat* and *Kellim*. That discussion presents us with
two options: when the Mishnah uses "Fathers" and "Offspring" in the
logical sense, as is the case in Shabbat laws, the Offspring are identical in
consequences to the Fathers; when the Mishnah uses "Fathers" and "Offspring" in the physical sense, as is the case in impurity laws, then the
Offspring are not identical to their Fathers. If the Talmud did not equate

14   Isaac Jacob Reines, *Hotam Tokhnit* [2nd ed.] (published by A. D. Reines; Jerusalem, 1933–34), 57–58. He terms them תולדות מדעיות and תולדות טבעיות, "scientific" and "natural" Offspring.
15   See Weiss, *Damages*, 50. See also below, n. 39, for Halivni's reconstruction of Rav
Papa's teaching.

the existence of dissimilar Offspring with physical derivation, the suggestion that such Offspring exist in damages law would not sound so implausible.

It is further surprising, therefore, that our *sugya* goes on to insist on a strictly logical derivation of Offspring from Fathers in damages laws. A prominent example of this insistence is the Talmud's discussion of the three Fathers pertaining to animal damages: "Foot," "Tooth," and "Horn." These three Fathers, we are told earlier in the *sugya*, are included in the Mishnaic Father Ox. Generally speaking, "Foot" is a category that includes all common damages caused unintentionally by an animal in motion in its regular course of action; "Tooth" includes all common damages caused unintentionally by an animal from which the animal gained benefit; "Horn" includes damages caused intentionally by the animal when it acted in an atypical, unexpected manner.[16]

The Talmud expresses its view of how Offspring may be derived—and how they may *not*—when it lists damages caused by biting, reclining (on something), and kicking as Offspring of Horn.[17] Immediately, the *stam* voices possible objections to this list: "But biting is an Offspring of Tooth!"—No, the *stam* explains, since Tooth is a category of damages in which benefit is gained by the animal, biting cannot be considered a derivative case of Tooth. "But reclining and kicking are an Offspring of Foot!"—No, since Foot is a category for damages caused by the animal's normal course of action, kicking and reclining cannot be considered a derivative case of Foot (*b. B. Q.* 2b).[18] These rhetorical objections may emphasize the counterintuitive nature of the classification, but including them also serves to assert the cogency and legal utility in focusing on logical rather than physical derivation. Once the Offspring are defined as logical derivations, the *stam* has no doubt that they should carry the same legal consequences as their Fathers. This, for example, is the conclusion of the discussion of Horn:

> But, the Offspring that are not like them, which Rav Papa mentioned, to which [Father do they relate]? If we say [he referred] to these [i.e., the Offspring of Horn], how does [the case of] Horn, in which there is intent to damage, [the damage is caused by] your property and is for you to prevent, differ [from these cases]? [In] these [cases] also, there is an intent to damage, [the damages are caused by] your property and are for you to prevent?

16   These are Talmudic abstractions from the Mishnah. See also *y. B. Q.* 1:1 for the process of abstraction, and Rubenstein, "Abstract Principles," 68 n. 136.

17   See below, n. 20, for the Tannaitic and Yerushalmi parallels for this list.

18   In fact, the Bavli's list of Horn derivatives (like the lists in the Yerushalmi and the Mekhilta) is itself connected to the list of "uncommon" or "unattested" damages in *m. B. Q.* 1:4. See more below in the section titled "The Pebbles' Trajectory."

Rather, an Offspring of Horn is like Horn. And what Rav Papa said was about Tooth and Foot. (*b. B. Q.* 2b)

The same formula repeats itself throughout the *sugya* with respect to each group of Offspring.

The Talmud's treatment of Fathers and Offspring owes much to previous developments in rabbinic tort law. The process of expanding the biblical cases into rules begins already in the Tannaitic period and continues through the Amoraic period: these early sources apply biblical law to a variety of cases by identifying essential similarities between these cases and the biblical precedents.[19] But the Talmud's discussion of Fathers and Offspring is also innovative. Tannaitic sources never use the term "Offspring" for the tort cases they derive from Scripture;[20] Amoraic sages use the term rarely and vaguely, and while they do group cases together they do not equate the ruling in a certain case with its assignment to one of the Fathers; nor do *amora'im* debate the assignment of cases to Fathers.[21] The necessary, universal identity, between the ruling in a primary case and the ruling in cases derived from it, appears in its systematic form only in the Talmud's anonymous layer.

We can observe this development in the *stam*'s gloss on one of Rava's questions about the case of pebbles: "Rava asked, is there an attestation process for pebbles or is there not an attestation process for pebbles [dam-

19   Thus, the laws of Ox are expanded to other animals (*t. B. Q.* 6:18), Pit to a variety of caves and trenches (*m. B. Q.* 5:5). See Rubenstein, "Abstract Concepts," 67–69, and Moscovitz, *Talmudic Reasoning*, 108. See also, ibid., 344–51 for a general chronology of conceptualization in rabbinic literature.

20   Compare the Mekhilta d. R. Yishmael (Neziqin, 12; Horowitz-Rabin 289), which comments on Exod. 21:35, "If it butts": "*included in* butting [בכלל נגיפה] are goring, pushing, biting, reclining and kicking"—with the Yerushalmi, "the *Offspring* of Horn [תולדות הקרן] are goring, butting, biting, reclining, kicking and pushing" (cf. R. Hiyya's *baraita* in *y. Shabb.* 7:2 9d). What in the Tannaitic *midrash* is an expansion of the verse becomes in the Yerushalmi a list of derivative cases. The difference is significant: saying that a certain verse may be applicable to a variety of actions is not like saying that any case of biting, for example, should be judged in accordance with the rules of goring. Cf. Moscovitz, *Talmudic Reasoning*, 107; Halivni, *MM BQ*, 8 and n. 11; Rubenstein, "Abstract Concepts," 63 n. 113; and Zohar, "Scripture," 197.

21   In the Yerushalmi, R. Yitzhak twice contests the status of Offspring, but in both cases he does not argue they should be categorized as Offspring of a different Father but rather that they should be seen as part of the Father itself (*y. B. Q.* 1:1 2a, once on Horn and once on Tooth). Later in the Yerushalmi (accepting Lewy's emendation, *Interpretation des I.–VI. Abschnittes des pälast. Talmud-Traktats Nesikin* [Heb. and Ger.; Breslau, 1895–1914; repr. Jerusalem: Kedem, 1970], 27), coals are rejected as an Offspring of Fire because they do not spread (the rejection is either by R. Yosi or by the Yerushalmi's *stam*). It is not clear what Father he would assign coals to (Pit?) or what the implication for ruling is. See also below, n. 23, on Rav and Shmuel.

ages]? Do we conceptualize it as Horn or is it an Offspring of Foot?"[22] (*b. B. Q.* 18b). The second half of the question ("Do we . . .") is clearly a later Talmudic addition (the first half is in Hebrew, the second in Aramaic; the second part glosses on the first). Rava's original question concerned a particular aspect in the legal treatment of pebbles damages. The *stam* rephrases his question in terms of the assignment of the case to one of the Fathers, equating the difference in ruling with a difference in classification.[23]

Our *sugya*, then, presents an innovative argument for using systematic categorization as a tool for ruling in damage cases.[24] The Bavli shows us that if we strictly use Offspring to describe cases that share all essential characteristics with an archetypal case, we can rule on a large number of cases simply by assigning these cases to one of a very short list of archetypal cases. As one medieval commentator noted, "all of the *sugya* comes to prove that the Offspring are like their Fathers."[25]

Rav Papa's teaching is, then, not only at odds with the general notion of Fathers and Offspring appropriate to the case of damages; it also stands in tension with the Talmud's own agenda. On the one hand, the Talmud's opening moves prepare the ground for Rav Papa's teaching. As Halivni and others have shown, the *stam* legitimates Amoraic dicta by introducing them as responses to already-existing questions, as if the dicta were

22   בעי רבא יש העדאה לצרורות או אין העדאה לצרורות לקרן מדמינן ליה או דלמא תולדה דרגל הוא; see also the similar question in *b. B. Q.* 19b.

23   The *stam* in our *sugya* refers to another Amoraic dispute on categorization, concerning property that was left in the public domain, but not abandoned by its owners, and caused damage: Shmuel derives ruling on this damage from Pit whereas Rav derives it from Ox (*b. B. Q.* 3b). Shmuel's statement does seem to be genuinely Amoraic, but it differs from the *stam*'s approach in important ways. First, Shmuel's dictum (כולם מבורו למדנו, "we learned all these cases from Pit") does not use the term "Offspring." Second, where Shmuel's exposition is found in full (*b. B. Q.* 28b) it is aimed at a specific question—whether damage to utensils is liable for restitution or not in the kind of damage discussed there—and it is not clear that he would rule in each aspect of that damage as he would in the archetypal case (cf. *b. B. Q.* 50b). Note also that the opinion ascribed to Rav, that these damages are derived from Ox, seems to be inferred by the Talmud precisely because Shmuel cites his derivation of these cases from Pit as a reason to object to Rav's ruling on utensils; there is no other evidence that Rav held this opinion.

24   Abstraction also figures in the parallel *sugya* in the Yerushalmi. In the first Fathers it mentions—Horn, Pit, and Foot—it relies on traditional Tannaitic material to determine their Offspring, with no appeal to abstraction. But when it examines Tooth and Fire (accepting Lewy's emendation, *Interpretation*, 27), it first offers Offspring that are rejected, then comes up with a counterintuitive Offspring that it justifies by appeal to shared characteristics with the respective Father (*y. B. Q.* 1:1 2a). While this *sugya* is similar to the Bavli's, it does not focus on the implication of abstraction for ruling in these cases, and it lacks that *sugya*'s rhetoric of systematic revision.

25   See Shita Mequbezet to *b. B. Q.* 2a, s.v. תולדותיהן.

inevitable responses;[26] the parallel discussion in the Yerushalmi lacks the dichotomy between similar and dissimilar Offspring, which the Talmud derives from Rav Papa's teaching.[27] On the other hand the Talmud's creators set up the discussion in a way that emphasizes, rather than hides, the teaching's incompatibility with their own conception of the relationship between Fathers and Offspring.

THE CONCLUSION OF THE *SUGYA* (1)

This tension is never resolved. The *stam* calls attention to the incongruence between Rav Papa's teaching and its own inquiry in the conclusion by repeating a question it had already posed. The first time this question is raised, the *stam* offers its own answer. In the conclusion, the *stam* supplies an answer that validates Rav Papa's teaching. The conclusion also refers back explicitly to the first discussion, inviting us to compare these two parts of the *sugya*. I quote here both the first discussion of Foot and the conclusion, along with the key sentences that drive the discussion from one point to the other:

> And what Rav Papa said [about the existence of dissimilar Offspring refers] to an Offspring of Foot. What is an Offspring of Foot? When it [the animal] caused damage while in motion either with its body or with its hair, or with the load which was upon it, or with the bit in its mouth, or with the bell on its neck. Now, why should these cases be different? Just as Foot is a common damage and, being your possession, is under your control, why should not this also be the case with its Offspring, which similarly are common damages and, being your possession, are under your control? An Offspring of Foot is, therefore, identical to Foot, and what Rav Papa said was about an Offspring of Pit... an Offspring of Pit is, therefore, identical to Pit, and what Rav Papa said was about an Offspring of *mav'eh*... an Offspring of *mav'eh* is, therefore, identical to *mav'eh*, and what Rav Papa said was about an Offspring of Fire... an Offspring of Fire is, therefore, identical to Fire, and what Rav Papa said was about an Offspring of Foot.

---

26 See Halivni, *Midrash*, 89–90; *MM BB*, 43–44.

27 See *y. Shabb.* 7:2 9d, of which the beginning of our *sugya* is otherwise a rather faithful reworking (the order there is damages, impurities, and Shabbat—since the topic there is Shabbat). The general structure of this part of the *sugya*, then, is quite early, even though the terminology of the *stam* here (מדקתני . . . מכלל דאיכא) might be evidence of a late, "Saboraic" provenance of its formulation (compare the examples in Nehemia Brüll, "Die Entstehungsgeschichte des Babylonischen Talmud als Schriftwerkes," in idem, *Jahrbücher für Jüdische Geschichte und Literatur II* (Frankfurt: W. Erras, 1876), 1–123 (44), and see, e.g., *b. Ket.* 12b).

THE ALTERITY OF TRADITION

Foot?! But we have established that an Offspring of Foot is identical to Foot! [Rav Papa referred to] the half damage [paid in the case] of pebbles, about which they had learned a tradition. (*b. B. Q.* 3b)

The first time Foot is examined, the Talmud offers a few derivative cases and explains that since legal variables (frequency of the damage, ownership, and responsibility over the damaging element) are equal in the original case (Father) and its derivatives (Offspring), there should be no difference in consequence between the original case and the cases we derive from it. The Talmud then goes on to examine, in the same fashion, other possible referents of Rav Papa's teaching, referring on its way to various legal distinctions and biblical verses.

The second time Foot is mentioned, where the solution is finally revealed, there is no analysis of legal properties. The solution is maintained only by a vague "tradition." This conclusion stands not only in contrast with the previous appearance of Foot, but with the *sugya* as a whole: nothing in the Talmud's long investigation leads to its solution, which could have been offered right at the beginning, without the comprehensive investigation; the abrupt, arbitrary conclusion stands in contrast to the long, painstaking process that is supposed to lead to it. The artful composition of the *sugya* in general, and the way it builds up to this conclusion—both documented so well by Jacobs—make it unlikely that the repetition of the Foot question or the abruptness of the conclusion are instances of sloppy editing; the contrast between the conclusion and the rest of the inquiry is part of the careful design of the text.

This contrast is further expressed by the pronouns the Talmud uses in this conclusion. In the *stam*'s protest at the suggestion that the referent might be, after all, an Offspring of Foot, the reference to the previous inquiry is marked with the first-person plural pronoun: "But *we* have established that an Offspring of Foot is like Foot!"; the answer uses the third-person plural pronoun: "[Rav Papa referred to] the half damage [paid in the case of] pebbles, about which *they* had learned a tradition." While the phrase "they had learned a tradition" appears in several places in the Talmud, its deployment here pits "us"—the authors and audience of the *sugya*, who have been engaged in a diligent examination to achieve compelling results—with "them"—they who learned a tradition that we must consider in our discussion.

The Talmud uses the phrase "they had learned a tradition" in several places to explain the origin of laws or knowledge that it cannot (or will not) trace to scriptural or legal reasoning.[28] Here, ostensibly, the "tradi-

---

28   This phrase and similar phrases (such as גמרא גמירי לה) appear throughout the Talmud with varying functions and subject matters. For a survey of the occurrences, see

tion," or *hilkheta*, to which the Talmud refers is the ruling that in the case of pebbles the damaging party pays for only half of the damage; we will see why and how this ruling was traced to a special tradition in the following section. But the Talmud also links this tradition with Rav Papa's teaching: if there was no tradition reducing the restitution in the case of pebbles, there would not be any dissimilar Offspring and Rav Papa's tradition would be invalid.[29]

Read in the light of the other elements in the *sugya* that distance Rav Papa's teaching from the Talmud's own inquiry, this association between that teaching and the phrase "they had learned a tradition" works to expand the meaning of "tradition" so as to include in it Rav Papa's teaching itself. The Talmud's creators invite us to think that just as we are compelled to obey the law of pebbles even though we cannot justify it, so we are bound to Rav Papa's teaching even though it is alien to what "we" have just established.

THE PEBBLES' TRAJECTORY

The case that the Talmud identifies as the sole dissimilar Offspring is that of damage caused by pebbles that shot out from under the feet of an animal as it was walking. Reines, who is followed by Jacobs, notes that since this damage is caused by something that physically touched the animal's feet, it can be classified as a physical Offspring of Foot. He continues to argue that this solves the problem with Rav Papa's teaching: we thought that we would never find a "physical Offspring" in tort law, but here it is.[30]

While the Talmud's creators might be leading us to this harmonizing interpretation, they also immediately invalidate it: the Talmud traces the difference between the pebbles case and Foot to a special tradition, not to the fact that they are physically rather than logically connected; and in the final lines of the *sugya*, it supplies a legal reason for the connection between pebbles and Foot, which would be impossible if it indeed conceived pebbles as a physical Offspring. The Talmud, in our *sugya*, does not explain how the pebbles case is logically derived from Foot—but we can reconstruct this derivation by looking at the history of the case.

David Halivni, "Reflections on Classical Jewish Hermeneutics," *PAAJR* 62 (1996), 19–127 (107–11). Halivni also notes that this phrase always appears in the *stam* except for one occurrence (which happens to be attributed to Rav Papa); ibid., 109.

29 Some versions and commentators take the connection between Rav Papa's teaching to the *hilkheta* even further—see below, n. 38.

30 Reines, Ḥotam, 58–62; Jacobs, *Studies*, 144–45.

The ruling that the animal's owner must pay for only half of the damage in a pebbles case has a complex history in Talmudic sources.[31] The case is first mentioned in the Mishnah, in the context of the distinction between "attested" (common, expected, normal) and "innocent" (uncommon, unexpected, abnormal) damages. The Mishnah first lists five from each category and then explains that common damages carry full liability (since the damage should have been expected and prevented by the damaging party) while uncommon damages result in a payment for only half of the damage. One of the common causes of damages the Mishnah lists is "the foot [of an animal], attested to break [things] as it walks" (m. B. Q. 1:4).

This clause is interpreted in the passage that follows: "How is the foot attested to break [things] as it walks? An animal is attested to walk in its normal way and break [something]. [But] if it was kicking, or if pebbles shot out from under its feet and it broke vessels—he [its owner] pays half of the damage" (m. B. Q. 2:1). The cases of pebbles and kicking are mentioned to show that not all damages an animal causes with its foot are considered common damages; these cases are examples of uncommon damages that occur as an animal walks. The original reason for the reduced restitution in the case of pebbles was, then, that this damage was seen as uncommon or "innocent."

Most animal damages that are designated as "innocent" in rabbinic law are so designated because they are instances in which the animal deviates from its normal behavior. Since it is not normal for domestic animals, generally speaking, to gore people or to consume vessels and clothing, these damages are classified as "innocent" and the damaging party is assigned only half of the payment. Specific animals can become attested for certain damages according to their observed behavior: if my ox is particularly aggressive and has gored the neighbor's ox three times, testimonies may be submitted to have this ox designated as attested for goring; I will have to pay the full amount the next time it gores. The classification

31   The two classical studies of this case's development are Samuel Atlas, "Towards a Development of the *sugya* and the *halakha*" (Heb.), *HUCA* 17 (1942), 1–12, and Weiss, *Damages*, 229–70. Both have been supplanted by Avishalom Westreich, "The Crystallization and Development of the Pebbles Ruling in the Words of the Tannaim, in the Words of the Amoraim and in the Talmuds" (Heb.), *Sidra* 19 (2004), 77–100 (see ibid., 87–88, for a critique of Atlas and Weiss).

While the account given here builds on Westreich's, it differs from it significantly. Westreich identifies as the seminal point the expansion of the dispute between Symmachus and the sages (ibid., 84), but he does not explain what motivated this expansion. Here, the main point of shift is ascribed to an ambivalence inherent in the case itself and the explication of this ambivalence in the Yerushalmi. It seems that Westreich dates the *baraitot* that appear in the Bavli and are clearly reworked to an earlier date than the Yerushalmi's *sugya* (ibid., 84, 94–95).

of cases as "innocent" or "attested," then, is generally based on the animal's behavior.

The case of pebbles, in contrast, is designated as "innocent" not because it is abnormal for an animal to sprinkle pebbles as it walks, but rather because the probability that the pebbles will damage property is low. This probability depends more on the direction and angle in which the pebbles shot out—and on the location of the property—than on the animal's behavior. We could say that it is "attested" for an animal to walk in such a way that causes pebbles to shoot out, but it is "not attested" for the pebbles to damage property.

Since the laws that distinguish "attested" damages from "innocent" damages are premised on the correlation between the animal's behavior and the likelihood of the damage, the designation of the pebbles damage as "innocent," which is not based on such correlation, raises some problems. One problem stems from the laws pertaining to the location of the damage. Generally, attested damages are not eligible for restitution if both the damaging party and the damaged property are in the public domain (*reshut ha-rabbim*) since the damaged party should have protected their property from damages that they could have reasonably expected to occur and since the damaging party has equal rights in the public domain (if I leave my formal china in the middle of the highway, I cannot expect full restitution if a car runs over it).[32] This reasoning, however, cannot be applied to damages caused by pebbles an animal shot out: neither the damaged party nor the owner of the animal could have reasonably expected the damage to happen.

This is precisely the problem that stands at the center of the Palestinian Talmud's discussion of our *mishnah* (*y. B. Q.* 2:1 2d), a discussion that presents a seminal development in the rabbis' understanding of the pebbles ruling. The Yerushalmi's discussion is premised here on a *baraita*, preserved in the Tosefta (*t. B. Q.* 1:5; 2:22–3:24) but omitted in the Yerushalmi, which assigns restitution for pebbles damages even if the damage occurred in the public domain.[33] The Yerushalmi challenges this ruling: "But is it not normal for an animal to sprinkle pebbles as it walks [and therefore, should not the owner be exempt from paying if the damage was caused in the public domain]?" The Yerushalmi then cites a se-

32 Noam Zohar recently suggested that originally the variables of attestation and place of damage were part of discrete systems of case classification. See Zohar, "Scripture," 199–203.

33 According to Lewy's reconstruction; he suggests that the *baraita* was omitted due to a *homoioteleuton* (Lewy, *Interpretation*, 45). Alternatively, the Yerushalmi assumes that the Mishnah itself assigns payment for pebbles damage even if it was done in the public domain, and asks why. See Joseph Hirsch Dünner, *Ḥidushei ha-riṣad* (4 vols.; Jerusalem: Mosad Ha-Rav, 1981–99), 3.433, for a different reconstruction of the text.

ries of sources. The first two sources interpret the ruling as applicable only in very specific cases. The third source, a teaching from R. Eleazar, explains that when the animal causes damages through something "outside its body" it is irrelevant where the damage occurred, and half a payment is due in both public and private spaces.

R. Eleazar *does not* intend to provide the reasoning for the reduced restitution when he characterizes the pebbles damage as caused by something outside the animal's body. Rather, his teaching comes to explain why the damage is eligible for restitution even in public spaces. In Babylonia, however, this indirect nature of the pebbles damage will replace the low probability of the damage as the *reason* that the payment is reduced to half. Moreover, "pebbles" in Babylonian teachings no longer refers to a specific case, but to a category of damages, a category that is defined as damages caused not by the animal's body directly but outside its body, indirectly. The characteristic that is made explicit in the Yerushalmi in order to explain one aspect of the ruling in a specific case becomes in Babylonia the defining characteristic of an abstract category.

The Bavli dedicates several discussions to the case of pebbles, the most important of which centers on a group of reworked Tannaitic sources (*b. B. Q.* 17b). The sources as they appear in most versions of the Bavli present a series of cases in which Symmachus disagrees with the rest of the sages: first, our case of an animal shooting out pebbles as it walks; second, the case of chickens who befouled food by hopping around and spraying dirt and pebbles on it; third, in the case of a chicken who, flying from one place to another, pushed the air with its wings in a way that broke vessels. In all three cases, the sages assign a payment for half the damage, while Symmachus assigns the full amount.

These sources seem to indicate that there is a principled dispute between the sages and Symmachus on the question of indirect damages: for the sages, the indirect damage implies reduced liability; for Symmachus, it does not. This is how the Bavli interprets these sources, applying the dispute between Symmachus and the sages in the case of pebbles to a large number of cases (*b. B. Q.* 17b–19a). The result is that the ruling of reduced payment in pebbles (and a series of other cases) is no longer traced to the low probability of this damage, but to its indirect nature.

The Tannaitic sources the Bavli cites are also preserved in the Tosefta, where there is no trace of a principled dispute between Symmachus and the rabbis or even that there was a dispute on indirect damages. Symmachus and the sages simply dispute whether the damage is "attested" or not, as we have seen in the Mishnah and as is the case in other Tannaitic disputes.[34] It is difficult to say with much certainty at what point these

34 For a discussion of the Tosefta's sources in comparison with the Bavli's, see West-

Tannaitic sources transformed into a systematic dispute on indirect damages,[35] but the process probably has its origins in a juxtaposition of the Yerushalmi and the Tosefta. R. Eleazar's teaching in the Yerushalmi makes explicit the indirect nature of the pebbles damage. This teaching employs terminology similar to that of the Tosefta's account of the Symmachus dispute: the Tosefta contrasts damage the chicken caused "with its body" (be-gufo) with damage it caused by moving air; R. Eleazar says the pebbles are "outside the animal's body" (ḥuṣ le-gufo).[36] When the Tosefta is read with R. Eleazar's teaching in mind, it implies that Symmachus does not distinguish between direct and indirect damages, while

---

reich, "Pebbles," 80–85. The Bavli's versions (and to a lesser extent, the Yerushalmi's) was so compelling it led even Saul Lieberman and Abraham Goldberg to "emend" the Tosefta in light of the dispute on indirect damages (see Westreich, ibid., 82, pace Lieberman, Tosefta Ki-fshuta [Heb.; 10 vols.; New York: Jewish Theological Seminary, 1955–88], 9.16, and Goldberg, Tosefta Bava Kamma: A Structural and Analytic Commentary [Heb.; Jerusalem: Magnes, 2001], 56; Goldberg does note the Bavli's addition of pebbles to the first baraita; ibid., 49).

35   On the one hand, the Yerushalmi already has one of these Tannaitic sources transformed: t. B. Q. 1:1 rules that in the case of a chicken who damaged food by bouncing dirt on it, the owner of the chicken pays for the full damage (this is the text that Lieberman and Goldberg emend—see previous footnote); in the Yerushalmi, possibly because this was already seen as an instance of "pebbles" or indirect damage, the payment is set at half (y. B. Q. 2:1 2d). On the other hand, the Yerushalmi is not aware of the other changes introduced to these Tannaitic sources. Furthermore, we can trace some of the evolution to the stam itself (the first baraita is emended because of the stam's argument, הזיק פשיטא! אלא התיז והזיק, and see there also the Bavli's comment on the introduction of pebbles—צרורות מאן דכר שמייהו).

The version of the baraitot in Ms. Florence of the Bavli is peculiar. In the first baraita, where the common version mentions "pebbles" in Symmachus's words, Ms. Florence, like the Tosefta, does not. Furthermore, the baraitot in this manuscript always rule for the full payment, which makes the manuscript closer to the Tosefta in other instances (e.g., in the baraita about the chicken and dirt), though by ruling for full payment in the first part of this baraita this version is more distant from the Tosefta. The comments in the margin emend the version according to the common version. It is possible to dismiss these variations as yet another example of the infamous "ignorance" and "incompetence" of this manuscript's scribe (for which, see Rabbinovicz, Variae on San., 1, and David Rosenthal's introduction to the manuscript's facsimile edition, Babylonian Talmud: Codex Florence [Jerusalem: Makor, 1972], 3). But they might alternatively indicate that the formulation of the baraitot (or at least the first one) was still fluctuating during the Bavli's transmission period.

36   R. Eleazar's teaching itself is not in the Bavli, but a parallel teaching, attributed to R. Yohanan, is cited on b. B. Q. 19b, אמר ר' יוחנן אין חצי נזק חלוק לא לרשות היחיד ולא לרשות הרבים. It is likely this is a version of R. Eleazar's teaching, as teachings attributed to R. Eleazar are often attributed elsewhere to R. Yohanan (and vice versa; see Chanoch Albeck, Introduction to the Talmud, Babli and Yerushalmi [Heb.; Tel Aviv: Dvir, 1969], 226), even though this teaching does not mention explicitly the indirect nature of the damage (thus allowing the Bavli to suggest it discusses the half payment in the case of Horn).

the sages do, and that it is this distinction that leads the sages to the ruling on reduced compensation.

At the end, however, even this interpretation of the pebbles case was
replaced. The Talmud attributes to Rava a discussion of the dispute between Symmachus and the sages that challenges the reasoning for the
reduced payment:

> Rava said: All is well for Symmachus, who believes that [a damage an ani-
> mal caused with] its force is equivalent to [damage it caused with] its body;
> but for the rabbis, if [that damage] is equivalent to [damage it caused with]
> its body, he [the owner] should pay for the entire damage, but if it is not
> equivalent to [damage it caused with] its body, let him not pay even for half
> the damage? Later Rava said: Everyone agrees that [damage the animal
> caused with its force] is equivalent to [damage it caused with] its body, and
> the half payment in pebbles is learned from tradition. (b. B. Q. 17b)

Rava rejects the logic that the indirect nature of the damage should lead
to a partial reduction in payment (as we have seen, this indeed was not
the original reason for the ruling). Instead, he traces the Mishnah's ruling
to a special tradition that lies beyond legal reasoning. But at least as it is
taken by the Bavli, Rava's statement does not completely disconnect the
indirect nature of the damage from the reduction in restitution. Since the
Bavli uses the word "pebbles" for all damages caused indirectly (with the
animal's "force"), the special tradition about pebbles is also a general
tradition concerning indirect damages: all indirect damages are assigned
half of the restitution, and this ruling is derived from a special tradition
rather than from the characteristics of indirect damages.

THE CONCLUSION OF THE *SUGYA* (2)

These developments allow us to appreciate better the abruptness with
which the *sugya* is concluded. As we have now seen, the pebbles case
raises substantive questions about its legal classification: is it predict-
able or unpredictable? Is there a substantive difference between indirect
and direct damages? Rabbis throughout the Talmudic period gave different answers to these questions, but the authors of our *sugya* choose to
defer these questions for now. This is not because they shy away from
excursions off the main narrative: throughout the *sugya*, the Talmud
takes many opportunities to explain various concepts and discuss various distinctions, even when they do not relate directly to the relationship between Fathers and Offspring (e.g., that people have a *mazal*
whereas animals do not, on 2b; the distinctions between complete and

partial destruction and autonomous or non-autonomous movement, both on 3a). The Talmud, I suggest, avoids presenting answers to this question at this point precisely in order to achieve an abrupt conclusion contrasted with reasoned discourse.

The history of the pebbles case illuminates the very last part of the *sugya*, where the Talmud asks why pebbles are considered an Offspring of Foot:

> And on what account is it called an Offspring of Foot? So that the restitution would come even from the best assets. But according to Rava, this is uncertain! For Rava questioned, "the half payment in pebbles, is it paid only from the animal's body or even from the best assets?" For Rava it is uncertain, for Rav Papa it is certain [that the payment can be collected from the best assets]. And for Rava, for whom this matter is under question, on what account is it called an Offspring of Foot? In order to exempt it [when it occurs] in the public domain. (*b. B. Q.* 3b)

The Talmud's answers diverge from previous instances of establishing links between Fathers and their Offspring. Earlier in the *sugya*, the connection between Fathers and Offspring was established by noting their shared characteristics: the common or uncommon nature of the damage, whether the damage was caused in motion or not, the extent to which the damaging party benefited from the damage. From our survey of the history of the pebbles case, we know that the common characteristic shared by the Foot case and the pebbles case is that both concern damages caused in the course of an animal's regular behavior while in motion.

Here, however, the Talmud does not discuss what characteristics Foot and the pebbles case might have in common. The connections that the Bavli does draw are of desirable consequence: we need pebbles to be an Offspring of Foot so that, as with Foot cases, the damaging party will be exempt if the damage occurred in the public domain, or so that we may collect the reparations from all of the damaging party's assets. We are not even told *why* these consequences are desirable in the case of pebbles.[37]

---

37 The sense that the derivation of pebbles from Foot is a given to be justified rather than the result of a reasoned process is created not just by the form of the Bavli's answer but also by the question itself. The question, "and on what account is it called an Offspring of Foot?" (ואמאי קרי לה תולדה דרגל), echoes the beginning of the *sugya*, in the discussion of Shabbat. After it notes that for R. Eliezer there is no practical difference between the performance of labors designated Fathers and labors designated Offspring, the Talmud asks, "And on what account [a labor designated Father] is called Father and [a labor designated Offspring] is called Offspring?" (ואמאי קרי ליה אב ואמאי קרי לה תולדה). In both cases, these identically formulated questions seek reasons for already established facts; both the distinction between Fathers and Offspring in Shabbat and the derivation of the pebbles case from Foot are taken for granted.

The Talmud's answers are so unsatisfactory that they led some medieval commentators to argue that we must know that pebbles is an Offspring of Foot from that same tradition that taught us the reduced restitution.[38]

In its answer, the Bavli also creates a dispute between Rava and Rav Papa, arguing that Rav Papa believed that the restitution for pebbles damages may be collected from any of the damaging party's assets, while Rava (as we know from other places) was uncertain about this. This dispute is both unlikely and unnecessary: unlikely, since we have no tradition from Rav Papa indicating he took a stance on this question; unnecessary, since Rav Papa also seems to agree that pebbles are not eligible for restitution in the public domain, and therefore it would suffice to say that this was the reason for deriving pebbles from Foot. Whatever other reason the Talmud might have had to create this dispute,[39] it also contributes to the sense of arbitrariness of the conclusion.[40]

38   The version that survives in Ms. Vatican in the margin and in the Venice edition, as well as in a few medieval commentators (see Rabbinovicz, *Variae BQ*, 4 n. 8), relies on the distinction between restitutive payments and punitive payments, saying that the tradition teaches us that half damage paid in pebbles is restitutitve (דהלכתא גמירי לה דממונא הוא, "about which they had a tradition that it is restitutive"). This line of understanding (see, e.g., Rashi, ad loc.) goes on to point out that though we would have expected the pebbles case to be an Offspring of Horn, given that the payment is set as in Horn cases at half the damage, the fact that the payment is restitutive and not punitive (as it would be in Horn cases) teaches us that it is an Offspring of Foot.

This interpretation relies on the Talmud's statement in *B. Q.* 15b that the payment in pebbles is restitutive, which indeed reads, חצי נזק צרורות דהלכתא גמירי לה דממונא הוא, just like the version in Ms. Vatican of our *sugya*. As Westreich showed, however, this interpretation is based on a wrong parsing of this phrase, which ought to be translated "the [payment for] half the damage in pebbles, about which they had a tradition, *and* which is restitutive [וממונא הוא]"—which is the version in several manuscripts; the *hilkheta* thus delineates the amount rather than nature of the payment. See Westreich, "Pebbles," 93.

This interpretation is further unlikely since Rav Papa himself does not believe that the half payment in Horn damages is punitive (see *b. B. Q.* 15a) and therefore for him—whose opinion the Talmud is allegedly reconstructing—the restitutive nature of the damage would not necessarily mean it is an Offspring of Foot. Finally, how could the Talmud even ostensibly ask "why is the case of pebbles called an Offspring of Foot?" if that designation was derived from tradition?

39   Halivni, *MM BQ*, 10–11, offers two alternative solutions. In the first solution, he suggests that Rav Papa's teaching itself already included the identification of pebbles as the dissimilar Offspring and that the *stam* entered the whole *sugya* between both parts of Rav Papa's teaching—the assertion that both kinds of Offspring exist and the identification of pebbles as the dissimilar one. The second solution is that the two different justifications ("Rava's" and "Rav Papa's") derive from different layers of the *stam*.

40   The discussion in the Bavli here seems to imply that everyone is certain that pebbles damages are exempt in the public domain. The Yerushalmi, as we have seen, had a different position. More important, in *b. B. Q.* 19a the Bavli cites R. Yirmiah, who leaves this question open ended. It seems possible then that our *sugya* was unaware of that *sugya*.

Our *sugya* revolves around Rav Papa's teaching, and in its final moves our *sugya* maintains it, but this teaching is divorced from the Talmud's theoretical framework rather than embedded in it. The very structure of our *sugya* communicates this ambivalence. On the one hand, the opening moves are designed to prepare the ground for Rav Papa's teaching. On the other hand, they do so in a way that constructs or emphasizes the tension between the system implied in teaching and the one implied in the Talmud. The conclusion of the *sugya* validates this teaching, but only outside the Bavli's systematic inquiry. The incongruity between the conclusion and the earlier inquiry is emphasized, we have seen, by the return to the question about the Offspring of Foot and by the different rhythm and standards of proofs this conclusion presents. Like the other texts we will examine in this part of the book, our *sugya* is instructive precisely because it does not reject tradition, but rather combines a commitment to preserving and maintaining tradition with a move to distance or undermine it. The scholars who shaped this *sugya* quoted and eventually maintained Rav Papa's dictum; but by creating a literary structure that contrasted their own reasoning with the implication of this tradition they also showed us that the offspring may be very much unlike their fathers.

Chapter Two

THE DIVISION INTO LAYERS

Our ability to separate the words of the Talmud's creators from the traditions they quote depends on the omnipresent literary distinction in the Bavli between the anonymous literary framework and the attributed traditions embedded in it. Most scholars today believe this distinction reflects the Talmud's literary history: the dicta were produced first and the *stam* was woven around them by later scholars.

This chapter explores the possibility that this distinction is constructed, that it is a strategy pursued by the Talmud's creators. The distance between the dicta and the *stam,* I argue, is not simply a reflection of their different provenances. Rather, it may also be the outcome of a particular pattern of organization and technique of differentiation that was maintained throughout the Talmud and even imposed on materials in which it did not exist. We will see in this chapter how the Bavli takes Palestinian texts and divides them into layers, assigning dynamic, narrative, and deliberative material to the anonymous layer and static and apodictic material to the dicta. It is this strategy that produces the "Talmud's voice" as distinct from its traditions, this pattern that separates tradition from analysis. The gap between the two layers is not the mark of a historical gap that the Talmud's creators tried to overcome, but a literary gap that these scholars produced. The conclusion of this chapter argues that this strategy allowed those who shaped the Talmud to balance the conflicting demands of transmission and innovation in the oral performances in which our Talmud originated.

THE DEBATE OVER THE LITERARY HISTORY OF THE TALMUD

The contemporary consensus in American scholarship follows the work of Shamma Friedman and David Weiss Halivni in dating the *stam* as later than the Amoraic dicta. These scholars and others support this chronology by demonstrating that the anonymous parts of the Talmud depend on or refer to the dicta attributed to Amoraic sages;[1] that anonymous parts differ from the dicta in language and style—whereas dicta tend to be brief and in Hebrew, anonymous parts are verbose and mostly in Aramaic;[2] that the anonymous parts present new ideas and developments absent in the dicta;[3] that without its anonymous parts, the Babylonian Talmud is much more similar to the earlier Palestinian Talmud;[4] and that manuscripts and other textual witnesses present more variation in the anonymous parts than in the dicta.[5] All these considerations suggest to Friedman, Halivni, and their followers that the Talmud holds two separate literary corpora of different provenances—the early dicta and the late *stam*.[6]

Because the *stam* plays such a central role in structuring the discussions in the Talmud and in bringing the different traditions into a conversation, the question encompasses more than just the date of this or that component of the Talmud; at stake is how the Talmud, as a text, came about. Halivni argues that prior to the composition of the *stam*, rabbinic traditions circulated as legal rulings without discussion or narration, at most paired with one another; only through the late composition of the *stam* were these traditions woven into the elaborate *sugyot* we know today.[7] Daniel Boyarin concludes that we should not associate the compos-

---

1   Richard Kalmin, *The Redaction of the Babylonian Talmud: Amoraic or Saboraic?* (Cincinnati: Hebrew Union College Press, 1989), is dedicated to a comprehensive demonstration of this claim. See also Shamma Friedman, *Talmudic Studies: Investigating the Sugya, Variant Readings, and Aggada* (New York and Jerusalem: Jewish Theological Seminary, 2010), 11–12 and 19–20, and David Halivni, *Sources and Traditions: A Source Critical Commentary on the Talmud: Tractate Baba Bathra* (Heb.; Jerusalem: Magnes, 2007), 14–17.

2   See Friedman, *Talmudic Studies*, 22–23 and the literature cited there in n. 60, as well as Hyman Klein, "Gemara and Sebara," *JQR* 38 (1947), 67–91 (75).

3   For a compelling example, see Leib Moscovitz, *Talmudic Reasoning: From Casuistics to Conceptualization* (Tübingen: Mohr Siebeck, 2002), 303–13 and 346–50.

4   Friedman, *Talmudic Studies*, 21, and the literature cited in n. 57 there; cf. Yaacov Sussmann, "Ve-shuv li-yerushalmi neziqin," in *Talmudic Studies I* (ed. Y. Sussmann and D. Rosenthal; Jerusalem: Magnes, 1990), 55–134 (101–7).

5   Friedman, *Talmudic Studies*, 25–26.

6   This particular formulation is from David Halivni, *Sources and Traditions: From Yoma to Hagigah* (Heb.; Jerusalem: Jewish Theological Seminary, 1974), 8. While Sussmann also argues that the distinction between the Amoraic nucleus and the late Babylonian *sugya* "is the essence of the study of the Bavli" ("Yerushalmi," 113), he is extremely critical of what he sees as the transparentness of the distinction in Halivni's formulation, which does not, in his view, do justice to the permeability and fluctuation in and between both layers (ibid., and especially 109 n. 204).

7   Halivni, *MM BB*, 115. Halivni concedes that limited couplings occurred before the *stamma'im*—see *MM BB*, 37–45, 52 and the conclusion, ibid., 139—but there is solid evidence for a more extensive redactional activity prior to the composition of the *stam*.

ers of the *stam* with the redaction of the Talmud, "as if there were a Talmud already to be redacted," but rather with the "production" of the Talmud.[8] Friedman allows for greater compositional activity prior to the *stam*, positing the existence of skeletal arrangements of traditions before the composition of the anonymous layer. Still, even for Friedman, only with the *stam*'s narration and interpretation did these clusters of tradition become what we now recognize as the Talmud.[9]

Robert Brody recently offered a critique of the late dating of the *stam*. At the center of his critique are passages in which, he claims, Amoraic statements refer to content found in the anonymous layer.[10] In addition to these examples, Brody also offers arguments against the strong connection other scholars make between the form of Talmudic material and its provenance. He explains the different styles of presentation—Aramaic vs. Hebrew, brief vs. verbose, anonymous vs. attributed—not as indicators of different periods but as different conventions for transmitting material with different functions. It may be, Brody argues, that rulings were formulated in Hebrew and attributed to specific rabbis while the deliberations on these rulings were formulated in Aramaic and transmitted anonymously, but that does not imply that they belong to different periods.[11] He also points to cases in which we can document the transformation of a comment that appears attributed in one place in rabbinic literature and then anonymously in another place (because, he argues, the attribution was forgotten); anonymous statements may thus contain early material.[12]

Friedman too discusses these transformations of material from one form to another. But whereas Brody attributes such transformations to

8   Daniel Boyarin, "Hellenism in Jewish Babylonia," in *The Cambridge Companion to the Talmud and Rabbinic Literature* (ed. C. E. Fonrobert and M. S. Jaffee; Cambridge: Cambridge University Press, 2007), 336–63 (342).

9   Friedman, *Talmudic Studies*, 58. See also 54: יש והבחנת החטיבות זו מזו עשויה להבליט סידור קדום של תלמוד אשר בו הברייתות והמימרות בלחוד, לעומת התוספת של משא ומתן של דברי סתם התלמוד שהיא מאוחרת לו בקביעתה הספרותית. The words בקביעתה הספרותית might indicate that Friedman is not saying that the *stam* was added to clusters of *baraitot* and *memrot* but rather that this layer existed all the time but only became fixed at a later date; but the analyses on pp. 44–47 and again especially the account on p. 58 indicate that he conceives of arrangement and narration as two different stages.

10   Robert Brody, "The Anonymous Talmud and the Words of the Amoraim" (Heb.), in *Iggud: Selected Essays in Jewish Studies: Volume 1* (Heb.; ed. B. J. Schwartz, A. Shemesh, and A. Melamed; Jerusalem: Magnes 2009), 213–32 (226): "The determinative proof must come from examples in which, it can be shown with a great degree of probability, that a certain *amora* referred to an existing anonymous material." He adduces sixteen examples from *b. Ket.* in an appendix on pp. 228–32.

11   Brody, "Anonymous Talmud," 223.

12   Brody, "Anonymous Talmud," 225, and idem, "Sifrut ha-ge'onim veha-ṭeqsṭ ha-talmudi," in *Talmudic Studies I* (ed. Y. Sussmann and D. Rosenthal; Jerusalem: Magnes, 1990), 237–303 (277–78).

the accidents of oral transmission, Friedman and other scholars—including Yaacov Sussmann—have emphasized that in some cases, it is the Talmud's creators who change the form of the material. They create or modify what appear to be *baraitot* and *memrot*, expressing their own ideas and concerns through sources attributed to the past; and they assimilate into their own anonymous deliberations material that originates in earlier attributed sources.[13]

The fluctuation of material from one form to another dictates that we treat separately the dating of *content* found in the *stam*, on the one hand, and the dating of the composition of the *stam* as a layer, on the other hand.[14] Passages in which Amoraic sages react to objections, statements, or interpretations that now appear in the Bavli's anonymous layer cannot in themselves prove that these sages knew these materials in the form of an anonymous dialectic discussion similar to the one we find in our Talmud. The dates of specific ideas or formulations should be determined, as both Brody and Friedman agree, on a case-by-case basis, but such dating does not necessarily teach us about the formation of the layers as layers.

While this disconnect between form and provenance might conceal from us the origins of the Talmud's sources, it might also disclose something significant about the creation of the Talmud itself. Friedman focuses on the gap between the scholarly interest in classifying the layers and the actual provenance of the sources. But the fact that the creators of the Bavli maintain the stylistic distinctions between the layers regardless of the material's provenance shows us that the division into layers is not just a product of modern scholarship; it is, in large part, the action of the Talmud's creators themselves. It is the Talmud that uses certain citation terms for *baraitot* and *memrot*, and no citation terms for the anonymous layer.[15] It is the Talmud that, more often than not, presents *baraitot* and *memrot* in Hebrew—even when they have been modified or produced at a later stage; and Aramaic for the anonymous deliberations and glosses— even when it incorporates earlier materials into these anonymous discussions.[16] The distinction between attributed or cited sources and an anonymous deliberation of these sources is not simply a phenomenon observed

---

13   Friedman, *Talmudic Studies*, 48–50 and especially 59–72; Sussman, "Yerushalmi," 109 n. 204.

14   Cf. Sussmann, "Yerushalmi," 110 n. 210.

15   In the conclusion of this chapter, I suggest that it is this distinction—i.e., "cited" vs. "citing"—that distinguishes between the layers, and not the more common "attributed"–"not attributed" distinction. Most *baraitot* are "anonymous," and we would never think of including them in the anonymous layer because they are *cited*; and we even have *memrot* that are cited anonymously (בכדי; see Brody, "Anonymous Talmud," 225)—but it is precisely because these *memrot* are cited that we should not include them in the anonymous layer.

16   See the references in n. 13.

by scholars—it is also a representational strategy pursued by the Talmud's creators and a basic organizing principle of the Talmud's structure.

As noted above, scholars have seen this organizing principle, which correlates function and style, as original to the material—whether, like Friedman and Halivni, they believe it is the result of chronological difference, or like Brody, they imagine it as reflecting different conventions of transmission. But the observation that the Talmud's creators did, on occasion, reshape their sources in the form of either layer, raises the possibility that they could also manufacture this structure themselves by dividing the material into layers.

This chapter compares a *sugya* in the Bavli with a similar *sugya* preserved in the Palestinian Talmud. In the Palestinian version, there is no clear distinction in function or characteristics between attributed and anonymous material. In the Bavli's reorganization of the material, we can see a move toward a distinction between a narrating and deliberating anonymous framework and the attributed sources that it discusses. The Babylonian adaptation does not consist of weaving an anonymous layer around an existing cluster of traditions; it produces both the Amoraic teachings and the anonymous commentary, and most important, the division between them.

The layered structure of the Talmud, Moshe Benovitz notes, implies at least a relative chronology: it seems reasonable that the literary framework would be later than the sources it discusses in any given *sugya*.[17] In fact, despite the impression one might get from some modern scholarship,[18] the understanding that the *stam* presents the words of the Talmud itself, which are by definition later than the Talmud's sources, has been intuitive for many readers of the Talmud for a long time.[19] This chapter not only joins other scholars in claiming that, at least in some cases, a

---

17 Moshe Benovitz, *BT Shevu'ot III: Critical Edition with Comprehensive Commentary* (Heb.; Jerusalem: Jewish Theological Seminary, 2003), 8. I find Benovitz's argument that certain anonymous parts of that tractate must be early *qua anonymous parts* since they seem to have affected the Yerushalmi, unconvincing—for as he himself seems to imply (when he says, ibid., "dependence of a *sugya* in the Yerushalmi on a *sugya* in the Bavli, *or* Babylonian material that appears in the *stam*"; my emphasis) it might be that while this material appears now in the *stam* it had its origin in a different form.

18 See, e.g., David Halivni, *Sources and Traditions: A Source Critical Commentary on the Talmud: Tractate Baba Metzia* (Heb.; Jerusalem: Magnes, 2003), 8, who writes against the "communis opinio" and the reference to Albeck there. It is interesting that while Halivni always represents his approach as innovative, Friedman chooses to represent his as turning an old interpretive approach into a systematic method (e.g., in *Talmudic Studies*, 12–15).

19 See both traditional and academic commentators cited by Friedman, *Talmudic Studies*, 12-15 (but see my discussion in the Conclusion of this book on the limits of this observation). The famous chapter in Halevy's *Dorot ha-rishonim*, which undertakes to prove the existence of early anonymous material, opens with the sentence: "We have been accustomed to think that the *stam* is in every place and occasion only from the time

thorough investigation shows that this dating is false; it argues that it is the very structure chosen by the Talmud's creators that gives us this impression of a chronological distance between the Talmud's voice and its sources.

THE BAVLI AND THE YERUSHALMI

The Palestinian Talmud, or the Yerushalmi, completed centuries before the Babylonian Talmud in the second half of the fourth century,[20] is essential to our investigation of the Bavli's layers in two ways. First, in some cases, the Yerushalmi allows us to approximate what the Talmud's sources looked like when they were received by the Talmud's creators. How much of the Yerushalmi the Babylonian scholars knew remains under debate.[21] There is, however, extensive documentation of passages in the two Talmuds—including those discussed in this chapter and elsewhere in this book—which share not just a tradition or two but an ordered sequence of material.[22] In such cases it is reasonable to posit either that the creators of the Babylonian *sugya* had something like the Palestinian *sugya* before them or that both *sugyot* depend on some kind of an "early Talmud" that circulated before the formation of the documents we have.[23] This phenomenon itself already complicates the notion that rab-

of the Talmud's completion." Isaac Halevy, *Dorot ha-rishonim* (Frankfurt: Jüdische Literarische Gesellschaft, 1906), 2.550.

20 Leib Moscovitz, "The Formation and Character of the Jerusalem Talmud," in *The Cambridge History of Judaism IV: The Late Roman-Rabbinic Period* (ed. S. T. Katz; Cambridge: Cambridge University Press, 2006), 663–77 (665–67).

21 See Alyssa Gray, *A Talmud in Exile: The Influence of Yerushalmi Avodah Zarah on the Formation of Bavli Avodah Zarah* (Providence: Brown Judaic Studies, 2005), 1–33. On the question of using the Yerushalmi to date the anonymous layer, see Gray, ibid., 175–95, and Robert Brody, "The Contribution of the Yerushalmi to the Dating of the Anonymous Material in the Bavli" (Heb.), in *Melekhet Mahshevet: Studies in the Redaction and Development of Talmudic Literature* (ed. A. Amit and A. Shemesh; Ramat Gan: Bar Ilan University Press, 2011), 27–37.

22 Friedman, *Talmudic Studies*, 44–47; Noah Aminoah, "Qit'ei talmud mi-sidur qadum be-masekhet rosh ha-shanah," in *Studies in Rabbinic Literature, Bible, and Jewish History* (ed. Y. D. Gilat; Ramat Gan: Bar Ilan University Press, 1982), 185–97; Alyssa Gray, "A Bavli *sugya* and its Two Yerushalmi Parallels: Issues of Literary Relationship and Redaction," in *How Should Rabbinic Literature Be Read in the Modern World?* (ed. M. Kraus; Piscataway, NJ: Gorgias, 2006), 35–77; see also the examples discussed in Chapters 3 and 4 of this book.

23 Influential statements of this "early Talmud" hypothesis include Israel Lewy, *Interpretation des I.–VI. Abschnittes des pälast. Talmud-Traktats Nesikin* (Heb. and Ger.; Breslau, 1895–1914; repr. Jerusalem: Kedem, 1970), especially pp. 3–5 of the Introduction; Eliezer S. Rosenthal, "Le-'arikhat masekhet pesaḥ rishon: bavli" (Ph.D. dissertation, He-

binic traditions were circulated as discrete rulings before they were woven together into the Talmud by the composers of the *stam*: at least in those cases, the creators of the Talmud received their sources already structured in some kind of sequence.

More important, the Yerushalmi offers us a critical perspective on the Bavli's layered structure because the Yerushalmi, in general, is not structured in the same way. There are, to be sure, anonymous materials in the Yerushalmi, but, as Leib Moscovitz observes, they are "of a piece, both substantively and stylistically, with the attributed material."[24] The Yerushalmi may employ different styles for "apodictic" and "dialectic" functions, but those functions are taken up just as frequently by attributed teachings as they are by anonymous teachings; the result is that the chronological distance between a "narrating" layer and a layer of "rulings" that we find in the Bavli does not exist in the Yerushalmi. This difference between the Talmuds invites us to see the Bavli's structure not as an inevitable result of the way Amoraic material was formulated but as part of representational habits or choices of those who shaped the later Talmud. Furthermore, this is not simply a difference between two parallel alternatives for presenting rabbinic literature: the chronological priority of the Yerushalmi and the large number of cases in which the Bavli seems to depend on Palestinian *sugyot* make it likely that the Bavli's creators knew this earlier form of representing Talmudic material and replaced it with their own.

Let me make these suggestions concrete with a brief preliminary example. The Palestinian Talmud reports, in the name of Hanan bar Ba, that when Rav recited the prayer, he used to bow as he was saying the words "blessed are you" and then rise again before he mentioned God's name. Shmuel then offers scriptural support for Rav's practice with Ps. 146:8, "YHWH lifts those who are bowed down." R. Ami objects with Mal. 2:5, "and before my name he bowed," a verse that seems to indicate

---

brew University of Jerusalem, 1959); David Rosenthal, "'Arikhot qdumot ha-meshuq'ot ba-talmud ha-bavli," in *Talmudic Studies 1* (ed. Y. Sussmann and D. Rosenthal; Jerusalem: Magnes, 1990), 155–204; Friedman, *Talmudic Studies,* 46–47; Sussmann, "Yerushalmi," 98–106. For Alyssa Gray's critique of this hypothesis, see below, n. 55.

24   Moscovitz, "Jerusalem Talmud," 672. Even Nurit Be'eri, who goes much further than Moscovitz in the degree of uniqueness she attributes to the Yerushalmi's *stam,* concedes that it is difficult to distinguish anonymous material in the Yerushalmi from material attributed to the last generation of sages in that Talmud, and that the two largely overlap. Nurit Be'eri, *Exploring Ta'aniot: Yerushalmi, Tractate Ta'aniot: Forming and Redacting the Traditions* (Heb.; Ramat Gan: Bar Ilan University Press, 2008), 146, 149–50. See also Brody, "Anonymous Talmud," 224–25. I follow Be'eri here in differentiating the anonymous voice from the transmitting voice—which is also anonymous (see Be'eri, *Ta'aniot,* 110); indeed what the Bavli does can be described as a unification of these two functions.

that the divine name should be accompanied with bowing rather than rising. R. Abin replies that R. Ami's objection would have indeed been appropriate if the verse said "*at* my name," but since it says "*before* my name" the verse in fact supports Rav's practice.

The Bavli records a discussion that is so similar we must posit that its creators knew a text close, if not identical, to the passage preserved in the Yerushalmi. But in contrast with the Yerushalmi, the Bavli's presentation of this material conforms to the structure of an attributed ruling followed by an anonymous dialectic discussion. First, we do not receive a report of Rav's practice but rather a dictum attributed to him that rules on the issue;[25] Shmuel's explanation, too, is transmitted as a dictum rather than as part of an exchange. More important, while the Bavli maintains both R. Ami's objection and R. Abin's solution, it presents them in the anonymous voice.

b. Ber. 12a	*y. Ber.* 1:4 3d
And Rabbah b. Hinana the elder said in the name of Rav: When one prays, he bows at "blessed are you" and rises back at [the mention of] the divine name.	Hanan bar Ba said to the associates: Let me tell you something good I saw Rav doing—and when I told it to Shmuel he rose and kissed me on the mouth—
	"Blessed are you," he [Rav] bows. When he comes to utter the name, he rises.
Shmuel said: What is Rav's reason? For it was written: *YHWH lifts those who are bowed down* (Ps. 146:8).	Shmuel said: I will tell you the reason: *YHWH lifts those who are bowed down* (Ps. 146:8).
They object, *And before my name he bowed* (Mal. 2:5).	Said R. Ami: This does not stand to reason, because of *And before my name he bowed* (Mal. 2:5).

25 This is according to all manuscripts in the first unit. In the last unit of the passage, however, some manuscripts do record a report on Rav's behavior. Where the printed edition and a Genizah fragment (JTS ENA 2673.29) have "I will tell you something good your father said" and Ms. Paris 671 has "I will tell you something good I heard from your father," Ms. Florence II-1.7, Ms. Munich 95, and Ms. Oxford have "I will tell you something good your father *did*." Again, all extant versions, including these manuscripts, record a teaching attributed to Rav at the beginning of the passage; but the variation in the anecdote about Rav's son shows us that the shift from a deed to a teaching was not uniformly applied in the Bavli. The production of teachings based on precedents and other teachings is of course a broader phenomenon that applies to both Talmuds; see Abraham Weiss, *The Talmud in its Development* (Heb.; New York: Feldheim, 1954), 114–40 and especially 134–38, including examples of Yerushalmi *memrot* that are anecdotes in the Bavli.

But does it say "at my name"? It says *before my name*. [Some manuscripts[26] present here an Aramaic equivalent of the last sentence in the parallel Yerushalmi unit, which is in Hebrew].

Shmuel said to Hiyya b. Rav: Son of the Torah! Come and I will tell you something excellent your father said. For thus said your father: "he bows at 'blessed are you' and rises back at [the mention of] the divine name."

Said R. Abin: If it were written, "at my name he bowed," it would be correct. But it says *before my name he bowed*. Prior to mentioning the name he is already bowed.

[Compare last unit in the Bavli to the first unit in this column]

Without the Yerushalmi, we would have had the impression that a ruling by Rav and a brief support with a verse by Shmuel were subjected to an anonymous give-and-take composed by the Bavli's creators.[27] The comparison with the Yerushalmi shows us not just that the give-and-take is older than the Bavli, but, more important, that it was originally presented through attributed teachings. It is possible, as Zacharias Frankel suggested, that the names of R. Ami and R. Abin were simply forgotten,[28] or even that the give-and-take itself was lost and then reconstructed by the Babylonian creators (under Halivni's model). But given the fact that otherwise the Bavli here parallels so closely the Yerushalmi's *sugya*, and given what we have learned in recent decades about the creativity of the scholars who shaped the Bavli, it is just as likely, if not more, that the tale was turned into a dictum and the give-and-take was anonymized (and in the manuscripts that record a fuller version, Aramaicized) to fit the Bavli's pattern of representation.

The comparison undertaken here between the Talmuds is meant to highlight the constructed nature of layerization in the Bavli. My argu-

26 Mss. Munich, Florence, Paris, and JTS 2673.29.

27 We might have even been tempted to rely on the fact that the objection and solution shift around in the manuscripts to argue that they are late additions; but note that Shmuel's statement moves as well. The printed edition and Ms. Oxford produce the objection and solution between Shmuel's support and the anecdote about him and Rav's son; so does Ms. Florence, but a scribe then added a different version of the objection in the margins and indicated it should be placed before. Ms. Munich and Ms. Paris likewise have the objection and solution before Shmuel's words. The JTS fragment goes straight from the *memra* to the anecdote about Rav's son and only then produces both Shmuel's support and the objection and solution.

28 Zacharais Frankel, *Einleitung in den Jerusalemischen Talmud* (Heb.; Breslau, 1870), 43a; this explanation is adopted by Moshe Benovitz, *BT Berakhot: Chapter I* (Heb.; Jerusalem: The Society for the Interpretation of the Talmud, 2006), 598.

ment is not that such reorganization is typical of Babylonian adaptations of Palestinian *sugyot*. Still, the process observed here may enrich our understanding of the general difference between the Talmuds with respect to the layers. Scholars previously reasoned that the Babylonian *stam* appears so distinct from Amoraic traditions because it was composed much later than these traditions and took longer to develop than its Palestinian counterpart.[29] The process studied here, in contrast, shows that this distinctiveness of the anonymous layer can be the result of a literary adaptation in the service of a particular literary strategy.

THE PALESTINIAN *SUGYA* (*Y. PES.* 2:1 28C)

At the heart of this chapter stands a comparison between two texts, one in the Yerushalmi and one in the Bavli, which allows us to observe clearly the process by which a layered structure was introduced into a Palestinian *sugya*. This section examines this Palestinian *sugya* as it appears in the Yerushalmi. The aim of this *sugya* is to identify which of the consumption prohibitions in the Torah, if any, also implies a prohibition on deriving benefit from the prohibited substances (e.g., making a bandage from the flesh of an animal that is prohibited for consumption as food, or selling this flesh to gentiles). The Yerushalmi presents three Amoraic positions and teachings associated with these positions. The first section presents a teaching R. Abbahu cites in the name of R. Eleazar, and follows with a series of objections to and defenses of that teaching:

1.
    a. R. Abbahu in the name of R. Eleazar, "Wherever it is said—*you* [sing.] *shall not eat, you* [pl.] *shall not eat, they shall not eat*—you should perceive a prohibition on deriving benefit just as you perceive a prohibition on eating, until a verse comes and specifies to you otherwise, as it specifies to you regarding taking a limb from a living animal and regarding an animal that died naturally [Heb.: *nevelah*].
    b. And what did it specify to us regarding taking a limb from a living animal? *You shall not eat flesh torn by beasts in the field; you shall cast it to the dogs* (Exod. 22:30). And what did it specify to us regarding an animal that died naturally? *You shall not eat anything that dies of itself—give it to the resident* [Heb.: *ger*] *in your community to eat, or you may sell it to a foreigner* (Deut. 14:21).
    c. Hezekiah teaches and disputes, {"And is it prohibited for a dog?[30]}

29   See Sussmann, "Yerushalmi," 72–73, 121–24.
30   The text here seems either incomplete or corrupted. As it stands now, Hezekiah is

d.

    i. And, lo, it is written, *You shall not eat any fat of ox or sheep or goat* (Lev. 7:23). Now, do you perceive here a prohibition on deriving benefit just like a prohibition on eating?

        It is different, for it is written, *Fat from animals that died or were torn by beasts may be put to any use, but you must not eat it* (Lev. 7:24).

    ii. And lo, it is written, *But you shall not eat of the blood* (Deut. 12:16). Now, do you perceive here a prohibition against deriving benefit just like a prohibition on eating?

        It is different, for it is written, *You shall pour it out on the ground like water* (ibid.). Just as water is permitted for deriving benefit, so blood should be permitted for deriving benefit.

    iii. And lo, it is written, *This is why the children of Israel to this day will not eat the thigh muscle* (Gen. 32:33).

        Said R. Abbahu, "I explain it as referring to the thigh muscle of an animal that died naturally [which is permitted to be given to a gentile, along with its thigh muscle]."

    iv. And lo, it is written, *Until that very day you shall not eat bread or parched grain or fresh ears* (Lev. 23:14).

        Said R. Abba Mari the brother of R. Yose, "It is different, for the verse has set a time for that prohibition."

    v. And lo, it is written, *You shall not eat them among all the things that swarm upon the earth . . . for they are an abomination* (Lev. 11:42). Said R. Mana,[31] [with the word *them* Scripture] removes the prohibition on deriving benefit [in this verse].

---

quoting a *baraita* that is said to contradict R. Eleazar's teaching. This *baraita* seems to refer to the prohibition on torn flesh in Exod. 22:30, asking why it was necessary to say in the verse that the flesh will be cast to the dogs and implying that this permission is self-evident. Hence, this *baraita* must contradict R. Eleazar's position because according to R. Eleazar, Exod. 22:30 does imply a benefit prohibition that is then revoked by the permission to cast the flesh to the dogs. Such an interpretation works best if this *baraita* is understood to be truncated since as it stands now it lacks what should be its point—the alternative interpretation of Exod. 22:30. Saul Lieberman (*Hayerushalmi Kiphshuto* [2nd ed.] [Heb.; ed. M. Katz; New York and Jerusalem: Jewish Theological Seminary, 2008], 390), following some traditional commentators (e.g., R. Elijah Fulda), refers to the *baraita* Hezekiah cites in §4c.iv and suggests reconstructing the text: "And is it prohibited for a dog? What then does the teaching say concerning *You shall cast it to the dog*? You cast *it* to the dogs, but you do not cast to the dog profane animals that were slaughtered in the Temple's courtyard." Baer Ratner (*Ahawath Zion We-Jeruscholaim* [10 vols.; Vilnius: Garber, 1917], 4.223), possibly following Sirilio, writes that the words וכי מי אסרו לכלב, "do not belong where they are," but leaves תני חזקיה ופליג. See n. 43 below for my suggestion, which combines Lieberman's solution with Ratner's. For other (in my opinion, unlikely) solutions, see the Vilna Gaon and Solomon Sirilio on the parallel in *y. ʿOrlah*.

31   The text here reads אמר ר' מיעט, without any name, but R. Mana's name, which is

R. Abbahu quotes R. Eleazar's position that each of the prohibitions on consumption in the Torah must also be perceived as a prohibition on deriving benefit from the forbidden substance, unless the verse explicitly indicates that the substance is permitted for use (§1a–b). A series of objections to this position follows, focusing on prohibitions on the consumption of substances that are, according to rabbinic tradition, permitted for use. In each of the cases, R. Abbahu or someone else defends R. Eleazar's position, demonstrating that the prohibition in question is unrepresentative (§1d).

In the second section, Rabbi Abbahu cites an opinion that contradicts the former teaching:

2.

    a. R. Abbahu in the name of R. Yohanan: "One who makes a bandage from the fat of a stoned ox or from leaven that has passed through Passover[32] is not liable for a lashing, for its negative injunction is not clear. [One who makes a bandage] from mixed seeds in the vineyard is liable for lashes. . . ."

    b. A teaching disputes with R. Yohanan: "It is evident in that which is written, [*when an ox gores a man or a woman to death,*] *the ox shall be stoned* (Exod. 21:28); do we not know that that its meat is forbidden to be eaten? What then does the teaching say concerning *and its flesh shall not be eaten* (ibid.)? It comes to inform you that just as it is prohibited to eat it so it is prohibited to derive benefit from it.

    c. What does R. Yohanan do with this latter part of the verse? He solves it with the case in which the owners went and slaughtered the ox before the judgment was rendered.

3.

    a. R. Zeira asked before R. Abbahu, "Here you say this and here you say this?!"

    b. He said to him, "One is in the name of R. Eleazar, and the other is in the name of R. Yohanan."

R. Yohanan's exempts from flogging a person who uses the flesh of a stoned ox or leaven because the prohibition on deriving benefit from these substances is not explicit (§2a). His position is challenged and sustained.

---

omitted in our version because of an *homoioarcheton*, can be added according to the parallel text in *y. 'Orlah* 3:1 62d, אמר ר' מנא.

32 See Ratner, *Ahawath Zion*, 6.21, and Lieberman, *Hayerushalmi Kiphshuto*, 390, on the text here.

In the third section, R. Zeira notes before R. Abbahu that the two traditions the latter cited contradict one another: the first tradition, R. Eleazar's, argues that prohibitions on consumption are to be understood as
prohibitions on deriving benefit as well, whereas the second tradition, R.
Yohanan's, exempts from punishments those who use substances prohibited for consumption because the benefit prohibition is not explicit (§3a).
R. Abbahu replies that the traditions came from different rabbis who are
in disagreement (§3b).

In the fourth section, R. Abbahu presents another teaching from R.
Yohanan (§4a), now transmitted also through the "Rabbis of Caesarea," a
collective name for Caesarean sages who flourished after R. Abbahu's
death:[33]

4.

 a. The Rabbis of Caesarea, R. Abbahu in the name of R. Yohanan:
    "Whenever it is said, *you shall not eat* [sing.], *you shall not eat* [pl.],
    you should not perceive a prohibition on deriving benefit as well as a
    prohibition on eating; [whenever it is said] *you shall not have it eaten,
    it shall not be eaten*—you should perceive a prohibition on deriving
    benefit as well as a prohibition on eating."[34]
 b. And the construction of the principle for all of those cases is from *But
    no sin offering may be eaten from which any blood is brought into the
    Tent of Meeting for expiation in the sanctuary; any such shall be con-
    sumed in fire* (Lev. 6:23).
 c. Hezekiah teaches in support of R. Yohanan:
    i. "It is evident in that which is said: *You shall not eat fat of ox or sheep
       or goat* (Lev. 7:23) [that fat may not be eaten]. For what purpose
       is it said, *Fat from animals that died or were torn by beasts may be
       put to any service (but you shall not eat it)* (ibid.)?—[it is usable]
       even for the service of the Most High.
    ii. "It is evident in that which is said, *But you shall not eat the blood*
        (Deut. 12:16), [that blood may not be eaten]. For what purpose is
        it said, *You shall pour it out on the ground like water* (ibid.)? Just as
        water makes something susceptible to impurity, so blood should
        make something susceptible.
    iii. "It is evident in that which is said, *You shall not eat anything that
         has died a natural death* (Deut. 14:21), [that such animal may not
         be eaten]. For what purpose is it said, *Give it to the resident in your
         community to eat, or you may sell it to a foreigner* (ibid.)? It comes to

---

33 See Frankel, *Einleitung*, 123a–b.
34 See below, n. 36 for textual variants.

inform you that a resident alien may eat animals that died a
natural death.

iv. "It is evident in that which is said, *You shall not eat flesh torn by
beasts in the field* (Exod. 22:30), [that torn flesh may not be eaten].
What then does the teaching say concerning *You shall cast it to the
dogs* (ibid.)? You cast *it* to the dogs, but you do not cast to the dogs
profane animals that were slaughtered in the courtyard of the
Temple."

In this teaching, R. Yohanan makes a distinction between two kinds of
consumption prohibitions: those that use the active form of the verb
("shall not eat") and those that use the passive form ("shall not be eaten");
while the former do not imply a prohibition on deriving benefit, the latter do. He supplies as a scriptural proof a case in which the verb appears
in the passive form and a prohibition on use is explicitly stated (§4b).
Hezekiah then cites a Tannaitic teaching (or teachings; see the following
section) that supports Rabbi Yohanan: it explores a series of cases in
which consumption prohibitions formulated in the active voice are accompanied by what may be constructed as benefit permissions, but in
each case it interprets the latter as teaching something other than benefit
permission, implying that such permission is not necessary.

The fifth and final section of the *sugya* centers on a *baraita* that reports
a dispute between two Tannaitic sages on the verses supporting the prohibition on leavened food. The Yerushalmi uses the *baraita* to tie the entire *sugya* together by noting that each side of this dispute can be read as
corresponding to the differing opinions that have occupied the *sugya*, the
opinions of R. Eleazar and R. Yohanan, and that therefore there is authoritative support for each of these general principles:

5.

a. A Tannaitic source supports this one and a Tannaitic source supports
that one.

b. A Tannaitic source supports R. Eleazar: "'*And leavened food shall not
be eaten* (Exod. 13:3), [this comes] to equate the one who feeds it
with the one who eats it. You say [it comes] to equate the one who
feeds with the one who eats it; but does it not come only to prohibit
deriving benefit from it? But when it says *You shall not eat with it
anything leavened* (Deut. 16:3), then it teaches us that it is prohibited
to derive benefit from it. What does the teaching say about *And
leavened food shall not be eaten*? To equate the one who feeds it with
the one who eats it.'—These are the words of R. Yoshiah. R. Yitzhak
says, 'It is unnecessary [to use Exod. 13:3 for the purpose of equating

feeding and eating]. If in the case of creatures that swarm upon the earth, which is a light [prohibition], Torah equates the one who feeds them [to others] with the one who eats them, then is it not a clear outcome that in the case of leavened food, which is a grave [prohibition], that the one who feeds it be equated with the one who eats it? And what does the teaching say about *And leavened food shall not be eaten*? This verse comes only to prohibit deriving benefit from it.' "

c. [The prohibition], then, is because *shall not be eaten* is written; from *you shall not eat*, then, he [R. Yitzhak] does not derive anything.[35] And this supports R. Yohanan.

LITERARY CREATIVITY IN THE PALESTINIAN VERSION

The relationship between the different sections of this *sugya* betrays an interesting literary history. First, the second and fourth sections offer contradictory reports of R. Yohanan's position. In §4a, R. Yohanan argues that prohibitions on consumption that use the passive forms should be perceived as prohibitions on use as well, but in §2a R. Yohanan exempts from punishment the use of a stoned ox's flesh, a substance that is prohibited for consumption in a verse that uses the passive form (Exod. 21:28, cited here in §2b).[36]

---

35 On this phrase and its use here, see Leib Moscovitz, *The Terminology of the Yerushalmi: The Principal Terms* (Heb.; Jerusalem: Magnes, 2009), 361 n. 423.

36 This contradiction is less pronounced in the version of the *sugya* preserved in the Ms. Leiden version of *y. 'Orlah* 3:1 62d, which has only the negative part of R. Yohanan's teaching, reading only "Whenever it is said you shall not eat (pl.), you should not perceive a prohibition on deriving benefit as well as a prohibition on eating," without the positive part, "you shall not have it eaten, it shall not be eaten—you should perceive a prohibition on deriving as well as a prohibition on eating." The argument, therefore, can be made that R. Yohanan never intended to implicate consumption and benefit prohibitions at all. This interpretation, however, is undermined by the fact that the scriptural proof that follows even in the text in *'Orlah* proves the positive part of the teaching. The omission of this part in *'Orlah* seems, then, to be a result of *homoioteleuton*.
    It is possible to harmonize these two teachings attributed to R. Yohanan by observing that the first focuses on the punishment and the second focuses on the prohibition. R. Yohanan says that while there is a prohibition on deriving benefit implied in לא תאכל prohibitions, there is no flogging since the benefit prohibition is not explicitly stated (see, e.g., *Itur*, cited in Lieberman, *Hayerushalmi Kiphshuto*, 390). While this interpretation may reflect R. Yohanan's original intention, it cannot be applied to the Yerushalmi's understanding of these teachings. The Yerushalmi, R. Zeira, and R. Abbahu accept (in §3) that R. Yohanan's teaching in §2a contradicts R. Eleazar's teaching in §1a. R. Yohanan's teaching in §4a is identical to R. Eleazar's teaching with respect to the ox's flesh. He therefore must be understood as claiming that there is an explicit prohibition, contradicting the teaching attributed to him in §2a.

The structure of the fourth section parallels the structure of the first section,[37] almost perfectly: §1a and §4a use identical phrasing ("whenever it is said ... you should/should not perceive") to state mutually exclusive positions, in a teaching presented by R. Abbahu; §1b and §4b present a scriptural proof for these positions; §1c and §4c each present a teaching ascribed to Hezekiah; and §1d considers a list of prohibitions that roughly parallels the list in §4c. If we remove the second section entirely, and place the third section after the fourth section, our *sugya* would have a clearly symmetrical structure: R. Abbahu's presentation of R. Eleazar's teaching ("you should perceive"), scriptural proof for this teaching, and a tradition from Hezekiah (§1); R. Abbahu's presentation of R. Yohanan's teaching ("you should not perceive ... you should perceive"), scriptural proof for this teaching, and a tradition from Hezekiah (§4); R. Zeira's question to Abbahu—how can he transmit two contradictory teachings?—and Abbahu's answer (§3). The last component of the *sugya* (§5) complements this symmetry by citing a Tannaitic source that supports both teachings.[38]

The attribution of §4a to the Rabbis of Caesarea, the contradiction between R. Yohanan's words in this section and his words in §2a, and the way in which R. Yohanan's words here parallel R. Eleazar's words at the beginning of the *sugya*—all suggest that what we see here, in §4a, is an *artificial formulation*. R. Yohanan's casuistic, local opinion from §2a was reformulated as a general rule that expresses the contradiction between his opinion and R. Eleazar's in the clearest way, presenting two different systematic approaches to the question at hand.

The symmetrical structure of the *sugya* is constituted in part by the parallel structure between the series of objections and answers that supports R. Eleazar's teaching in §1d and Hezekiah's *baraita* that supports R. Yohanan's teaching in §4a. There is no reason to suspect Hezekiah's Tannaitic teaching in itself. It may evince the creative, paraphrastic Amoraic use of Tannaitic sources:[39] most of the exegetical remarks cited in this *baraita* have good Tannaitic parallels, but the collection as a whole, with its particular purpose, is not found in Tannaitic literature.[40] Still, there is

---

37   There is also a structural parallel, to a lesser extent, between the first and second sections: both begin with a statement about the relationship between consumption prohibitions and benefit prohibitions (§1a, 2a), then a Tannaitic source disputes is cited to dispute the statement (§1c, 2b).

38   This *baraita* parallels *Mek.*, *Bo*, §16 (Horowitz-Rabin 61–62). See n. 52 for the original function of this *baraita*, before it was reinterpreted by the Yerushalmi.

39   See especially concerning *baraitot* attributed to Amoraic rabbis, Chanoch Albeck, *Studies in the Baraita and the Tosefta and their Relationship to the Talmud* [2nd ed.] (Heb.; Jerusalem: Mosad Ha-Rav, 1969), 15–43.

40   Fat: *Sifra, Tzav*, 10:1; blood: *Sifre Deut* §126; limb: *Sifra, Nedava*, 15:2; it is inter-

no evidence of editorial manipulation here: the terminology in Hezekiah's teaching may not be Tannaitic, but it does conform with other *baraitot* taught by Hezekiah.[41]

In contrast, the series of objections and answers in §1d seems to have
been created to parallel Hezekiah's *baraita* in its structure. The *baraita*
examines four forbidden substances: fat, blood, the flesh of an animal
that died naturally (i.e., without proper slaughter), and the limb of a live
animal. The series in §1d follows this order, which is not the order of the
verses in the Bible. The first two items in the series, like in the *baraita*, are
fat and blood. While the list departs from the order of the *baraita* by proceeding to the verse prohibiting the thigh muscle, R. Abbahu's argument,
that the verse actually speaks about the thigh muscle of an animal that
died naturally, maintains the parallel between the sections. We would
not expect the fourth element of Hezekiah's *baraita* to be paralleled in the
support of R. Eleazar's teaching since the verse regarding flesh torn from
a live animal was already used by that teaching itself.

It is suggestive that the next two elements in the series, which are not
paralleled in the *baraita*, are attributed to sages from the fifth generation
of *amora'im* (R. Aba Mari, brother of Rav Yosi, and R. Mana), whereas the
previous objections were answered either anonymously or by R. Abbahu
(third generation). If we remember that R. Yohanan's teaching in its reformulated version was attributed to the Rabbis of Caesarea (i.e., third-
to fifth-generation *amora'im*), we can suggest that just as these rabbis
formulated R. Yohanan's teaching (§4a) in the image of R. Eleazar's
teaching (§1a), they formed the series of teachings supporting R. Eleazar
(§1d) in the image of the *baraita* that supports R. Yohanan (§4c); the two
last objections in the series were added later.[42] The structural parallelism
was completed by adding a reference, in §1c, before the series of objections, to Hezekiah's *baraita* in §4c.[43]

---

esting that, for the *nevelah*, the *baraita* does not cite R. Yehuda's opinion from *Sifre Deut*
§104—see below, n. 61.

41   Our *sugya* holds two of several instances in which a *baraita* is ascribed to Hezekiah, son of R. Hiyya. The majority of these *baraitot*, including both instances here, present *halakhic* exegesis that could have originated independently of the discussion in the
sugya in which they are quoted, and thus could certainly be Tannaitic (see *y. Ta'an.* 2:1
65a, *y. Bez.* 1:8 60d, *y. Pes.* 5:4 32b, *y. Yeb.* 11:1 11d~*y. San.* 9:1 26d, *y. Ket.* 3:1 27a and
4:3 28b, *y. Naz.* 6:1 54c and 6:2 55a, *y. Qidd.* 1:1 58b, *y. Shav.* 1:1 32d and 4:3 35c; but
see, in contrast, *y. Ber.* 2:8 5d = *y. Shab.* 1:2 3a and *y. Ter.* 1:6 40d).

42   Note also that in the Bavli's parallel, *b. Pes.* 22b, at least the first objection (in the
Bavli's order, the thigh muscle) is attributed to R. Yitzhak (or a Tannaitic source that he
cites: מתיב ר' יצחק בר נפחא), a late third-generation *amora* and a junior contemporary of Abbahu; this fits with the dating of the list of objections proposed here.

43   This also suggests a solution for the textual problem in §1c (see above, n. 30). If
the clause "Hezekiah teaches and disputes" is a *reference* rather than a formula introduc-

The extent of creativity in the composition of the Yerushalmi's *sugya* is important to recognize not only in its own right but also in order properly to appreciate Babylonian literary activity. All too often, in comparisons between the Talmuds, the Yerushalmi is presented as an artless background matter with a construction devoid of agency—as if it preserves some unredacted original Talmud, which is then contrasted with creative, "artificial" Babylonian composition.[44] An appreciation of the Yerushalmi's own art and of the ways this art is different from the Bavli's promises a more accurate picture of the history of rabbinic literary practices.

THE BABYLONIAN DISCUSSION

The *sugya* in the Babylonian Talmud, *b. Pes.* 21b–23b, shares enough material with the Palestinian *sugya* studied above that it is reasonable to suppose that the creators of the Bavli's *sugya* received a *sugya* that resembled the Yerushalmi's and reworked it.[45] The dependence of the Bavli

---

ing a citation, then we can erase the words "and is it for a dog." These words were probably a comment in the margins of the Yerushalmi near §4c.iv (where they appear in Sirilio's text) or they were intended as an explanation of the reference in §1c and were entered by error here because the scribe wanted to supply the "missing" teaching. I doubt that these words were originally part of the *baraita* since they diverge from its uniform style (cf. Lieberman, cited above, n. 30). On the phenomenon of the Yerushalmi referring to sources without spelling them out, see Frankel, *Einleitung*, 36a–37a.

44   On appreciating the literary construction of the Yerushalmi, see Jeffrey Rubenstein, "Some Structural Patterns of Yerushalmi 'sugyot,' " in *The Talmud Yerushalmi and Graeco-Roman Culture III* (ed. P. Schäfer; Tübingen: Mohr Siebeck, 2002), 303–13 (especially 304 and n. 7 for previous scholarship).

45   See Yaakov Elman, "Orality and the Redaction of the Babylonian Talmud," *Oral Tradition* 14.1 (1999), 52–99 (87–92). While Elman's treatment reveals the dependency of the Babylonian version on the Palestinian version, it is too influenced by the former. First, Elman identifies the series of objections and answers (§1d in the Yerushalmi) as the "core" of the *sugya*, dubbing the rest "additional material" that is not "incorporated into the core" (ibid., 87). But it is only from the perspective of the Bavli, in which the list of objections is indeed used to frame the better part of the *sugya*, that this list can be called a "core." In the Yerushalmi, it is an appended part to one element of the *sugya*, R. Eleazar's opinion, whereas the *sugya* revolves around the three Amoraic teachings (as we have seen). The "additional material" that is not "incorporated into the core" simply has a different function in the Yerushalmi. This reading of the Yerushalmi's structure as an imperfect version of the Bavli's structure also leads Elman to see R. Yohanan's first teaching, in §2a, as a "test case" that continues the inquiry of the various prohibitions in the list of objections and answers (ibid., 89). As we have seen, however, this teaching is independent of that list and is brought here because it contradicts R. Eleazar's principle. Elman's disregard of the Yerushalmi's structure is also evident in his assertion that the discussion hinges on "the dispute between two Palestinian sages ... Hezekiah ... and R. Abbahu," and in his subsequent dating of the Yerushalmi's *sugya* on the basis of "the

on the Yerushalmi is best observed in the long series of objections and defenses, which is not reproduced here (see *b. Pes.* 22a–23a).[46] Our focus will be on the opening moves of the Babylonian *sugya*, which show clearly the structural differences between the two texts:

1.
   a. Hezekiah said: How do we know it is forbidden to derive benefit from leavened food in Passover? Because it is said, *leavened bread shall not be eaten* (Exod. 13:3), that is, there shall not be in it permission for eating.
   b. The reason, then, is because the Merciful One wrote, *leavened bread shall not be eaten*; but if *shall not be eaten* was not written, I would say: it implies a prohibition on eating—it does not imply a prohibition on deriving benefit.

2. Now he differs from Abbahu, for R. Abbahu said: "Wherever it is said, *it shall not be eaten, you* [sing.] *shall not eat, you* [pl.] *shall not eat,* both prohibitions, of eating and of benefit, are implied, until Scripture spells out otherwise, as it does with an animal that died naturally that may be given to a resident or sold to a foreigner."

3.
   a. For it was taught: "*You shall not eat of anything that dies of itself; to the resident in your community you may give it to eat, or you may sell it to a foreigner* (Deut. 14:21). . . . (*b. Pes.* 21b)

A few differences between the Talmuds may be noticed immediately. First, the Bavli opens with the matter of leavened food, which ties the *sugya* with the *mishnah* to which it is appended in *Pesahim*; in the Yerushalmi, one must wait until the end of the *sugya* to see how the two opinions apply to leaven.[47] In the Bavli, the two opinions regarding the impli-

---

coupling" of these two sages (ibid., 88). Only the Babylonian version presents a real dispute between R. Abbahu and Hezekiah. In the Yerushalmi, the dispute is between R. Eleazar and R. Yohanan, *both* of whose opinions are transmitted by R. Abbahu. Hezekiah's *baraita* indeed supports R. Yohanan and does not support R. Eleazar, but the discussion does not pit them one against the other, which is only true for the Bavli. See more below, n. 47.

46 See Elman, "Orality," and also n. 53 below on the Bavli's adaptation of this segment.

47 Elman, "Orality," 89, writes, "the Palestinian redactor(s) did not really incorporate leaven into their *sugya* but merely hinted at its relevance by placing it in tractate Pesahim and adjacent to the same *mishnah* as the Bavli does, naturally the one dealing with the prohibition of deriving benefit from leaven on Passover." Again, I think Elman looks in the Yerushalmi for the connection that is made in the Bavli and when he cannot find it he concludes that leaven was not incorporated, that it is only hinted at by location.

cation of benefit prohibitions in consumption prohibitions appear side by
side and are immediately contrasted; in the Yerushalmi, each of the opinions is cited and discussed on its own. Finally, the Bavli introduces a new
source, the *baraita* cited at §3a. This source does not appear at all in the
Yerushalmi, and here it is the subject of an extended discussion, to be
expounded in the following section.

This section focuses on the emergence in the Bavli of the division between attributed sources, on the one hand, and anonymous narration and
interpretation, on the other. The analysis here centers on two components of the *sugya*. First, it shows that the basic narrative of the *sugya*,
which in the Yerushalmi is carried through both attributed and anonymous comments, is carried in the Bavli only by the *stam*. Second, it demonstrates that while the Yerushalmi attributes to R. Yohanan both a specific ruling and a general principle, the Bavli's anonymous voice presents
that same general principle as an explication from a more specific teaching. In other words, the Babylonian version does not simply *add* to our
text the anonymous layer's characteristic functions—elucidation, gener-
alization, and, most important, narration. Rather, the Bavli divides the
material it received in a new way so that these functions are taken on by
the anonymous layer.

The first of these transformations is evident in the different roles
played by R. Abbahu and Hezekiah in the two versions. The difference
may at first appear trivial: the opinions that in the Yerushalmi are attributed to R. Eleazar (§1a) and R. Yohanan (in two variations, §2a and §4a)
are attributed in the Bavli to R. Abbahu[48] (§2a) and Hezekiah (§1a). Dif-

---

But leaven is incorporated: the *sugya* is concluded with a *baraita* about leavened food
(§5), and the Yerushalmi explicitly ties it with the different positions (§5b–c). See also
below, n. 50, on the Bavli's incorporation of this *baraita*.

48   The parallel texts in *b. Qidd.* 56b, *b. B. Q.* 41a, and *b. Ḥul.* 114b, as well as some
of the manuscripts in our *sugya*, indeed trace the teaching to R. Eleazar, reading "Said R.
Abbahu in the name of R. Eleazar" (see Rabbinovicz, *Variae*, ad loc.), as we have it in the
Yerushalmi. But even in these manuscripts, the Bavli treats the teaching as R. Abbahu's
position, introducing it by noting that Hezekiah "disputes with R. Abbahu" and referring
to the position as R. Abbahu's throughout the *sugya*. David Halivni (*Sources and Traditions: A Source Critical Commentary on the Talmud: Tractates Erubin and Pesaḥim* [Jerusa-
lem: Jewish Theological Seminary, 1982], 336 n. *1), refers to the version in a responsum
cited by Lewin (*Otzar*, 3.17) which reads "R. Abbahu in the name of R. Yohanan," to
argue that this version "explains the connection to the *memrot* of R. Yohanan cited beginning 24b." But it seems better to treat the *memrot* in 24b as relating to R. Yohanan's
teaching in the Yerushalmi, §2b; the position ascribed to him there that prohibitions in
the Torah only incur punishment through consumption rather than deriving benefit
seems to be an abstraction of R. Yohanan's teaching in the Yerushalmi about the flesh of
an executed ox, whereas the opposite teaching seems to be a reversal of that abstraction
(on opposite teachings as variations of the same traditions, see Sussmann, "Yerushalmi,"
98 n. 180).

ferences in attribution are commonplace in rabbinic literature, either between two given documents or even within the same document, and are often insignificant. This particular difference, however, deserves our close attention.

In the Yerushalmi, R. Abbahu and Hezekiah do not give their own opinions on the matter at hand. Abbahu quotes two opposing Amoraic rulings—R. Eleazar's and R. Yohanan's, while Hezekiah quotes a source that supports one and objects to the other.[49] With R. Zeira, who notes the contradiction between the positions (§3), these rabbis structure the *sugya*. The Bavli reorganizes the material altogether. It assigns R. Eleazar's position, and only R. Eleazar's position, to R. Abbahu; it assigns R. Yohanan's position to Hezekiah; it takes R. Zeira's indication of the contradiction between the teachings and voices it in its anonymous layer; and, as we shall see, it removes what in the Yerushalmi was R. Eleazar's second example and presents it as the conclusion of its own dialectic process.

The result is that in the Bavli, R. Abbahu, and Hezekiah are the narrated rather than the narrators. The *sugya* becomes a text about them, not by them. The function these rabbis held in the Yerushalmi is now assumed by the voice of the anonymous Bavli: it is this voice, not R. Abbahu's, which is the omniscient narrator who can cite two contradicting opinions; this voice, not R. Zeira's, which indicates the contradiction; this voice, not Hezekiah's, which adduces a related Tannaitic source.

The second instance of layerization in the Bavli concerns not the narrating function of the *stam* but more specifically its role as extracting from a specific ruling a broad rationale or general principle. While the teaching the Bavli attributes to R. Abbahu parallels an Amoraic teaching in the Yerushalmi, the exegetical teaching that it attributes to Hezekiah (§1a) has no such parallel. The Bavli combines several elements from the Yerushalmi to produce this teaching, to attribute it to Hezekiah, and subsequently to extract from this teaching the position that in the Yerushalmi is expressed by Rabbi Yohanan. The attribution of this teaching and this position to Hezekiah stems from the fact that, in the Yerushalmi, Hezekiah teaches a *baraita* in support of Rabbi Yohanan and in opposi-

---

49 It is explicitly stated in the Yerushalmi that R. Abbahu does not give his own opinion but rather transmits two traditions from his predecessors, even though in §1d.iii he defends R. Eleazar's teaching against an objection. Hezekiah's case is less clear. On the one hand, he never explicitly adopts either of the two positions. On the other hand, from the Yerushalmi text as we have it now, it can be understood that he supports R. Yohanan's position since he teaches a *baraita* that in §1c is said to contradict R. Eleazar and in §4c supports R. Yohanan. It is possible then that the Bavli is relying on Hezekiah's *baraita* in support of R. Yohanan (see *infra*) and Abbahu's defense of R. Eleazar's teaching when it ascribes to the *amora'im* these respective positions. Cf. the examples in Frankel, *Einleitung*, 41b.

tion to Rabbi Eleazar (§1d and §4c in the Yerushalmi). The new teaching itself is drawn from Rabbi Yitzhak's teaching in the *baraita* quoted by the Yerushalmi at the end of the *sugya* (§5b).[50] The principle that the Bavli derives from the teaching, and thus the general position it attributes to Hezekiah, is based on Rabbi Yohanan's second teaching in the Yerushalmi (§4a) and on the anonymous comment at the end of the *sugya* there (§5c), which is very similar to the Bavli's comment here.[51]

The Babylonian *sugya* divides these earlier materials into two elements: an exegetical teaching attributed to Hezekiah in Hebrew (§1a) and an anonymous and analytical comment in Aramaic (§1b). Without the Yerushalmi parallel, we might have been tempted to rely on this distinction and argue that Hezekiah's dictum was produced earlier than the anonymous comment. This chronology would posit a plausible intellectual development: Hezekiah, a first-generation Palestinian *amora*, did not intend to offer a general principle but rather a specific scriptural justification for a ruling on leavened bread;[52] only later did the Babylonian editors extract from his teaching a wide-ranging principle concerning the difference between prohibitions with passive verbs and active verbs.

The comparison with the Yerushalmi shows us how misleading this chronology would have been. The *stam*'s inference appears almost word for word in the Yerushalmi. More important, the general position that this inference extracts from Hezekiah's teaching already appears in Rabbi Yohanan's second teaching in the Palestinian *sugya*. The ostensibly early dictum attributed to Hezekiah, with its more local concerns, appears only in the later version. Both elements in the Bavli—the dictum and its interpretation—incorporate material from a variety of Palestinian sources.

50   Jacob Epstein, *Introduction to Amoraitic Literature: Babylonian Talmud and Yerushalmi* (Jerusalem: Magnes, 1962), 168, writes that this *baraita* was not known to the Bavli, but I think it is more likely, in light of the dependence of the Babylonian *sugya* on the Yerushalmi, that the Bavli synthesizes the *baraita* into Hezekiah's *memra*. An alternative explanation to the one presented *here* is that the Bavli understood the *baraita* Hezekiah cites in the Yerushalmi to be precisely the *baraita* that contains R. Yitzhak's words (rather than the *baraita* quoted by Hezekiah in our versions of the Yerushalmi). It is even possible that the version the Bavli received simply had Hezekiah teach that *baraita* without quoting it as a *baraita*. These possibilities reduce the extent of the Bavli's creativity here, but they do not change the fact that the division between ruling and principle is introduced here by the Bavli.

51   The Yerushalmi there (§5) reads (in *y. 'Orlah*): בגין דכתיב לא יאכל הא מלא תאכל לית שמע. מינה כלום, while the Bavli here reads, טעמא דכתב רחמנא לא יאכל חמץ הא לא כתב לא יאכל הוה אמינא איסור אכילה משמע איסור הנאה לא משמע.

52   This is likely the original meaning of R. Yitzhak's exegetical comment as it appears in the Mekhilta and in the Yerushalmi. It deduces the benefit prohibition not from the passive form but from the redundancy of the prohibition; the Yerushalmi interprets it as supporting R. Yohanan's distinction between passive and active forms, and the Bavli follows the Yerushalmi in its incorporation of this exegesis into the dictum it creates for Hezekiah.

The division between the two elements reflects not their different provenance but rather their different functions. It is the result of the Talmud's strategy of representation, which differentiates between "sources" and "discussion," between brief or local remarks and broader exegetical implications: the former are expressed in attributed Hebrew dicta; the latter in anonymous Aramaic commentary.

The possibility, raised in the previous section, that Rabbi Yohanan's teaching in the Yerushalmi is itself a late literary abstraction highlights rather than undermines this observation. My argument is not that the Yerushalmi presents to us the *sugya* as it was successively authored by the rabbis it names while the Bavli is the result of an artificial literary process. The contrast is between two different designs. It is possible that when the Palestinian rabbis wanted to produce a general principle based on Rabbi Yohanan's ruling, they formulated a teaching that they attributed to him. The Babylonian rabbis, in contrast, produced a formal distinction between a specific teaching and its broader implications, expressing them in different voices. We are seeing here two kinds of literary design, two ways, as it were, to tell a story. In the Palestinian version, both attributed and anonymous material is used to move the plot forward; in the Bavli, the narrative relies mainly on the anonymous layer.

To be sure, important elements of the Yerushalmi's *sugya* are anonymous—the reference to Hezekiah's *baraita*; the objections to R. Eleazar's teaching and two of the responses to these objections; and the introduction of and brief comment on the *baraita* in the final section. Moreover, the functional division between anonymous and attributed material in the Bavli is not absolute. Unlike in the case of R. Yohanan's position, the Bavli does not bifurcate R. Eleazar's position into a ruling and an inference but rather reports the general principle in Abbahu's name (again, this difference may be explained by the possibility that the *sugya* before the Bavli did not have R. Yohanan's general statement but did have R. Eleazar's general statement). We also find one discursive element, the objection regarding the thigh muscle, which appears anonymously in the Yerushalmi but is attributed to Rabbi Yitzhak Nappaha in the Bavli (22a). Still, the comparison shows us a general move, though not a systematic one, toward the familiar organizing principle of an anonymous layer discussing and explicating attributed sources.

In this case, then, Babylonian composition did not consist of weaving a narrating and justifying layer around apodictic attributed traditions that lacked such functions. Before the Bavli's creators a structure with a literary framework of its own was already extant.[53] The Babylonian au-

<hr />

53 There might be indication that the reorganization of our *sugya* occurred after several generations in which it was transmitted in Babylonia in its original structure. In the Yerushalmi, the first list of objections and answers appears after R. Eleazar's teaching,

A Summary of the Differences between the Bavli and the Yerushalmi

Bavli	Yerushalmi
The *stam* quotes a *memra* from Hezekiah and comments on it (§§1a–b).	Hezekiah himself quotes a source to support R. Yohanan's position and object to R. Eleazar's (§1c, §4c). The elements in the Yerushalmi that compose Hezekiah's *memra* in the Bavli and the *stam*'s comment are R. Yohanan's position (§4a), the fact that Hezekiah supports this position (§4c), and the anonymous comment on the *baraita* that concludes the *sugya* (§5b–c).
The *stam* quotes a *memra* from R. Abbahu (§2).	R. Abbahu himself quotes two opposing teachings (one of them in two versions; §1a, §2a, and §4a).
The *stam* points out that the teachings oppose one another (2).	R. Zeira points out the opposition in a dialogue with R. Abbahu (§3a), who responds that these are in fact two opposition positions (§3b).
The *stam*'s discussion necessitates Exod. 22:30 as support for R. Abbahu's position (§3c)—see following section.	R. Abbahu (in the name of R. Eleazar) himself alludes to Exod. 22:30 (§1a)—see following section.

but before R. Yohanan's. As a result, even though some of these objections may apply to R. Yohanan's teaching, they are only examined against R. Eleazar's position. In the Bavli, the same series of objections and answers is examined against both positions (*b. Pes.* 22a–23a) since both have already been discussed.

Most of that part of the Bavli's discussion is anonymous except for three cases in which the answers are attributed to Babylonian rabbis of the fourth through sixth generations: Rav Shma'ayah, Rav Papa, Rav Ashi, and Mar Zutra. In all three cases, the answer is to a question regarding R. Abbahu's position. There are no attributed answers pertaining to Hezekiah's position even though the discussion routinely refers to that position. This contrast is clearest in two of the three cases, where an answer on behalf of Abbahu, which is attributed to a Babylonian rabbi, prompts a question on Hezekiah's position, which is then answered anonymously. It is difficult to explain this distinction as a result of the *stam*'s function (since both are answers to objections) or of arbitrary transmission. Interestingly, all three cases may be understood as supplanting the Yerushalmi's series: the priests' share and the Nazirte's wine are not discussed anywhere in the Yerushalmi's *sugya*. The third case, new produce, is shared by both versions, but unlike the other shared cases, it is solved very differently in each of the Talmuds, making it likely that even though the case appears in the Yerushalmi, it may not have appeared in the version received by the Bavli.

thorship took over the narration and one of the dialectic components and voiced them in the anonymous layer; the rulings it left attributed to authoritative rabbis.

It is this reorganization that creates the impression of independent dicta that only came into a conversation through the *stam*; it this reorganization that gives us the sense, in the case of Hezekiah's dictum, of a local tradition that is expanded by the Talmud's own narrative. Halivni's theory can be applied here not as an account of the Bavli's literary history, but as an explication of the Bavli's self-representation. Friedman's model, which posits the existence of unnarrated clusters of attributed tradition prior to the composition of the *stam*, also fails to account for our case. The Bavli here shares with the Yerushalmi not just attributed rulings or traditions but also anonymous elements and narrative elements; more important, the fact that the Bavli reworks Palestinian traditions into both layers shows us that the Bavli redraws distinctions between "sources" and "interpretations." It does not add a literary framework to material that had none; it replaces one literary framework with another. The differences in presentation between the Talmuds here should not be attributed to the lack of narrative in what the Bavli received, but to the liberty of representation typical of creative transmission. The scholars who shaped the Babylonian version had before them a structure close to the Yerushalmi's, which they were committed to transmit, but they also took the liberty to present the material in their own way.

There are good reasons to believe that this process of reorganization and layerization was broader than the cases studied here. Scholars have already identified a significant number of Bavli passages that share a sequence of sources with earlier texts, not just the Yerushalmi.[54] Such passages show us that at some point, generations before the crystallization of

These features of the list of objections may thus indicate that the Palestinian *sugya* was received in Babylonia by the time of Rav Shema'ayah (fourth generation); that the aforementioned Babylonian scholars then added their own answers to new cases when the list still applied only to R. Eleazar's opinion; and that after their time, when the *sugya* was reorganized and the list was made to apply to both opinions, the *stam* added references to Hezekiah's position as well.

54   For the Yerushalmi, see above, n. 22; David Brodsky, *A Bride Without a Blessing: A Study in the Redaction and Content of Massekhet Kallah and its Gemara* (Tübingen: Mohr Siebeck, 2006), 265; scholars have also used hypothesized early structures to explain parallels within the Bavli itself—e.g., Friedman, *Talmudic Studies*, 47–48 n. 61—and even to explain variation in the development of the Bavli's text—e.g., Vered Noam, "The Later Rabbis Add and Innovate: On the Development of a Talmudic *Sugya*" (Heb.), *Tarbiz* 72 (2003), 151–75 (151–52, 174–75). While this last type of evidence may tell us of a much later period, the compositional process that emerges from it, in which clusters of traditions are expanded in different ways, is similar to the one that emerges from comparisons between the Bavli and earlier texts.

the Bavli, rabbinic traditions began circulating not only independently but also as part of complicated structures.[55] Friedman and others posit that these sequences circulated as clusters of unnarrated attributed traditions. But it is more plausible that such sequences circulated for purposes that required a literary framework to introduce the traditions and to draw connections between them—say, a presentation in a pedagogical setting. The evidence of the Yerushalmi also shows us how Amoraic traditions, especially later ones, play just as much of a role in this narration and explication as anonymous comments.

It is possible that Talmudic material was transmitted in textual cores, that is, memorized or even written elements of earlier performances, which were then re-expanded in a new performance;[56] but as our case shows, the distinction between core and expansion, between the material that was reproduced and the material that was changed or added, did not necessarily correspond to the Bavli's distinction between the *memrot* and the *stam*. The conclusion of this chapter suggests that it was the adoption of the layered structure that brought about such correspondence precisely in order to create a certain boundary between transmission and innovation. Our comparison here between the two versions of our *sugya* as well as more broadly between the Talmuds' modes of presentation warns us against understanding the Bavli's structure and its effects as the necessary result of the way rabbinic traditions were produced.

TRANSMISSION AND COMPOSITION IN PERFORMANCE

In the previous section, we saw the emergence of the anonymous layer as part of the Babylonian adaptation of the Palestinian *sugya*. This section explores the way this layer functioned in the subsequent transmission

---

55   See n. 23 for scholarship on the hypothetical "early Talmud." Gray, *Talmud*, 15–33, offered a critique of this theory. In her work on tractate *Avoda Zarah* in both Talmuds, she argued that the Bavli's creators had access to a redacted, written Yerushalmi, and that appealing to a hypothetical Q-like document is unnecessary when we can posit a direct relationship between the two. Such a model would strengthen the central argument of this section. But even if Gray's model applies to the entire Yerushalmi (which she is cautious not to argue), the hypothesis may still explain connections between the Talmud and other texts or among different *sugyot* in the Bavli (see previous note).

56   See Martin Jaffee, "What Difference Does the 'Orality' of Rabbinic Writing Make for the Interpretation of Rabbinic Writings?" in *How Should Rabbinic Literature Be Read in the Modern World?* (ed. M. Kraus; Piscataway, NJ: Gorgias, 2006), 11–33 (17–18). I do not think we can ascertain in our case whether our *sugya* was transmitted from Palestine to Babylonia in writing or orally—Elman, "Orality," 91–92, finds evidence for both kinds of transmission in the different passages of the *sugya*.

and composition of our text. There are good indications that Talmudic *sugyot* originated in oral presentations by scholars in the academy.[57] This section and the conclusion of the chapter suggest that the *stam* offered these scholars a way to preserve the teachings they were committed to transmit while also showcasing their own scholarly virtuosity through new composition.

The focus of this section is the Bavli's discussion of R. Abbahu's position and the biblical verses that may support it. In the Yerushalmi, at §1b, two verses are given in support of the opinion that benefit prohibitions are also consumption prohibitions: Exod. 22:30 (which prohibits a limb from a living animal) and Deut. 14:21 (which prohibits an animal that died naturally). In the Bavli, R. Abbahu's statement of the same position (§2) mentions only the latter. It is only after a new source, a *baraita* on a dispute between R. Meir and R. Yehuda on Deut. 14:21,[58] that Exod. 22:30 is mentioned as a possible support for R. Abbahu's position:

2. Now he [Hezekiah] differs from R. Abbahu, for R. Abbahu said: "Wherever it is said, *It shall not be eaten, you* [sing.] *shall not eat, you* [pl.] *shall not eat*, both prohibitions, of eating and of benefit, are implied, until Scripture spells out otherwise, as it does with an animal that died naturally, that it may be given to a resident or sold to a foreigner."

3.

   a. For it was taught: "*You shall not eat of anything that dies of itself; to the resident in your community you may give it to eat, or you may sell it to a foreigner* (Deut. 14:21). I know only that it may be given [as a gift] to a resident or sold to a foreigner; how do I know that it may be sold to a resident? The teaching says: *to the resident in your community you may give it to eat or you may sell it.* Given to a foreigner? The teaching says: *you may give it to eat or you may sell it to a foreigner.* You end up saying that the law is identical, whether it is to a foreigner or to a resident, whether sold or given. So are the words of R. Meir. R. Yehuda says: Things are as they are written: it may be given to a resident or sold to a foreigner."

---

57 See David Rosenthal, "'Al ha-qitzur ve-hashlamto," in *Meḥqerei Talmud III* (ed. Y. Sussmann and D. Rosenthal; 2 vols.; Jerusalem: Magnes, 2005), 791–863 (791–96), who provides fascinating examples of the vestiges of those oral presentations in the Talmud, and see the literature cited there. On the composition involved in those oral presentations, see Yoav Rosenthal, "On the Early Form of Bavli *Mo'ed Katan* 7b–8a" (Heb.), *Tarbiẓ* 71 (2008), 45–69 (especially 64–65). Though his discussion applies to a period when the Talmud was more fixed, it seems to me it applies all the more so to the formative period discussed in this chapter.

58 The *baraita* is preserved in some variation also in *Sifre Deut* §104 (ed. Finkelstein, 163), where R. Meir's opinion is the anonymous opinion.

  b. What is R. Yehuda's reason? If your opinion is as R. Meir said, let the
     Merciful One write, "to the resident in your community you may give
     it to eat, *and* you may sell it to a foreigner"; why state "or"? Infer
     from this that things are as they are written. And R. Meir? "Or"
     prioritizes giving to a resident over selling to a foreigner. And R.
     Yehuda? This does not need a verse. Since you are commanded to
     maintain a resident and you are not commanded to maintain a
     foreigner, a verse is unnecessary—it stands to reason.
  c. It is all well with R. Meir, who said that the law is identical—whether
     it is to a foreigner or to a resident, whether in selling or in giving.
     Since a verse was needed to permit deriving benefit from an animal
     that died a natural death, [we can infer that] all things forbidden in
     the Torah must be forbidden both with respect to eating and with
     respect to benefit. But as for R. Yehuda, who says things are as they
     are written, how does he know that all the things forbidden in the
     Torah [for consumption] are forbidden [also] with respect to benefit?
     It is derived for him from [*you shall not eat any meat that is mangled by
     beasts in the field;*] *you shall cast it to the dogs* (Exod. 22:30). "It" you
     may cast to the dogs, but you may not cast to dogs any of the other
     things forbidden in the Torah. And R. Meir? "It" you may cast to the
     dogs, but you may not cast to the dogs profane animals that were
     slaughtered in the courtyard of the Temple. And the other [R.
     Yehuda]? The law about profane animals that were slaughtered in
     the courtyard of the Temple is not in Scripture. (*b. Pes.* 21b–22a)

    Why does the Bavli defer the mention of Exod. 22:30 until after the
baraita? Halivni notes in his commentary on our *sugya* that R. Abbahu's
use of Deut. 14:21 may be understood in two ways: either as a scriptural
proof for his position (this verse prohibits eating the flesh of an animal
that died naturally but permits deriving benefit from it; why would such
permission be necessary if consumption prohibitions did not generally
imply benefit prohibitions?) or as an example of exceptions to the rule
(generally, we believe that consumption prohibitions entail benefit prohibitions, except for prohibitions in which the Torah explicitly states otherwise, as it does in Deut. 14:21).
    In the Yerushalmi, the verses are certainly put to the latter use: they
are examples of explicit exceptions;[59] this seems to be their function even
in the Bavli's formulation of R. Abbahu's statement.[60] In contrast, the

59 Halivni, *MM 'Er. Pes.*, 336–37.
60 The formulation "until Scripture specifies . . . the way it specifies in the case of an
animal" implies that there are other cases of which this is an example. *Pace* Halivni, *MM
'Er. Pes.*, 336.

Bavli's *stam* in its discussion of the *baraita* as well as later in the *sugya* takes these verses as alternative scriptural proofs. It uses Exod. 22:30 only to explain how, under R. Yehuda's "literal" understanding of Deut. 14:21, proof may still be found for R. Abbahu's general principle (§3c): "since a verse was needed to permit deriving benefit, [we can infer that] all things forbidden in the Torah must be forbidden [in both respects]. . . . But for Rabbi Yehuda, who says things are as they are written, how does he know [that]?" In the Yerushalmi, there is no particular reason why both of our verses, Deut. 14:21 and Exod. 22:30, appear as examples. In the Bavli, the appearance of both verses becomes significant. Each of them is presented as the only proof possible (and necessary) for each side of the dispute between R. Meir and R. Yehuda.[61]

There is some indication in this segment that the *sugya* had several versions even within its Babylonian career. The initial formulation of R. Abbahu's position in §2b seems to be at odds with the discussion about the *baraita* in §3c. The latter concludes that R. Abbahu's position may be supported by Deut. 14:21 only if the verse presents a general permission of use, as Rabbi Meir holds, and not a specific instruction that it may be "given to a resident or sold to a gentile," as per Rabbi Yehuda. But according to most manuscripts, when Rabbi Abbahu supports his position with Deut. 14:21, he further specifies it with the interpretation and formulation associated with Rabbi Yehuda: "Rabbi Abbahu said: ' . . . until Scripture spells out otherwise, as it does with an animal which died naturally, that it may be given to a resident or sold to a foreigner.' "[62] There is a problem even in versions that do not have this specification. When R. Abbahu's statement is read in light of the discussion that assumes the two verses as alternatives proofs, its use of Deut. 14:21 necessarily implies

61 While the Yerushalmi does not quote the *baraita*, a certain parallel to the Bavli's use of the *baraita* is found in the *baraita* Hezekiah quotes to support Rabbi Yohanan (at §4.c.iv): the exegetical aim there, it may be remembered, is to show that an explicit benefit permission would *not* be necessary in the case of Deut. 14:21, and therefore that source interprets the verse as a necessary permission for *gerim* in particular to eat *nevelot*, implying that otherwise we would think they are forbidden to do so. This touches on the contested issue of which biblical laws apply to *gerim*; in the discussion of this problem in *y. Yebam.* 8:3 8d, R. Hilai actually alludes to R. Yehuda's opinion in our *baraita,* to show that perhaps such explicit permission for *gerim* is not necessary and the verse therefore instructs selling to a gentile and giving to a *ger.*

62 Rashi (ad loc.) removes the specification from the text, and it is indeed missing in some manuscripts (Mss. Munich 95, Oxford) but present in most (Mss. JTS, Munich 6, Sassoon-Lunzer, Vatican 125, Vatican 109). It also appears in the overwhelming majority of the textual witnesses of the other occurrences of Rabbi Abbahu's teaching in the Talmud in *b. Qidd.* 56b, *b. B. Q.* 41a, and *b. Ḥul.* 114b. In light of this evidence and because it is easier to explain the abbreviation than it is to explain an addition here, the fuller formulation seems likely to be the original. See also Tos. on *b. Ḥul.* 114b (especially s.v. *ke-derekh* but also s.v. *'ad*) and Epstein, *Amoraitic Literature,* 164.

that he agrees with R. Meir; yet it is not typical of the Talmud to create an association of this sort between two rabbis without noting it.[63] It is possible, then, that the discussion of the *baraita* was spliced in from a different version of the *sugya*, which did not include the further specification in R. Abbahu's statement and which explicitly identified his position with R. Meir's.

Regardless of its origins, this move in §3c reveals how reverently this layer of the *stam* treated the structure it had inherited. In its presentation of the verses, it transformed them from chance examples to necessary outcomes of legal reasoning, lending more significance to the original structure of the *sugya*. This transformation does not follow from a particular reading of Scripture or of R. Abbahu's position. It is motivated by the *stam*'s commitment to the structure of the earlier *sugya* and by the desire to further bolster and justify the earlier structure.

At the same time, the delayed appearance of Exod. 22:30 is also a particularly interesting example of the Bavli's exercise of authorial independence. The support from Exod. 22:30, which is presented in the Palestinian version as part of an Amoraic tradition, is presented here as the result of the *stam*'s own reasoning. Modern scholarship has shown us again and again how the *stam* projects its ideas and terminology onto the words of past authorities, but here we see the reverse action: the *stam* combines what originally was presented as the words of an *amora* into its own inventive discussion.[64] This move bestows more authority on the *stam* itself, authority that is deflected from the cited tradition. It invites the audience of the *sugya* to believe that only through the anonymous commentary would it have gained access to this information.

The discussion about the *baraita* was most likely composed for one of the *sugya*'s oral performances—that is, one of the sessions in which it was presented in the academy. The scholar responsible for this presentation

---

63   Halivni, *MM 'Er. Pes.,* 337, points to this second difficulty, but does not suggest that it may result from patchwork within the *stam*.

64   This phenomenon is different from the cases examined by Hauptman and Friedman, where *baraitot* are presented as the result of the *stam*'s discussion even though they must have been in place before the *stam* in question was composed. What makes the instance in b. *Pes.* particularly telling for this study of the relationship between the Bavli and its traditions is that the element that is made to look "invented" is not just the placement of a certain source in a discussion, but a part of the source itself. In the cases Hauptman and Friedman refer to, we are not misled to think the *baraita* itself is part of the *stam*, its own composition; in this case, we *are* led to believe that the second part of R. Abbahu's/Eleazar's teaching is an innovation of the anonymous layer. See Judith Hauptman, *Development of the Talmudic Sugya: Relationship Between Tannaitic and Amoraic Sources* (Lanham: University Press of America, 1988), passim, and Shamma Friedman, *BT Bava Meẓiʿa VI: Critical Edition with Comprehensive Commentary: Commentary* (Heb.; Jerusalem: Jewish Theological Seminary, 1990), 1, 57.

had memorized the building blocks of the text from a previous performance he had heard.[65] He introduced this new discussion when he presented the *sugya* to his students and colleagues. Having at his disposal the distinction between the attributed sources and the dynamic narrative and interpretation of the *stam*, he could use the anonymous layer to foreground his inventive addition.

One possible reading of the *stam* here, then, is that it is not only the narrative voice in the structural literary sense, but also the voice of the actual narrator of the *sugya*—the scholar who presented it in a particular session. Anonymity has of course become the identifying characteristic of the anonymous layer, but that is, at least to a certain extent, a function of the complicated process by which *sugyot* transformed into a written Talmud. In an oral performance, it would be clear which scholar presented the *sugya*. It is hard to imagine that the audience of Talmudic *sugyot*—who were exposed to numerous Talmudic discussions that speculate about the authors of anonymous teachings and that frequently read teachings in light of their putative authors—would not have been sensitive to the identity of those presenting these *sugyot* to them.

A particular aspect of the oral-performative culture in which the Talmud was produced invites us to consider the possibility that the original contribution of an individual scholar would have been recognized in such presentations. Martin Jaffee argued that because rabbinic students were expected to have memorized a large amount of material, a scholar presenting a certain text could rely on his audience to have access to a vast nexus of other texts. An accurate reconstruction of what rabbinic texts meant to their earliest audiences must therefore consider the knowledge that these presentations assumed.[66] While Jaffee discusses how the performance of one text could have meant to evoke another, we can extend his model to understand the relationship studied here between two performances of the "same" text: our two versions of the *sugya*.

The original audience of the Bavli included advanced students as well as scholars.[67] It is plausible to posit, then, that some of those more experienced members of the audience would have heard a previous performance of the *sugya* and memorized it just as the scholar presenting it had. If that was indeed the case, then the scholar who composed the discussion about the *baraita* might have expected those members of his audience to recognize how brilliantly that addition had changed the meaning of the structure with which they were familiar. Much as a Barenboim

---

65   See n. 56 above.
66   Jaffee, "Orality," 20.
67   David Kraemer, "The Intended Reader as a Key to Interpreting the Bavli," *Prooftexts* 13 (1993), 125–40.

trusts that his audience perceives his virtuosity by comparing his version to a recording by a Richter, the performer of our *sugya* trusted his audience would appreciate the way his performance outdid the version they had heard before.

The foreknowledge of the audience provides one way in which innovation could have been recognized in the presentation of the *sugya*. But even if this knowledge was not accessed in that way, the discussion on the *baraita* still shows us how the layered structure was in part a move toward a more marked form of innovation. The separation of a layer of sources from a layer of interpretation meant that interpretive virtuosity took place less in the attributed statements and more in the words of the Talmud itself; in fact, as we have seen, the Talmud here claims more for its own interpretation, merging into its discussion of the *baraita* R. Abbahu's second example. The conclusion of this chapter focuses on this foregrounding of interpretation as the feature that made the layered structure desirable for the scholars who used it.

CONCLUSION: TOWARD A NEW APPRECIATION OF THE *STAM*

In the case we have examined, the division between the layers does not, as we usually assume, represent the different provenances of Talmudic materials; it is the result of a reorganization by the Talmud's creators. If we see in the layered structure an indication that the Talmud was created out of unnarrated and unexplained "apodictic" sources, we are not only telling an inaccurate story about the Talmud's sources; we are missing the work of the Talmud's creators themselves. Above, I noted that there are good reasons to believe that this case is at least in some sense representative of broader phenomena in the Talmud's formation. But regardless of how representative this case is, the process observed here can shed light on the question of the layered structure in general because it invites us to think of this structure as something the Bavli's creators could desire; it raises the question of what they found appealing about this structure and why they maintained it throughout the Talmud; and it allows us to consider the particular character this structure gave to Talmudic literary creativity. The following paragraphs offer tentative reflections toward such a new account of the *stam*.

Walter Ong has observed that in oral transmission, the line between transmitter and transmitted is blurred.[68] It is difficult for agents to distinguish and distance themselves from the knowledge they transmit, or

68   Walter Ong, *Orality and Literacy: The Technologizing of the Word* (London and New York: Routledge, 1989), 45–46.

to objectify it, when this knowledge is embodied not in an external written source but in their own performance. The division between the *stam* and the *memrot* does just that—it separates the transmitter from the transmitted.

More than a division between an "apodictic" layer and a "dialectical" layer or even a division between an "attributed" layer and an "anonymous" layer, the division in the Bavli is between a quoting layer and a quoted layer. The attribution of sources in the Bavli certainly lends these sources the authority of past masters and is often used to determine *halakhic* coherence among the teachings of a single sage. But this attribution also functions as a buffer that separates any given teaching from the Talmud's narrator; even unattributed sources, such as anonymous *baraitot* or *memrot*, are introduced with such a buffer in the form of citation terms. The use of Hebrew for the *memrot* might indicate that Hebrew was still used as a language of instruction or express a sort of deference toward Amoraic teachings; but it also functions to distinguish further the voice of the narrator from the sources it cites.[69] The effect of the pervasive use of these mechanisms in the Bavli is evident when contrasted with the Yerushalmi: in the earlier Talmud, attributed teachings work together with anonymous teachings to create a conversation; in the later Talmud, the division between attributed rulings and anonymous narrative implies a chronological distance between the earlier "sources" and the later "interpretation." It is this division between the *stam* and the *memrot* that produces traditions as objects belonging to the past, waiting to be explicated and expanded by a later interpretation.

The oral presentations that eventually transformed into our written Talmud had two ends that stood in a certain tension. On the one hand, these presentations were vehicles for transmission. Even when they did not, as in our case, follow already composed sequences, they still revolved around the traditions of the past and were intended to communicate such traditions. On the other hand, these presentations were also occasions for creative composition and scholarly innovation. As we have seen in this chapter, and as other scholars have shown with other cases, this was true not just when these presentations brought together different

---

69 Neusner argued for this function of the Hebrew-Aramaic division as distinguishing the Talmud from its sources (see, e.g., Jacob Neusner, *The Discourse of the Bavli: Language, Literature, Symbolism* [Atlanta: Scholars Press, 1991], 1–32). Neusner sees the division as distinguishing "authoritative" statements from deliberation, whereas here it was argued that sometimes it is the anonymous layer that is presented as more authoritative on account of its superior knowledge. Neusner also understands this division as allowing the Bavli to be "systematic"—whereas here I argue that this division is precisely what enables the Bavli to be unsystematic, i.e., to contrast tradition with its own system and not let one completely prevail over the other.

sources for the first time but also when they offered new renditions of existing *sugyot.*

The innovative aspect of these presentations was not simply a tolerated consequence of the fluidity of oral transmission: it was expected and celebrated. The ambition and quality of variants between different versions of the same sequence show us that even after the initial formation of *sugyot,* their presentation was given not to professional memorizers who could repeat them but to advanced scholars who could revise and augment them with new sources and discussions.[70] This conforms with the well-known emphasis on creativity in the Talmudic ideology of Torah study, which we will examine in Chapter 4. For now, it is important to emphasize that scholarly innovation was prized in the culture that produced the Talmud, and was part of the task with which the scholars who shaped its *sugyot* were charged.

The layered structure provided a solution for the tension between these two ends. It created a literary distinction between the body of teachings that was transmitted and the interpretation that was open to innovation. It combined a commitment to a faithful transmission of tradition and an independent and flexible engagement with that tradition. It allowed Babylonian scholars to contrast their own approaches with the teachings of the past, whether to showcase the scholarly virtuosity of an individual scholar or more generally to mark the distance between a classical past and their own age. The adoption of this structure was a move toward a more marked distinction between tradition and innovation.

To be sure, the anonymous narration cannot be identified straightforwardly with the scholars who presented the *sugyot* in the academy. The written form we have is far from an exact transcription of such presentations; the *stam* itself, both as it was orally presented and especially as it was transferred into writing was a patchwork of many sources, as we have seen throughout this chapter. More important, we need to apply here the well-known distinction between "author" and "narrator": the *stam* as the narrator of the *sugya,* with its typical formulations and endless inquiries, is itself a literary character that follows the conventions of the genre.

We can, however, posit that for the purpose of the session, these scholars assumed this role of the narrator. For the duration of the presentation, they were the ones who were quoting the sources, they were the ones who were narrating the *sugya,* and the narrative of the *sugya* became

70   See Rosenthal, "Early Form," 65. The transmission process Rosenthal discusses is later than the one discussed here, inasmuch as it is the transmission of fairly fixed *sugyot,* whereas here we are dealing with *sugyot* that were already formed but could vary dramatically in structure—but this difference makes it even more likely that they were transmitted and recomposed by advanced scholars.

theirs to change and expand. In other words, the adoption of a separation between attributed rulings and anonymous narrative invited subsequent scholars to approach the former as fixed and belonging to the past and to identify themselves with the latter. The distinction between *stam* and *memrot* allowed the performer of the *sugya* to base his claim to authority both on the accurate transmission of fixed, brief, archaic-sounding Hebrew traditions and on the virtuosity of his inventive, dialectical Aramaic.

The observation that the layered structure was a literary strategy, maintained and sometimes introduced by the scholars who shaped the Bavli in the performances of the *sugyot* in the academy, offers us a new perspective on the features of the Talmud that have been central to discussions of the layers' dating. It is true that very often *memrot* preserve approaches different and earlier than those presented in the *stam*, and that in early versions of the Talmud the *memrot* are relatively stable while the *stam* fluctuates significantly from one version to another. But we need not take these features as indications that a late anonymous narrative was woven around early apodictic sources. Rather, it was the function of the layered structure that resulted in a distinction between a relatively stable layer, which Babylonian scholars transmitted more conservatively, and a dynamic layer of interpretation, which could vary from one performance to another and which increasingly presented the interpretations and approaches of later scholars.

Thus to the extent that we can detect a difference between the *memrot* and the *stam*, it is not *despite* the attempt by late Babylonian scholars to hide themselves or despite their unconscious retrojection of their views into past teachings. We can detect this difference *because* these scholars adopted literary practices that distinguished the preservation of older materials from the presentation of new interpretations by freezing the teachings of the past and embedding them in an evolving layer of interpretation.

As we have seen, however, this distance between an attributed source and its anonymous interpretation did not always correlate with a difference between earlier and later material. Still, even in such cases the presentation of tradition as independent from and earlier than its interpretation is significant. The Talmud thus demonstrated to its audience how an innovative inference from an existing tradition works. More important, it initiated its students into a particular relationship with tradition that was premised on discontinuity: on the one hand, it "canonized" tradition, fixing it and authorizing it; on the other hand, because it presented attributed traditions as detachable from interpretation and context, it invited students to an independent and creative engagement with these traditions in a quest for better interpretations and broader inferences. In other

words, even when the Talmud did not offer its own original interpretation, the layered structure thematized and demonstrated an innovative
approach to tradition.

The layered pattern of representation was developed and practiced for
a long span of time and applied to a large number of texts by many different people. It was probably more often the result of habitual practice, by
which received materials were formulated in conventional forms, than
the result of conscious reorganization; it cannot be explained as an expression of a unified ideological statement on tradition. This structure
was adopted so overwhelmingly because it served important functions
for the individuals who created and maintained it and for their audiences. These functions, it was suggested here, were connected precisely
with the ability of this structure to create or highlight the very alterity of
tradition which, according to its modern readers, it was designed to
overcome.

Chapter Three

COMPOSITION AS CRITIQUE

The authors of the *stam* were also the "redactors," "editors," "compilers" of Babylonian *sugyot*; that is, we attribute to them not just the composition of the anonymous layer but also a series of more "silent" activities: juxtaposition, arrangement, reformulation of traditions, and the adaptation and composition of narratives. Since these modes of composition do not involve the division between attributed traditions and anonymous commentary, they have provided good examples for the "voiceless" model of Talmudic composition that we encountered above.

This chapter aims to show that the Talmud's creators produced the same critical space that we have seen in the previous chapters, the same gap between themselves and their sources, even in their role as compilers, adaptors, and storytellers. It focuses on a thematic series of *sugyot* in *b. Qidd.* IV, dedicated to the genealogical division of the Jewish people. These *sugyot*, I argue, develop a particular strategy to present a certain kind of traditional knowledge and at the same time offer a critique of this knowledge. The traditional knowledge in question is genealogical knowledge: statements, rulings, bits of information that the rabbis transmitted in the matter of Jewish genealogy, in particular, the classification of certain persons, families, or regions as genealogically "unfit" or "impure" for the purpose of marriage.

The critique is achieved with a number of literary devices, which are designed to train the audience of these *sugyot* to be suspicious about the production of genealogical traditions. Through the reinterpretation of statements, rulings, and biblical commentary, and through the presentation of certain stories, the Bavli here shows us that this kind of knowledge, even when entrusted to the rabbis, does not reflect natural or even legal reality but rather is produced and manipulated by powerful people with various motives.

This situation of knowledge instills in us a suspicion that is then activated when the genealogical traditions themselves are deployed; we no longer see in them a reliable representation of reality. Thus only part of the work here is done through new composition, whether of anonymous commentary or reformulation of earlier materials. Even when the creators of our *sugyot* presented some traditions without commentary or reformulation, I argue, they were relying on the material they formulated and the commentary they introduced to guide their audience to a critical disposition toward these traditions. The redactional disengagement from some traditions, that is, the choice not to change them or manipulate them, can also work as a measure of distanciation. The old question— whether "the framers of the Bavli serve as conservators of a received tradition or as active participants in the framing of a statement of their own"[1]—is misleading: conservation can bear a message very different from, and even critical of, what is being conserved.

THE BAVLI ON GENEALOGY

Rabbinic law divides the Jewish people into marital castes or genealogical classes. The Mishnah, in *m. Qidd* 4:1, lists these classes and details the permissible unions among them. In order to prevent the unions proscribed by rabbinic law, the rabbis were concerned with keeping genealogical records and with developing procedures to ensure that each individual was assigned to its correct class. This concern with genealogical knowledge was particularly urgent because this knowledge, given its consequences for personal lives and social status, was likely to be manipulated and abused.

The Bavli dedicates a series of *sugyot* to a general discussion of this genealogical division. The Talmud's discussion shares with previous rabbinic texts a concern with genealogical knowledge. Surprisingly, though, its authors choose to focus on the instability of this knowledge and its contingent nature.

This chapter focuses on two parts, or *sugyot*, of this Talmudic discussion. Both of these *sugyot* take as their point of departure the gap between innate genealogical identities, on the one hand, and ascribed genealogical identities on the other. While earlier rabbinic texts were certainly aware of this gap, the Talmud's discussion departs from those texts in important ways. First, the Bavli presents a special interest in the social processes that lead to the production or manipulation of innate genealogical identities. It links this production with personal interest and political power. Furthermore, in contrast with its predecessors, the Talmud does not perceive socially ascribed identities as mere errors to be reversed by divine action or rabbinic procedure; in one passage, the Tal-

---

1   Jacob Neusner, *The Bavli's One Voice: Types and Forms of Analytical Discourse and their Fixed Order of Appearance* (Atlanta: Scholars Press, 1991), xvii.

mud goes so far so as to say that God approves the human processes that lead to the creation of these identities.

More important, rabbinic procedure itself is portrayed as the origin of the perversion and abuse of genealogical knowledge. The Talmud does not present to us a reasoned rabbinic discourse that salvages innate, fixed genealogical information from social deception or misperception. Rather, the rabbis are represented as the most authoritative participants in the dynamic processes that produce genealogical knowledge. Rabbinic decisions are shown to be motivated by personal passions, collective interests, and power struggles.

The Bavli's discussion is indebted to earlier developments in the rabbinic treatment of genealogy but it takes them in different directions. If earlier rabbinic texts invested more prestige in achieved or ascribed status than in innate status,[2] the Bavli blurs the distinctions between them. If earlier texts bestowed some power on humans to change birth-determined conditions,[3] the Bavli is concerned with the problems, advantages, and responsibilities associated with this power.

Scholars have documented the importance of genealogy in many aspects of rabbinic culture in general and Babylonian Jewish culture in particular. It played a central role in the Babylonian community's self-perception,[4] its religious and public life,[5] the shape of its academic leadership,[6] the relations between rabbis and non-rabbis,[7] and, naturally,

2 See, e.g., the famous text in *m. Hor.* 3:8, which presents a hierarchy of the Jewish people based on descent, only to conclude with the general principle, "a *mamzer*, who is a scholar, and a high priest, who is an ignoramus: the *mamzer* scholar takes precedence over the ignorant high priest." For a re-evaluation of the rabbis' position on descent as a hierarchy-determining factor, see Martha Himmelfarb, *A Kingdom of Priests: Ancestry and Merit in Ancient Judaism* (Philadelphia: University of Pennsylvania Press, 2006), 160–80.

3 See *m. Qidd.* 3:13: "Rabbi Tarfon says: '*mamzerim* may be purified. How so? A male *mamzer* that has married a female slave, (according to the law) their offspring is (genealogically) a slave.'" See the discussion in Christine E. Hayes, *Gentile Impurities and Jewish Identities* (Oxford: Oxford University Press, 2002), 278 n. 51.

4 Isaiah Gafni, *The Jews of Babylonia in the Talmudic Era* (Heb.; Jerusalem: Zalman Shazar Center, 1990). See also idem, *Land, Center and Diaspora* (Sheffield: Sheffield Academic Press, 1997), 54–55.

5 Aharon Oppenheimer, "Purity of Lineage in Talmudic Babylonia" (Heb.), in *Sexuality and Family in History* (ed. I. Gafni and I. Bartal; Jerusalem: Zalman Shazar Center, 1998), 71–82.

6 Jeffrey Rubenstein, *Talmudic Stories: Narrative Art, Composition and Culture* (Baltimore: Johns Hopkins University Press, 1999), 201–6. Rubenstein also dedicates a whole chapter to genealogy in his reconstruction of Talmudic culture; idem, *The Culture of the Babylonian Talmud* (Baltimore: Johns Hopkins University Press, 2003), 80–101. Both of these studies build on the arguments in Goeffrey Herman, "Ha-kohanim be-bavel bi-tequfat ha-talmud" (master's thesis, Hebrew University, 1998), especially those about the place of priestly lineage as a criterion for leadership (85–90).

7 Richard Kalmin, "Genealogy and Polemics in Literature of Late Antiquity," *HUCA* (1996), 77–94.

marriage.[8] Scholars have also noted that the importance accorded to lineage in Babylonian Jewish culture corresponds to Iranian attitudes toward lineage.[9] The Bavli is critical of the connection between genealogy and society not despite the prominence of genealogical concerns in the culture in which it was written, but because of that prominence. The creators of our *sugyot* were engaging here in a critique of their own Babylonian rabbinic culture. In some sense, it was the implication of genealogy with power in that culture that allowed them to concentrate so intensely on the processes and structures of authority that construct genealogical identities; but they achieved this critique using common Talmudic literary techniques—and it is these techniques, rather than the topic of genealogical stratification itself, which stand at the center of our discussion.

This chapter focuses on two principal sections of the Bavli's discussion of *m. Qidd.*, each illustrating a different aspect of Talmudic composition. The first is a conversational *sugya*, which focuses on the purification of Israel. It is a treatment of a group of traditions that the Talmud's creators received already structured into a discussion. An earlier version of this discussion is recorded in the Palestinian Talmud (the Yerushalmi), and a comparison between the two versions illuminates the reformulation of this discussion in Babylonia. While the Bavli's creators remain faithful to the structure they received, they undermine its premises. The second segment has at its center a long story about Rav Yehuda, and it concludes with a list of genealogical traditions. Here the Bavli advances its agenda not by revising an existing structure but by arranging distinct traditions into a new structure. It uses sequence, juxtaposition, and narrative to subvert the traditions reproduced in its beginning and end.

THE PURIFICATION OF ISRAEL

The genealogical division described by the Mishnah prohibits some of the classes from coming into union with most Jews. The most prominent of these "prohibited" classes is the class of *mamzerim* ("bastards," or off-

8   See Michael Satlow, *Jewish Marriage in Antiquity* (Princeton, NJ: Princeton University Press, 2001), 151–56, for Babylonian peculiarities, and more generally on rabbinic culture on pp. 133–61; Adiel Schremer, *Male and Female He Created Them* (Heb.; Jerusalem: Zalman Shazar Center, 2004), 147–58, especially his comparison between Palestinian and Babylonian traditions (148–52).

9   Richard Kalmin, *The Sage in Jewish Society in Late Antiquity* (New York: Routledge, 1999), 8–10 and 58–59; Rubenstein, *Talmudic Stories*, 205–6; and Satlow, *Jewish Marriage*, 152; on lineage in Iranian culture, see Maria Macuch, "Zoroastrian Principles and the Structure of Kinship in Sasanian Iran," in *Religious Themes and Texts of Pre-Islamic Iran and Central Asia* (ed. C. Cereti et al.; Beiträge zur Iranistik 24; Wiesbaden: Reichet, 2003), 231–46.

spring of illegitimate unions). The first text that I want to offer for analysis addresses some of the problems that stem from the existence of these prohibited classes.

This text is interesting not just because of its content but also because we are able to trace its fascinating literary development by comparing it with an earlier version of the same discussion recorded in the Palestinian Talmud.[10] The parallels between the Talmuds can be seen in the following synopsis:

Palestinian Talmud, *Qidd.* 4:1 65c	Babylonian Talmud, *Qidd.* 70b–71a
R. Yohanan: *derashah* on the beginning of Mal. 3:3. God will purify only Levites in the future to come.	R. Hama: *derashah* on the beginning of Mal. 3:3. When God will purify the tribes, he will begin with the Levites.
R. Zera: As a person who drinks from a clean cup.	
	R. Yehoshua b. Levi: *derashah* on Mal. 3:3. Money purifies *mamzerim*.
R. Hoshaya: And we shall lose out since we are Levites?	
R. Hanina: *derashah* on the other half of Mal. 3:3. God will show grace to them.	*stam:* Question about the other half of Mal. 3:3. R. Yitzhak: *derashah* on Mal. 3:3. God showed grace to Israel. . .
R. Yohanan: We do not inquire after families in which a disqualified person was mixed.	. . .A family that was intermingled remains intermingled.
	Gufa: All lands are dough to Palestine. . . . A story about Rabbi Yehuda and his students. A story about Rabbi Pinehas and his students.

10 The parallels were noted, without analysis, by Noah Aminoah, *The Redaction of the Tractate Qiddushin in the Babylonian Talmud* (Heb.; Tel Aviv: Rosenberg School, 1977), 322. See also Shamma Friedman, *Talmudic Studies: Investigating the Sugya, Variant Readings, and Aggada* (New York and Jerusalem: Jewish Theological Seminary, 2010), 40–41 and n. 24. The analysis undertaken in this section suggests that the version in the Yerushalmi is closer to the original. For a general discussion of this kind of parallels, see Chapter 2 above.

[See last row of this column for the Yerushalmi parallel of this teaching]

Rabbi Yohanan: "By the Temple! It is in our hands, but what can I do, that the greatest men of the generation were intermingled in it."
He was of the same opinion as R. Yitzhak:
"A family that was intermingled remains intermingled."

R. Shimeon: The Mishnah instructs this as well:
m. Eduyyot 8:7: 'The family of Beit Ṣerifa was on the right bank of the Jordan. . . ."

Abaye: we have learned this in the Mishnah as well:
m. Eduyyot 8:7: "The family of Beit Ṣerifa was on the right bank of the Jordan . . . like these Elijah comes to render pure or impure. . . ."

stam:
'Like these' — which are known.

And still there was another one there, and the sages did not want to publicize it, but they do transmit it to their sons and their students two times every seven years (cf. t. Eduyyot 3:4).

And still there was another one there . . . and the sages did not want to reveal it. But they do transmit it to their sons and their students once every seven years (cf. t. Eduyyot 3:4).

R. Yohanan, "By the Temple service! I know them, but what can I do, that the greatest men of the generation were mixed in them."

[See Rabbi Yohanan's teaching above for the Bavli parallel for this teaching]

Let us begin with a brief description of the version in the Yerushalmi and then proceed to see how the Bavli completely transforms it in a few powerful acts of redaction.

1.
  a. R. Issa in the name of R. Yohanan: Even in the future to come the Holy One, blessed be he, only deals with the tribe of Levi. What is the proof [for this]? *And he shall sit as a refiner and purifier of silver and he shall purify the sons of Levi* (Mal. 3:3).
  b. Said R. Zeira: As a person who drinks from a clean glass.
  c. Said R. Hoshaya, And because we are[11] Levites, we shall lose out?

11 Both Ms. Leiden and the printed edition read "because we are not Levites," possibly under the influence of the Bavli. My translation omits the word "not" based on the parallel in *y. Yebam.* 8:3 9d as well as on interpretive considerations; see n. 13 below.

   d. Said R. Hanina b. R. Abbahu: Even in the future to come the Holy
      One, blessed be he, will show them grace. What is the proof? *And
      they shall offer unto the Lord minḥa offerings in righteousness* (Mal. 3:3).

2.
   a. Said R. Yohanan: We do not meticulously inquire after a family in
      which a disqualified person was mixed.
   b. Said R. Shimeon ben Lakish: The Mishnah [already] said so: "The
      family of Beit Ṣerifa was across the Jordan, and Ben Zion distanced it
      [i.e., rendered prohibited] using force. And there was another one
      there that Ben Zion brought closer [i.e., rendered permitted] using
      force. (*m. Eduyyot* 8:7). And the sages did not wish to reveal them.
      But the sages transmit them to their sons and students twice every
      seven years."
   c. Said R. Yohanan: [I swear by] the [Temple] service! I know them,
      and what can I do, that the greatest of the generation were intermin-
      gled with them. (*y. Qidd.* 4:1 65c)

This passage comes after a discussion that describes how God purges society of members of one of the prohibited classes, the *mamzerim*. In that
discussion, we learn that God kills *mamzerim* every sixty or seventy years,
lest they be intermingled with families of the permitted classes. The
Yerushalmi goes on to point out that along with these *mamzerim*, God
kills some members of the permitted classes in order not to expose the
identity of the *mamzerim*. It then concludes that this purging only affects
mamzerim whose status is unknown (since there is no danger that members of the permitted classes will marry known *mamzerim*). Known
mamzerim are therefore unaffected by the purge. The significance of God's
actions is that we human beings cannot, and should not, concern ourselves with the presence of hidden *mamzerim* among us. God will purge
them, but in a discreet way that does not make their identity public.[12]

   It is in this context that the Yerushalmi adduces R. Yohanan's Midrashic comment on Mal. 3:3 (§1a). Even in the Messianic era, God will
continue this discreet treatment of intermingled disqualified persons.
Since, however, the Levites will be called once again to serve in the Temple, God will expose the status of those Levites who are genealogically
blemished and therefore disqualified from service, setting them apart
from the rest of the tribe. We learn this in Mal. 3:3, a verse that describes

---

   12   On this discussion in the Yerushalmi and its parallel in Leviticus Rabbah, see Tzvi
Novick, "'They Come Against Them with the Power of the Torah': Rabbinic Reflections on
Legal Fiction and Legal Agency," *Studies in Law, Politics and Society* 50 (2009), 1–17
(8–12).

an eschatological purification but mentions only the Levites. R. Zeira's teaching (§1b) compares God's unwillingness to tolerate disqualified Levites and priests in the Temple to the unwillingness of a person to drink from a contaminated glass. R. Hoshaya objects to this discrimination against the Levites (§1c),[13] but R. Hanina uses the second half of Mal. 3:3 as evidence that God had actually shown them grace (§1d).

The second part of the Yerushalmi's discussion begins with R. Yohanan's teaching, "we do not meticulously inquire after any family in which a disqualified person was mixed" (§2a). This dictum builds on the general conclusions of the Yerushalmi's discussion. Since God takes care of the *mamzerim* by removing them from society, and since even God is careful not to make prohibited genealogical identities public, we should not be particular about families in which a disqualified person was intermingled.

R. Shimeon comments that this lenient policy toward intermingled families could already be seen in a Tannaitic source or a *baraita* that comments on a tradition from the Mishnah, tractate *Eduyyot* (§2a). That tradition tells of two families whose genealogical identities had been violently changed. The *baraita* observes that the Mishnaic tradition only identifies the family that was originally permitted and is now considered disqualified. The family that benefited from the violent manipulation, that is, the intermingled disqualified family, remains anonymous, though the *baraita* assures us that the sages transmit its name discreetly.[14] We may therefore conclude that the Mishnah wished to limit investigation of intermingled disqualified families. This part of the discussion concludes with R. Yohanan, who exclaims that he knows the identity of the origi-

---

13   The version transmitted in *y. Qidd.* (as opposed to *y. Yebam.*; see n. 11 above) that has R. Hoshaya say, "because we are *not* Levites" (בגין דלית אנן לויים), might be the result of a positive understanding of the purification, perhaps influenced by the Bavli. The Yerushalmi, however, seems to perceive the purification as a negative necessity. R. Hoshaya's exclamation protests the irony and injustice of punishing the most selected, dedicated tribe.

14   Michael Satlow writes that "R. Shimeon ben Lakish's dictum deliberately blurs the boundaries of the *mishnah* he cites, thus implying greater authority to his assertion" (Satlow, *Jewish Marriage*, 151). It seems, though, that R. Shimeon's dictum, like Abaye's in the Bavli parallel, is not just citing the *mishnah* but also a *baraita* (which itself treats the *mishnah* as a lemma). The "intermingling" of *baraita* and *mishnah* in this manner is not uncommon, especially in the Yerushalmi. See Jacob Epstein, *Introduction to the Mishnaic Text* [3rd ed.] (Heb.; 2 vols.; Jerusalem: Magnes, 2000), 2.799–801, with reference to our text on 2.801. See also Chanoch Albeck, *Studies in the Baraita and the Tosefta and their Relationship to the Talmud* [2nd ed.] (Heb.; Jerusalem: Mosad Ha-Rav, 1969), 3, for the general lack of citation terms for *baraitot* in the Yerushalmi, and ibid., 53, on the meaning of *tana* as a citation term for *baraitot* that present commentary on other Tannaitic materials, just as it is found in the Bavli parallel of R. Shimeon's teaching (attributed there to Abaye).

nally prohibited family and laments that it is now intermingled with prominent members of society (§2c).[15]

The Bavli's version, in contrast with the Yerushalmi's, does not proceed from a discussion of the purification of *mamzerim*.[16] Rather, it opens a new discussion of the eschatological purification:

1.
    a. Said Rabbi Hama b. Hanina, "When the Holy One, blessed be he, purifies the tribes, he will first purify the tribe of Levi, for it was said, *And he shall sit as a refiner and purifier of silver, and he shall purify the sons of Levi* (Mal. 3:3).

    b. R. Yehushua b. Levi said: Money purifies *mamzerim*, as it was said, *and money shall sit as a refiner and purifier* (ibid.).[17]

    c. What is [meant by the end of that verse] "*and they shall offer unto the Lord minha offerings by grace [ṣedaqa]*"?

    d. R. Yitzhak said: The Holy One, blessed be he, showed grace to Israel: a family that was intermingled—[remains] intermingled.

2.
    [Units 2a–c are reproduced later in this section.]

    d. Said R. Yohanan: "[I swear by] the Temple! It is in our power. But what can I do, that the greatest men of the generation were intermingled in it."

    e. He was of Rabbi Yitzhak's opinion, for R. Yitzhak said, "A family that was intermingled—[remains] intermingled."

    f. Said Abaye: We have also learned so in the Mishnah:

    g. The family of Beit Ṣerifa was across the Jordan, and Ben Zion distanced [i.e., rendered prohibited] it using force. And there was another one there that Ben Zion brought close [i.e., rendered permitted] using force. [Families] like these Elijah comes to purify or declare impure, to distance or bring closer' (*m. Eduyyot* 8:7)."

    h. "Like these"—which are known, but a family that was intermingled—[remains] intermingled.

    i. It was taught on Tannaitic authority: "And there was another one there [which ben Zion brought closer by force'; *m. Eduyyot* 8:7], and

15 The interpretation of the Yerushalmi offered here follows, roughly, the *Pnei Moshe* on *y. Yebam.* 8:3.

16 The idea that God purges *mamzerim* does appear in the Bavli, in *b. Yebam.* 78b, but the discussion here, in *b. Qidd*, is not connected with it and in fact seems to contradict it.

17 In its original context, this part of the verse reads: "And he shall sit as a refiner and purifier of silver (*kesef*) and he shall purify the sons of Levi." This *derashah* takes *kesef* to be the subject of the sentence and as a reference to money.

the sages did not want to reveal it. But they do tell it to their sons[18] and students once every seven years." And some say, "twice every seven years." (b. Qidd. 70b–71a)[19]

The most important difference between the Talmuds in the first part of the discussion concerns the nature of the purification. In the Yerushalmi, God purifies the Levites by setting apart the disqualified members of the tribe. In the Bavli, we learn, with R. Yehoshua b. Levi (§1b), of a very different purification. The target of that purification is *mamzerim* whose wealth was sufficiently enticing to members of the permitted classes that they married them, and who thus became intermingled with these permitted classes and came to be perceived as pure. Their purification is constituted by the process through which their socially ascribed pure genealogical status prevails over their innate impure status.[20] The Talmud's question regarding the second half of Mal. 3:3, and R. Yitzhak's answer (§1c–d), extend this process of purification to all sorts of intermingling, not just that motivated by wealth. A family that was intermingled will remain intermingled, its prohibited status written off by God as part of the grace he has shown Israel.

The idea that in the Messianic era God will render the members of the classes permissible or pure appears in earlier rabbinic texts,[21] but the way this purification is understood here is surprising. Essential to the Bavli's discussion is the idea that often there is a difference between people's innate or natural identity, on the one hand, and the identity society as-

---

18   "Their sons" is missing in both Ms. Munich 95 and Ms. Vatican 111.

19   All subsequent citations in this chapter are from b. Qidd. unless otherwise noted.

20   Following Rashi, ad loc. See Hayes, *Gentile Impurities*, 186: "This is a remarkable and counterintuitive reading of Mal 3:3, which on the face of it suggests purification by means of *purging* than by means of dilution, absorption, and ultimate assimilation" (emphasis original). The remarkable nature of this reading is even more noticeable when compared with the Yerushalmi's more conventional reading, which was replaced in the Babylonian reformulation.

21   The earliest recorded manifestation of this idea in rabbinic literature is in the following *baraita*, which appears in the Tosefta and both Talmuds: "*Netinim* and *mamzerim* become pure in the future to come" — the words of R. Yosi. R. Meir says, "They do not become pure." R. Yosi said to him, "But has it not been said, *And I will sprinkle clean water upon you?*" (Ezek. 36:25). R. Meir said to him, "*From all your impurities, and from all your idols*" (ibid.)." R. Yosi said to him, "What does the teaching say (concerning the words), *I will cleanse you* (ibid.)?—even from the *netinut* from the *mamzerut*" (t. Qidd. 5:4, 294–95). See Saul Lieberman, *Tosefta Kifshutah VIII: Seder Nashim* (New York: Jewish Theological Seminary, 1973), 971–72, and Hayes, *Gentile Impurities*, 185–86 and 191. Both Talmudic passages under study (i.e., b. Qidd 70b–71a and y. Qidd 4:1 65c) contradict R. Yosi (in their own way), even though elsewhere in both Talmuds his opinion is cited positively, without referring to any contradictory opinion but that of R. Meir (b. Qidd. 72b and y. Qidd. 3:13, 64d, following Lieberman's emendation in *Tosefta Kifshutah*, ibid.).

cribes to them, on the other. The passage argues that God would approve the transformation of the former into the latter, even if the latter identity was created under dubious conditions (and R. Yehoshua's statement on money hints at one example of such conditions).

Two significant editorial actions contribute to the reinterpretation of the Palestinian discussion in the Bavli. First is the addition of Rabbi Ye-hoshua b. Levi's interpretation of the word "silver" as pertaining to the wealth of the *mamzerim*. This statement, which is the only one the Bavli adds (rather than modifies) in this part of the discussion, suggests a human motivation behind the formation of genealogical identities.[22]

The second act of redaction is more intriguing. R. Yohanan's teaching in the Yerushalmi (§2a) and R. Yitzhak's teaching in the Bavli (§1d) are two versions of the same fundamental teaching or tradition.[23] Read on its own, this teaching is a *halakhic* instruction that aims to limit the in-quiry into genealogical blemishes through legitimizing the status quo attained by each family or person (presumably because of the clear moral and social difficulties inherent in such an inquiry). The variations in terms and attribution between these versions are typical of such inter-Talmudic parallels and do little, in themselves, to change the meaning of the instruction.

This tradition, however, receives different meanings in the two Tal-muds. The Bavli unifies what in the Yerushalmi were two different, unre-lated sources and points, creating one teaching: R. Yitzhak's teaching parallels not only R. Yohanan's teaching (§2a), but also the *derashah* that precedes it (§1c). The Bavli sets up the two traditions as an argument ("an intermingled family remains intermingled") and its proof (Mal. 3:3). The *derashah* in the Yerushalmi answers R. Hoshaya's question about the mistreatment of Levites; the *derashah* in the Bavli buttresses R. Yitzhak's point on intermingled families. The *derashah* in the Yerushalmi is applied only to Levites and the "future to come"; the *derashah* in the Bavli applies to the present and to all of Israel (God *has shown* grace to *Israel*).[24]

The result of this literary manipulation is that R. Yitzhak's teaching is no longer simply a *halakhic* instruction, but also a factual statement about

---

22   This is emphasized by the parallel placement of R. Yehoshua b. Levi's tradition in the Bavli and R. Zera's tradition in the Yerushalmi (see synopsis). If the former speaks of human motives, the latter speaks of God's motives (though with human imagery, similar to the one employed in the famous discussion in *b. Git.* 90 a–b on husbands' attitudes to-ward their wives).

23   See Friedman, *Talmudic Studies*, 40–41.

24   In his brief comment, Friedman (*Talmudic Studies*) does not discuss these differ-ences, and therefore it is not clear whether he sees the Midrashic part of the teaching in the Bavli as original or not. In my opinion, since the *stam* asks the Midrashic question, it is not likely that the teaching originally included the reference to Mal. 3:3.

the transformation of genealogical identities: a person's intermingling, that is, the achievement of legitimization by society, affects the genealogical identity that will be given by God in the process of purification. R. Yohanan's parallel teaching in the Yerushalmi is never understood as being anything but a *halakhic* instruction; the principle behind it does not affect the reality of genealogical identities.[25] The facts that in the Yerushalmi are assumed to be natural or divine in origin are represented by the Bavli as being determined by human processes and conditions.

The next three units in the Bavli differ from the trajectory common to the two Talmuds to such an extent (see the synopsis) that it would be best to defer full treatment of them until later and discuss them here only briefly. Using the Talmudic term *gufa* (the "body" of the matter), the first of these units indicates that the discussion is returning to a statement that was cited earlier in passing. In our case, this is Shmuel's genealogical hierarchy (all lands are considered genealogically mixed, "dough," compared to Palestine, and Palestine is considered "dough" compared to Babylonia).[26] The interpretive effect of this *gufa* statement is significant, especially in terms of the differences between the Talmuds. It applies all subsequent sources in the Bavli to a matter that is not mentioned in this part of the Yerushalmi at all. The two stories that follow tell how Palestinian sages tried to reverse this genealogical hierarchy to no avail.

The Bavli then quotes a statement by R. Yohanan: "[I swear by] the Temple! It is in our power. But what can I do, that the greatest men of the generation were intermingled in it" (§2d). In this context, the statement means that Palestinian sages have the ability to reverse the genealogical hierarchy, subordinating Babylonia to Palestine in genealogical reputation. But unfortunately, R. Yohanan exclaims, "the greatest men of the generation" were already intermingled in it (in the mixed "dough" that is Palestine) through marriage with originally prohibited families. An in-

25   While R. Yohanan's dictum in the Yerushalmi is clearly a description of rabbinic policy ("we do not inquire"), R. Yitzhak's words in the Bavli, "a family which was intermingled — (remains) intermingled," lend themselves to being understood as a description of reality rather than a normative instruction. This difference in wording in itself may have occurred before the teaching was given its new meaning. Still even if the Bavli's creators had it before them as we have it now (and it is not unlikely that they would have changed a teaching's wordings to better fit its new context), the formulation itself does not at all necessitate the Bavli's interpretation.

26   The term "dough" (עיסה) may also be rendered "admixture." The hierarchical teaching argues that in all lands, the genealogical classes are more mixed with one another (i.e., through intermarriage) than they are in Palestine; in Palestine, the classes are more mixed with one another than they are in Babylonia. The more genealogically suspect the place one comes from, the more inquiry is needed before marriage is allowed. For the history of the term עיסה, see Satlow, *Jewish Marriage*, 155–56, and Hayes, *Gentile Impurities*, 191–92.

quiry into the genealogical identities of all Jews in Palestine, one that aims to identify the genealogical ingredients of the Palestinian Jewish community and which will make sure the classes do not mix, should be avoided because it will expose the blemished identity of prominent members of that community.

This statement by R. Yohanan, it may be recalled, appears in the Yerushalmi as well (§2c). There are two differences in the roles it plays in each of the Talmuds; one is more obvious, but the other is more significant. The first and more obvious difference is that in the Yerushalmi the statement is not connected to the hierarchy between Palestine and Babylonia, but rather to the issue of hidden prohibited families.

The second and more important difference is in the nature of the statement. In the Yerushalmi, the function of the statement is not to suggest R. Yohanan's reason for not exposing or inquiring into these families. That reason has already been supplied by R. Yohanan himself, when his instruction not to inquire appeared earlier, and was exemplified in the Mishnah (§2a–b). The Bavli, however, suggests that the fact that the "greatest of the generation" were intermingled is itself the reason for R. Yohanan's non-action. Unlike the Yerushalmi, the Bavli uses the word "but" to link the first part, "it is in our power," to the second, "the greatest generations have intermingled," suggesting a causal connection. In order to justify R. Yohanan's decision not to act, the Bavli speculates that "he was of R. Yitzhak's opinion, for R. Yitzhak said, 'A family that was intermingled—[remains] intermingled.' "

The Talmud's interpretation of R. Yohanan's motive emphasizes again that genealogical identity is affected by social factors: earlier in the discussion it was wealth, now it is a more general kind of prominence, most probably rabbinic prominence.[27] Still, this source adds an important element to the picture. By having a rabbi approve of the situation, even reluctantly, the Talmud implicates the rabbinic establishment itself in the production and manipulation of genealogical information.

Rabbinic control of genealogical information is also the topic of the next step in the Talmud's discussion. In the Yerushalmi, R. Shimeon quotes

---

27 Cf. Kalmin, *Sage in Jewish Society*, 55. Kalmin's thesis that rabbinic policies of genealogical knowledge are connected with the rabbis' attitude toward prominent non-rabbis is very persuasive, but he frequently marginalizes the possibility that these policies also reflect inner rabbinic tensions. In any event, while Kalmin is interested in the reconstruction of rabbinic policies in the Amoraic period, my interest here is in the Babylonian *sugya*, which seems to be more concerned with the problems stemming from *rabbinic* manipulations of genealogical knowledge. On the "greatest men of the generation" as rabbis in the Bavli and non-rabbis in Palestinian sources, see Shamma Friedman, "The Transformations of עולם" (Heb.), in *Sha'arei Lashon: Studies in Hebrew, Aramaic, and Jewish Languages Presented to Moshe Bar-Asher* (Heb.; ed. A. Maman et al.; 3 vols.; Jerusalem: Bialik Institute, 2007), 2.272–85 (280–281).

a *mishnah* about families whose class identity was altered violently (§2b). In the Yerushalmi this *mishnah* is adduced to support R. Yohanan's policy of leniency toward intermingled families: since the Mishnah is discrete concerning the intermingled family's name, and since the *baraita* tells us that the name is transmitted confidentially, we know we should not inquire after intermingled families. In the Babylonian version, the same *mishnah* is adduced by Abaye to support the same policy (which in the Bavli is attributed to R. Yitzhak).[28] The Bavli's addition of an interpretive comment on the *mishnah*, however, significantly changes this part of the discussion.

After it tells us of the two families, the Mishnah in *Eduyyot* promises that the original identities of families "like these" would be restored by Elijah at the end of times (§2g; this clause is not cited by the Yerushalmi). That is to say, Elijah will remedy the corrupt state of affairs in which families are assigned to a class not originally theirs, but one that was forced on them.[29] The Bavli draws our attention to this clause and adds an interpretive comment on the words "like these," stating that Elijah will only restore identities that "are known, but a family that was intermingled—[remains] intermingled."[30]

This comment is puzzling, almost outrageous: Elijah was summoned by the Mishnah to dispel genealogical uncertainty and misperception, not to preserve it! The task of genealogical restoration is assigned to the prophet Elijah precisely because he can see beyond the intermingling and recognize true genealogical identities. When the Talmud limits Elijah's mission to families that are known, surely it does not imply that there are families that are not known to him. To whose knowledge, then, does the Talmud refer?

The answer lies in the conclusion of the Tannaitic teachings quoted by the Talmuds (§2i in the Bavli), which tell us that even though the name of

28   The fact that Abaye's teaching is part of a complete discussion adapted from a Palestinian source qualifies, I think, the extent of the particular agency Kalmin ascribes to Abaye when he states that "the fact that Abaye asserts that this Palestinian view [R. Yitzhak's–R. Yohanan's] is 'also taught in a *mishnah*' suggests strongly that he agrees with it; further support for my characterization of later Babylonian attitudes" (Kalmin, *Sage in Jewish Society*, 56). In fact, the Bavli simply attributes to Abaye the same teaching attributed to R. Shimeon in the Yerushalmi.

29   As it explicitly says before Ben Zion is first mentioned: "R. Yehushua said: I have received a tradition from R. Yohanan b. Zakkai . . . that Elijah will not come to pronounce impure or pure, to put distance or to bring near, but to distance those who were brought close by force and to bring near those who were distanced by force." This *mishnah* seems to contradict other views on the eschatological purification (see n. 21 above).

30   My reading of this comment as an addition made by the Bavli, rather than part of Abaye's teaching, is based on the following considerations: first, R. Shimeon's parallel teaching in the Yerushalmi, similar to Abaye's in every way, does not include the comment; the comment may be easily excised; the gloss separates the *mishnah* from the *baraita* that interprets it.

the family is not mentioned in the Mishnah, it is secretly transmitted by the sages. This reference to rabbinic transmission explains the Talmud's comment on the Mishnah: by "those who are known," it means those who are known to the rabbis. This is also a reinterpretation of the term "intermingled." Since one of the families is known only to the rabbis, who do not publicize its name, the term now signifies families whose names have not been transmitted by the rabbis.

Rabbinic transmission, then, is the final catalyst and criterion by which genealogical identity will be determined. Elijah will come to change the genealogical identities only in those cases in which the rabbis chose to transmit names. This move also solves for the Bavli the contradiction between its interpretation of R. Yitzhak's assertion, "a family that was intermingled remains intermingled," and the Mishnah's promise of genealogical restoration.

The Bavli thus departs from the tradition recorded in the Mishnah, the *baraita*, and the Yerushalmi.[31] For the Mishnah, as we have seen, the important distinction was between those families whose genealogical status was violently manipulated and those families who were not victims of such action. Elijah will restore the status of the former. By not stating the name of the family whose original status was prohibited, the Mishnah also makes an implicit distinction between families whose situation would be made worse by having their status made public, and those families whose situation would be ameliorated. This implicit distinction is acknowledged by the *baraita*.

In the Yerushalmi there are also two operative distinctions. The first distinction is between families whose original status is known to the public and families whose status is unknown. The second distinction, as in the Mishnah, is between families who were originally prohibited and families who were originally permitted. Thus, R. Shimeon uses the *mishnah* and the *baraita* to show that the sages avoided exposing families whose original status, now unknown to the public, was prohibited.

For the Bavli, the emphasis is on the rabbinic demarcation of genealogical identities through the production or transmission of genealogical knowledge. This emphasis is most evident in those passages in which the

---

31 Satlow, *Jewish Marriage*, 151, similarly observes that this is an "assertion that the rabbis controlled genealogical knowledge." While Satlow's comment refers to the Yerushalmi, I think it is more applicable to the Bavli and less to the Yerushalmi or the *baraita*. In the latter sources, it seems more of a reassurance: do not worry, even though the name is not mentioned, we transmit it. It is only in the Bavli, where the transmission actually affects genealogical identities by determining Elijah's list of clients, that the argument is made for absolute rabbinic control of genealogical knowledge. See also Satlow's important observation that Kalmin (*Sage in Jewish Society*, 54), who reads in this source only an expression of rabbinic discretion in genealogical matters, "neglects to take into account the implicit power of secret knowledge, the mere mention of which serves notice that it can, if needed, be instantly deployed" (Satlow, *Jewish Marriage*, 327 n. 143).

Bavli significantly diverges from the line common to both Talmuds. The Babylonian addition (see synopsis) begins with a discursive reference and continues with two stories very similar in form:

2.
  a. *Gufa*: Said Rav Yehuda said Shmuel: All lands are dough to Palestine, and Palestine is dough to Babylonia.
  b. In the days of Rabbi [Yehuda the Patriarch] they [Palestinian students] sought to make Babylonia dough to Palestine. He said to them, "Thorns you are putting in my eyes! If you wish, R. Hanina b. Hama will join [issue] with you." R. Hanina b. Hama joined [issue] with them and told them: "This I have in tradition from R. Ishmael son of R. Yosi who stated on his father's authority: 'All lands are dough to Palestine and Palestine is dough to Babylonia.' "
  c. In the days of R. Pinehas they [Palestinian students] sought to make Babylonia dough to Palestine. He said to his slaves: "the moment I have said two things in the *beit-midrash*, take me in my chair and run!" When he entered [the *beit-midrash*] he told them [the scholars]: "Slaughter of fowl has no basis in Scripture." As they were seated and [were preoccupied] studying this [teaching], he told them: "All lands are dough to Palestine, and Palestine is dough to Babylonia." They [his slaves] took him in the cradle and ran, and they [the scholars] ran after him but did not reach him. They sat and examined [matters genealogical], until they encountered danger, and quit [investigating]. (71a)

Both of these stories tell us of attempts by Palestinian scholars to over-turn the genealogical hierarchy of the Jewish world so as to favor their own Palestinian community.[32] While both stories have a similar structure and probably bear a similar message, the second story expresses the Tal-mud's point more clearly. R. Pinehas devises a plan to evade his students' demand for thorough genealogical investigation of Palestine. He will dis-tract them with an unrelated, difficult subject, and as they struggle with it he will utter Shmuel's teaching of genealogical hierarchy and make a

---

32   These stories at first seem to be nothing but Babylonian propaganda. But is it pos-sible that they originated in Palestine? Kalmin seems to presuppose as much when he takes them as reliable evidence for the Palestinian position (*Sage in Jewish Society*, 55). I find it improbable that the stories as they now appear in the Bavli came from Palestine; but it is possible that they were not originally concerned with the genealogical hierarchy between the two communities. Just as R. Yohanan's exclamation ("it is in our hands," etc.) appears in the Bavli in direct relation to the regional hierarchy while in the Yerush-almi it is a general statement about genealogical inquiry, so also these stories might have at first dealt with a general discussion concerning inquiry into disqualified families, with-out any connection to the hierarchy between the two communities.

colorful exit with the help of his slaves (the irony of having Rabbi Pinehas use slaves, one of the low genealogical classes, to help him evade the consequences of his opinion on this matter is surely intended). While at first it seems that the Talmud portrays R. Pinehas as a comical coward with his clumsy diversion tactics and evasive maneuvers, his students also end up backing down after encountering danger, presumably political. Once again, the Talmud represents genealogical knowledge as arbitrary and contingent on the politics of Jewish society.

In fact, the story does more than that: it suggests that rabbinic discourse is itself politicized and arbitrary. From the very beginning, the students' motivation is self-serving: they want their community to be in a better position than Babylonia. R. Pinehas's behavior, though justified by the story, is in any event not a good example of reasoned discourse. He never justifies his support for the genealogical hierarchy. The topic he chooses as a diversion is not accidental: just like the slaughter of fowl, the story implies, the issue of genealogy is not based on scriptural reasoning but on rabbinic authority.[33]

These two stories are then followed by R. Yohanan's statement (§2d), discussed above, that the inquiry required to overturn the hierarchy is undesirable because prominent members of society are in danger of being downgraded in status. Read together, the two stories and R. Yohanan's statement (§2b–d) expose the motivations that affect rabbinic decisions.

The personal motivation behind rabbinic decisions on genealogical matters is even more explicitly presented in two statements that are quoted later in the Bavli. These statements appear in a discussion that seeks to determine which settlements are included in the superior pedigree zone of Babylonia. In the case of two such settlements, suspicion arises about a certain rabbi's reason to include or exclude the settlement:

Hanan ben Pinehas says: "[The district of] Ḥavel Yama is the blue [i.e., the best] of Babylonia; Šunya, Guvya, and Ṣiṣura are the splendor of Ḥavel Yama." Rav Papa said: "But now foreigners [lit. Cutheans] have intermingled in these [places]"; and this is not [so—rather,] he [Rav Papa] wanted

---

33   The story about Rabbi Yehuda is less clear, though Rashi (ad loc.) suggests an interpretation with which my interpretation of the *sugya* coheres. Rashi explains Rabbi Yehuda's reaction as personally motivated. The Patriarch's family, as was well known, went back to Hillel, who famously emigrated from Babylonia; an inquiry that would undermine Babylonia's claims to purest descent would also undermine the Patriarchal family's genealogical status. R. Hanina is appointed to block the new effort. At first, his answer seems to be a mere reassertion of the situation the students wanted to revise. If we stick to the logic of Rashi's explanation, though, we may be able to make good sense of it. If Rabbi Yehuda's reaction had to do with his personal Babylonian interest, R. Hanina's answer might have aimed to assure the students that this kind of Babylonian interest was not behind the genealogical hierarchy by attributing it to a Palestinian tradition (R. Ishmael b. Rabbi Yosi, from his father).

[to marry] a woman from them [the people of these places)], and they did not let him [and he has been resentful ever since.]. . . .

Said Rav Ika bar Abin in Rav Hananel's name, citing Rav: "Helwan Niha-wand is like 'Exile' [i.e., Babylonia] with respect to genealogy." Abaye said to them: "Do not heed him! A *yevama* [his dead brother's widow, whom he should according to law either marry or release] has fallen for him [Rav Iqa] there [and he wanted to marry her]." He [Rav Iqa] said: "is this [teaching] mine?! It is Rav Hananel's!" They went and asked Rav Hananel who told them, "Thus said Rav—Helwan Nihawand is like 'Exile' with respect to genealogy." (72a)

In both instances we are exposed (either by the Talmud itself or by a tradition the Talmud adduces) to the possibility that rabbinic instruction itself may be used to manipulate genealogical information and that this manipulation is motivated by the personal interests of individual rabbis. The Talmud thus chooses to draw our attention to the problems inherent in rabbinic control of genealogical information.[34]

The passage on the purification of Israel ends with a brief discussion about the configuration of rabbinic transmission. It may be recalled that in §2i, we were offered two accounts of how frequently the sages trans-mit the name of intermingled families: "'they tell it to their sons and stu-dents once every seven years.' And some say, 'twice every seven years.'" The Bavli proceeds to discuss this difference:

> j. Rav Nahman b. Yizhak said: "he who says 'once every seven years' is of the more probable opinion, as we have learned in a Tannaitic source: [when someone takes a vow saying] 'I shall be a Nazirite if I shall not reveal [the genealogical identities of] families—he should be a Nazirite rather than revealing [the genealogical identities of] families.'"
>
> k. Rabbah b. b. Hana said in the name of R. Yohanan: "the [divine] name of four letters is transmitted by the rabbis to their students once every seven years" and some say: "twice every seven years." Rav Nahman b. Yizhak said: "he who says once every seven years is of the more probable opinion . . ." (71a)

Rav Nahman supports the version that would have the transmission oc-curring less frequently. He demonstrates that publicizing names of genea-logically blemished families is treated elsewhere with utmost severity. The Talmud then goes on to cite a similar discussion. Then we hear again

---

34 The tradition about Havel Yama is also brought in *y. Qidd.* 4:1 65c without the addition of Rav Papa's reservation and the *stam*'s comment.

of a tradition about esoteric transmission of a name, though this time it is
the divine name (or names) rather than family names; this tradition also
has two versions.

The discussion then concludes with passages that at first seem to come
in by mere "free association" from the discussion of divine names and
have no bearing on the discussion of genealogical identity:

l. It was taught: "At first, the name of twelve letters was transmitted to
every person. But when the morally corrupted had become many it was
transmitted only to the most pious of the priesthood, and the most pious
of the priesthood would silence it in the singing of their brethren the
priests." It was taught: "R. Tarfon said: 'I once climbed up after my
mother's brother to the stand, and I tuned my ear to the high priest, and
I heard him silence the name in the singing of his brethren the priests.'"

m. Rav Yehuda said in Rav's name: "the name of forty-two letters is not
transmitted but to he who is pious and humble, and is in his middle
age, and does not get angry nor drunk, and does not insist on his rights.
And he who knows it and uses it carefully and preserves it with purity,
is beloved in the heavens and beloved on earth, and is feared by people
and has a part in both worlds—this world and the world to come."
(71a)

The juxtaposition of these passages places the two divine names in a clear
hierarchy: the first is shorter than the second; the first used to be common knowledge; the second bestows on its knower all sorts of rewards
that are not mentioned regarding the first. The first is transmitted by
priests (or, more correctly, was transmitted by priests, as the transmission is set in a Temple ritual), but the transmission of the second name,
the more important one, does not necessitate priestly status. In other
words, it stipulates no genealogical merit. Everyone—a *mamzer*, convert,
slave—may know it and transmit it, if he is pious and humble and of the
right age, conduct, and character. In this sense, this passage expresses
one side of the Talmud's ambiguous relationship with hierarchies based
on heredity.

This passage, however, is also a statement about the authority to transmit knowledge. We learn that rabbinic tradition has replaced priestly
tradition in the transmission of *theological* knowledge. The priestly tradition is reduced to a nostalgic anecdote about R. Tarfon's uncle in the
Temple. The rabbis, in contrast, continue to transmit better, more re-
warding theological knowledge. This passage is placed at the end of a
discussion that conferred on the rabbis the absolute control of *genealogical* knowledge. The implied message with which the Bavli concludes the
discussion, then, is that the rabbis replaced the priesthood in genealogi-

cal matters just as they replaced it in theological matters.[35] This statement closes this part of the Talmud's discussion.

The comparison between the Palestinian and Babylonian versions of the discussion demonstrates that the latter is derivative in nature. A clear manifestation of this derivative nature is already found in the first tradition reproduced in the Bavli (§1a): the statement that the Levites will be the first to be purified has little to do with the point of the Bavli's discussion (as opposed to that of the Yerushalmi) and it does not work in the exegetical framework the Bavli offers; the only reason it is there is because it was in the earlier structure, and it had to be reformulated so as to not contradict its new context.

This derivativeness is a source of creativity. The Talmud pursues its ideas by creating unlikely connections between its received sources and giving them interpretations that often go far beyond whatever original meaning we could imagine they had. It relies on its traditions' particular literary form (or transforms it to fit its needs) and on the earlier context in which it found them, and it plays with how they can function in new contexts.

The Talmudic discussion we analyzed invokes the conditions under which genealogical knowledge is produced and transmitted. The Talmud draws our attention to these conditions, shows us how they may change *halakhic* reality, and even argues that the human processes that modify or manipulate this knowledge are approved by God. The focus throughout the second part of the discussion on the rabbinic reproduction and manipulation of knowledge brings us to our next *sugya*.

RAV YEHUDA'S TRIAL

The story of Rav Yehuda's trial, introduced about halfway through the series of *sugyot* on genealogy, can be read as a long meditation on the problems inherent in rabbinic authority over genealogical demarcation.[36]

---

35 The Yerushalmi's *sugya* also concludes with a polemic against the priesthood, though one of a different nature: "Said R. Joshua b. Levi, 'Pashur ben Immer had five thousand slaves, and all of them were mixed up with the high priesthood; indeed they are the arrogant among the priesthood.' Said R. Eleazar, 'Complaint is inherent in them—*For with you is my contention, O Priest* (Hos. 4:4)' " (y. *Qidd.* 4:1 65c as well as y. *Yebam.* 8:3 9d). Note, however, that while the Bavli's polemic focuses on the transmission of knowledge, the Yerushalmi focuses on exposing the "natural" prohibited genealogical identities. The Pashur comment is also found in the Bavli; see below, n. 37, and the conclusion of the story about Rav Yehuda).

36 The story has received two illuminating recent treatments: Zvi Septimus, "Trigger Words and Simultexts: The Experience of Reading the Bavli," in *Wisdom of Bat Sheva: The Dr. Beth Samuels Memorial Volume* (ed. B. S. Wimpfheimer; Jersey City: Ktav, 2009),

The Talmud introduces the story with a brilliant sequencing that changes the course of the *sugya*. The sequence is found after several admonitions against marrying into the prohibited classes, the last of which reads:

> *Tanna*: "Elijah writes everyone, and the Holy One, blessed be he, puts his signature: woe to him, who disqualifies his progeny and taints his family; that is, to him who marries a woman who is not genealogically fit for him. Elijah binds him and the Holy One, blessed be he, whips him. And whoever disqualifies is [himself] disqualified, and he never speaks in praise [of others]." And Shmuel said: "[He, who disqualifies,] disqualifies with his [own] defect." (70a)

This teaching, introduced as Tannaitic, addresses one of the moral problems of the Jewish genealogical system. Jewish law practically excommunicates whole families for generations because of their ancestors' sins. This source is a clear and harsh admonition against such a sinful ancestor who disqualifies his family by entering into a prohibited union. We are promised that God will punish him for the ruin he has brought on his descendants.

The following clause, "and whoever disqualifies is [himself] disqualified," is less clear. If we maintain the terminology used in the previous lines, the subject of this assertion is the person who disqualifies his own family through a prohibited union. The meaning of the assertion, then, is that this person himself, and not only his descendants, should be viewed as disqualified—morally or perhaps even genealogically. This meaning fits well with the source's attempt to censure the one responsible for genealogical disqualification rather than the disqualified offspring.

This interpretation of the clause, however, does not conform with the concluding statements of the passage. What is the connection between a person who disqualifies his own family and the statement that he "never speaks praise"? Furthermore, how can Shmuel's interpretive addition, "he disqualifies with his [own] defect," be applied to someone who is not himself already disqualified, but rather disqualifies his descendants?

163–85, and Barry S. Wimpfheimer, *Narrating the Law: A Poetics of Talmudic Legal Stories* (Philadelphia: University of Pennsylavnia Press, 2011), 149–69, which builds in part on an earlier version of this chapter (Moulie Vidas, "The Bavli's Genealogy Discussion of Genealogy in Qiddushin IV," in *Antiquity in Antiquity: Jewish and Christian Pasts in the Greco-Roman World* [ed. G. Gardner and K. Osterloh; Tübingen: Mohr Siebeck, 2008], 285–326). Especially revealing is the use by both authors of the story's intertexts—an inquiry that I have therefore not undertaken here. See the conclusion of this chapter for a discussion of Wimpfheimer's theoretical insights.

The use of the teaching in the story about Rav Yehuda's trial, which follows our passage, provides an answer to these questions. In the story, the disqualifier is not someone who married an unfit woman and thus disqualified his own descendants, but rather someone who *says* a certain person is of the prohibited, disqualified classes. Our teaching thus asserts that whoever disqualifies in that way must himself already be disqualified. This instruction is rooted in the intuitive psychological observation that someone who goes around ascribing genealogical blemishes to other people might have some blemishes of his own to hide (an observation shared by other Talmudic sources dealing with genealogy).[37] Shmuel comments on this principle, adding that a person disqualifies using his own defect: a *mamzer* is likely to call others *mamzerim*, a slave is likely to call others slaves, and so forth.

When this observation is given *halakhic* significance and codified in a rabbinic teaching, it makes negative genealogical judgment impossible: if I say so and so is a slave, *mamzer*, or convert I will be seen as a slave, *mamzer*, or convert myself.[38] This teaching was originally conceived for the purpose of limiting genealogical slander. The term "disqualifier," then, changes its meaning in the middle of the passage.

I suggest that this passage includes two originally unrelated teachings that were unified by the creators of their *sugya*. The first teaching concerned the disqualification of one's own family and a description of the horrible punishment it incurs ("woe to him, who disqualifies his progeny . . ."); the second concerned genealogical speech ("and whoever disqualifies is disqualified . . .").

The Bavli blurred the distinction between these two teachings by putting them one after another without separation, taking advantage of the

37 Silence and peacefulness are associated with good pedigree in a number of traditions quoted at 72b: Ulla's advice to Rav Yehuda in selecting a bride of prime stock for his son is "Follow the silence. Just as the Palestinians examine: if two are fighting with each other, they see who becomes quiet first, and they say: 'he is of better pedigree' "; Rav's teaching, "Silence, in Babylonia, means good genealogy"; and two very similar traditions from Babylonia and Palestine: "Said Rav Yehuda in Rav's name, 'If you see two persons quarreling with each other, there must be some (genealogical) defect in one of them' "; "Said R. Yehoshua b. Levi, 'If you see two families quarreling with each other there must be some defect in one of them.' " See also the comment that Pashur ben Immer's slaves, now intermingled into the priesthood, account for those priests who are belligerent (70b). Some of these sources are quoted by Schremer, *Male and Female*, 156. Kalmin (*Sage in Jewish Society*, 60–61) takes the dialogue between Ulla and Rav Yehuda to represent precisely the difference between the Palestinian and Babylonian societies for which he argues; but the same position is also quoted by Rav Yehuda himself in Rav's name.

38 The problems in legal application of the general psychological observation is apparent in what seems to be a later addition to the statement: "and he never speaks praise"; i.e., since this behavior (of disqualifying people) now has consequences, it has to be more severe, otherwise anyone could be suspect.

ambiguity in the term "disqualifier."[39] The blurring of this distinction between the two manners of disqualification, the first through a prohibited union and the second through the attribution of prohibited status to another, parallels the blurring of the distinction between ascribed and natural genealogical identities seen in the previous section. Genealogical identity is as much the result of human speech as it is of procreation.

This almost covert rhetorical jump has a dramatic effect on the course of the *sugya*. As noted above, our passage comes after harsh admonitions aimed at the first, "physical" disqualifier; it is immediately followed by the story about Rav Yehuda, after which the Talmud cites teachings that stress the importance of genealogical purity.[40] By equating the two disqualifiers and adding the story about Rav Yehuda, which revolves around the second type of disqualifier (and is cited because of the rule concerning that disqualifier), the Talmud shifts the entire focus of this section of the discussion. The harsh criticism leveled against the first disqualifier is thus shifted to the disqualifier by speech, who is assigned an equal share of the responsibility for genealogical impurity.

---

39   The account of the creators' work here as the mere placement of sources one after the other is admittedly "conservative" in that it assumes that both sources were similar in the first place and that the Bavli's creators simply exploited this similarity. It is certainly possible, especially considering the recent work done on *baraitot* in the Talmud, that the shared terminology employed by the sources (i.e., terming both different actors as "disqualifiers") is itself already due to some editing process (see, e.g., Shamma Friedman, "Uncovering Literary Dependencies in the Talmudic Corpus," in *The Synoptic Problem in Rabbinic Literature* [ed. S. J. D. Cohen; BJS 326; Providence: Brown University Press, 2000], 35–57).

40   After a discussion regarding the words "came up from Babylonia," the *gemara* goes on to specify, using verses from Ezra and Nehemiah, how we know each of the classes was part of the immigration to Palestine. The Bavli identifies the *mamzerim,* children and foundlings in Neh. 7:61 ("The following were those who came up from Tel-melaḥ, Tel-ḥarsha, Cherub, Addon, and Immer, but they could not prove their ancestral houses or their descent, whether they belonged to Israel"), through interpretations of the place names. The verse is also used by both Rabbi Abbahu and Rabbah b. b. Hana to state the importance and holiness of genealogical purity.

The latter's teaching ("Everyone who marries a woman unfit for him, Scripture says of him that he plowed [*ḥarash*] the entire world and sowed it with salt [*melaḥ*], as it was written: 'and the following were those who came up from Tel-melaḥ, Tel-ḥarsha' ") is of special importance because in association with it the Talmud presents three more teachings that exhort against marrying an unfit woman. The discussions appended to each of these exhortations stretch the citation over almost two full Talmudic pages, most of which are taken up by our story and the appended declarations. After the declarations, the Talmud returns to one more exhortation against he who marries an unfit woman, then goes on to remark that God's *shekhinah* resides among families of good pedigree. It continues with two negative sayings about converts, before proceeding to the discussion of the purification of *mamzerim.*

The story itself is no less interesting than the manner in which it is introduced. It begins as a person from Nehardea asks for a piece of meat in a butcher shop during a visit to Pumbedita. He is told that he will have to wait until one of Rav Yehuda's servants comes to pick up the prominent rabbi's order. The Nehardean customer is outraged and curses Rav Yehuda. Upon hearing this, the rabbi is himself infuriated and decides to excommunicate the Nehardean. Moreover, after hearing that this Nehardean frequently calls people "slaves," the rabbi declares him to be of slave stock. In response, the Nehardean sues Rav Yehuda, who is then summoned to Rav Nahman's court in Nehardea. After some deliberation, the trial begins.

Throughout the story, legal and genealogical knowledge is represented as context-dependent in various ways.[41] This representation is pushed into the foreground in the conversation between the Nehardean, Rav Yehuda, and Rav Nahman. The Nehardean, the complainant, uses a strange argument to prove that contrary to the claims made by the defendant, Rav Yehuda, he is not of inferior, but rather excellent stock:

> Said that complainant to Rav Yehuda: "You call me a slave, I, who descend from the royal house of the Hasmoneans!?" He [Rav Yehuda] replied: "So said Shmuel: 'Whoever says, "I come from the house of the Hasmoneans" is a slave.'" He [Rav Nahman, the arbiter] said to him [Rav Yehuda]: "[But] do you not agree with that [teaching] that Rav Abba said in Rav Huna's name who said in Rav's name: 'Any scholar who issues a ruling: if he had said it before the event [to which he wishes to apply the ruling] he is heeded, but if [he did not] he had not heeded [because we suspect he invented the principle for the purpose of the case]'?" (70b)

Rav's rule, cited at the end of this passage, expresses a concern with rabbinic partiality: it is suspicious of rabbis who issue rulings after the fact

---

41   In fact, the very existence of the trial is contingent on politics. Twice the trial is almost avoided: once because Rav Yehuda is not legally obliged to appear in a court of an equal, Rav Nahman, and then because Rav Nahman himself (who first forgets about the subpoena) is reluctant to judge Rav Yehuda. In both instances, the reason for continuing with the trial is political. First, Rav Yehuda is advised by Rav Huna to attend the court "because of the honor of the exilarch," a political consideration whether this has to do with Rav Nahman's personal connection to the exilarch (of which we can be skeptical) or more generally with the rabbinic accountability as a desideratum of the political leadership. Second, after Rav Yehuda shows the subpoena to Rav Nahman, the latter notes that they should proceed with the trial lest it be said that the rabbis are going easy with one another. The tension in the story between rabbis and other prominent members of the community (for which, see Kalmin, *Sage in Jewish Society*, 51), as well as the tension between the two Babylonian Jewish communities (Nehardea and Pumbedita), are both parts of the story's implication of genealogical discourse with power struggles.

and is concerned about potential ad hoc inventions of tradition. This suspicion itself stems from the perception of rabbinic decisions as being intrinsically connected to the situation in which they are made. As the conversation continues, the extremely detailed mode of literary description draws the reader's attention to this matter:

> He [Rav Yehuda] said to him, "Rav Mattena is here; may it stand according to him." Rav Mattena had not seen Nehardea in thirteen years, but came that day. [Rav Yehuda] said to him, "Does his mastership remember what Shmuel said as he was standing with one leg on the bank [of the river], and one foot on the ferry boat?" [Rav Mattena] said, "So said Shmuel: 'Whoever says, "I come from the house of the Hasmoneans" is a slave.' " (70b)

Rav Yehuda and the Talmudic narrator present details concerning the situation of legal procedure and instruction. These details aim to stabilize what is understood to be unstable knowledge; to prove that Rav Yehuda's teaching was reliable tradition; and to meet the requirements set up by Rav's rule. Rav Mattena cannot have been affected by the event because he had not been in Nehardea for thirteen years, and Rav Yehuda's question is phrased indirectly, without mentioning the subject matter, lest he be accused of begging the answer. These details, especially as they are specified in Rav Yehuda's question—down to the location and bodily posture of its instructor—also illustrate the localized context of *halakhic* information.

Rav Yehuda uses two rabbinic traditions to justify his declaration that the person from Nehardea is genealogically a slave; we have encountered both. The first tradition is the circular principle, "whoever disqualifies is himself disqualified," with Shmuel's addition, "he disqualifies using his own defect." Since the Nehardean "regularly declares" that certain people are of slave stock, he is, according to Shmuel's interpretation of the Tannaitic teaching, of that stock himself. That is the original justification given by the story for Rav Yehuda's declaration that the Nehardean is a slave. The second tradition is that any person claiming to have Hasmonean descent is genealogically a slave. As we have seen, the Nehardean claimed at Rav Nahman's court to be a descendant of that house.

Rav Yehuda's original reasoning is rejected by Rav Nahman, who understands the circular principle discussed above to be a good reason to *suspect* that someone is disqualified, not to declare him disqualified. He is compelled, though, to declare the complainant a slave after the latter claims to be a Hasmonean and after Rav Matenna confirms Rav Yehuda's tradition that the descendants of the Hasmoneans are slaves. Rav Yehuda is victorious.

From the beginning, however, the story invites us to think about Rav Yehuda's motives. We know that he wanted to punish the Nehardean for insulting him. At first it seems to us that the punishment, at least, follows rabbinic protocol: when Rav Yehuda was told (by his own circle) that the Nehardean calls other people slaves, the rabbi applied the circular principle and declared him to be a slave. This declaration, however, loses its original reasoning in the trial: first, Rav Nahman refuses to accept the application of the circular principle, and second, the declaration is only validated by a fact that Rav Yehuda had not known at the time. Rav Yehuda's original decision, then, is reduced to simple revenge.

I suggest that both of the traditions Rav Yehuda uses, along with a third one, constitute an effort by Shmuel to remove genealogical stratification from daily interaction. Adiel Schremer has already suggested that the intention behind Shmuel's hierarchical teaching, "All lands are dough to Palestine, and Palestine is dough to Babylonia," was to create in Shmuel's immediate social environment a space free of genealogical suspicion.[42] The two traditions used here by Rav Yehuda seem to have a similar intention. We have already seen how the circular principle, "whoever disqualifies is disqualified," can operate to limit genealogical slander. The instruction concerning Hasmonean descent should probably be read not just in terms of a rabbinic assertion regarding the historical house of the Maccabees (though it is was certainly understood to be so later),[43] but also as targeting genealogical boasting by honor-seeking or match-seeking Jews who affiliated themselves with the Jewish royal house in order to boost their genealogical status.[44]

---

42   Schremer, *Male and Female*, 155. He interprets other statements, some ascribed to Shmuel and some to other sages, in the same vein, on pp. 155–57.

43   In the printed edition, the Talmud supports Shmuel's teaching with a historical anecdote about the last of the Hasmoneans proclaiming, on the verge of suicide, that her house is of slave stock (found also in *b. B. B*). This story is lacking, though, in both Ms. Munich 95 and Ms. Vatican 111.

44   This understanding of Shmuel's intention, with Schremer, undermines the case for Kalmin's reconstruction of Amoraic attitudes toward genealogical discretion. Kalmin argues that whereas Palestinian rabbis supported discretion in genealogical matters, Babylonian rabbis had no qualms about publicly exposing blemished genealogies, and that they directed this discourse against non-rabbis (*Sage in Jewish Society*, 52–58). Kalmin himself writes that Shmuel's comment, "he disqualifies with his own defect," means that he "knows and comments on the Palestinian view" (ibid., 57; Shmuel not only knows of this view, but accepts it as a *halakhic* policy). Though Kalmin may be correct in his assessment of what the story does with Shmuel's teaching, I think his interpretation does not account for the teaching itself. Kalmin's study might have drawn too sharp a line between Palestinian and Babylonian *amora'im* on this matter (see also n. 37 above). One story in the Yerushalmi, not cited by Kalmin, seems to present precisely the opposite picture as it tells us of a Babylonian surprised by Palestinian *indiscretion* in genealogical matters and then protests against it with a Babylonian tradition from Rav Huna: "When R. Zera came up here [Palestine], he heard people calling (this person) a *mamzer*, (that one) a female

If these two traditions seek to pre-empt the abuse of genealogical language for the personal advantage of the speaker and to prevent further social stratification, Rav Yehuda (or rather, his literary character) uses them for precisely the opposite purposes. He abuses genealogical discourse, subordinating it to his own vengeful agenda. Whatever problem he may have had with the Nehardean, it had nothing to do with the man's genealogical status. Rabbinic decision-making is represented as an arbitrary process.

The conclusion of the story is most revealing in the Talmud's treatment of Rav Yehuda's character. In order to appreciate this part of the story, however, we must first turn to another story that appears in the Talmud's discussion a few pages after the story about Rav Yehuda. That story is cited at the end of a discussion in which the status of converts is examined. The male convert emerges as a borderline case between the permitted classes and prohibited ones: on the one hand, he may marry a female *mamzer* (*mamzeret*), which is prohibited to the permitted classes; on the other, he may come in union with a woman of priestly stock, which is prohibited to the prohibited classes.[45] The story describes the communication of this law in the Jewish suburb of the Persian capital:

> Rabbi Zera lectured in Mahoza, "A convert may take a *mamzeret* for a wife!" Everyone pelted him with their citrons. Said Rava, "Is it possible to lecture this way in a place full of converts?!" Rava lectured in Mahoza, "a convert may take a woman of priestly stock for a wife!" Everyone loaded him with silk garments. He then said: "A convert may take a *mamzeret* for a wife." They told him, "You have spoiled the first [teaching]." He replied, "I have done what is best for you. If he wants, he can marry from this [stock]; if he wants, he can marry from that [stock]!" (73a)

Rava is astonished that in the presence of so many converts R. Zera should emphasize the aspect in the convert's legal status that is similar to that of the prohibited classes. He then gives a more balanced presentation that opens with the more crowd-pleasing law. This Talmudic story again focuses on the way context affects the transmission of knowledge (though in a more modest way—it affects here only the way *halakhah* is presented, not *halakhic* status or genealogical reality).

---

mamzer. He told them, 'What is this? but R. Huna said . . . , 'A *mamzer* not live more than thirty days' [How can you say this? There are not supposed to be so many *mamzerim* around]" (*y. Qidd.* 4:1 65c).

45   On the *halakhic* discussion itself, see Hayes, *Gentile Impurities*, 168–71, with citation of the story on p. 171.

The story about Rava in Mahoza invites a comparison with the conclusion of our story, about Rav Yehuda, which tells us what happened after the court's dramatic decision:

> He [Rav Nahman, after Rav Mattena approved Rav Yehuda's teaching] declared [the Nehardean] to be a slave. On that day, several marital contracts were torn up in Nehardea. As he [Rav Yehuda] went out [of the court, citizens of the town] came out after him to throw stones at him. He said to them, "If you will be silent, I will be silent, but if not, I reveal upon you that which Shmuel said, 'two lineages are in Nehardea. One is called the House of the Dove and one the House of the Crow, and the mark [through which one is to know their different natures] is that the impure is impure, and the pure is pure.' " They threw away those stones from their hands, and a great levee rose in the Royal River. (70b)

The tale about Rava celebrates his rhetorical use of the flexibility inherent in the law to adapt legal presentation to social circumstance. In contrast, Rav Yehuda uses his authority to create turmoil and stratification rather than peace. Rava avoided the "fruity stoning" mentioned above through an instruction of the law; Rav Yehuda stops the "rocky stoning" by concealing the law.[46] He is forced to compromise the genealogical zeal that brought him to this situation in the first place, revealing that he pursues genealogical purity only when he can use it as a punitive instrument to defend his honor but will abandon it when his well-being is in danger.

The Talmud's best joke at the expense of rabbis who abuse genealogical knowledge extends beyond the literary boundaries of the story to the following literary unit, which includes teachings by Rav Yehuda, Rava, and other rabbis:

> Rav Yehuda announces in Pumbedita: "Ada and Yonatan—slaves; Yehuda bar Papa—*mamzer*; Bati bar Tuvia—in haughty spirit did not take a *get* of manumission." Rava announces in Mahoza: "The Belans, Denans, Telans, Melans, and Zegans are all disqualified." Said Rav Yehuda: "The people of Guvai—Givonites; Durnunita—a town of *netinim*" [*guva'e—giv'ona'e; durnunita'—dura' denetina'e*[47]]." Said Rav Yosef: "That (settlement in) Kube of Pumbedita—all of them are slaves." Said Rav Yehuda in Shmuel's name:

46   The comparison between the two rabbis is made more explicit in the version recorded in Ms. Vatican 111. In that manuscript's version of the story about Rava in Mahoza, the "insensitive" rabbi is not R. Zera but Rav Yehuda. Chronologically, however, Rabbi Zera makes more sense.

47   According to all manuscripts; printed editions have the version *dara'ei netina'e* (pedigrees of *netinim*), which maintains the sound similarity.

"Pashur ben Immer had four hundred slaves—and some say four thousand slaves—and they all intermingled into the priesthood. And any priest who displays impudence is descended from them." (70b)

The Talmud adduces these declarations in connection with the public declaration of the Nehardean as a slave. They appear immediately after a story that showed us how a person entered a butcher shop, and, because he angered a rabbi, wound up being branded a slave, unworthy of marriage.

By reproducing these declarations after this story, the Talmud is inviting us to be suspicious of the decisions these declarations represent. Each of them might be a product of a similar blend of emotions, politics, personal interest, and truth. The punning used in Rav Yehuda's penultimate declaration, "The people of Guvai— Givonites; Durnunita—a town of *netinim*," seems in this context to be a parody of the arbitrariness of the production of genealogical stratification.

The Talmud first redirects the conversation about genealogical stratification when it blurs the distinction between the person who disqualifies by prohibited union and the one who disqualifies by speech, shifting the focus to the latter. The story about Rav Yehuda's trial further focuses the conversation on a particular kind of disqualifying speech when it exposes us to the complicated dynamics of rabbinic legal discourse. The production of prohibited families is still the problem, but it occurs not in the bedroom but in the rabbinic courtroom. This sequence creates a critical framework for the genealogical traditions that appear at the end of the story. There is no reason, of course, to believe that the Bavli is not committed to the legal validity of these traditions; but they are now seen in a completely different light that undermines any reading of them as straightforward revelations of genealogical truths faithfully transmitted by the rabbis.

CONCLUSION

The two long segments analyzed in this chapter, the *sugya* on the purification of Israel and the story about Rav Yehuda with its surrounding passages, create a similar effect. Both move from innate genealogical identity to attributed genealogical identity to the rabbinic production and control of genealogical knowledge. The Talmud's approach here, as in other cases, is at once "conservative" and "critical" in our terms. On the one hand, both specific genealogical traditions and the genealogical system in general are preserved; on the other hand, the Talmud draws our attention to the conditions in which this system is produced, exposing the social processes and structures of authority that construct genealogical status.

The congruity between the dialectical *stam* and the narratives of our *sugyot* is important to emphasize. First, this congruity complicates recent studies of the Talmud. In his *Narrating the Law*, Barry Wimpfheimer constructs a far-reaching contrast between two genres in the Bavli. Talmudic narratives show the law to be informed by a broad set of discourses of emotions, social interactions, and values, and their protagonists behave in ways that defy not only specific norms but also norm-making. The anonymous commentary in the dialectical *sugya*, Wimpfheimer argues, works against both of these characteristics, reducing this heterogeneity of law into a single-voiced, rules-oriented discourse that is as coherent as it is flat.[48] Daniel Boyarin's *Socrates and the Fat Rabbis* generally accepts this contrast, but he objects to Wimpfheimer's attribution of this reductionism to "the Talmud" as a whole. Instead, Boyarin posits two elements in the Talmud, two implied authors or voices: the monologizing voice of the *stam* and the voice of the bizarre and wild stories that are "deeply antithetical to the legal *sugya*," joined together by the (implied) "author of the Talmud as a whole."[49] The approach offered here is more similar to Boyarin's in the sense that it attributes the use of narrative as a feature that expands or opens up legal discourse to the same authorship that is responsible for the shaping of the Talmud generally. But it seems to me that both Wimpfheimer and Boyarin overestimate the question of genre and therefore overlook important features of the dialectical *stam*.

The narratives of our *sugya* indeed operate much in the same way as Wimpfheimer and Boyarin describe them, exposing the implication of legal discourse in a broad array of social and psychological phenomena; they show the rabbis, as in Boyarin's genre of "wild stories," to have extreme conduct motivated by anger or jealousy.[50] But similar functions and modes of representations apply also to the non-narrative elements in our texts. First, the dialectical *stam* itself sometimes engages in narrational discourses—when it tells us, for example, that Rav Papa only taught that Havel Yama is no longer pure to revenge their refusal to marry him to one of their women. We have seen how in the dialectical *sugya* on the purification of Israel, short narratives and Amoraic and Tan-

---

48 Wimpfheimer, *Narrating*, 147–48. Wimpfheimer (149, 159–60) agrees that the creators of the *stam* also engaged in the "narrative" form of legal discourse—in their creation of long Talmudic narratives such as the one about Rav Yehuda's trial; but the dialectical *stam* itself, in the "conversational *sugya*," remains in opposition to this discourse.

49 Boyarin, *Socrates*, 133–242 (see especially 165–67, 202–7). Wimpfheimer, *Narrating the Law*, 177 n. 91, seems to concede Boyarin's argument at least with respect to one text.

50 Boyarin, *Socrates*, 201.

naitic legal traditions are all woven together to offer the same perspective on the situated nature of rabbinic legal discourse. That perspective
there, I argued, is created chiefly through the reformulation and recon-
textualization of sources by the Talmud's creators, and it is intensified by
their brief anonymous commentary. This chapter shows how narrative
works together with and serves the same voice in the Talmud with which
Wimpfheimer and Boyarin contrast it. More important, when we appreciate that the "narration" of rabbinic legal discourse can be achieved both
through the Talmud's stories and through the dialectical *sugya*, we can
also see how the subversive and critical potentials of this narration,
which these scholars describe so well, may be harnessed to create the
same distance from tradition that we have observed in the dialectical *sugyot* studied in the two previous chapters.

The focus of our *sugyot* on the conditions in which rabbinic knowledge
is produced dislodges that knowledge from the "eternal yesterday," presenting it as the result of particular moments in the past, informed by interests of historical individuals or groups. To be sure, the Bavli's critique
of rabbinic genealogical knowledge is informed by particular aspects
connected with this knowledge, such as the tension between innate and
ascribed, or the political importance of genealogical status in the Jewish
community. But the historicizing move we see here applies to rabbinic
tradition in general and is the result of features that are pervasive in the
Talmud: the interest of the *stam* in the parameters of rabbinic transmis-
sions; its inclusion of narratives about scholars; the juxtaposition of such
narratives with legal traditions; the attribution of traditions to particular
scholars that together with these other components work to connect rabbinic teachings with characters that have emotions, interests, and histories. The *sugyot* studied here may present a case where the effects of these
features is intensified; but to some degree, these typical components of
Talmudic composition always produce rabbinic tradition as an object of
the past by inventing or putting on display this tradition's genealogy.

PART II

Chapter Four

SCHOLARS, TRANSMITTERS, AND
THE MAKING OF *TALMUD*

The first part of this book offered an interpretation of the literary practice of the Talmud's creators, deriving their approach to tradition by examining the literary strategies through which tradition is produced in the Talmud. This second part of the book focuses on how the creators of the Talmud themselves understood the project with which they were engaged, on the place of the transmission of tradition in this self-conception, and on the way this self-conception was informed by a debate with other elements in these creators' environment.

Scholarship on the Bavli's ideology of Torah study has demonstrated that, in contrast with other rabbinic works, the Bavli prioritizes analysis and innovation over memorization and transmission. In passages that distinguish between two kinds of Torah scholars, the one who is able to retain tradition by repeated recitation and memorization, and the one who is able to arrive at new insights through the analysis of received tradition, the Bavli tends to favor the latter.[1] The passages studied in this chapter

---

1 One of the most influential earlier treatments is Louis Ginzberg, *A Commentary on the Palestinian Talmud IV* (Heb.; arranged and edited posthumously by D. Halivni; New York: Jewish Theological Seminary, 1961), 19–31. More recent treatments include David Rosenthal, "The Transformation of Eretz Israel Traditions in Babylonia" (Heb.), *Cathedra* 92 (1999), 7–48 (30–36); Jeffrey L. Rubenstein, *The Culture of the Babylonian Talmud* (Baltimore: Johns Hopkins University Press, 2003), 39–53; Daniel Boyarin, *Border Lines: The Partition of Judeo-Christianity* (Philadelphia: University of Pennsylvania Press, 2004), 151–201; idem, "Hellenism in Jewish Babylonia," in *The Cambridge Companion to the Talmud and Rabbinic Literature* (ed. C. E. Fonrobert and M. S. Jaffee; Cambridge: Cambridge University Press, 2007), 336–63 (343–56). Also related is Sussmann's argument, that in Palestine the Mishnah was studied on its own whereas in Babylonia it was studied as part of "Talmudic study" (even before "The Talmud," as a text, was completed). See Yaacov Sussmann, "Manuscripts and Text Traditions of the Mishnah" (Heb.), *Proceedings of the Seventh World Congress of Jewish Studies: Volume 3: Studies in the Talmud, Halacha*

can be read as employing a particular variation of this distinction. They associate with the "conservative," transmission-oriented aspects of Torah study the occupation with the two bodies of knowledge that the rabbis received: the Written Torah (Scripture) and the Oral Torah (rabbinic tradition). Many passages in the rabbinic corpus, including some of the Palestinian sources reworked by the *sugyot* studied here, see in the reading of Scripture and the recitation and memorization of rabbinic tradition the totality of rabbinic knowledge. Such passages are mostly concerned with those who have mastered the former but not the latter, those who have Scripture but not tradition—no doubt a concern motivated by the rabbis' emphasis on their own authority. The passages studied in this chapter, in contrast, present these two kinds of study as insufficient. In the first passage we will examine, both the reading of Scripture and the recitation of tradition are construed as inferior to *talmud*, understood here as the "creative," analysis-oriented kind of Torah study.

This chapter argues that this dichotomy between the transmission of texts and the creation of new knowledge was central to the way the creators of the Talmud understood themselves, to the way they wanted to be perceived, and to the way they distinguished themselves from others. One of the passages studied in this chapter harshly condemns those who do not recognize the rabbis' originality. It insists on a public image of the rabbis as innovators, showing us how they resisted prominent members of the Babylonian Jewish community who portrayed them as mere transmitters of Scripture and oral tradition. The same passage is also concerned with the image of the rabbis within the rabbinic academy, criticizing a student who does not recognize the innovation of his master.

At the heart of this book stands a tension within the rabbinic community which, I argue, informed this self-conception of the rabbis who created the Talmud. Our passages wholly identify with those who occupy themselves with the creative and analytical study—the "masters of *talmud*" (*ba'ale talmud*). More important, they exclude those who do not engage in *talmud* from their definition of "the sages" and equate them with some of the rabbis' classical opponents. This exclusion applies to the "masters of Scripture" (*ba'ale miqra*) as well as to the persons who only "read [Scripture] and recited [tradition]"; but, we shall see, these passages focus particularly on those who were engaged in the transmission of rabbinic tradition: the "masters of tradition" (*ba'ale mishnah*) or the *tanna'im*, the "repeaters" or "reciters" who were in charge of the memorization of rabbinic tradition and its deployment through constant recitation. The creators of our passages present these transmitters as "haters"

and Midrash (Jerusalem: Perry Foundation; World Union of Jewish Studies, 1981), 215–50 (236–41).

or enemies of the rabbis, say that they are "the destroyers of the world," and admonish the Talmud's audience not to associate with them. The creators of our passages, I argue, construct these "masters of tradition" and reciters as their "others" in order to portray the scholar as the opposite of the transmitter. In other words, when the creators of the Talmud thought of what made them the "masters of *talmud*," they thought of themselves in opposition to those who focused on transmission.

Some of the types that are criticized by the Talmud here do not represent distinct ideological or social groups—they seem to be stereotypes of bad conduct or personifications of different specializations in the rabbinic world. But the deliberate drawing of boundaries we see in these passages, their polemical tone, and the existence of rabbinic texts that are at odds with our passages make it likely that the Bavli here is staking a position in a real conversation with other ideological positions and perhaps also other groups within the academy.

Previous accounts of the Bavli's celebration of dialectic and marginalization of memorization have explained it either in temporal terms—as a stage in the development of rabbinic thought and institutions, or in geographical terms—as one of the differences between the two rabbinic centers in Palestine and Babylonia. It is true that we can understand the Bavli's position better by comparing it with earlier Palestinian texts; but the urgency of these passages indicates that the issues are still very much alive, and there is nothing in them to suggest that the division between Palestine and Babylonia is at stake for their creators. If our *sugyot* needed to assert their ideology of Torah study against the reciters of the academy or those who focused on the transmission of rabbinic traditions, the Bavli's ideology was not the only possibility in the time and place in which it was formed; the Talmud is staking a contested position that had rivals even within the academy itself (even if not in its leadership), as part of a conversation on the appropriate place and nature of the transmission of tradition.

The reconstruction of this conversation can illuminate the literary characteristics studied in the first part of the book. If the "masters of *talmud*" defined themselves and their practices in opposition to the "masters of *mishnah*" and the reciters, and if these other groups had their own ideology or position concerning the nature of Torah study, then we can posit a sharper and richer opposition between *talmud* and recitation as literary practices reflecting different approaches to the interface between Jews and their tradition: one that distanced tradition and separated analysis from transmission in order to highlight innovation, and one that internalized tradition through memorization and focused on transmission. This chapter examines the Bavli's side of this debate; the following chapter seeks to shed light on both sides by comparing this opposition with the Jewish community with similar oppositions in the Christian and Zoroastrian communities of late ancient Mesopotamia; the final chapter examines Hekhalot traditions which, I will argue, may have been shaped by the Bavli's opponents.

"WISDOM—BUT NOT *MISHNAH*"

Our first *sugya*, at *b. B. M.* 33a–b, confronts the question of rabbinic identity explicitly, from its beginning. The Mishnah states that if a person is simultaneously required to attend to property lost by his father and property lost by his rabbi, his rabbi's property takes priority over his father's. The reason given in the Mishnah is that a person's father is responsible for his existence in this world, but a person's rabbi (i.e., teacher), "who taught him wisdom," is responsible for his existence in the world to come (*m. B. M.* 2:11).[2] The Talmud then raises the question of who counts as one's rabbi. The discussion opens with a *baraita* citing different answers to this question:

> Our rabbis taught: "The 'rabbi' they mention here is the rabbi who taught him wisdom and not the rabbi who taught him Scripture and *mishnah*"—[these are] the words of R. Meir. R. Yehuda says: [The rabbi referred to in the law is] any rabbi from whom [he derived] most of his wisdom. R. Yosi says: Even if he only opened his eyes regarding a single tradition, he counts as his rabbi." (*b. B. M.* 33a)

R. Meir's words are presented here as a gloss on the Mishnah's definition of the rabbi as the "rabbi who taught him wisdom" (even though he may have referred to an earlier version of the Mishnah that did not include this definition).[3] He explains that in using the word "wisdom," the Mishnah seeks to exclude from the law rabbis who taught the person Scripture and *mishnah*, meaning, not the text we know by this name, but rabbinic

---

2 Similar ideas appear in other ancient texts. See, e.g., the argument attributed to Isocrates in the *Exercises* of Theon: "Honor teachers ahead of parents. For the latter have been only the cause of the living but teachers are the cause of living well." George A. Kennedy, *Progymnasmata: Greek Textbooks of Prose Composition and Rhetoric* (Leiden: Brill, 2003), 18.

3 See Ginzberg, *Commentary IV*, 24, and his useful explanation of the development of the tradition in the Tannaitic period. See also David Halivni, *Sources and Traditions: A Source Critical Commentary on the Talmud: Tractate Baba Metzia* (Heb.; Jerusalem: Magnes, 2003), 111 n. 2, who makes the same argument (without reference to Ginzberg) in order to solve the contradiction the *stam* points in R. Yohanan's ruling; but Halivni himself (ibid., 113) concedes that this is unnecessary. Both are preceded by Joseph Hirsch Dünner, *Ḥidushei ha-riṣad* (4 vols.; Jerusalem: Mosad Ha-Rav, 1981–99), 150.

oral tradition in its entirety.[4] The parallel of this *baraita* in the Tosefta, and in a partial parallel in the Yerushalmi that is not attributed to R. Meir, the comment reads, "the rabbi who taught him wisdom, and not the rabbi who taught him Scripture," without reference to *mishnah* or tradition at all.[5] The Bavli's version, then, adds the teaching of tradition to what *does not* qualify a teacher to be a person's rabbi.

The meaning of this opposition between "wisdom" on the one hand and "Scripture and tradition" on the other is explained only indirectly, after a brief discussion of the *baraita*, when the Talmud quotes another Tannaitic source:

> Our rabbis taught: Those who occupy themselves with Scripture—this is a merit and not a merit; [those who occupy themselves] with *mishnah* [i.e., oral tradition]—this is a merit, and they receive reward on its account; [those who occupy themselves with] *talmud*—there is no greater merit. But always run to the Mishnah more than to the *talmud*. (ibid.)

This teaching mentions Scripture and tradition, the two elements of study that were contrasted above with wisdom, but it also introduces a new term that we have not heard yet in this discussion: *talmud*,[6] which stands above the first two in a three-part hierarchy. The clear implication of the

---

4   See, e.g., Wilhelm Bacher, *Die Exegetische Terminologie der Jüdischen Traditionsliteratur* (Leipzig: J. C. Hinrichs, 1905), 1.122: "Bezeichnung der mündlichen Lehre und ihres Studiums." Similarly the word *miqra*, translated here as "Scripture," is better interpreted as "the study of the written Torah" (see, e.g., Bacher, *Terminologie*, 1.117), but since the gap between this sense and the translation "Scripture" is narrower than in the case of *mishnah*, I use "Scripture" for the sake of fluency.

5   See *t. B. M.* 2:30 and *y. Hor.* 3:7 48b. Later in the same *sugya* in the Yerushalmi, there is a fuller parallel of our *baraita*, which appears also in *y. M. Q.* 3:7 83b and *y. B. M.* 2:11 8d, which lacks the interpretive gloss attributed here to R. Meir altogether, instead attributing to him the anonymous Toseftan opinion that the rabbi in question is the rabbi who taught the student first. On the Yerushalmi there, see Lieberman's comments in Eliezer S. Rosenthal and Saul Lieberman, *Yerushalmi Neziqin* (Heb.; Jerusalem: Israel Academy of Sciences and Humanities, 1983), 138–39, and Louis Ginzberg, *Yerushalmi Fragments from the Genizah* (New York: Jewish Theological Seminary, 1909; repr. Hildesheim: Georg Olms, 1970), 202.

A parallel in tractate *Kallah*, §24 (for which see David Brodsky, *A Bride Without a Blessing: A Study in the Redaction and Content of Massekhet Kallah and its Gemara* [Tübingen: Mohr Siebeck Siebeck, 2006], 28–31), ascribes to R. Meir essentially the same opinion as the Tosefta, reading: "his rabbi . . . taught him *mishnah* and *talmud*, but not Scripture."

6   Many of the manuscripts read *gemara* instead of *talmud*, and this is also the version in several of the texts of Rashi's interpretation of our *sugya*; but this is the result of censorship (self-imposed or otherwise); see on our *sugya* and others, Chen Merchavia, *The Church Versus Talmud and Midrashic Literature* (Heb.; Jerusalem: Bialik Institute, 1970), 325–26.

Bavli, then, is that the term "wisdom" encountered in the first *baraita* is equivalent to the term *talmud* in this *baraita*.

As with the first two terms—*miqra*, or the study of Scripture, and *mishnah*, or the study of oral tradition—*talmud* is a stage[7] or a type of Torah study. The specific meaning of this term changed during the rabbinic period. In the Tannaitic and early Amoraic periods, *talmud*, in the sense of a discipline of Torah study, denoted scriptural exegesis, specifically legal exegesis of the Torah, what we now call *midrash halakhah*.[8] If this *baraita* is indeed a Tannaitic source—and as we shall see, this is not at all certain—its original sense might have been that *talmud* supersedes both *mishnah* and Scripture because *midrash halakhah* exegetically links both Scripture and tradition and presupposes knowledge of both.

By the time we reach the Bavli, the term *talmud* has come to refer to the analytical, dialectical kind of Torah study, the examination of the reasoning behind both Scripture and tradition.[9] This shift gives the teaching a meaning similar to that of other teachings in rabbinic literature that privilege analytical and dialectical study over memorization.[10] Read back into the beginning of the *sugya*, the import of this teaching is that only

---

7   While the *baraita*—at least as it is deployed in the *sugya*—treats these as kinds of study with which people are identified rather than stages, other passages describe the study of Scripture and the study of *mishnah* as successive stages, and some of them also add *talmud* as an additional stage. The most famous source for that is the *baraita* that was appended to *m. Avot* in the Geonic period: "A five-year-old (is initiated) in Scripture; a ten-year-old, in *mishnah*; a thirteen-year-old, in the commandments; a fifteen-year-old in *talmud*" (on this *baraita*, its attribution, and its late inclusion in tractate *Avot*, see Yitzhak Gilat, "Ben shelosh 'esre le-mitzvot?" in *Talmudic Studies I* [ed. Y. Sussmann and D. Rosenthal: Jerusalem: Magnes, 1990], 39–53 [39-41]) and Shimon Sharvit, *Language and Style of Tractate Avoth Through the Ages* [Heb.; Beer-Sheva: Ben Gurion University of the Negev Press, 2006], 121–22). The division of the curriculum into three stages parallels the division in the Greco-Roman educational system, which also divides the instructing body into three types of teachers and scholars, and also presents a progression from memorization and recitation of texts to creative use of language in rhetoric. See Henri-Irénée Marrou, *Histoire de l'éducation dans l'antiquité* [6th ed.] (Paris: Éditions du Seuil, 1965), 243, and see the warning against perceiving this division as rigid in Robert Kaster, "Notes on 'Primary' and 'Secondary' Schools in Late Antiquity," *Transactions of the American Philological Association* 113 (1983), 323–46. Kaster's demonstration of the versatility of the grammarian offers an interesting parallel to the versatility of the *tanna* explored later in the chapter.

8   Bacher, *Terminologie*, 1.201: "Der 'Talmud' in diesem engeren Sinne hat die Schriftauslegung und . . . die halachische Schriftauslegung zum hauptsächlichen Inhalte." On our *baraita*, see Jacob Epstein, *Introduction to the Mishnaic Text* [3rd ed.] (Heb.; 2 vols.; Jerusalem: Magnes, 2000), 2.750–51.

9   See Chanoch Albeck, *Introduction to the Talmud, Babli and Yerushalmi* (Heb.; Tel Aviv: Dvir, 1969), 3–7.

10   Thus, Louis Ginzberg, *A Commentary on the Palestinian Talmud I* (Heb.; New York: Ktav, 1971), 139. Ginzberg applies this interpretation to the *baraita*'s supposed Tannaitic meaning as well as its occurrence in the Yerushalmi, but, even if the "full" *baraita* indeed

the rabbi who initiates one in this creative kind of study (*talmud*, or "wisdom"), in contrast with the one who teaches oral tradition (*mishnah*), counts as one's rabbi.

The *baraita* appears in several rabbinic texts and may have had a complicated composition history. Aaron Amit has recently argued that, rather than a Tannaitic-era teaching, the Bavli's *baraita* is a late Amoraic-era creation that presupposes the Yerushalmi's *sugya*. The composers of this tradition, Amit argues, paraphrased and combined a number of Tannaitic and Amoraic statements found in *y. Hor.* 3:8 into a single, ostensibly Tannaitic teaching. The original *baraita*, according to Amit, contrasted the non-exegetical study of Scripture with the study of rabbinic tradition; the parts of it concerning *talmud* were formulated by later scholars based on traditions that appear in the Yerushalmi.[11] It should be noted though that at least some of the scholars who contributed to the development of our *sugya* in the Bavli saw the *baraita* as a single unit, and therefore the composition of the *baraita* pre-dates at least some of the *sugya*'s formation.[12]

The Yerushalmi's discussion (*y. Hor.* 3:8 48c) is important for our understanding of the Bavli whether or not it was the source of the *baraita* quoted by the latter. In the Yerushalmi, as in the Bavli, the question is the hierarchy between the two different kinds of scholars: the *sodran* (the arranger or memorizer of traditions) and the *pilpelan* (the analytic, dialectic, creative scholar). It is in this context that the Yerushalmi quotes either the *baraita* we know from the Talmud in truncated form or the brief Tannaitic teaching that transformed into that *baraita*. Yet if both Talmuds are similar with respect to the question, they differ with respect to the answer: the Yerushalmi is much less sympathetic to *talmud* or to the "masters of *talmud*" than the Bavli. The Yerushalmi begins with a Tannaitic teaching that declares the superiority of the memorizer, which is

---

occurs in the Yerushalmi, this interpretation seems only to be applicable to its occurrence in *y. Hor.*

11   Aaron Amit, "The Homilies on Mishnah and Talmud Study at the Close of *Bavli Bava' Metsi'a'* 2 and *Yerushalmi Horayot* 3: Their Origin and Development," *JQR* 102 (2012), 163–89 (170–82). I find most of Amit's analysis persuasive, but I leave here open the option that the *baraita* is genuine. The "full" *baraita* does appear in *y. Shab.* 16:1 15c (Amit, ibid., 175 n. 31, argues that it was was mistakenly copied there from the late tractate *Soferim* but does not elaborate), and the fact that in other contexts in the Yerushalmi only part of what is the Bavli's *baraita* is quoted and the fact that a part of the *baraita* appears in the Yerushalmi without a citation term both apply to authentic Tannaitic *baraitot* in the Yerushalmi. The discussion *here* keeps the main argument applicable to both scenarios.

12   Otherwise, the *stam* would not have been able to object, *ha gufa qashya!*—"this teaching contradicts itself!" Amit, "Homilies," 178, attributes the composition of the *baraita* to "a Babylonian editor," but admits that it might as well have been the work of Palestinian scholars.

essentially affirmed throughout the *sugya*; the only teaching that stands out in the Yerushalmi is Rabbi Yohanan's statement that "*talmud* precedes *mishnah* [in importance]," a statement which, we shall see, is tempered by the rest of the Yerushalmi's discussion.

As the Bavli itself notes, the *baraita* is self-contradictory: on the one hand, it states that the study of *talmud* is the most excellent merit, while, on the other hand, it recommends that the student "always run more to *mishnah* rather than to *talmud*." According to Amit, this contradiction reflects the *baraita*'s composite nature. These statements were not originally part of a single teaching: the statement that Talmud is the most excellent kind of study is a paraphrase of R. Yohanan's teaching in the Yerushalmi, mentioned above, whereas the recommendation to study *mishnah* is an anonymous statement there. Be that as it may, R. Yosi b. R. Bun offers a harmonization of these statements, whether he saw them as two parts of a single *baraita* or as two separate Amoraic statements:

> Said R. Yosi b. R. Bun, "What you say [i.e., "always run to *mishnah*," was only valid] as long as Rabbi [Yehuda the Patriarch] did not embed in it [i.e., in *talmud*] many Tannaitic traditions [*mishnayot*]. But from the time Rabbi [Yehuda the Patriarch] did embed in it many traditions, run always to *talmud* more than to *mishnah*. (*y. Hor.* 3:8 48c, adding R. Yosi's name from the parallel in *y. Shab.* 16:1 16c).

R. Yosi b. R. Bun explains that the last statement ("always run...") was true when *talmud* did not include many oral traditions, but, since such traditions are embedded in *talmud*, there is no reason to study *mishnah* by itself anymore.[13] It is not clear how the Patriarch's action—presumably the redaction of the Mishnah—has caused *talmud* to be replete with Tannaitic traditions,[14] or even whether *talmud* here means a kind of study or some kind of work of *midrash halakhah* or Mishnaic interpretation.[15] For our purpose, however, what is crucial is that even when a

---

13   Following Lewy, "Vorwort," 19 n. 3, and Ginzberg, *Commentary I*, 140.

14   Saul Lieberman, *Hayerushalmi Kiphshuto* [2nd ed.] (ed. M. Katz; New York; Jerusalem: Jewish Theological Seminary, 2008), 193–94, suggests (citing an interpretation he had "seen, but forgotten where") that because R. Yehuda selected the most important Tannaitic materials for inclusion in the Mishnah, the rest were now studied through *talmud* (it is not clear how Lieberman understands the term). Ginzberg (*Commentary I*, 140) amends here "Rabbi" to "rabbis" based on some versions in tractate *Soferim*. Amit reads "in it" as referring to the Mishnah rather than to *talmud*. According to him, R. Yosi means that the redaction of the Mishnah made the study of *mishnah* less urgent. I find this interpretation less convincing, but at any event according to this interpretation too the Yerushalmi will only acknowledge the greater importance of *talmud* only if the study of *mishnah* is secured.

15   See the suggestion by Amit, "Homilies," 178.

rabbi in the Yerushalmi's *sugya* defends the superiority of *talmud*, he does so with the argument that *talmud* already includes *mishnah*, not by pointing to the preferability of analysis to transmission.

The Bavli's discussion is very different:

> This [*baraita*] is self-contradictory! You say "in *talmud*—no greater merit," and then you say "and always run to *mishnah* more than to *talmud*"?!
>
>   Said R. Yohanan: "This tradition was taught in the time of Rabbi [Yehuda the Patriarch]." Everyone abandoned the Mishnah and pursued *talmud*. As a result, he expounded to them, "always run to *mishnah* more than to *talmud*." (*b. B. M.* 33a–b)

What follows the question is a Hebrew answer attributed to R. Yohanan as well as an Aramaic explanation of this answer.[16] The Hebrew component is different in important ways from R. Yosi b. R. Bun's answer to the similar question in the Yerushalmi,[17] but, standing on its own, it may be interpreted as saying essentially the same thing: the recommendation to study *mishnah* is now obsolete and only applied to the period of R. Yehuda the Patriarch.

The explanation of this answer by the *stam* takes it into a completely different direction. First, while in the Yerushalmi it is uncertain whether R. Yosi b. R. Bun understands the recommendation to study *mishnah* or the Mishnah, here it is clearly the latter: when the *stam* tells us "everyone left the Mishnah" it uses neither the Hebrew word employed by the *baraita* earlier, *mishnah*, nor its Aramaic equivalent, *matnita*, but rather the word *matnitin*, "our Mishnah," the ubiquitous term in the Bavli for *the* Mishnah. More important, while in the Yerushalmi the recommendation to study *mishnah* was said to *apply* to the time of the Patriarch, here the teaching is attributed to the Patriarch himself. It is the Patriarch who spoke the words, "but always run to the Mishnah more than to the Talmud."

The fact that it is *the* Mishnah that is at stake explains why the Patriarch defends it; after all, it is *his* Mishnah.[18] The recommendation to

---

16 I have placed the Aramaic outside of the quotation marks. The original reads: אמר ר' יוחנן: בימי רבי נשנית משנית זו. שבקו כולא עלמא מתניתין ואזלו בתר תלמודא. הדר דרש להו, ולעולם הוי רץ למשנה יותר מן התלמוד.

17 To begin with, it refers to the teaching under study as *mishnah*, which assumes it is a *baraita*; it says that the teaching is "taught" in a certain period rather than that it applies in a certain period; and it says that it is *in the days* of Rabbi rather than *before* Rabbi's literary activities. The last two changes could be seen as connected with the interpretation of the *stam*, but again on their own I do not think they necessitate it.

18 For the attribution of the completion of the Mishnah to Rabbi Yehuda in both Talmuds, see Chanoch Albeck, *Introduction to the Mishna* (Heb.; Jerusalem: Bialik Institute and Tel Aviv: Dvir, 1959), 99.

study the Mishnah is thus explained by the Bavli as the Patriarch's defense of his own unpopular creation despite the inherent superiority of *talmud*. In the Yerushalmi, the general assumption is that *mishnah* is more important than *talmud*, and even R. Yohanan's teaching, which argues that *talmud* is more important than *mishnah*, is defended by R. Yosi only because now *talmud* includes *mishnah*. In the Bavli, the superiority of the Talmud is never questioned, and the recommendation to study the Mishnah is understood as a self-serving teaching by the Mishnah's compiler.

This interpretation of the Bavli might sound too light-hearted, but it is supported by the fact that when the Bavli explains what the Patriarch said to convince people to come back to the Mishnah, it puts in his mouth a warning, even a threat, rather than a reason:

> What did he[19] expound [so that everyone returns to the Mishnah]? As R. Yehuda b. R. Ilay expounded: What is [the meaning of] that which is written, *Announce to my people their crime, to the house of Jacob their sin* (Isa. 58:1)? *Announce to my people their crime*—these are the sages, in whose case unintentional transgressions count as intentional crimes; *and to the house of Jacob their sin*—these are the common people (*'am ha-'ares*), in whose case intentional transgressions count as unintentional sins.
>
> And this [conforms with] what we study [in the Mishnah, *m. Avot* 4:13], R. Yehuda b. Ilay says: Be careful in *talmud*, for an unintentional error in *talmud* counts as an intentional transgression. (*b. B. M.* 33b)

R. Yehuda b. R. Ilay's *derashah* maps the dichotomy between the "sages" and the *'am ha-'ares*—the "common people," or non-sages—onto a verse from Isaiah. What enables this mapping is that if we apply to this verse the routine Midrashic understanding of biblical parallelism, in which each of the parallel parts has its own meaning, the verse is making a distinction between two groups: "my people" and "the house of Jacob." Since the "house of Jacob" denotes Israel, and since the other group is called "my people" by God, the latter must be a group within Israel that is even closer to God. The *derashah* then identifies the select group as the rabbis, and the rest of the people as their "others" par excellence, the *'am ha-'ares*.

---

19   Thus ("what did he expound," third-person singular past: דרש) in Mss. Hamburg, Florence; Ms. Vatican 115 and the printed edition use the plural: "what did they expound?" (מאי דרוש). Since this question clearly refers to R. Yehuda the Patriarch's action immediately preceding it, the first version is preferable; the second version might be influenced by Rashi's interpretation that the question refers to the anonymous *baraita*'s first part, hence the common impersonal expression "what did they expound" (see below, n. 21).

The *derashah* further observes that the verse uses different nouns to describe the transgressions of each group: "crime" (*pesha'*) for the first group and "sin" (*hatat*) for the second. Since the latter term is the name of the sacrifice that is offered in the case of unintentional transgressions (see, e.g., Lev. 4:27–29), the *derashah* reasons that the difference in nouns correlates with the difference in status, under the common biblical logic that the more select group is dealt with more harshly. Immediately following this *derashah* the Talmud quotes R. Yehuda's teaching from *Avot*, which says that an "unintentional error in study [*talmud*] counts as an intentional transgression" (*m. Avot* 4:13).

The connection between the two sources, the *derashah* and the teaching from *m. Avot*, might be genealogical; the *derashah*, which is also attributed to R. Yehuda, might be a later construction, making his warning a scripturally sanctioned rule that distinguishes sages from non-sages. On the other hand, the relatively moderate approach this *derashah* takes to the *'am ha-'ares* might indicate that it is not reworked by the late *stam*, as passages that were reworked or composed by late Babylonian sages use harsh language and describe a much sharper divide between sages and "commoners."[20]

Whether the *derashah* is R. Yehuda's or a later Midrashic elaboration on his teaching, it is clear that both sources are put by the Bavli to a purpose very far from their original ones. The teaching in *Avot* warns its audience, fellow sages, that Torah study is such a holy task that even erring unintentionally in it carries the punishment of intentional crimes; the *derashah* fortifies the status of the sages as God's people within God's people, while also protecting the *'am ha-'ares* by implying that God takes a lenient line with their crimes.

In the Bavli, both the *derashah* and teaching appear as a reconstruction of how Rabbi Yehuda the Patriarch tried to convince the sages, who were all running to *talmud*, to come back to his Mishnah.[21] This new function builds on the specific wordings of these sources. R. Yehuda b. Ilay's teaching from *Avot* uses the word *talmud* for Torah study. While there is no reason to believe that *talmud* in his teaching is anything but an abbrevia-

---

20 See Stephen G. Wald, *BT Pesahim III: Critical Edition with Comprehensive Commentary* (Heb.; New York and Jerusalem: Jewish Theological Seminary, 2000), 211–39; Rubenstein, *Culture*, 123–42; Stuart Miller, *Sages and Commoners: A Philological Inquiry into Local Traditions in Talmud Yerushalmi* (Tübingen: Mohr Siebeck, 2006), 314–27.

21 Rashi maintains that the question "What did he expound?" goes back to the beginning of the *baraita*, and specifically to the statement that *talmud* study is better than *mishnah* study. Under this interpretation, R. Yehuda b. Ilay's *derashah* presents a scriptural grounding for this *baraita*. This seems to me unlikely. The verb used in the question, "expounded," *darash*, clearly goes back a few words to the *stam*'s explanation that R. Yehuda expounded (*darash*) to the people that they should "always be running" to the Mishnah.

tion of *talmud torah*, the common, generic term for Torah study, the juxtaposition of this teaching with the distinction between *mishnah* and *talmud* gives it a specific meaning: the teaching's warning is made valid only for the part of Torah study termed *talmud*. What R. Yehuda the Patriarch tells the sages running to the Talmud is that they should come back to *mishnah*, where errors will be dealt with more leniently. In *talmud*, their unintentional errors will count as intentional ones. The boundary the *derashah* draws between sages and non-sages is now mapped onto the distinction between the different kinds of sages. The source is all but implying that if the sages would heed R. Yehuda and return to *mishnah*, they would count as outsiders, non-sages, equal in status to *'am ha-'areṣ*.

The move the Bavli makes here is outrageous. First, it interprets the last part of the *baraita*, which recommends *mishnah* study over *talmud* study, as a self-serving teaching of the Mishnah's "author"; second, it creates an expectation that R. Yehuda b. Ilay's teaching from *Avot* and his *derashah* will support the merit of the study of *mishnah*, but in fact harnesses these sources to do the opposite, presenting *mishnah* as a less dangerous but also less important occupation; and most important, for our purpose, it redraws the boundaries of rabbinic identity, claiming this identity for one type of study—*talmud,* and one type of sage—the master of Talmud.

This redefinition of rabbinic identity becomes all but explicit at the conclusion of the *sugya*, with another *derashah* attributed to R. Yehuda b. R. Ilay:

> R. Yehuda b. R. Ilay expounded: What is [the meaning of] that which is written, *Hear the word of the Lord, you who tremble at his word said your brothers, those who hate you and those who reject you in my name, "Let the Lord be glorified and we shall see your joy." But it is they who shall be ashamed?* (Isa. 66:5) *You who tremble at his word* (ibid.)—These are the sages; *said your brothers* (ibid.)—these are masters of Scripture (*ba'ale miqra*); *those who hate you* (ibid.)—these are masters of *mishnah* (*ba'ale mishnah*); *those who reject you*—these are the common people (*'am ha-'areṣ*). Lest you say they have no hope and their chances are null, the teaching says: *and we shall see your joy* (ibid.). Lest you say Israel shall be ashamed, the teaching says:[22] *and they shall*

22   A large number of good manuscripts (e.g., Ms. Munich, Ms. Florence, Ms. Vatican 115, Ms. Hamburg) omit the words: "Lest you say Israel shall be ashamed, the teaching says." The version reproduced *here*, found in Ms. Vatican 117 and the printed edition (and also seems to be at the basis of Ms. Escorial), presents two rejected readings of the verse. The first possible reading is that the groups who are not the sages will not be redeemed ("they have no hope and their chances are null"), which is rejected by the verse's use of the first-person plural pronoun "we": since this implies that these groups will be

ashamed—the gentiles will be ashamed and Israel will be joyous. (*b. B. M.* 33b)

Like the previous *derashah*, this one also concerns a verse that can imply a division among God's people. On the one hand, it is addressed to those who tremble at God's word; on other hand, those who are opposed to these people who fear God want to cast them off in God's name, so they cannot be gentiles. God is understood by the *derashah* to be addressing the sages, "those who tremble at his word." Unlike the previous *derashah*, which was only connected to the hierarchy between the different kind of sages by its context in the Talmud, this *derashah* does explicitly mention two of the three kinds of scholars we encountered: those who occupy themselves with Scripture and those who occupy themselves with *mishnah*; it also mentions another group we encountered, *'am ha-'areṣ*, or the non-sages. It is clear why this *derashah* describes the latter, *'am ha-'areṣ*, as those who reject the sages: the enmity between them and the scholars appears in several rabbinic sources, and in the Bavli in particular.

It is less clear, and more surprising, that the *derashah* would identify those who hate the sages with those who occupy themselves with rabbinic tradition. In part, this identification is premised on a pun between the participle for hate, *son'e* (שונא), used here by the verse, and the participle for reciting or "repeating" tradition, *shoneh* (שונה, from the same root as *mishnah*).We will return to the enmity this *derashah* posits between the sages and those who occupy themselves with *mishnah*. For now I would just note that if this *derashah* is more positive toward the "masters of Scripture" (they are the sages' brothers) than toward the "masters of tradition," it stands in contrast with the *baraita* that opened this section of the *sugya*, which puts scriptural study below the study of tradition.

More important is the absence of "those who occupy themselves with Talmud," and the clear implication of this absence in the context of the *sugya*—especially given the previous *derashah*—is that that group is completely identified with the sages. This is a dramatic move: the term for sages here, *talmidei ḥakhamim*, is the designation of rabbinic identity par excellence throughout the rabbinic corpus; its identification in the Bavli with scholars of Talmud—that is, those scholars who focus on the analytical, innovative aspect of study, effectively denies rabbinic identity to

---

there to witness the sages' joy, it means they will not perish during the Messianic era. The second reading is that while these groups will be there, they—who constitute most of Israel—will be ashamed at their inadequacy, which is rejected by the verse's use of the third-person pronoun "they" for those who shall be ashamed. The other version does not distinguish between these two readings and two rejections.

all other types of scholars, who stand here in distinction with the sages just like *'am ha-'areṣ*.[23]

This *derashah* is not preserved in any other of the classical rabbinic works, and as it serves the Bavli's agenda so well I think it is likely to have been composed by the Bavli's creators. A version of the *derashah* is preserved in some post-Talmudic compilations, the most famous of which is the *Seder Eliyahu Zutta*:

> *Hear the word of the Lord, you who tremble at his word* (Isa. 66:5). They said, greater is the hatred which the *'am ha-'areṣ* feel toward the sages, than the hatred felt toward us by the nations. For it was said *Hear the word of the Lord, you who tremble at his word*—"despise his word" is not said, but "tremble at his word." *Said your brethren, those who hate you and those who cast you off. Your brethren*—these are masters of Scripture, who hate masters of *mishnah*; those *who hate you*—these are masters of *mishnah* who hate masters of *talmud*; *those who cast you off*—these are teachers of young children, who read [Scripture] but do not recite [tradition], and if they do read and recite they have no knowledge; and they may not be respected, and the one who respects them inherits hell for himself. (*Seder Eliyahu Zutta* 16)[24]

While this version might still imply that the "masters of *talmud*" are at the top of the hierarchy, it does not identify them with the *talmidei ḥakhamim*, or the sages par excellence. Furthermore, the final accusation against the "teachers of young children" (or in other versions, *minim*) is that they "read but do not recite," that is, they have Scripture but not tradition;[25] this stands in contrast with the Bavli's version, which puts those who

---

23   The distinction between *talmid ḥakham* on the one hand, and Scripture or *mishnah* specialists (*tanna* and *qara*) on the other, is also evident in other texts in the Bavli— see b. *Qidd.* 49a–b and also b. *Meg.* 28b, in Rav Ashi's answer to Rav Aha (אי צורבא מרבנן הוא לימא הלכתא ואי תנא הוא לימא מתני׳ ואי קרא הוא לימא פסוקא), and though those passages are about *tanna'im* (for which see below) rather than *ba'ale mishnah*, as we shall see the Bavli treats these categories similarly. While those passages present the categories of scholars in a casual, by-the-way matter, our *sugya* shows us their construction in action, as well as the polemical context of this construction. Finally, the only other *sugya* that I know in the Bavli that compares *ba'ale mishnah* to *'ame ha-'areṣ*—is b. *Sot.* 22a (קרא ולא שנה הרי זה עם הארץ; also *Derekh Eretz Zutta* 10:4)—this text is discussed below in the section titled "The Destroyers of the World."

24   See Meir Friedmann, *Pseudo-Seder Eliahu Zuta* (Heb.; Vienna: Aḥi'asaf, 1904), 5. See also the parallel versions discussed in Saul Lieberman, *Yemenite Midrashim* (Heb.; Jerusalem: Bamberger and Wahrman, 1940), 27–30; in some versions, the last section is directed against *minim* rather than the teachers of children—see, e.g., Michael Higger, *Masekhtot ze'irot* (Heb.; New York: Bloch, 1929), 69.

25   See, however, Lieberman, *Yemenite Midrashim*, who believes that this version is a scribal error, and that the group coupled with "those who cast you off" is the *minim*; the teachers of young children are the subject of the following section, and the scribes con-

focus only on Scripture in a better position than those who focus on tradition. In this aspect, this version in *Seder Eliyahu* is similar to the many hostile references in rabbinic literature to those who value the Written Torah, but discount rabbinic tradition or the Oral Torah.

The messy reality of later *midrashim* does not allow us to pin down a provenance for this version. The date and place of the *Seder Eliyahu* are still under dispute,[26] though we can say that it was compiled before the ninth century.[27] Urbach's study of the first chapter of *Seder Eliyahu* demonstrated that variations in passages found both in this work and in "classical" rabbinic works, such as the Talmuds, are best explained as adaptations of the material from the latter works by the author of *Seder Eliyahu*, rather than seen as independent parallels stemming from different textual sources.[28] Another problem is that our passage appears in a chapter that Meir Friedmann deemed not an authentic part of the work; rather, Friedmann argues, this chapter and two other chapters usually transmitted in *Seder Eliyahu Zutta*, are a compilation from the kind of material included in the *Derekh Eretz* tractates.[29]

As cautious as we ought to be given the state of the scholarship on this document, I would like to suggest that the *derashah* from *Seder Eliyahu Zutta* (or *Pseudo-Seder Eliyahu Zutta*, as Friedmann would call it) is a *Babylonian* adaptation of the Bavli's version or of a version similar to the Bavli's. The *derashah* is introduced in the *Seder* as a proof that the 'am ha-'areṣ hate the sages more than the gentiles hate Israel. This is a paraphrase of a source cited as a *baraita* in the Bavli (*b. Pes.* 49b) but which is either Babylonian in origin or heavily reworked by the Bavli's creators, as Wald has shown.[30] Given that the *derashah* in *Seder Eliyahu* does not refer to 'am ha-'areṣ, this introduction makes sense only if it originally did refer to that group, like the version in the Bavli. Already from the beginning of the unit, then, we can see both that this version is familiar with Babylonian material and that it is dependent on the Bavli's version of the *derashah*. Another suggestive piece of evidence comes from the body of the

---

flated and abbreviated these two units. On the place of the teachers of young children in the rabbis' hierarchy, see *b. Pes.* 49b.

26 See W. G. Braude and I. J. Kapstein, *Tanna debe Eliyyahu: The Lore of the School of Elijah* (Philadelphia: Jewish Publication Society, 1981), 3–15, and Albeck's literature survey in his translation of Leopold Zunz, *Die Gottesdienstlichen Vorträge der Juden Historisch Entwickelt* [2nd ed.] (Heb.; trans. and ed. Ch. Albeck; Jerusalem: Bialik Institute, 1974), 292–98.

27 See Albeck's comments, *Die Gottesdienstlichen Vorträge*, 55–57.

28 Ephraim E. Urbach, "Li-she'elat leshono u-meqorotav shel sefer 'seder eliyahu,' " *Leshonenu* 21 (1957), 183–97 (197).

29 See Friedmann, *Pseudo-Seder Eliahu*, 1; but see also the criticism in Max Kadushin, *Theology of Seder Eliahu* (New York: Bloch, 1932), 15–16.

30 See Wald, *BT Pesahim III*, 238; see also the other studies cited above, n. 20.

derashah. As we have seen, the hook that allows the *derashah* to identify the "masters of tradition" with the "haters" in the verse is the similarity between the word for "reciters of tradition" and "haters." In the version in *Seder Eliyahu,* the "masters of tradition" are still identified as the "haters," but so are the "masters of Scripture." The logic of the *derashah* in the Bavli, then, is more specifically tied with the verse, which makes it more likely to be the original version. More generally, there is evidence that *Seder Eliyahu* was compiled in Babylonia[31] though most of it comes from parts other than those chapters Friedmann attributes to the *Derekh Eretz* tradition.[32]

If this conjecture is correct, we have here two versions, *both* rabbinic and *both* Babylonian, with different views of the place of the "masters of *talmud*" in the rabbinic hierarchy: the version of *Seder Eliyahu* might imply that they are at the top of this hierarchy, but only the version in the Talmud gives them a monopoly on rabbinic identity and excludes the "masters of tradition" from that identity. This suggests that the view we find in the Bavli here does not represent "Babylonian Judaism" or even "Babylonian rabbinic Judaism," but only the Bavli itself, a point to which I will return again in this part of the book. Even if this conjecture is wrong, however, the version in *Seder Eliyahu* is still useful to us in accentuating the particular agenda of the creators of our passage in the Talmud.[33]

Another difference between the two versions of the *derashah* can help us see the coherence of the Talmud's move as a whole. In *Seder Eliyahu,* the *derashah* is anonymous; in the Bavli, the *derashah* is attributed to R. Yehuda b. R. Ilay. Omissions or changes in attributions are routine in

31   Jacob Mann, "Changes in the Divine Service of the Synagogue Due to Religious Persecutions," *HUCA* 4 (1927), 241–310 (249–51 and the appendix dedicated to *Seder Eliyahu* on pp. 302–10), surveys the evidence for *Seder Eliyahu Rabbah* and *Zutta,* defined narrowly as the material Friedmann deemed authentic; Kadushin, *Seder Eliahu,* 12, adds evidence from the other part of the *Pseudo-Seder Eliyahu Zutta,* the Rabbi Eliezer chapters.

32   Still such evidence is found even within the *Derekh Eretz* chapters. See, e.g., the statement in *PSEZ* 16 (Friedmann, 13) on the genealogical boundaries of Babylonia, which, while textually corrupt, is given in its Babylonian version (see *b. Qidd.* 72a) rather than its Palestinian version (*y. Qidd.* 4:1 65c); the very inclusion of this teaching, which is not immediately relevant to the author's discussion there, may betray Babylonian interests.

33   Another option is that this version, if indeed it can be included in *Seder Eliyahu Zutta,* reflects that composition's more "democratic" approach to the study of Torah—which, Adiel Kadari argued, was developed in response to the Karaite schism. See Adiel Kadari, "'Talmud Torah' in Seder Eliyahu: The Ideological Doctrine in its Socio-Historical Context" (Heb.), *Daat* 50–52 (2003), 35–59 (44–46). See also Lennart Lehmhaus, "'Were not understanding and knowledge given to you from Heaven?': Minimal Judaism and the Unlearned 'Other' in Seder Eliyahu Zuta," *JSQ* 19 (2012), 230–58.

intra-rabbinic parallels. However, especially given the likely possibility that the version in *Seder Eliyahu* is dependent on the Bavli's, this difference invites us to think about the function of this attribution of both of the *derashot* on Isaiah in our *sugya* to R. Yehuda b. R. Ilay. One function, as we have seen, is the reinterpretation of R. Yehuda's teaching in *Avot*. Another, more important function is to link the second part of the *sugya*, the discussion of the three disciplines of Torah and their hierarchy, with the first part, the discussion of the law of lost possession. This Rabbi Yehuda b. R. Ilay is the same Rabbi Yehuda who, in the first *baraita* cited in the *sugya*, said that the law is applicable to "any rabbi from whom he [the student] derived most of his wisdom." In its discussion of this *baraita*, the Bavli quotes two contradicting opinions from Rabbi Yohanan: the first is that the law is according to Rabbi Yehuda's opinion, and the second is that the law is according to the anonymous opinion in the Mishnah. The Bavli notes the contradiction: after all, Rabbi Yehuda stipulated a condition, that it would be the rabbi who taught the student *most* of his wisdom, which the Mishnah, saying "the rabbi who taught him wisdom," did not. How can Rabbi Yohanan say that the law is both?[34] To solve this contradiction, the Bavli reinterprets the Mishnah as if it already implies the stipulation of Rabbi Yehuda. The attribution of the *derashot* at the end of the *sugya* to the same rabbi whose opinion was linked to the Mishnah itself not only achieves coherence throughout the *sugya* but also gives these *derashot* an authority they would not otherwise have.

Our *sugya* opens with the question of "who counts as one's rabbi," and while it seems to travel a long way, it also concludes with an answer to this question. Already in the first *baraita*, which discusses lost property, the Bavli began the process of identifying "wisdom" with "*talmud*" by adding the word *mishnah* to R. Meir's definition of what does not count as "wisdom." Since the name for rabbis or sages, *ḥakhamim*, is derived from the same root as wisdom, *ḥokhma*, the definition of the former, achieved by middle of the *sugya*, obviously prepares the definition of the latter.

The creators of our *sugya* clearly identify with the "masters of *talmud*"; they present them not only as superior but as the "real rabbis," the only ones worthy of the name "sages." Those occupied with other kinds of Torah study are not only excluded from this category but are equated with non-rabbinic Jews. The text seems to be particularly interested in the difference between the "masters of *talmud*" and the "masters of *mishnah*": it is the latter rather than the "masters of Scripture" that draws its rhetorical energies from the very beginning, through the discussion of the Patriarch's defense of the Mishnah, until the presentation of the en-

---

34 On this question see Epstein, *Introduction to the Mishnaic Text*, 1.243–44; Halivni, *MM BM*, 112–13.

mity these "masters of tradition" supposedly feel for the Talmudists. We will return to this enmity later in this chapter.

"OF WHAT USE ARE THE RABBIS TO US?"

We are used to seeing the rabbis defending or legitimizing their innovations; in the *sugya* studied in this section, however, we find members of the Jewish community accusing the rabbis of not being innovative enough. The topic of the discussion is the meaning of the category *apikoros,* "an Epicurean," which is listed in *m. San.* 10:1 among the kinds of persons who do not take part in the world to come.[35] The Talmud quotes several teachings identifying the sort of conduct that makes one an Epicurean, all of which involve irreverence toward the sages.[36] Since the sages are in a sense the embodiment of Torah, the Talmud must also distinguish between the Epicurean, who compromises their honor, from another, more offensive type of person: the one who compromises the honor of the Torah itself, the one "bares [his] face to the Torah."[37] After

35 On the *apikoros* in rabbinic literature, see Jenny R. Labendz, "'Know What to Answer the Epicurean': A Diachronic Study of the 'Apiqoros in Rabbinic Literature," *HUCA* 74 (2003), 175–214. I thank Azzan Yadin-Israel for pointing me to this article.

36 Relying on the similarity between Epicurus's name and the Aramaic word for irreverence, אפיקרותא, which appears explicitly on the following page in the Talmud. The interpretation of Epicurean as irreverence toward the sages is already evident in *y. San.* 10:1 27d, which has parallels in our *sugya*. See Labendz, "Epicurean."

37 This term first appears in Tannaitic literature (*Mekhilta d. R. Yishmael, pisha,* §5, Horowitz-Rabin 15; *Sifre to Numbers, shalaḥ,* §112, on Num. 15:30, ed. Kahana *13–14, and Num. 15:31, ibid., 121, which gives an exegetical reasoning for a tradition also cited in *m. Avot* 3:11) and its precise meaning was debated by *amora'im*. In the Yerushalmi's discussion of *m. San.* 10:1, this category of people is added to the Mishnah's list of those who take no part in the world to come. At first, the Yerushalmi cites a tradition equating it with the denial of the Torah's divine origin, but after it is objected that that offense was already mentioned by the Mishnah itself, another tradition is cited that interprets the term as a reference to public transgression of the Torah's words. The Bavli provides several interpretations. One explains that it is to act like Menashe b. Hezekiah, probably referring to what is said earlier in the *sugya*, that Menashe "was sitting and expounding queer legends" (*b. San.* 99b), i.e., biblical stories that are embarrassing (or made embarrassing by the interpretation). This interpretation led to an understanding of the term that understands the exposed face to refer to the Torah's face rather than the person's, rendering the term "he who reveals aspects of the Torah." This puzzled readers—what could be wrong with revealing aspects of the Torah?—leading to an addition in most versions of the Mishnah and of the Talmud in our *sugya*: "exposing faces [i.e., aspects] of *torah not in accordance with the law*" (מגלה פנים בתורה שלא כהלכה). This interpretation was accepted by many scholars (see, e.g., Ephraim E. Urbach, *The Sages: Their Concepts and Beliefs* [Heb.; Jerusalem: Magnes Press, 1969], 23–24, 263–64); but the original meaning of the term, in all classical rabbinic sources, is to act impudently (or "barefacedly") toward the Torah; see Sharvit, *Language and Style*, 84–86.

a certain suggestion is rejected, the Bavli follows with a series of possibilities for what it would mean to dishonor the rabbis:

1. An Epicurean—such as whom?
2. Said Rav Yosef: Such as those who say, "How do the rabbis benefit us? They read [Scripture] for themselves and recite [traditions] for themselves!"
3. Abaye said to him: But this can also [be entered under the category] of one who bares his face to the Torah; for it is written, *Thus says the Lord: if it were not for my covenant studied*[38] *day and night, I would not have placed the ordinances of the heaven and the earth.* (Jer. 33:25). R. Nahman b. Yitzhak says: you may also derive it from here, where it says, *I will forgive the whole place for their sake* (Gen. 18:26).
4. Rather, such as one sitting in front of his master, and a tradition occurs to him in a different place [than the one in which the tradition was originally said], and [quoting this tradition,] he says, "This is what we said there," and does not say, "this is what the master said."
5. Rava said: Such as those of the house of Benjamin the Physician, who say, "How have the rabbis benefited us? They did not permit the raven nor did they prohibit the dove."
6. Rava, whenever they would bring before him a defective animal of Benjamin's house, if he saw a reason to permit it he would say to them, "behold as I permit you a raven!" and if he saw a reason to prohibit it, he would say to them, "behold as I prohibit for you a dove!" (b. San. 99b)

The Talmud supplies three examples of irreverence here, and while each of them might have its own meaning, they all also concern a lack of recognition, on the part of the Epicurean, for rabbinic innovation. Rav Yossef gives the example of those who say that the rabbis are useless as they only read Scripture and memorize tradition for their own sake (§2). Part of this charge is that the rabbis' study of written and oral sources has no public benefit, and it is this aspect to which the answers from Abaye and Rav Nahman (§2a) relate.[39] But the accusation also targets the *kind* of

---

38   The NRSV reads: "Thus says the Lord: Only if I had not established my covenant with day and night and the ordinances of heaven and earth"; I have changed the translation to fit the rabbinic interpretation, which understands "covenant" here as Torah and, probably taking "day and night" as an allusion to Josh. 1:8 ("This book of the law shall not depart out of your mouth; you shall meditate on it day and night"), takes the verse to be implying the dependence of the order of the world on Torah study.

39   Both Abaye and Rav Nahman use verses that argue for the benefit of Torah study to the world or the community (Rav Nahman's is a bit more obvious; for Abaye, see previous note). The implication in the Talmud seems to be that because the rabbis' benefit is

study, not just its utility. The verbs here, "study" and "recite," are familiar to us from the hierarchy of study examined in the previous section as the two less-favorable, less-productive kinds of study. The irreverent accusers, then, are in accord with Talmudic ideology: simply reading Scripture and reciting tradition are unproductive; innovation is necessary.

The accusation of the rabbis by the family of Benjamin the Physician (§4) is similar. Again the utility of the rabbis is in question, and again it is their lack of innovation: what is already prohibited will stay prohibited, and what is already permitted will stay permitted, regardless of the rabbis' actions. Rava counters this accusation by boasting before this family of his power to prohibit and permit according to his own "reasons" (§4b). Yaakov Elman argued that this passage pits the "written Torah" against the "oral Torah," "Biblical authority" vs. "rabbinic authority."[40] But Benjamin's family accepts rabbinic authority; otherwise they would not have brought their defective animals before Rava to see if they are fit to eat, and their accusation does not contain any reference to the dichotomy between Oral Torah and Scripture. Furthermore, Rava does not cite any rabbinic tradition when he prohibits or permits the animal, but rather appeals to a "reason" (ta'ama), which can refer to the sage's own exegesis or reasoning. The context of the passage also does not support Elman's interpretation, as the accusation in §2 refers to the study both of Scripture and of rabbinic tradition. It is doubtful therefore that the distinction between them is at stake here. In both of these definitions, then, the alleged Epicuri accuse the rabbis of traditionalism: they read whatever is written and repeat whatever is transmitted; they prohibit the prohibited and permit the permitted.

The example of irreverence that the Talmud supplies between these two (§3) seems different at first. The interpretation offered by most commentators (see, e.g., Ramah ad loc.) is that the student is irreverent because he compromises the honor of his master by taking partial credit for a teaching he had heard from him, ascribing the teaching to "us" rather than to the master. Read with the two other definitions in our passage, however, I think the student is said to be irreverent for the same reason the non-rabbinic accusers are: he does not recognize rabbinic creativity.

---

acknowledged in Scripture (and in one instance in the Torah proper), then doubting it in this way is to dishonor the Torah itself. But there is a certain tension between this claim and the claim in the anonymous discussion prior to the examples that implies that dishonoring the sages is dishonoring the Torah by definition, not only when the dishonoring in question also happens to contradict Scripture.

40 Yaakov Elman, "Middle Persian Culture and Babylonian Sages: Accommodation and Resistance in the Shaping of Rabbinic Legal Tradition," in *The Cambridge Companion to the Talmud* (ed. C. E. Fonrobert and M. S. Jaffee; Cambridge: Cambridge University Press, 2007), 165–97 (176–77).

The student introduces the teaching by saying, "we say there"—as if this teaching has always existed and is in consensus, not recognizing that this teaching was his rabbi's innovation. Traditionalism figures here again, but it is not a characteristic ascribed to the rabbis by outsiders but rather a condemned characteristic of an insider, a rabbinic student.

The fact that this student's conduct is condemned here by the *stam* (§3 is the only example that the Talmud supplies itself), along with the use in the first charge of the Talmud's own hierarchy of study, indicates that while the accusers are condemned as examples of irreverence, the Talmud in a sense sympathizes with the charges. In other words, the Talmud's criticism of the accusers is not ideological (the accusers do not understand, or value, what their rabbis are supposed to be doing) but factual (the accusers correctly understand that the rabbis ought to innovate and value this innovation, but they are incorrect that this innovation is not happening).

Do the charges we see here present us with real voices from outside the rabbinic establishment, or do they reflect internal rabbinic anxieties, attributed to outsiders precisely because they challenge the very legitimacy of the rabbis?[41] I do not think we can answer this question in full, but it is possible to estimate whether these sources were reworked by the *sugya*'s creators. Both charges share a core that is identical except for the tense of the verb ("How do the rabbis benefit us?" in §2; "How have the rabbis benefited us?" in §4). The first charge is not attributed to a specific group, and the second part of it, beyond the shared core, employs rabbinic technical terms for ideological effect, as we have seen above. The second accusation is ascribed to a relatively unfamiliar family—which appears only once more in the Talmud[42]—and it employs imagery that is used by the Talmud elsewhere but is not part of the technical terminology of the rabbinic academy.[43] While the first example, then, could have been constructed at a late time (perhaps even using the second charge as a source), I think it is likely that the second charge, and at least part of its narrative setting, were already extant before the creators of our *sugya*. Since these creators were probably not suspicious of the story's historicity, they "knew" that there was criticism from the community of the rab-

---

41 On this problem in general, see Christine E. Hayes, "Displaced Self-Perceptions: The Deployment of 'mînîm' and Romans in b. Sanhedrin 90b–91a," in *Religious and Ethnic Communities in Later Roman Palestine* (ed. H. Lapin; Bethesda: University Press of Maryland, 1998), 249–89.

42 See *b. Shab.* 133b, also in a story with Rava, but with another variant of the name (בני מניומי אסיא); see Epstein, *Introduction to the Mishnaic Text*, 2.1333, and Rabbinovicz, *Variae*, on *b. Shab.* 133b.

43 For "raven" and "dove" as symbols for permitted and prohibited, see *b. Qid.* 70b, discussed above in Chapter 3.

bis' traditionalism; but they encountered this outside criticism, whatever its origin, in a story transmitted and adapted by rabbinic storytellers. The creators of our passage combine criticism from the outside of rabbinic traditionalism (whether real, perceived, or imagined) with their own criticism of traditionalism within the rabbinic community by employing the terms "read" and "recite" and by juxtaposing the two similar charges with the critique of the student in §3.

This passage equates rabbinic honor with rabbinic creativity: to dishonor the rabbis is to underestimate their originality, to think of them as teaching only received knowledge or instructing only established laws. Like our previous *sugya*, this passage is about who the rabbis are, and like that *sugya*, it rejects the conception of the rabbis as transmitters who merely read what is already in Scripture and recite what is already in tradition. The fact that this self-conception is presented here in part as a response to claims made from outside the rabbinic community may suggest a certain context for that *sugya*'s insistence that the "sages" are *not* those who focus on Scripture or *mishnah*; but it is difficult, as we have seen, to determine whether these claims are projections of the rabbis' own concerns or whether they represent concerns of members of the community whom the rabbis were trying to impress. Our next passage, I think, suggests more clearly a social context for understanding this rabbinic self-conception.

"THE DESTROYERS OF THE WORLD"

Like the previous passage, our final text is concerned with offering examples of a certain type of person. In the Mishnah (*m. Sot.* 3:4), R. Yehoshua offers a list of types of people who are "destroyers of the world."[44] One of these types is a person who is "evil and cunning." The Talmud then quotes seven rabbinic traditions that identify types of behavior that count as "evil and cunning":

1. R. Yohanan said: He who makes his case to the judge before the other party to the lawsuit arrives.
2. R. Abbahu says: He who gives a *denar* to a poor person, to round him up to two hundred *zuz*. For we have learned [in *m. Pe'ah* 8:8], "Anyone who has two hundred *zuz* may not partake in gleanings, abandoned sheaves, the corner [produce], and the poor tithe; but should he have two

---

44 On the variant in the Hebrew of the Mishnah here, see Eduard Kutscher, "Marginal Notes to the Article of Mrs. Japhet" (Heb.), *Leshonenu* 31 (1967), 280–82 (282).

hundred *zuz* minus one *denar* even if a thousand [people] give him [these charities] at once, he may take [it]."

3. R. Asi said in the name of R. Yohanan: He who advises [male orphans] to sell [their] small [inherited] estate. For Rabbi Asi said in the name of R. Yohanan: male orphans who sold [their] small estate [before the orphaned daughters had the chance to claim the small estate, to which they have a right according to *m. B. B.* 9:1], the deal is valid.

4. Abaye said: He who advises to sell property [using the opinion of] Rabban Shimeon b. Gamaliel. For it was taught, ["If a person said, 'I give] my property to you and after you to so-and-so,' and the first [buyer] sold [the property] and ate up [the proceeds], the second person can claim restitution from the purchasers—these are Rabbi's words. Rabban Shimeon ben Gamaliel says, the second person only has whatever was left by the first [a *baraita* also cited in *b. B. B.* 137a].

5. R. Yosef b. Mama said in the name of R. Sheshet: He who induces others to follow in his ways.

6. Rabbi Zerika said in the name of Rav Huna: He who is lenient with himself and strict with others.

7. Ulla said: He who read [Scripture] and recited [*mishnah*] but did not attend to the sages. (*b. Sot.* 21b–22a)

Most of the conducts condemned in this list necessitate a thorough knowledge, on account of the "evil and cunning" person, of rabbinic law. Two of the three that do not specifically refer to rabbinic traditions—the person lenient on himself and strict on others and the person convincing others to walk in his ways—are clearly models of bad rabbinic behavior; to a lesser extent, this can be applied also to the person who manipulates the legal system.

One function of this list is pedagogical—it tells the audience of the Talmud, which consists of sages or aspiring sages, how not to take advantage of their knowledge and position, and teaches them a few rabbinic traditions on charity, inheritance, and business. But it also offers a particular interpretation of the Mishnah: the "cunning and evil" person is someone who has mastered significant amounts of Torah knowledge (therefore, he is "cunning" or "wise"), but abuses this knowledge or otherwise conducts himself badly (therefore, he is evil). The Bavli also makes the point that we, rabbis, should look for the "evil" close to home. In these aspects, the Bavli's treatment of the Mishnah generally resembles the Yerushalmi's (see *y. Sot.* 3:4 19a).

The final element in the list is Ulla's identification of the "cunning and evil" person with someone who "read [Scripture] and recited [tradition] but did not attend to the sages." This phrase, also found in other contexts, juxtaposes a person's intellectual achievement—by reading and reciting he has mastered both the written and oral elements of Torah—with his lack of service to the sages. This conduct fits the previous items in the list: knowledge of Torah, on the one hand, and lack of piety or bad behavior on the other. But there is a sense in which this item is different. As Martin Jaffee has shown, rabbinic ideology makes a strong connection between Torah, rabbinic authority, and discipleship; the sages are the Torah's exclusive mediators and therefore true mastery of Torah can only be achieved through constant interaction with, observation of, and service to them.[45] Unlike the other "cunning and evil" people on the list, whose misconduct does not necessarily affect their knowledge of Torah, here the lack of service to the sages must also decrease the extent of that person's Torah learning. Such an interpretation of the phrase is explicit in one of its other occurrences:

> If a person read [Scripture] and did not recite [tradition], he still stands outside. If he recited [tradition] but did not read [Scripture], he still stands outside. [But even if] he read [Scripture] and recited [tradition], and [yet] he did not attend to the sages, he is like someone from whom the mysteries of Torah are withheld. (*Seder Eliyahu Rabbah*, 6; ed. Friedmann 37)

This passage appears in the printed editions of the early Palestinian work *Leviticus Rabbah*, but it was in fact appended to that work from *Seder Eliyahu Rabbah*.[46] It comes after a string of interpretations of the biblical phrase, "the maidens love you" (Song 1:3). The *derashah* builds on the similarity between the word for maidens, *'alamot*, and the root for mysterious things, *'l.m.*,[47] to imply that the love of God must go through the mysteries of Torah. It first tells us that focusing exclusively on Scripture or tradition will leave one "outside" the Torah. It goes on to say that even reading and reciting, if not complemented by serving the sages, will still leave one without the "mysteries" of Torah. Scripture and tradition might be accessible—the first in written form, the second in oral form—without interaction with the sages; but to know the mysteries of Torah one must have attended to the rabbis. The social and political import of this tradition is clear.

45   Martin Jaffee, *Torah in the Mouth: Writing and Oral Tradition in Palestinian Judaism 200 BCE–400 CE* (Oxford: Oxford University Press, 2001), 126–52.

46   See Mordechai Margulies, *Midrash Wayyikra Rabbah: A Critical Edition Based on Manuscripts and Genizah Fragments with Variants and Notes* (Heb.; 5 vols.; Jerusalem: Ministry of Education and the Epstein Fund of the American Academy of Jewish Research, 1953–60), 1.72. On the general phenomenon of addition to Lev. Rab. from *Seder Eliyahu*, see ibid, 1.32.

47   See Margulies, *Midrash Wayyikra Rabbah*, 1.74.

The verb "attend" (*shimesh*) here may have a range of meanings, including "serving" and "obeying"; but nothing in the expression itself, nor in its deployment in Ulla's statement or in *Seder Eliyahu Rabbah*, prepares us for Rashi's explanation on its use in the Talmud: "And he did not attend to the sages: to study the logical deductions (*sevara*) of the Talmud concerning the reasons of the Mishnah." Rashi is reading into this expression the tripartite division of Torah study that we have encountered earlier. Since the person is reported to have engaged in the first two disciplines of Torah study, having read Scripture and recited tradition, the problem must be that he neglected the third discipline, *talmud*.

While Rashi's interpretation might be far from the original sense of the phrase as Ulla used it, it certainly prepares its readers for the direction in which the *sugya* is heading.[48] The Bavli will indeed go on to imply that there is something missing in simply "reading and reciting," that is, in mere transmission. This becomes clear at the next stage of the *sugya*:

> It was said: "He read and recited and did not attend to the sages."
>
> R. Eleazar says: He is an 'am ha-'areṣ.
>
> R. Shmuel b. Nahmani says: He is uncultivated [*bur*].[49]
>
> R. Yanai says: He is a Cuthean.[50]
>
> R. Aha b. Yaakov says: He is a magus.
>
> Rav Nahman said: It seems reasonable that it is like Rav Aha b. Yaakov's opinion. As they say: "The magus mumbles but he does not know what he is

---

48   The Bavli itself, in a different but thematically related *sugya*, certainly understands the service rendered to sages as personal service. In *b. Meg.* 28b the Bavli contrasts the opinions of Resh Lakish and (our) Ulla on whether a sage can accept service (*le-hishtamesh*) from someone "who recites traditions." Resh Lakish objects to such use, and a story is quoted to illustrate his opinion: Reish Lakish was walking in a road and arrived at a pool of water. A certain person came, put him up on his shoulder, and was taking him across. Reish Lakish asked him, "Did you read [Scripture]?" He said, "I have read." "Did you recite [tradition]?" "I have recited the four orders of the Mishnah." He told him: "You have hewn for yourself four mountains, [and yet] you carried the son of Lakish [me] on your shoulder?!" Clearly, all three actions referred to in the expression "he read and recited but did not serve the sages" appear here too: Resh Lakish asked whether he has read and recited, and the service is in the form of the person giving the rabbi a ride on his shoulders.

49   On *bur*, see Saul Lieberman, *Tosefta Ki-fshuta* (Heb.; 10 vols.; New York: Jewish Theological Seminary, 1955–88), 1.121.

50   Heb. כותי, the normal rabbinic term for Samaritan, often used in rabbinic literature as a generic term for a foreigner, and sometimes replacing, as an act of censorship (either self-imposed or not), terms for *minim* or gentiles. As far as I know, there is no study about this term in the Bavli; for the Yerushalmi, see Andreas Lehnardt, "The Samaritans (Kutim) in the Talmud Yerushalmi," in *The Talmud Yerushalmi and Graeco-Roman Culture III* (ed. P. Schäfer; Tübingen: Mohr Siebeck, 2002) 139–60, and the bibliography noted there, 140, on studies covering all of the rabbinic period.

mumbling," the *tanna* recites and does not know what he is reciting.[51] (*b. Sot.* 22a)

This list is different from the list with which the *sugya* opened. That first list takes a negative category, "evil and cunning," and ties it to specific examples of bad conduct. The list here does the opposite: it takes a specific conduct—knowledge of Scripture and tradition without service to the sages—and ties it to various negative categories.

The point of these suggestions is that the Torah knowledge of our non-servant does not save him from counting as an outsider. He is counted either among those parts of Israel different from the rabbis ('am ha-'areṣ or *bur*) or a foreigner altogether (Cuthean). The last suggestion, R. Aha's, is in the same vein: it uses a group hostile to the rabbis, the Zoroastrian magi, to say that this kind of a person is an outsider or an enemy to us, the sages.

The Bavli takes an additional, crucial step with this last identification. Rav Nahman quotes a popular saying[52] to link the magus to a Jewish title, the *tanna* or the reciter of traditions, a title used from the Amoraic period on to designate those who, in the absence of written texts, were in charge of memorizing rabbinic oral traditions and deploying them through recitation in scholarly, and perhaps also liturgical, contexts.[53] In a story that appears elsewhere in the Talmud, the same Rav Nahman is asked to deliver a eulogy for such a scholar who excelled in the recitation or memorization of traditions. He refuses to do so, saying that the best thing he could say about him is that he was a "bag full of books" (*b. Meg.* 28b). Here Rav Nahman expresses a similar view: these *tanna'im* are merely "reciters" or "repeaters" (the primary meaning of the root t. n. y.); they know how to memorize tradition but they do not understand it. The Zoroastrian magi, as we shall see in the following chapter, also practiced the recitation of traditions, and since that recitation was mostly of Avestan material in a time when Avestan was no longer understood, and since this recitation did not necessitate analytical inquiry, Rav Nahman can

---

51   Translation follows the version in Ms. Oxford. Other versions have "does not know what he is saying" instead of "does not know what he is mumbling" and "does not know what he is reciting."

52   On a possible Manichean parallel to this saying, see below, Chapter 5, n. 3.

53   See Yaakov Sussmann, "Torah shebe-'al peh—peshuṭah ke-mashma'ah," *Talmudic Studies III* (2 vols.; ed. Y. Sussmann and D. Rosenthal; Jerusalem: Magnes, 2005), 209–384 (238–45, and the rich bibliography in 240 n. 51); on the Geonic period, Neil Danzig, "From Oral Talmud to Written Talmud: On the Methods of Transmission of the Babylonian Talmud and its Study in the Middle Ages," *Bar Ilan* 30–31 (2006), 49–112 (85–94). In addition to the references in these essays, see also the comprehensive list of Talmudic sources in Abraham S. Meir, *Institutions and Titles in the Talmudic Literature* (Heb.; Jerusalem: Mosad Ha-Rav, 1977), 38–63.

compare them to the Jewish *tanna'im*: both recite material that they do not necessarily understand.[54]

Through the comparison between the *tanna* and the magus the Bavli affects a dramatic change of meaning of the "read and recited" phrase. It might not be necessary, as Rashi does, to understand the phrase as "read [Scripture] and recited [tradition] but did not engage himself in *talmud* [the analytical study]"—but that interpretation now does not seem as far off as it did before this point in the *sugya*. At the very least, Rav Nahman's teaching takes advantage of the fact that the phrase mentions only the transmission-oriented kinds of Torah study to say that there is something lacking in mere transmission. As opposed to the original sense of the phrase and its other occurrences,[55] our *sugya* does not use it to contrast good knowledge of the Torah (mastering both written and oral components) with bad conduct—rather, our text says that knowledge of Torah that is constituted only by reading and recitation is in itself insufficient, and the one who practices might as well be a foreigner.

The Bavli attributes to Rav Nahman not only the comparison between the *tanna* and the magus but also the connection of this comparison to Rav Aha's teaching about the person who read, recited, and did not serve. It seems more likely, though, that this connection was made by the creators of our *sugya*. First, the connection is based on a significant reappropriation of Rav Aha's teaching. In its context in the list, that teaching is meant as a general condemnation (what *x* counts as) whereas Rav Nahman supports it with a specific identification (what counts as *x*). It is un-

---

54   On the comparison itself, see Jonas C. Greenfield, "רטין מגושא" (Eng.), in *Joshua Finkel Festschrift* (ed. S. B. Hoenig and L. D. Stitskin; New York: Yeshiva University Press, 1974), 63–69, and Eliezer S. Rosenthal, "For the Talmudic Dictionary—Talmudica Iranica," *Irano Judaica* 1 (1982), Hebrew section 38–134 (72–73), and see Chapter 5 in detail.

55   The other appearance in the Bavli may be somewhat similar to ours, at least according to one of its versions. A passage in *b. Ber.* 47b deals with the law that an *am ha-'areṣ* may not count for a *zimmun*. One definition given for the *'am ha-'areṣ* there is: "Others say: even if he read and recited and did not serve the sages he is an *'am ha-'areṣ*." A story follows: "Rami bar Hama did not count for a *zimmun* R. Menashia b. Tahalifa, who recited *Sifra* and *Sifre* and *Hilkheta*." When Rava says that Rami b. Hama's premature death was only due to his conduct with R. Menashia, the *stam* protests that he was simply acting according with the opinion that the one who read and recited equals *'am ha-'areṣ*. The description of R. Menashia b. Tahalifa as someone who has mastered a large body of Tannaitic teaching, as expected of a reciter or a master of *mishnah*, and the Talmud's understanding that he is a person who "read and recited and did not serve the sages," are similar to our *sugya*'s connection between that category and the *tanna*. But this characterization of Menashia is missing in Mss. Munich and Paris (though it is present in good manuscripts as well as a Genizah fragment), and since there is no immediate reason to omit the phrase it may present a secondary interpretation of this *sugya* in light of our *sugya* and the *sugya* from *b. Meg.* 28b.

likely that Rav Nahman, Rav Aha's contemporary, recontextualized his teaching so thoroughly. More important, this connection serves too well the ideological and structural line of the rest of our *sugya*.

This line continues, after two passages that consider the 'am ha-'areṣ and various combinations of Torah knowledge (reading but not reciting; reciting but not reading; neither reading nor reciting), when the Bavli quotes a *derashah* on the reciters:

> *My child, fear the Lord and the King, and do not intermingle with the* shonim ["those who differ," "the different ones"; also: "those who recite" or "reciters"] (Prov. 24:21). R. Yitzhak said: [The verse refers to] those who recite traditions [*shonei halakhot*].[56] But [why even teach that? Is not] this [the] simple [sense of the verse]?
>
> What [else] could you say? That they repeat their sins, and [the verse could be teaching something] like Rav Huna's [teaching], for Rav Huna said, "Because a person committed a transgression and repeated it, it feels permitted for him." This teaches us [that it is indeed those who recite traditions]. (*b. Sot.* 22a)

This *derashah* shares much with the *derashah* attributed to R. Yehuda b. R. Ilay in *b. B. M.* discussed earlier in this chapter. Both *derashot* are premised on the similarity or identity of the Hebrew word *shonim*—of which *tanna'im* is an Aramaic equivalent—to a word in their respective verses. Both *derashot* interpret a verse that distinguishes between an "in group" and an "out group"—here the addressees of the verse are the in group and those with which they are warned not to intermingle with are the out group—and both put those associated with tradition in the out group. Finally, both *derashot* are found only in the Babylonian Talmud (it is telling that late Palestinian works interpret this verse to fight their own "others," directing it against "those who say that there are two powers in the heaven").[57]

What makes this *derashah* even more striking than Rabbi Yehuda's *derashah* is that while the latter presented us with a static picture of the four different groups, this *derashah* indicates that the boundary between the addressees and the reciters of traditions is not so stable; apparently, the addressees of this verse—presumably, the sages—must be warned not to mingle with these reciters.

56   According to most manuscripts. Ms. Vatican 110 has "simple traditions" (*halakhot peshutot*), which could imply that this only refers to reciters who deal with particular kinds of tradition. But this version is most certainly a misunderstanding of the following clause in the Talmud, "simple," which was probably abbreviated in the version this scribe received and then expanded erroneously.

57   See *Tanḥuma* (Buber) 16, *Deut. Rab.* 2, and *Ex. Rab.* 15.

We usually think of the *tanna'im* as clearly distinguishable from the sages: they have a different function in the academy, they are of much lower rank and they command no respect, their engagement in Torah study is limited and superficial. Here, however, we can see that the Talmud is constructing a boundary that apparently was not that clear in reality. Is it possible that the two types of scholars, the analytical Talmudic sage and the "living book" who cannot understand what he repeats, are merely "ideal types" imagined by some Talmudic authors? The next passage in the *sugya* raises this question even more sharply:

It was recited [*tanna*]: The reciters [*tanna'im*] are the destroyers of the world.

Does it [really] occur to you that they are the destroyers of the world!?

Ravina said: Because they offer legal instruction from their tradition.

And this was also recited [*tanya nami hakhi*]: Rabbi Yehoshua said, "And are they the destroyers of the world? Do not they populate the world? For it was said, *the ways (halikhot) of the world are for him* (Hab. 3:6)—do not read *halikhot* but *halakhot*.[58] Rather [they are thus called] since they offer legal instruction from their tradition." (*b. Sot.* 22b)

A great irony of this passage's design is that these two sources against reciters are presented as recited sources. Given that these *baraitot* do not appear in compilations from the Tannaitic period itself,[59] it is possible that this attribution is deliberately ironic. Even if this attribution represents the real or perceived Tannaitic provenance of these sources, the irony could not have been lost on the audience of the *sugya*.

The condemnation of the *tanna'im* here as the "destroyers of the world" goes back to the Mishnah on which our *sugya* is appended, which contains a list of such "destroyers." It might also be related to the previous unit, the *derashah* on Proverbs 24, as Proverbs there refers to ruin and disaster.[60] The statement is so harsh that Ravina needs to explain that the *tanna'im* are destroyers not by definition, but because they instruct the

---

58   The crux of the Midrashic argument here ("do not read . . .") is missing in the printed editions and added here according to Ms. Oxford.

59   Even Epstein, *Introduction to the Mishnaic Text*, 2.673, classifies the first *baraita* as "Babylonian."

60   The following verse reads: "For disaster comes from them suddenly, and who knows the ruin that both can bring" (Prov. 24:22) where "both" probably refers to God and the king mentioned in the previous verse: the ruin and the disaster they bring is a punishment for associating with those who differ from or rebel against them. The Talmudic reading of the verse might again employ a pun, taking the word "both" (שניהם) to refer to "reciters" (שונים). Thus Prov. 24:21–22 would read: "Fear God, my son, and the king, and do not intermingle with the reciters; for disaster comes from them suddenly, and who knows the ruin that the reciters can bring."

law based on their recited traditions (more on this below). The second *baraita* (§3) is attributed to R. Yehoshua because the list of the "destroyers" in the Mishnah is attributed to him as well;[61] thus this late *baraita* is seen as continuous with the Mishnah that it expands. A similar *derashah* to the one appearing in the *baraita* appears in another purportedly Tannaitic source in the Bavli, where it is put in praise rather in condemnation of recitation:

> *Tanna de-vei Eliyahu*: Anyone who recites traditions [*halakhot*], it is promised to him that he takes part in the world to come. For it was said: *Eternal ways [halikhot olam] are for him* (Hab. 3:6). Do not read *halikhot* but rather *halakhot*. (*b. Sot.* 28b)

It seems likely that the *baraita* in our *sugya* in b. *Sot.* 22a is a later construction based on this *baraita* in b. *Sot.* 28b. The first *baraita* is suspect because it is formulated to reject an assertion (that the reciters are the destroyers of the world) which has has no parallel in rabbinic literature, and, more important, because what it adds to the *derashah* is paralleled word for word in a statement made by a very late sage (Ravina). The second *baraita* expresses a sentiment common in early rabbinic literature about the importance of memorizing *halakhot,* and it is not subordinated to an expansion of a Mishnaic list. This *baraita* is identified here as *tanna de-vei Eliyahu,* and in fact appears in *Seder Eliyahu Zutta,* where its form suggests an earlier date than that document's compilation.[62] Our *sugya* then takes this *derashah* in praise of recitation and reappropriates it into a text designed to criticize reciters.[63]

What is most striking about this text is that it shows us further the artificial nature of the boundaries that the Bavli is drawing here. If the previous unit, the *derashah* on Prov. 24:21, warned the sages not to intermingle with the *tanna'im,* this unit gives us the other side of the equation

---

61   Though this attribution seems to have been introduced late—all manuscripts have R. Shimeon instead of R. Yehoshua.

62   The version in *Seder Eliyahu Zutta* 2 is: "And it also says, *Eternal ways are for him* (Hab. 3:6): from here they said that 'anyone who recites *Halakhot* is promised a part in the world to come' " (ed. Friedmann, 173). That is, at least according to this version, the *derashah* was added as a prooftext to an already existing tradition. See Meir Friedmann's comment in his introduction, *Seder Eliahu Rabba und Seder Eliahu Zuta* (Heb.; Vienna: Ahi'asaf, 1902), 45, and the sources he cites there. While the interpretation of *halikhot* as *halakhot* is already in y. *Meg.* 1:4 70d, that reading there says nothing about the *tanna'im,* and thus it is likely that our two *derashot* in b. *Meg.* and b. *Sot.* are related to each other and not to this Palestinian original.

63   It is also interesting that the rejected possibility, that the *tanna'im* in fact populate or colonize the world, is comparable with what is said about the sages in b. *Shab.* 114b, "these are the sages, who are occupied with building the world their entire lives."

by condemning the *tanna'im* for overstepping their boundaries, for becoming too much like the sages: they dare to instruct the law.[64] The Bavli then is speaking here of two kinds of transgressions: scholars who associate with reciters, and reciters who act like scholars. Thus while the Talmud often presents us with a clear boundary between "sages" and "reciters," between "masters of *talmud*" and "masters of *mishnah*," between *halakhic* authorities and "living books"—we can see here that that boundary was at least partially the result of construction and deliberate separation.

CONCLUSION: TALMUDISTS AND RECITERS

The efforts we find in the Bavli to oppose sages with the "masters of *mishnah*," or the reciters, raise questions not only about the utility of this opposition for the composers of our passages but also about the identity of those whom these composers portray as their "haters." Who were the reciters, and why did they become such important "others" for the "masters of *talmud*"?

To a large and surprising degree, the Talmud's presentation of the reciters as mindless bags of books has been adopted by modern scholarship. The most recent treatment of the subject simply quotes Rav Nahman's statements on the reciters (from *b. Sot.* and *b. Meg.*) to support the claim that the *tanna'im* "were not great scholars but professional reciters who offered the traditions without interpreting them."[65] This image is problematic not only because it relies on texts with an obvious polemical tone, but also because it does not conform with much of the evidence about these *tanna'im*. Even if we limit ourselves to the Babylonian Talmud, the primary source for this negative image, we find the *tanna'im*

---

64   I think it is clear from the context, with the juxtaposition of this statement with the *derashah* on Proverbs 24, that what the Talmud has in mind here is the crossing of the boundaries between two identities, the scholar and the *tanna*. Ephraim E. Urbach, *The Halakhah: Its Sources and Development* (trans. R. Posner; Tel Aviv: Massada, 1986), 126–27, reads this statement in the context of the prohibition to teach the law based on texts or theoretical study. This might well have been the original meaning of this statement, and it may be observed in the version of the *baraita* in *PSEZ*: "and the *tanna'im* [emending the text that reads ותנאי] are the destroyers of the world. And do not they sustain the world? Rather, *anyone* who teaches from his *mishnah*, he is the destroyer of the world" (*PSEZ* 16, Friedmann 8). The Bavli, however, clearly uses it to contrast the sages with the *tanna'im*, rather than to discuss generally the ability of "anyone" to instruct law based on tradition. The Bavli also prohibits basing legal instructions on *talmud* (see *b. B. B.* 130b, according to manuscripts) and yet we would never imagine it saying that *ba'ale talmud* are the destroyers of the world.

65   Danzig, "Oral Talmud," 85.

engaged in a range of scholarly activities that go beyond memorization and recitation: they juxtapose traditions, offer their own emendations, interpret these traditions, and expand on them; and yes, there is some indication that, despite the objections of our *sugya*, they offered legal rulings.[66] The distinction between the reciter and the scholar, one on which our *sugyot* insist, was not always clear.[67]

Geonic literature complicates matters further. On the one hand, the *tanna* is a distinct office or position in the Geonic academy, clearly differentiated from the positions of scholars and students—a development that may be explained by the further institutionalization of the academy. On the other hand, several Geonic sources portray the *tanna'im* as central and respected members of the academic community, whose range of activities show interpretive capability and include much more than a simple reproduction of texts in aid of study.[68] Neil Danzig has recently argued that because we know from the Talmud that the *tanna'im* were not scholars and that their scope was limited to non-intellectual memorization, these sources must refer to different kinds of individuals. The title *tanna*, Danzig concludes, applied both to the office of the reciter and to "real scholars" (*ḥakhamim muvhaqim*) who were engaged in permanent study in the academy.[69]

While it is possible that the term *tanna'im* was used to refer to a wide range of individuals, it seems to me that the polemical nature of our *sugyot* should make us suspicious of their hostile or belittling relation to these reciters. The fact that even the Talmud, in non-polemical passages, can portray these reciters as capable and ambitious, may tell us that the

66   See the sources cited in Epstein, *Introduction to the Mishnaic Text*, 2.677–88. See also the sources in Amir, *Titles*, 44–53.

67   To this one can add that many sages are said in the Talmuds to recite traditions, and several are characterized with the sort of memorizing abilities associated with the *tanna'im*—see Amit, *Titles*, 44–45. It seems misleading to me, however, to say as Amit does that famous sages functioned in the Amoraic period as reciters of traditions—rather, as sages, they were also expected to recite traditions and memorize them, and it is only from the perspective of the Babylonian separation between "scholarship" and "transmission" that this would relegate them to a different function.

68   See the sources noted by Danzig, "Oral Talmud," and especially the sources published by Simcha Emanuel, "New Responsa of R. Hai Ga'on" (Heb.), *Tarbiẓ* 69 (2000), 105–26 (111–13). Several of these Geonic texts portray *tanna'im* as involved, respected, central to the activities of the academy, contributing much more than recitation of tradition: they participate in court discussions, contribute to the organization of the liturgy, and are consulted in the appointment of the exilarch; they also receive a stipend from the academy and seem to be well regarded by its leadership. Emanuel also reinterprets, in light of new textual evidence, one of the Geonic sources that was previously understood to draw a sharp distinction between the kind of study practiced by the sages and the one practiced by the *tanna'im*, with the dichotomy much less pronounced.

69   Danzig, "Oral Talmud," 85–87.

difference between the harsh statements in our *sugyot* and the more positive and diverse portrayal in Geonic sources has more to do with changes
in the rabbis' ideology than with a transformation in the nature of the
tanna'im themselves.[70] The image of the "mindless reciter" is, to a great
degree, a polemical and ideologically driven misrepresentation.

Our *sugyot* insist on the separation of scholars from reciters not because that separation was clear to everyone; rather, the Bavli is engaged
here in a discussion on what counts as scholarship, arguing that only
those involved in the analytical and innovative kind of Torah study, *talmud*, are worthy of the name. Those who focus on the transmission of
rabbinic tradition are portrayed as enemies of the rabbis and as equal in
status to the rabbis' classical opponents. Even if we grant that such polemical texts are often characterized by hyperbole, the lengths to which
our *sugyot* go to create this boundary are striking.

These texts do not, of course, object to recitation as such. For the
"masters of *talmud*," the reciters had a clear and important role in the
rabbinic academies: in the absence of written books, they were the primary sources of the traditions that could then be the subject of analysis in
the sessions of *talmud*. What the composers of our *sugyot* insist on is the
separation of scholars from transmitters and scholarship from transmission. They object to scholars who associate with reciters and to reciters
who act like scholars; they project an enmity between "masters of *mishnah*" and "masters of *talmud*" and present the reciters as "bags full of
books" because they did not want to think of them as anything more than
mere transmitters.

This connection between a particular ideology of Torah study and the
way the "masters of *talmud*" defined themselves gives us a context for the
literary practices analyzed in the first part of this book. They show us
that a determinative factor in the self-conception of these rabbis was not
just the ability to innovate but more specifically the separation between
transmission and innovation, a separation which, I argue, was central to
the formation of the layered structure. The insistence of our *sugya* in *b.
San.* that the rabbis are innovators supports the interpretation of the *stam*
as a form of showcasing analytical virtuosity. The representation of the
reciters may further correlate with this literary practice in the sense that
they provided for the Talmudists another way of externalizing tradition:
much like quotations served to confine traditions in Hebrew dicta waiting to be interpreted by the *stam*, the reliance on mindless transmitters
confined tradition in living books who were waiting to be read by "real"
scholars. The fact that, for the most part, the maneuvers we have seen in

---

70 On the more positive relation toward memorization in the Geonic period, see the
discussion in the Conclusion of this book.

this chapter belong to the redactional layer, suggest that we can connect their approach with the scholars who shaped the Bavli.

These *sugyot* also illuminate the Talmud's position by showing us its specificity and its contested nature. Their insistence on drawing the boundaries between transmission and scholarship, especially when juxtaposed with other types of evidence, betrays a reality different from the one the Talmud wishes to impose. They invite us to consider that outside the circles of the "masters of *talmud*," but still in Babylonia and within the confines of the rabbinic academy, transmission was not seen as inferior to and distinct from scholarship, but as continuous with it.

The ideological background of the Talmud's approach to the reciters and the evidence that suggests that they were engaged in more than mindless repetition raise the question of the reciters' own self-conception and approach to tradition. Here we have to be careful: we have no text that explicitly provides us with the reciters' perspective. When we consider that some Jews in late antiquity dedicated their lives to this demanding memorization and recitation of rabbinic tradition, the presentation of this recitation as mere aid to study becomes less satisfactory.

I suggest that as in other cultures, recitation of oral traditions in Judaism was a ritual in its own right.[71] This function of recitation may already be evident in the way it is described by Rav Nahman: the reciter may not understand what he is reciting, but that is not, as Rav Nahman himself says elsewhere, because he is an unintellectual "bag full of books," but rather because understanding the text was not the primary goal of its recitation.[72] Analytical activities such as emendations and interpretations were not separate from this activity; but they were not central to it either. Recitation of rabbinic tradition does become a ritual outside the study house later on—by the early Geonic period, both the *tanna'im* and recitation play a part in the liturgy of the synagogue; but there is no evidence that can tell us whether this was the case while the Talmud was forming.[73]

71   For this ritual, as opposed to scholarly, approach to sacred texts, see William A. Graham, *Beyond the Written Word: Oral Aspects of Scripture in the History of Religion* (Cambridge: Cambridge University Press, 1987); Barbara A. Holdrege, *Veda and Torah: Transcending the Textuality of Scripture* (Albany: State University of New York Press, 1995), 343–47, and see also the sources and studies quoted in Chapter 5 below for recitation as ritual in contexts closer to the Bavli.

72   In fact, if we separate Rav Nahman's statement from the *sugya* that presents the reciters as "cunning and evil," "destroyers of the world," or akin to the magi—they can be read more as a description and less as a criticism.

73   On the recitation of rabbinic texts as part of the Geonic-era liturgy, see Adiel Kadari, "Between Scholars and the General Public in the Synagogue during the Gaonic Period: On the Historical Development of Torah Reading and Scholarly Customs Associated with Public Prayer" (Heb.), *Sidra* 19 (2004), 135–58; on *tanna'im* in the synagogues,

If we understand the recitation of rabbinic tradition as a ritual with its own end, it may be posited as the opposite of the practice of *talmud*. Where the latter distances tradition and objectifies it for the purpose of intellectual analysis, the former internalizes it, literally embodying it by repeated memorization and recitation, uniting the sage and the sacred text. The following two chapters are dedicated to exploring the possibility of recitation as a ritual opposing the Bavli's scholastic practice, shedding light on this opposition from evidence outside the Talmud itself.

The texts studied in this chapter show us that their creators defined their intellectual activities by a particular relationship with tradition, one that not only emphasized analysis but also separated analysis from transmission. This is true of these texts even if we do not consider them against the possibility that ideological alternatives to the Talmud's approach existed in its immediate surroundings. But these passages do, I argue, suggest such alternatives, and the consideration of these alternatives offers us not only a certain social context for the development of the practice of *talmud*, but also a better appreciation of what *talmud* meant to the scholars who shaped it.

---

see also the texts noted by Danzig, "Oral Talmud," 85–87. It is possible, though unlikely, that the *deuterosis* and *deuterotai* that appear in some church fathers and in Justinian's Novella 146 may place *tanna'im* and *mishnayot* in Palestinian synagogues of late antiquity, but the identification of these Greek terms with the rabbinic terms is very problematic—see Seth Schwartz, "Rabbinization in the Sixth Century," in *The Talmud Yerushalmi and Graeco-Roman Culture III* (ed. P. Schäfer; Tübingen: Mohr Siebeck, 2002), 55–69 (especially 65–68). I do find suggestive that the chain of functions in Lev Rab 30:1, ותני קרייי קרוב ופויטס, lists the reader of Scripture and the reciter of tradition along with liturgical functionaries (the *paytan* and the *qarov*). But even if rabbinic traditions did play a role in the liturgy in such an early period, it was more likely as part of ritualized study rather than collective recitation—see Kadari, ibid., and see more in Chapter 6 below.

Chapter Five

THE DEBATE ABOUT RECITATION

The recitation of sacred texts was a common practice in antiquity, not only among Jews. This chapter examines some Zoroastrian and Christian texts on recitation and argues that the tensions between scholarship and recitation that we saw in the previous chapter should be read in the broader context of Mesopotamian late antiquity, beyond the Jewish community.

Each of the two sections of this chapter examines a way in which the Talmud's negotiation of reciters and of recitation was a product of its time and place. The first section shows that the distinction the Talmud makes between the "masters of *mishnah*" and the "masters of *talmud*" bears a striking similarity to a distinction Persian texts make between two kinds of Zoroastrian priests. Both distinctions concern the difference between reciting and analyzing, both distinctions describe animosity between the two groups, and both distinctions survive in sources that represent the scholarly group. What may at first seem to be a discussion completely internal to the Jewish tradition is in fact a Jewish version of a discussion that would be familiar to others in the Sasanian world.

The second section demonstrates that the representation of the Zoroastrian recitation of sacred texts in the Talmud shares both the rhetoric and function of the representation of this recitation in a Christian text. Both present the magi's ritual as performative murmuring and contrast it with intellectual engagement; in both cases, I argue, even though the ostensible target is Zoroastrian practice, this representation also functions to mark certain types of Jewish and Christian recitation as foreign rituals, serving a particular group in a debate on the appropriate Jewish or Christian approach to sacred texts. The differentiation of scholarship from traditional recitation—central, as we have seen, to the self-conception of the Talmud's creators—was shaped by the conversation with Zoroastrianism and, more important, with the kinds of Jewish and Christian practices the encounter with Zoroastrianism produced.

Much recent scholarship has focused on the extent to which Jews, Christians, Zoroastrians, and others in late ancient Mesopotamia shared spaces, practices, and ideas.[1] A related, but not identical, development has been the replacement of the model that posited autonomous, well-defined "religious communities" with an examination of the ways in which boundaries between these communities were imposed by some and transgressed by others.[2] This chapter builds on these developments to trace a particular debate about ritual and identity in late ancient Mesopotamia. This debate was one of the discursive spaces in which the literary practices that formed the Talmud took shape and in which the "masters of *talmud*" came to understand their project.

WHOSE MURMURING? THE *HĒRBED* AND THE *HĀWIŠT* IN THE ZOROASTRIAN TRADITION

In the previous chapter, we saw Rav Nahman comparing the *tanna* to a magus, who according to a popular saying[3] "does not understand what he

---

1   The number of recent publications on these matters, from Jewish, Christian, and Zoroastrian perspectives, is very large. See Shai Secunda, "Reading the Bavli in Iran," *JQR* 100.2 (2010), 310–42 (310–18 and n. 6 especially) for a survey of recent literature with emphasis on Jewish-Zoroastrian encounters; Michal Bar Asher Siegal, "Shared Worlds: Rabbinic and Monastic Literature," *HTR* 105 (2012), 423–56, with an emphasis on Jewish-Christian encounters. For an account from the perspective of Christian literature, see Joel Walker, *Legend of Mar Qardagh: Narrative and Christian Heroism in Late Antique Iraq* (Berkeley: University of California Press, 2006), 7–8 and passim. On "popular religion," see Shaul Shaked, "Popular Religion in Sasanian Babylonia," *Jerusalem Studies in Arabic and Islam* 21 (1997), 103–17.

2   On Zoroastrian polemic literature, see Albert F. de Jong, "Zoroastrian Religious Polemics and their Contexts," in *Religious Polemics in Context* (ed. T. L. Hettema and A. van der Kooij; Assen: Van Gorcum, 2004), 48–63; on Jewish polemics with Christianity, see, e.g., Shlomo Na'eh, "Freedom and Celibacy: A Talmudic Variation on Tales of Temptation and Fall in Genesis and its Syrian Background," in *The Book of Genesis in Jewish and Oriental Christian Interpretation* (ed. J. Frishman and L. van Rompay; Leuven: Peeters, 1997), 73–89, and Peter Schäfer, *Jesus in the Talmud* (Princeton, NJ: Princeton University Press, 2007). On the construction of the Christian community in relation to the Jewish community, see Adam Becker, "Beyond the Spatial and Temporal Limes: Questioning the 'Parting of the Ways' Outside the Roman Empire," in *The Ways That Never Parted* (ed. A. Becker and A. Y. Reed; Tübingen: Mohr Siebeck, 2004), 373–92.

3   I could not find another version of this saying, though it resembles the Christian representations of Zoroastrian recitation studied in this chapter. A similar formulation not too far from the Bavli's world may be found in a Parthian Manichean fragment that describes the oral storyteller, the *gōsan*, as someone "who expatiates on the great deeds of

is murmuring" (*b. Soṭ.* 22a). This vague reference to "magus" (like similar Christian references) lumps together—perhaps deliberately—a host of priestly titles and functions that were part of the complicated religious administration of Sasanian Zoroastrianism.[4] Jonas Greenfield's study of the comparison between the magus and the *tanna* uses material studied by Marie-Louise Chaumont on one kind of Zoroastrian title, the *hērbed*.[5] The *hērbed* was in the Sasanian period the priest in charge of religious education and the transmission of religious literature; given the absence of written texts in Sasanian Zoroastrianism, this education and transmission were carried through oral recitation and memorization.[6]

The illustration of the Talmudic passage with the position of the *hērbed* is attractive, but I would like to suggest that we can shed better light on the Bavli and its view of the *tanna* by examining the distinction in some Pahlavi texts between the position of the *hērbed* and the position of the *hāwišt*. In many Pahlavi texts, the *hāwišt* appears simply as a disciple of the *hērbed:* the latter instructs the former with the knowledge of the Avesta and the Zand and supervises his spiritual progression; the two are said to be bound in a teacher-disciple bond that is sanctioned and protected by the God Mihr (or Mithra) himself.[7]

In other texts this distinction between two levels of education becomes a distinction between two groups of priests that can be quite hostile to

---

rulers and heroes, but doesn't do a thing himself." See P. Oktor Skjærvø, "Reflexes of Iranian Oral Traditions in Manichean Literature," in *Literarische Stoffe und ihre Gestaltung in mitteliranischer Zeit* (ed. D. Durkin-Meistererst et al.; Wiesbaden: Ludwig Reichert, 2009), 269–86 (278). But the *gōsan* is lacking in activity (*ud xwad ēwiž nē karēd*) while the magus and the *tanna* lack in understanding.

4 For surveys on Zoroastrian priests in the Sasanian period, see Philippe Gignoux, "Die Religiöse Administration in Sasanidischer Zeit: Ein Überblick," in *Kunst, Kultur und Geschichte der Achämenidzeit und Ihr Fortleben* (ed. H. Koch and D. N. Mackenzie; Berlin: Dietrich Reimer, 1983), 252–66 (and see ibid., 257, 262–63, and the appendix on *magu-sha* and other titles in Syriac literature); Philip G. Kreyenbroek, "The Zoroastrian Priesthood after the Fall of the Sasanian Empire," in *Transition Periods in Iranian History* (Louvain: Association pour l'avancement des Études Iraniennes, 1987), 151–66; Michael Morony, *Iraq After the Muslim Conquest* (Princeton, NJ: Princeton University Press, 1984), 281–86. For more on Zoroastrian priests in the Talmud, see Shai Secunda, "Parva—a Magus," in *Shoshannat Yaaqov: Jewish and Iranian Studies in Honor of Yaakov Elman* (ed. S. Secunda and S. Fine; Leiden: Brill, 2012), 391–402.

5 Marie-Louise Chaumont, "Recherches sur le clergé zoroastrien: Le hērbad," *Revue de l'histoire des religions,* 158 (1960), in two parts: 55–80, 161–79. Chaumont herself already connects this office and its duties with the Syriac references to "murmuring magi" (62); these references are discussed in the second section of this chapter.

6 Chaumont, "Recherches," 61ff.; Firoze M. Kotwal and Philip G. Kreyenbroek, *The Hērbedestān and Nērangestān* (4 vols.; Paris: Association pour l'avancement des Études Iraniennes, 1992–2009), 1.15–20.

7 See Chaumont, "Recherches," 64–68.

one another, and the translation of *hērbed* as "teacher" and of *hāwišt* as "disciple" is no longer appropriate.[8] Most of this kind of evidence comes from the *Dādestān ī Dēnīg* (or "religious decisions"; henceforth *DD*), a ninth-century book containing the responsa of the Zoroastrian priest Manuščhir.[9] This text, like most of the texts used for the reconstruction of Zoroastrianism in the Sasanian period, post-dates the Sasanian period by a few centuries, and indeed, the competition for work between the *hērbed* and *hāwišt* that it describes seems to be the result of the financial crisis of the Zoroastrian establishment after the demise of the Sasanian state.[10] Still, Manuščhir's insistence on this distinction and his description of its nature in detail, even as other texts from the Islamic period reflect the merging of these two functions, suggest that his description reflects the reality in the Sasanian period at least in part.[11] The passages concerning the priesthood in *DD* have been edited and translated by Philip Kreyenbroek, and the following discussion is based on his work.[12]

Manuščhir discusses the distinction between these two kinds of priests in his answer to questions from his community. One question, which by itself is already very instructive, concerns a dispute that arose during the celebratory *myazd* (or *mēzd*) dinner:[13]

The 46th question and answer is that which was asked: at a *myazd* dinner of the faithful, at which 50 or 100 men ... are present, and seven men who have worked in the field of religion share the *myazd* with them; of these seven men there are some who have five *nasks* and some who have six parts of the Avesta by heart and can celebrate it and they have not memorized the Zand of a single *fragard*; and all seven are disputing about precedence. And one who has thirty *fragards* with Zand by heart says, "Precedence must be mine, and my status must be considered to be higher, and must be so, for I know the Zand and the *šāyist-nē-šāyist* best. ..." And those seven men say to him, "Our status must be higher, for each of us can celebrate a number of

8 See Shaul Shaked, "Esoteric Trends in Zoroastrianism," *Proceedings of the Israel Academy of Sciences and Humanities* 3 (1969), 175–221 (205).

9 For a general introduction to *Dādestān ī Dēnīg*, see Mamoud Jaafari-Dehagi, *Dādestān ī Dēnīg: Part I: Transcription, Translation and Commentary* (Paris: Association pour l'avancement des Études Iraniennes, 1998), 23–28.

10 See Kreyenbroek, "Zoroastrian Priesthood," 157.

11 Kreyenbroek, "Zoroastrian Priesthood," 159.

12 [Philip] G. Kreyenbroek, "The *Dādestān ī Dēnīg* on Priests," *Indo-Iranian Journal* 30 (1987), 185–208.

13 On this feast, see Anders Hultgård, "Ritual Community Meals in Ancient Iranian Religion," in *Zoroastrian Rituals in Context* (ed. M. Stausberg; Leiden: Brill, 2004), 367–88 (377–80).

nasks as a *zōt* in his own right."... Please enlighten us as to the inferiority and superiority in this matter: whether they belong to those who have more Avesta by heart, or to the one who knows the Zand and *šāyist-nē-šāyist* best, as we have asked.... (DD 46)[14]

The question contrasts the group of seven, on the one hand, with another person on the other. While the titles *hērbed* and *hāwišt* are not mentioned here, they appear in another chapter that deals with a very similar situation (*DD* 65, discussed later in this section), and Kreyenbroek therefore supplies them here, associating the group of seven with the *hāwišts* and the person who disputes them with the *hērbeds*.

The way the questioners distinguish between the two parties is by their different kinds of knowledge. The seven *hāwišts* know a considerable part of the Avesta by heart (the work is divided into twenty-one *nasks*; they know five), and they have the knowledge of how to "celebrate" (i.e., ritually recite) them. We are told, however, that none of these seven people have memorized the Zand (the Middle Persian translation, interpretation, and discussion of the Avesta); they do not even know a single *fragard* (the large "sections" to which each book of the Zand was divided). The other person (the *hērbed*) is in the reverse situation: he knows thirty *fragards* of the Zand (which could be the Zand of five or six Avestan *nasks*) but he does not know the Avesta nor can he celebrate it. He also knows the *šāyist-nē-šāyist*, literally the "permitted/not-permitted," the corpus of instructions on ritual matters. In the dialogue between them, the group of seven boasts that they can lead the ritual ("celebrate as *zōt*"—*zōt* being the term for the priest leading the ritual in any given session).

In other words, the *hāwišts* know by heart the text to be recited in the ritual, the Avesta, and are able to lead the ritual themselves; the other person, the *hērbed*, knows the interpretation and discussion of that text, as well as the instructions on how to perform the ritual properly. Both sides claim to be superior and want "precedence"—which entails more financial support from the community (as we shall see in Manuščhir's answer); the community members writing Manuščhir are asking him which of these two claims they should accept.

Manuščhir first avoids the answer, saying that the details supplied about the knowledge of the parties are not precise enough for him to determine which is superior; he wants to know exactly which *fragards*, which *nasks*, before he can give an answer (it might be that the absence here of the use of the terms *hērbed* and *hāwišt* is connected with this imprecise knowledge). After a caveat he is willing to supply a rule of thumb:

14 Kreyenbroek, "*Dādestān ī Dēnīg*," 198.

When . . . the superiority and inferiority of their qualifications are not precisely known, then it seems more reasonable to keep the one who knows more of the Zand by heart, and has celebrated more, more liberally supplied with food. And it is appropriate for both of them to be considered worthy of large rewards. . . . Mastery of the Zand and that of the Avesta are mutual helpmates, for those who recite the Avesta also have need of information from the Zand about ritual directions and about what is allowed and not allowed (*šāyist-nē-šāyist*) in the ritual, and the one who is more active in the field of the Zand will profit when their performance of the ritual is made to proceed better. They are both one; those who have mastery of religious subjects are friends to each other and help and praise and aggrandize each other . . . and even when they are heard to say hostile thing about one another, it is because of indigence or because of the oppression by the Adversary, and it is reasonable to be forgiving to them, and not to reduce their shares, and to guide them towards uniting their strength, and towards agreement. (*DD* 46)[15]

Between knowledge of the Zand and knowledge of the Avesta, Manuščhir prefers the Zand; he also associates it with seniority (the person who knows the Zand also "celebrated more"). For the remainder of the answer, Manuščhir tries to disarm the conflict between the two groups: he insists that these two types of knowledge, and the people who have acquired them, should be seen as complementary. He does all but deny the reality of the competition that is evident in the question posed to him (he emphasizes that they are "friends to each other"), and writes that if there is in fact a conflict, it is the result of the hard economic times or the result of intervention by "the Adversary" (*petyārag*), a reference to Ahrimen, the divine origin of evil and enemy of all good. Manuščhir takes a similar conciliatory approach in another response:

Essentially the status of a *hērbed* and that of *hāwišt* are connected. The *hērbeds* teach and the *hāwišts* teach[16] the knowledge of the religion, which is the Avesta and Zand. The *hērbeds* have been *hāwišts* in that they have learned from their own *hērbed*; and the *hāwišt* who has learned knowledge will be a *hērbed* to his students; in one person, the status of *hērbed* and *hāwišt* are combined. (*DD* 40)

15 Kreyenbroek, "*Dādestān ī Dēnīg* ," 200.
16 Here following Shaked's translation ("Esoteric Trends," 204). Kreyenbroek translates: "the *hērbeds* teach (or learn) and the *hāwišts* learn." Manuščcihr applies the same verb, which means both to teach and to study, to both groups: "*hērbedān hammōzēnd ud hāwištān hammōzēnd*." It is true that since the names of the groups themselves mean "teacher" and "disciple" the verb may take different connotations when applied to each, but I think here it is the similarity rather than the difference between the two that is emphasized, perhaps taking advantage of the verb's ambiguity.

Manuščhir asserts here the traditional functions of the *hērbed* as teacher and the *hāwišt* as disciple; these terms, he explains, are really just relative indications of seniority. This image, however, is at odds with most other representations in *Dādestān ī Dēnīg* of these two groups as different kinds of specialists (even when there is a clear hierarchy between them); in fact, it is at odds with the remainder of the same response:

> The *hērbed* has knowledge of the Zand, the *hāwišt* of the Avesta; in particular they can be known, the *hērbed* by his mastery of the texts and ritual directions of the *Yasna* and *Vīspered*, and his mastery of the Zand, the *hāwišt* by the fact that they know… [17] the directions of the rituals and the rules of ritual cleanness and uncleanness and purity and pollution, and by their mastery of the Avesta. (*DD* 40)[18]

Here again the *hērbed* is presented as proficient in the Zand, as well as in the directions for the Avestan rituals of the *Yasna* (the Avestan miscellany recited during the Yasna ritual) and the *Vīspered* (a text supplementary to the former that contains mostly invocations). The *hāwišt* is said to be master of the Avesta and also in possession of other, less specific knowledge of ritual and matters of purity.

The most programmatic distinction Manuščhir makes between the *hāwišt* and the *hērbed* is that the former is "performing" while the latter is "calculating and supervising":

> The worthiness of rewards for the *hāwišt*, which he is said to derive from the fact that he himself is a performer, and the worthiness of the *hērbed*, which is said to derive from his activities in the field of the religion [the *dēn*, or Zoroastrian tradition], constitute proper worthiness of large rewards for both of them; thus it is more reasonable if the *hāwišt* is the performer, and the *hērbed* the one who directs and seek to achieve a proper performance… but the worthiness from work, and the gratitude which it brings, one of them acquires by performing the ritual, and the other by calculating and supervising and arranging a pleasing performance. (*DD* 65)[19]

The questions and answers in *DD* present a consistent image of the differences between *hērbed* and *hāwišt*, despite occasional efforts by Manuščhir to blur these differences: on the one hand, we have the *hērbed*, who pos-

17   The omission here is of two words: the second is an undeciphered word, transliterated by Kreyenbroek as ‹dlštkʾ›; the first is the word *pād*, a preposition that usually carries such meanings as "in" or "with"; its meaning here would be determined by the undeciphered word.
18   Kreyenbroek, "*Dādestān ī Dēnīg*," 201–2.
19   Kreyenbroek, "*Dādestān ī Dēnīg*," 197–98.

sesses thorough knowledge of a secondary, interpretive text (the Zand) as well the ability to distinguish the permitted from the prohibited (*šāyist-nē-šāyist*), to "calculate" and to "supervise" the ritual; on the other hand, we have the *hāwišt*, the performer who knows by heart the primary traditional oral text (the Avesta), who is able, in contrast with the *hērbed*, to recite it, and is the *hērbed*'s junior. The two functionaries compete for prestige and for financial support from their community.

The similarities of the distinction between *hērbed* and *hāwišt* to the distinction between the Talmudists and the reciters are very suggestive. In both cases, the distinction originated as a distinction between different stages of study and at some point became a distinction between types of religious functionaries; in both cases, one type is associated with performance and recitation while the other is associated with scholarship, interpretation, and legal decision; in both cases, the "reciting" type is associated with knowledge of large amounts of ancient traditions whereas the "scholarly" type is associated with the newer, interpretive, secondary body of knowledge; in both cases, the two types are to some extent in a state of competition or hostility; and in both cases, the texts that we have accord the second, "scholarly" type more prestige. To be sure, there are also significant differences. Most important, while the *hērbed* has command of more scholarly material, he also takes pride in having it memorized, just like the *hāwišt* takes pride in having the Avesta memorized (the same expression, *warm*, is used for both);[20] the Talmudic typology, in contrast, distinguishes between memorization and analysis.[21] But the similarities are greater than the differences.

Several scholars have compared the place of the Zand in the Zoroastrian tradition to that of the Targum in the Jewish tradition. This comparison is in many ways apt: the Zand translates and expands on a scriptural tradition in a more accessible language.[22] But there are characteristics of the Zand—such as its citations of attributed opinions, its use of multiple sets of glosses,[23] as well as the work's scholastic character—that make a comparison with the Talmud more productive. The material concerning the *hērbed* and *hāwišt* strengthens the comparison of the Zand with the Talmud: knowledge of the Zand here is seen as more advanced

---

20 See *DD* 45 (Kreyenbroek, "*Dādestān i Dēnīg* ," 198) and *DD* 65 (ibid., 195–96).

21 It is true that there were, at least in later stages, functionaries in the rabbinic academy entrusted with memorizing Talmudic material as opposed to Tannaitic material—the *garsa'ei* and the *benei siyyume*—but this is clearly not what is meant by *ba'ale talmud*. See n. 7 in the Conclusion for more discussion of these functionaries.

22 See Dan Shapira, "Studies in Zoroastrian Exegesis: Zand" (Ph.D. dissertation, Hebrew University of Jerusalem, 1998), xxxi–xxxii and the literature cited there.

23 Both conceded by Shapira, "Studies," xxxii, though he believes the comparison with the Targum is best notwithstanding these elements.

than knowledge of the Avesta, which is true of Talmud (as more advanced than knowledge of the Mishnah) and not true of Targum (which as far as I know is not considered more advanced knowledge than Scripture).

A final difference in the treatment of the two types in *DD* and in the Talmudic texts we have seen is that while Manušchir, a *hērbed* himself, certainly maintains the superiority of the *hērbed*, he is also full of praise for the *hāwišt*. The Talmudic texts studied in the previous chapter are hostile to the *tanna'im* and the *ba'ale mishnah* (though other texts in the Talmud are certainly favorable to them).

This difference comes to a sharp relief in a mention of the *hērbed* and *hāwišt* in the *Zand ī Wahman Yasn* (hereafter *ZWY*; also known in the earlier transliteration as *Bahman Yasht*), the famous Zoroastrian apocalyptic miscellany compiled sometime in the early Muslim period.[24] In chapter four of this work the creator God Ohrmazd tells Zoroaster of the bad omens and evil happenings that will characterize the end of the millennium; one of these involves our two groups of priests:

> Those known as *hērbed* and *hāwišt* will wish evil of one another and will say false things . . . and Ahrimen and the *dēw*s will have conveyed evil onto them more. And three out of five sins that men commit will be committed by priests and disciples and they will be enemies of the good ones. That is, they will tell bad and false things one of the other. And they will accept the religious rites but will not perform them, and they will not have fear of hell. (*ZWY*, 4:39–40) [25]

The description of the animosity between the two groups here bears a striking resemblance to the way Manušchir describes it. As we have seen earlier, in *DD* 46, he, too, says that if the two groups are hostile to one

24 On the late dating of the *Zand ī Wahman Yasn*, see Philippe Gignoux, "Sur l'inexistence d'un Bahman Yasht avestique," *JAAS* 32 (1986), 53–64, and idem, "L'apocalyptique iranienne est-elle vraiment la source d'autres apocalypses?" *Acta Antiqua Academiae Scientiarum Hungaricae* 31 (1988), 67–78. For a survey of the scholarship Gignoux criticizes as well as a summary of his critique, see Anders Hultgård, "Bahman Yasht: A Persian Apocalypse," in *Mysteries and Revelations: Apocalyptic Studies since the Uppsala Colloquium* (ed. J. J. Collins and J. H. Charlesworth; Sheffield: JSOT Press, 1991), 114–34 (115–20).

25 The translation here is essentially the one published in Carlo Cereti, *Zand ī Wahman Yasn: A Zoroastrian Apocalypse* (Rome: Instituto Italiano per il medio ed estremo oriente, 1995), 155–56. I modified slightly the first clause. Cereti's translation is "Those who will be known as priests and disciples." In light of the above (and see also Shaked's comment, cited above n. 8), I prefer to maintain the Pahlavi terms, which are here *hērbedih* and *hāwištih*—literally *hērbed*-hood and *hāwišt*-hood, the states of being *hērbed* or *hāwišt*. I also chose to change this clause to the present tense ("are known"), which is also Shaked's choice (see above n. 8), and still reflects the Pahlavi.

another it is because of Ahrimen; he, too, writes that they "say hostile things about one another." The last sentence in this passage from the ZWY says that they "accept" (padīrēnd) the religious rituals—that is, they will accept performing the rite and the compensation that comes with this performance; this is the same "accepting" and compensation for which the two groups vie in the disputes that are recounted in DD.[26] This passage then seems to refer to the same problems Manušchir encounters in the ninth century, even if it is not necessarily dependent on it.[27] It is a *vaticinium ex eventu* of the troubles of the Zoroastrian priesthood in the period after the Muslim conquest.[28]

This text provides a surprising perspective on the *derashah* on Isa. 66:5 attributed in Bavli *B. M.* to R. Yehuda and its parallel in *(Pseudo) Seder Eliyahu Zutta*.[29] In the *derashah*, the hostility of the "masters of tradition" to the sages (in the Bavli, these are implicitly the "masters of *talmud*") seems contemporary; the version in *(Pseudo) Seder Eliyahu Zutta* uses the present tense (*she-son'in*), and the context in the Talmud seems to posit the contemporary, inherent superiority of the Talmudists as the source of the hostility. But the verse from Isaiah is, of course, eschatological—the rift it describes between the "haters" and those who fear God's word comes to expression in the future, like the rift described in ZWY.

It is unlikely that there is any genealogical connection between the *derashah* and the Zoroastrian prophecy, which as we have seen reflects the conditions of Zoroastrians well after the Muslim conquest. The comparison between these texts does, however, underline the different ways in which Zoroastrian intellectuals and the creators of the Talmud negotiated a substantially similar distinction between religious functionaries: in the Talmud, the hostility between the two types is used to describe the superiority of one of them; in the Zoroastrian text, this hostility is one of the feared, unwanted evils described in an eschatological prophecy.

26 On this "accepting" or "accepter" (padīrftār), see Kreyenbroek, "*Dādestān ī Dēnīg*," 188.

27 This is complicated by the fact that this passage contains a gloss, though the two editors of the text, Cereti and Anklesaria, disagree about the scope of this gloss. Cereti, *Zand ī Wahman*, 138, marks the gloss from from kū until dārēnd, i.e., in the translation from "that is" until the end of the passage; Anklesaria marks the gloss only until gowēnd, so only the speaking of bad things will be considered in the gloss whereas the "accepting of rites" stays original. See Tehmuras Anklesaria, *Zand-î Vohûman Yasn and Two Pahlavi Fragments: With Text Transliteration and Translation in English* (Bombay, 1957), 110.

28 This prophecy appears in the same chapter as the passages used most to date ZWY to the Muslim period, the passages that predict that authority will be taken from the Byzantines (the hrōmāyīg) and the Zoroastrians ("those who wear the kustī") and will be given to non-Iranians (ZWY 4:49–59). On these passages see Cereti, *Zand ī Wahman*, 191–93 and the literature cited there.

29 See pp. 126–31 above.

The Talmud uses the general term "magus" in the comparison between the *tanna* and the Zoroastrian priest, and there is no sufficient reason to think that the rabbis were familiar with the distinction between *hērbed* and *hāwišt*. Still, the existence of the distinction, and the discourses about it in *DD* and *ZWY*, are significant for our analysis of the Talmud. Some scholars have seen the Talmudic statement as making a contrast between the Jewish intellectual approach to the text and the Zoroastrian ritual approach; even if this is what the Talmud attempts to do, the distinction between *hērbed* and *hāwišt* shows us that, rather than presenting culturally different approaches to tradition, the two traditions debated this issue in a similar way.[30] Since both Manušchir and the Talmud construct the distinction between the scholars and reciters from the scholars' point of view, we may see these texts as an indication that recitation had a prominent and contested place in the religious life of late ancient Mesopotamia. The Christian representation of Zoroastrian recitation further illuminates both of these points.

"DO NOT DO AS THE MAGI DO"

Jonas Greenfield has shown that the Bavli's mocking representation of Zoroastrian recitation as mindless "murmuring" was common to other traditions in Mesopotamia, especially the Syriac Christian literary tradition, which also describes this recitation as murmuring (compare the *retna* in the Syriac to the *raten* in the Bavli).[31]

---

30 To be sure, distinctions and tensions between "creators" and "performers" and even between "scholars" and "reciters" are found beyond the Bavli and the Zoroastrian world. In classical Greece, the rhapsodes, or performers of poems, were the target of contempt by intellectuals such as Plato and Xenophon (see the discussion in Barbara Graziosi, *Inventing Homer: The Early Reception of Epic* [Cambridge: Cambridge University Press, 2002], 21–40). In discussions of Vedic recitation, which like the Zoroastrian one was ritual in nature, a similar tension arises—see Yaska's critique against the person who is "only able to recite the Veda but does not understand its meaning" (quoted in Radhakumud Mookerji, *Ancient Indian Education, Brahamical and Buddhist* [London: Macmillan, 1947], 239), deployed in the context of his defense of the Veda's meaningfulness. The same negative perception of recitation might be behind the famous frog-hymn, for which, see Wendy Doniger, *The Rig Veda: An Anthology* (Harmondsworth: Penguin, 1981), 232–35. The discourse on Vedic recitation is particularly important because of its connection with Avestan recitation. But it is the Zoroastrian distinction that is most important for our purposes—not just because of its specific affinities to the Talmudic distinction or its temporal and geographical proximity, but most importantly because it is the Talmud that makes the connection between the *tanna* and the Zoroastrian reciter.

31 Jonas C. Greenfield, "רטין מגושא" (Eng.), in *Joshua Finkel Festschrift* (ed. S. B. Hoenig and L. D. Stitskin; New York: Yeshiva University Press, 1974), 63–69.

In this section, I argue that Jewish and Christian authors used this representation of Zoroastrian recitation to mark certain reciting practices that were common among their audiences as foreign practices. In doing so, they not only imposed a boundary between Zoroastrian practice, on the one hand, and Jewish or Christian practice on the other; they also drew this boundary in a way that served their particular vision of Judaism and Christianity.

Previous scholarship on the representation of Zoroastrian recitation in Jewish and Christian sources assumes the communal boundaries that these sources are trying to create and the veracity of the worldview for which they argue. Greenfield writes that the sound of the Zoroastrian ritual seemed "strange" to Jewish and Christian authors, who as "outsiders" could not understand it and therefore termed it "murmuring."[32] But doesn't this presuppose too much of a cultural difference between groups that shared living spaces, economies, images, and ideas? How "strange" could a central ritual in Zoroastrianism seem to those who spent their entire lives with Zoroastrians, who borrowed technical legal ideas from Zoroastrians, and who disputed religious theologies with Zoroastrians? It is more likely that these polemical statements create difference just as much as they reflect it.[33] Greenfield and other scholars further argue that the Bavli's equation of the *tanna* with the magus is an apt comparison that observes the exclusive emphasis on memorization, as opposed to understanding, shared by these two religious functionaries.[34]

But Rav Nahman's comparison, at least as it is deployed in the Bavli, is not an innocent, cross-cultural observation. It is cited by the Bavli in a polemical passage that seeks to promote one form of Jewish religiosity (the study of *talmud*) over another (the recitation of *mishnah*). It leads up to a conclusion in which we learn that the *tanna'im* are the "destroyers of the world." This comparison uses the "mindlessness" of the magi—already a polemical construction in itself—both to create a difference between Jews and Zoroastrians and to claim Jewish identity for one form of Jewish engagement with the text. By associating the recitation of the

---

32 Greenfield, "רטין מגושא" (Eng.), 67; the sentence there refers only to Christians, but since it comes to explain the use of the word "murmuring," which also appears in the Talmud, it must be applicable to Jews as well.

33 See the methodological discussion of studying inter-religious discourse in Mesopotamia in De Jong, "Religious Polemics," 48–41.

34 See, e.g., Isaiah Gafni, *Babylonian Jewry and Its Institutions in the Period of the Talmud* (Heb.; Jerusalem: Historical Society of Israel; Zalman Shazar Centre, 1975), 112 n. 4; Neil Danzig, "From Oral Talmud to Written Talmud: On the Methods of Transmission of the Babylonian Talmud and its Study in the Middle Ages," *Bar Ilan* 30–31 (2006), 49–112 (85); Greenfield, "רטין מגושא" (Eng.), 69.

tanna'im with the mindless magi, it does more than mock these *tanna'im*; it implies that their practices are too Zoroastrian, too "foreign."[35]

I think a similar move may be observed in one of the Christian texts that mention the "murmuring magi." The seventh-century *Life of Isho'sabran*, composed by Isho'yahb III (later *catholicos*), tells of a person by that name who converted to Christianity from Zoroastrianism and was martyred under Khusrau II in 621.[36] At some point after his conversion, Isho'sabran decides it is high time he learned to read the Bible. He adopts a boy from the Christian community of a certain village to teach him. He asks the boy how to begin such study:

> The boy told him: "A person first studies the alphabet, then its pronuncia-tion, and after that he repeats [*tane*] the Psalms. Bit by bit he reads [*qare*] from all of the Scriptures. When he is trained in the reading of the Scrip-tures, then he proceeds to their interpretations."

The process of learning described here by the Christian boy bears similar-ity to the one we encountered in the Talmud—both in its components and, thanks to the shared language, in its terminology. It includes read-ing and reciting (here with the same roots as the Jewish Aramaic terms we encountered earlier: *t.n.'* and *q.r.'*), and both of these lead to "interpre-tation" (*pushaka*). To be sure, unlike the different activities in the rab-binic process, all these activities are part of scriptural study: the reciting is of Scripture, not of a separate body of tradition, and the interpretation

35   This phenomenon, in which something Jewish is connected with a negative por-trayal of something Zoroastrian in order to criticize the former, was observed in another text, *b. B. B.* 133b, by Yaakov Elman, "The Babylonian Yeshivot in the Amoraic and post-Amoraic Era" (Heb.), in *Yeshivot and Battei Midrash* (Heb.; ed. I. Etkes; Jerusalem: Zalman Shazar Center; Ben Zion Dinur Center, 2006), 31–55 (40–42 and 52–55). And while it is the *stam* there that makes the critique explicit, it is our Rav Nahman that makes the con-nection between the Mishnaic law and the Zoroastrian law to begin with! There is a cer-tain tension in Elman's explanation of Rav Nahman's intention: on the one hand, he seems to imply that being "acculturated" to Persian culture, Rav Nahman was "aware of the shortcomings" of the Persian court, and that explains his criticism; on the other hand, Elman sees in the reference a polemical maneuver designed both to critique a Jewish in-stitution and to keep Jews away from turning to Persian legal authorities. The latter ex-planation fits perfectly what we see in the Talmud in our case, and while it is possible that this polemical strategy observed in both *sugyot* really originated from the "Persian-ized" rabbi himself, it is also possible that he is used by the Talmud as a literary character particularly appropriate for this purpose.

36   The text was published with an introduction and a French summary by Jean-Baptiste Chabot, "Histoire de Jésus-Sabran: écrite par Jésus-yab d'adiabène," *Nouvelles archives des missions scientifiques et littéraires* 7 (1897), 485–584. On the author, see the helpful discussion in Wilhelm Baum and Dietmar Winkler, *The Church of the East: A Con-cise History* (London: Routledge, 2003), 642–45.

is scriptural exegesis, not a dialectical study of *halakhah*. Still, the fact that the process described here parallels the stages of education in Syrian schools,[37] the fact that the rabbinic tripartite division is also expressed in a division of the curriculum into three successive stages, and the fact that both divisions bear a structural similarity to the system presented by Greco-Roman schools[38] suggest that we see here different inflections of common schooling practices. The particular inflection in this passage, as Adam Becker pointed out, describes a process of learning typical of East-Syrian "scholastic" culture.[39]

Back in our story, the saint has no time for this long learning process:

> The saint told the boy: "But in the time I am not learning the letters, I could have ten Psalms memorized!"[40] He said so because he was used to receiving orally the murmuring of magianism [*retna demagushuta*], for the miserable learning of Zaradusht is not written in the letters of language. He convinced the boy . . . and when he [Isho'sabran] received the verses, he was making an industrious performance, moving his neck back and forth, as the magi do. The boy then stopped him and said, "Do not do as the magi do; rather, when you are at peace, speak only with your mouth." And like that, in little time, he chanted many verses.

Isho'sabran points out that recitation could be a more effective way of learning the Psalms, and Isho'yahb explains to us that this shocking position, so much at odds with the textual mode of learning described by the boy in the passage quoted above, is the result of the convert's Zoroastrian upbringing, in which oral recitation was the exclusive mode of study. The saint's Zoroastrian background comes to the foreground when the boy recites the Psalms and Isho'sabran begins a Zoroastrian ritual recitation with all its performative aspects. The Christian boy does not appreciate this Zoroastrified Bible reading, stopping the future saint from "doing as the magi do"; he teaches him the proper, Christian way to chant.

This text presents a certain form of ritualized recitation as foreign to Christianity; while at the end it is replaced by another form of ritualized recitation, this form is not only less physically elaborate, but is also placed in the context of the scholastic, intellectual learning process de-

37 For which, see Adam Becker, *Fear of God and the Beginning of Wisdom* (Philadelphia: University of Pennsylvania Press, 2004), 87–89.

38 See n. 7 in the previous chapter.

39 Becker, *Fear*, 206.

40 Greenfield ("רטין מגושא" (Eng.), 69) translates the verb here, ܐܠܐ, as an imperative: "by the time I get to learning the letters, recite for me ten psalms"; but the form of the verb is not imperative, and it seems preferable to take "psalms" here as the subject of the verb. I thank Joseph Witztum for this correction.

scribed at the beginning of the passage, with which Isho'sabran's performance is clearly put in contrast. Becker compares the saint's conduct here
to that of someone who converts to Christianity from Islam and then
prostrates himself when receiving the Eucharist.[41] Given the Talmud's
use of the murmuring magus in a polemic within the Jewish community,
it is possible that this scene is not only about a boy teaching a Zoroastrian
how to be a Christian, but also about Isho'yahb teaching his Christian
readers what practices are not acceptable in Christianity.

More specifically, I would like to suggest that Isho'yahb's criticism and
dehabilitation of Zoroastrian recitation are also directed against certain
Christian monastic practices. Becker dedicates a chapter in his study of
the East-Syrian school movement to the tensions between that movement
and other parties in East-Syrian monasticism.[42] In fact, one of the stories
with which Becker illustrates this tension concerns our own Isho'yahb,
who came into conflict with a group of monks over his decision, in his
capacity as *catholicos*, to build a school adjacent to their monastery.[43]
This anecdote raises the possibility that the same tension is reflected in
Isho'yahb's description of Isho'sabran's recitation.

The ritualized recitation of Scripture and particularly of the Psalms
was central to monastic life, both in Egyptian monasticism and in the
East.[44] The *Second Part* of the *Ascetic Homilies* of Isaac, the seventh-
century bishop of Nineveh, may be used here to illustrate the negotiation
of recitation in East-Syrian monasticism. Isaac's model of spiritual progress will be familiar to us: it begins with "laboring with a great deal of
recitation [*tenya*]", then "laboring in the reading of Scripture [*qeryana*],"
and then "laboring in meditation [*herga*]" (*Second Part* 22:1–3).[45] Again,
the basic activities, reading and repetitive recitation, are complemented
by an activity specific to a particular tradition—rabbinic *talmud*, scholastic *pushaka*, and monastic *herga*. But in Isaac's writing, recitation is
clearly not just a tool for an intellectual understanding of Scripture, as it
is in the *Life of Isho'sabran*. Not only does Isaac emphasize that the stages

41   Becker, *Fear*, 206.
42   Becker, *Fear*, 169–97.
43   Becker, *Fear*, 169–71.
44   On recitation in Egyptian monasticism, and the tensions surrounding it, see
Douglas Burton-Christie, *The Word in the Desert: Scripture and the Quest for Holiness in
Early Christian Monasticisms* (Oxford: Oxford University Press, 1993), 117–28. This practice figures prominently in Evagrius of Pontus—see Robert E. Sinkewicz, *Evagrius of Pontus: The Greek Ascetic Corpus: Translation, Introduction, and Commentary* (Oxford: Oxford
University Press, 2003), xxxii–xxxiv—which is particularly important since Evagrius's
writings, translated into Syriac, played "a major role in the monastic spirituality of the
Church of the East" (Becker, *Fear*, 175).
45   Translation and text are cited according to Sebastian Brock, *Isaac of Nineveh:
"The Second Part," Chapters IV–XLI* (2 vols.; Louvain: Peeters, 1995).

above do not replace one another (22:4); he numbers recitation with prayer, fasting, and reflection as one of the measures that pleases God and allows one to grow in wisdom (10:6), and he describes a monastic life focused on recitation as one equal to one focused on reading or prayer (30:4–5).

The monastic recitation itself was so physically and spiritually tasking that Isaac addresses in one of the chapters the possibility that "you have grown feeble and already become weary as a result of the labor of Psalmody, which takes the form of the assiduous recitation that is customary"[46] (21:1). If in this passage Isaac might be distancing himself somewhat from the form of recitation that is "customary," in another place he explicitly disapproves of the recitation practices of some in his environment, when he criticizes "those who read just for the sake of recitation"[47] (29:10), not for the sake of truth.

The image of *Christian* recitation in these two passages—"assiduous," physically tasking, and an end to itself in the eyes of some—is similar to the image of Zoroastrian recitation we have seen in other texts. Isho'yahb tells us that Isho'sabran performed his recitation "vigorously" or "assiduously"; the popular saying cited by the Talmud implies that the magi recited for recitation's sake, as opposed to understanding what is recited. The story about the convert and the boy, then, may be mocking Zoroastrian practice in order to make a point about a Christian practice in a divisive conversation within East-Syrian Christianity on the character of monastic life. It exhorts its readers: "Do not do as the magi do!"

CONCLUSION

The recitation of texts played a prominent role in pedagogical, literary, and ritual contexts in many ancient cultures, including the ancient Near Eastern and Greco-Roman cultures from which Judaism and Christianity developed.[48] It served important functions in the Palestinian rabbinic movement and in Egyptian monastic culture, both of which were foundational for the Mesopotamian culture studied in this chapter. But recitation assumed a special importance in Sasanian Zoroastrianism: in the absence of a written Avesta, it was the exclusive interface between Zoroastrians and their sacred texts;[49] the fact that these texts were trans-

---

46 ܟܠܗ ܕܡܙܡܘܪ̈ܐ ܕܗܘ ܕܘܒܪܐ ܕܗܘ ܕܝܠܢ.

47 ܗܢ. ܕܩܪܝܢ ܡܛܠ ܕܬܫܥܝܬܐ ܒܠܚܘܕ.

48 See David M. Carr, *Writing on the Tablet of the Heart* (Oxford: Oxford University Press, 2005), 71–73 on Egypt, 93–107 on Greece, and 134–39 on the biblical book of Deuteronomy.

49 On the absence of Avestan text and the process by which it eventually came into

mitted in a language that the majority of Zoroastrians did not understand at all and of which a select few had a limited command[50] meant that the memorization and recitation of these texts could assume a particular ritualistic character divorced from other, more scholastic forms of textual engagement; only in Zoroastrianism, recitation stood at the very center of the ritual and became the subject of extended, technical discussions regulating its details.[51]

If there were Sasanian Jewish "masters of tradition" or reciters who found in the memorization and recitation of oral traditions the ultimate expression of their Judaism; if there were Sasanian Christian monks who read "just for the sake of recitation" that took the form of an intensive bodily performance, as we hear from Isaac of Nineveh—then these Sasanian Jews and Christians simply approached religion and religious textuality like the practitioners of the state religion of the empire in which they lived. If we can speak of a particularly Sasanian structure of religion that crosses the boundaries imposed by the political and religious elites of these different traditions, recitation was one of its characteristics. It is against this background that we should see the polemical references to Zoroastrian recitation by the two "scholastic" movements, the Talmudic academies and the East-Syrian schools;[52] in these references we see these movements' efforts to define the boundaries of their respective communities and to fortify their claims to be the best representative of their respective traditions, Judaism and Christianity.

---

writing, see the classic discussion by Harold W. Bailey, *Zoroastrian Problems in the Ninth-Century Books* [2nd ed.] (Oxford: Oxford University Press, 1971), especially 149–76. See also Shaul Shaked, *Dualism in Transformation: Varieties of Religion in Sasanian Iran* (London: School of Oriental and African Studies, 1994), 99–119.

50   See Kotwal and Kreyenbroek, *Hērbedestān*, 1.19.

51   See Shaul Shaked, "The Yasna Ritual in Pahlavi Literature," in *Zoroastrian Rituals in Context* (ed. M. Stausberg; Leiden: Brill, 2004), 333–44. See also the three volumes of the translation of the *Nērangestān*, which is mostly dedicated to recitation details; Kotwal and Kreyenbroek, *Hērbedestān*, volumes 2–4, and especially the Introduction to the first volume, 2.13–19.

52   For an application of this term to the study of both developments, see Adam Becker, "The Comparative Study of 'Scholasticism' in Late Antique Mesopotamia: Rabbis and East Syrians," *AJS Review* 34.1 (2010), 91–113.

WORD OF THE WEEK
The Subject: God ordains certain men to hell on purpose

Isaiah 64:8 - 0 Lord, thou art our Father; we are the clay; and thou our potter; and we all are the work of thy hand.

> *work - Hebrew: Maaseh · an action (good or bad); product; transaction; business*

Romans 9:20-23 - Who art thou that repliest against God? Shall the thing formed say to him that formed it, why hast thou made me thus? Hath not the potter the power over the clay of the same lump, to make one vessel unto honour and another unto dishonour - What if God willing to show his wrath, and to make his power known, endured with much long suffering the vessels of wrath fitted to destruction: And that he might make known the riches of his glory on the vessels of mercy, which he hath afore prepared unto glory.

> *fitted - Greek: katartizo · to complete thoroughly; fit; frame; arrange; prepare. Thayer says this word speaks of men whose souls God has so constituted that they cannot escape destruction; their mind is fixed that they frame themselves.*

Men get angry to think that we serve a God that can do as it pleases him. They actually think that almighty God thinks the way they think and that he could not possibly form-fit a vessel to hell merely to show his wrath and power. Paul said he does. Men have difficulty perceiving a God that predestinates men (Rom. 8:29) on whom he desires to show his grace (unmerited favor) and mercy, that he may shower them throughout eternity with the riches of his glory. We like to believe that we must give him permission if he is to operate in our hearts and minds. The Lord said, "My thoughts are not your thoughts, neither are your ways my ways. As the heavens are higher than the earth, so are my ways higher than your ways and my thoughts than your thoughts (Isaiah 55:8,9)". Our God is in the heavens: he hath done whatsoever he hath pleased (Psalms 115:3). He doeth whatsoever pleaseth him (Eccl 8:3). Thou, 0 Lord, hast done as it pleased thee (Jonah 1:14). Whatsoever the Lord pleased, that did he in heaven, and earth, and in the seas, and in all deep places (Psalms 135:6). He does all his pleasure (Isa. 46:10; Isa. 44:24-28; Eph. 1:5,9; Philippians 2:13). It is Jesus that holds the keys to death and hell (Rev. 1:18), not Satan. God will intentionally cast these evil vessels of wrath into hell and lock them up for eternity because it is not his pleasure to draw them to him (John 6:44). This doctrine angers men, though it is taught throughout the pages of God's Holy Book. Men do not have a Biblical view of the living God when they think he is not in control of all things including the minds and hearts of all men. God is not only love to the vessels of mercy, but he is a consuming fire (Deut. 4:24) upon the vessels of wrath fitted to destruction. We do not serve a God who is Superman that can only shake mountains, implode blackholes, and explode quasars. The God of the universe can harden and soften the hearts of men at will (Rom. 9:18; Ezek. 36:26). He giveth not account of any of his matters (Job 33:13).

GRACE AND TRUTH MINISTRIES
P.O. Box 1109, Hendersonville, TN 37077
Jim Brown - Bible Teacher · Local: (615) 824-8502 | Toll Free: (800) 625-5409
https://www.graceandtruth.net/

Chapter Six

TRADITION AND VISION

The Talmudic position on Torah study, this book has argued, was part of a debate about the transmission of tradition and its place in Jewish intellectual life. This chapter suggests that Hekhalot literature provides us with the other side of the debate: that the *Sar ha-Torah* narrative from this corpus responds to the Talmudic academies' ideology of Torah study, presenting an alternative vision for Jewish culture in which retention and recitation are central rather than marginalized; that this response correlates with other Hekhalot texts that recruit powerful images such as heavenly vision, transformation, and angelic liturgy to the project of memorizing and reciting the Oral Torah; and that there is some evidence that the individuals whom the Bavli marks as its opponents—the *tanna'im*—had a role in the shaping of Hekhalot traditions.

Hekhalot literature is a diverse corpus of Jewish magical and mystical traditions arranged into a group of more-or-less redacted texts.[1] The historical context of these texts is still the subject of scholarly debate.[2] The texts themselves generally attribute the traditions they transmit to the great rabbinic sages of the Tannaitic period. Gershom Scholem located the development of the corpus in early rabbinic Palestine, seeing in this literature the "esoteric" core of rabbinic culture, hidden by the silence of the "exoteric" rabbinic canon.[3] An increasing number of scholars have

---

1   On the problem of redaction and tradition in Hekhalot literature, see Peter Schäfer, *Hekhalot-Studien* (Tübingen: Mohr Siebeck, 1988), 8–16; on the interaction of the magical and the mystical, see ibid., 277–95.

2   For a useful summary of the debates, see Michael Swartz, *Scholastic Magic: Ritual and Revelation in Ancient Judaism* (Princeton, NJ: Princeton University Press, 1996), 9–13.

3   See, e.g., Gershom Scholem, *Major Trends in Jewish Mysticism* [2nd ed.] (New York: Schocken, 1946; repr. 1995), 41–43. This view was designed as a critique of nineteenth-century historiography that was motivated to push the dating of these texts late into the Muslim period to save the "rational" character of classical rabbinic literature. On this move in the context of Scholem's general historiographical approach, see David Biale,

moved away from this view, dating formative stages of the corpus's literary development to the late Talmudic and Geonic periods, suggesting Babylonia rather than Palestine as the tradition's provenance, and positing a more complicated relationship between this corpus and classical rabbinic literature.[4]

This chapter contributes to this effort to fix the provenance of Hekhalot texts. It not only argues that some of these texts engage Babylonian Talmudic culture, but also connects this engagement to a particular fact of the transmission of this corpus. One of the earliest and most famous references to Hekhalot texts ties them to the *tanna'im*—not the sages of the Tannaitic period to whom the texts are attributed, but rather to those reciters of traditions we have seen as the target of the Bavli. In a discussion of the vision of the heavenly palace, the tenth-century Ga'on Rav Hayya tells his correspondents that "there are two *mishnayot* which the *tanna'im* recite on this matter, and they are called *Hekhalot Rabbati* and *Hekhalot Zutarti*."[5] This chapter argues that these *tanna'im* did not merely transmit this corpus, as Rav Hayya indicates, but actively shaped it, and that this fact may account for the centrality of memorization and recitation in Hekhalot traditions and perhaps for their critical engagement with Talmudic culture.

The argument here is not, of course, that all the Hekhalot traditions mentioned in this chapter (let alone the entire corpus) were composed by Babylonian reciters or that they were informed by a debate with Tal-

---

Gershom Scholem: Kabbalah and Counter History (Cambridge, MA: Harvard University Press, 1982), 52–56.

4   Ephraim E. Urbach, "The Traditions on Merkavah Mysticism in the Tannaitic Period" (Heb.), in *Studies in Mysticism and Religion* (ed. E. E. Urbach, R. J. Weblowsky, and Ch. Wirszubski; Jerusalem: Magnes, 1967), 1–28; Peter Schäfer, *The Origins of Jewish Mysticism* (Tübingen: Mohr Siebeck, 2009), 330, 343–48; Swartz, *Scholastic Magic*, 212–13; Ra'anan S. Boustan, *From Martyr to Mystic: Rabbinic Martyrology and the Making of Merkavah Mysticism* (Tübingen: Mohr Siebeck, 2005), 277–78 and especially 281–88; idem, "The Emergence of Pseudonymous Attribution in Heikhalot Literature: Empirical Evidence from Jewish 'Magical' Corpora," *JSQ* 14 (2007), 18–38.

5   Benjamin M. Lewin, *Otzar ha-Geonim: Volume IV: Tractate Jom-Tow, Chagiga and Maschkin* (Heb.; Jerusalem: Hebrew University Press Association, 1931), Hag. resp. §20 p. 14. James Davila, *Descenders to the Chariot: The People behind the Hekhalot Literature* (Leiden: Brill, 2001), 5, understands *tanna'im* here as the sages of the Tannaitic period, but I think it more likely (perhaps even from the tense of the verb, שֹׁנִין, if not only from the way this word is used in Geonic literature) that it refers to reciters contemporary with R. Hayya. See also Lewin, *Otzar*, Hag., p. 14 n. 6, and the articles by Emanuel and Danzig noted in the last section of this chapter. It seems very unlikely to me that R. Hayya would simply invent the connection between the reciters and Hekhalot compositions—but he might have emphasized this connection in order to distance himself and the rabbis from these compositions or even to imply that the *tanna'im* have tampered with these traditions (see below, n. 90).

mudic values. The diversity of our texts suggests different intentions and agendas, and therefore also different places and different times. But this chapter also aims to go further than placing the production of this or that element of the corpus in a particular context. Rather, by focusing on transmission rather than composition, it explores how central themes or aspects of this corpus as a whole—such as vision, transformation, and esotericism—could be understood in a given moment of its transmission, even if these themes or aspects themselves did not originate in that moment.

THE *SAR HA-TORAH* NARRATIVE

The narrative of *Sar ha-Torah*, transmitted in *Hekhalot Rabbati* §§281–98,[6] recounts the heavenly and earthly events that led to the revelation of the name of Sar ha-Torah (Prince of Torah), known from other texts as the angel whose adjuration allows perfect memorization of study material without effort.[7] Our text certainly had, in some form, a life independent of the compilation in which it was transmitted in the medieval manuscript tradition.[8] A possible indicator of the period in which this piece was written is God's promise in §291 that "town judges will be elected on your authority," which might invoke the term *reshut* in its Geonic-period sense of jurisdictional unit.[9] Since a version of the narrative's poetic part is quoted in ben Yeruhim's *Wars*, that part at least has a definite tenth-century *terminus ante quem*.[10] This section suggests that the text critically engages the Talmudic academies in Babylonia. This criticism lacks any particular claim to Palestinian superiority, and while there is nothing in

6 All references to Hekhalot texts in this chapter are according to Peter Schäfer (ed.), *Synopse zur Hekhalot-Literatur* (Tübingen: Mohr Siebeck, 1981).

7 Swartz, *Scholastic Magic*, is a comprehensive study of texts relating to Sar ha-Torah; he offers a translation and analysis of the narrative discussed here on pp. 92–108. On the magical practice itself in the context of similar practices and phenomena, see Yuval Harari, "La'asot petihat lev: praqitqot magiyot li-yedi'ah, le-havanah u-lezkhirah bi-yehadut ha-'et ha-'atiqa uvi-yemei ha-beinayim," in *Shefa Tal: Studies in Jewish Thought and Culture* (Bracha Zack Festschrift; ed. Z. Greis et al.; Beer Sheva: Ben Gurion University of the Negev Press, 2004), 303–47.

8 See the analysis of manuscript evidence in Schäfer, *Hekhalot-Studien*, 212–13.

9 See Urbach, "Traditions," 24 and n. 111; on *reshuyot* in the Geonic period, see Robert Brody, *The Geonim of Babylonia and the Shaping of Medieval Jewish Culture* (New Haven: Yale University Press, 1998), 39, 58–59, and 123–26. David Halperin, *Faces of the Chariot: Early Jewish Responses to Ezekiel's Vision* (Tübingen: Mohr Siebeck, 1988), 436, writes that if "we could take §291's allusion to patriarchs (*nesi'im*) at face value, it would guarantee a date before 425 A.D.," but that is unlikely.

10 Peter Schäfer (ed.), *Übersetzung der Hekhalot-Literatur* (Tübingen: Mohr Siebeck, 1987–91), 2.xxi.

the text that allows us to determine whether it was written in Palestine or Babylonia, this lack makes this question secondary: the text itself is interested in criticizing Babylonia, not in praising Palestine.

The action of the narrative is set immediately after the return from the Babylonian exile at the time of Zerubbabel. Israel is in Jerusalem and the people are preoccupied with the reconstruction of the Temple. They complain to God that the effort and time required by the construction work prevent them from fulfilling their other obligation, the study of Torah. God is open to their argument; he regrets punishing Israel so severely by sending them into exile. His solution is "the secret of the Torah," a magic ritual that enables the memorization and study of Torah with no effort or expenditure of time, enabling Israel to continue building the Temple while still ensuring that this progress will not cause Torah to cease from their mouths. The angels object, pleading with God not to make human beings like angels and arguing that God's glory is affirmed when they forget their study material and study it again. God, however, decides to stick with his plan, reasoning that there is no better gift he can give Israel after all their suffering.

In the second part of the narrative, the focus returns to earth. The people are on strike from building until they succeed in compelling God and his angels to give them the magical secret of the Sar ha-Torah. In a remarkable scene, God's *shekhinah* descends to the Temple and the people witness the throne of God. The people prostrate themselves in fear but God invites them rather to sit with him. The plot ends when Zerubbabel stands up and lists before the people the divine names needed to adjure the Prince of Torah.

The conflict between building the Temple and studying the Torah, which sets the entire narrative in motion, is also the key to understanding the purpose of the text. This conflict is artificial—it is set up as a permanent problem requiring a permanent solution, but even in the logic of the narrative the problem is only a temporary one: there will be no conflict once the Temple is built. The move our text makes in constructing this conflict is similar to that of other rabbinic texts that set Torah study against other activities to make a point about cultural priorities. One such text resembles ours both in historical setting and in the conflict it presents:

> Said Rav, or say, Rav Shmuel b. Martha, "Torah study is greater than the building of the Temple: as long as Baruch ben Nerya was alive, Ezra did not leave him to come up [to Palestine]." (*b. Meg.* 16b)

The aim of teachings of this sort is to present a hierarchy of duties and pursuits, a sorting of agendas. That is also the concern of our narrative. Like Rav in the Talmud, our author chooses a very apt historical setting, in many respects the beginning of both Temple and the study of Torah, to set two of the most important activities associated with Israel's commitment to the covenant—Temple sacrifice and Torah study—against each other and to ask, "which shall we embrace and which we shall we abandon?" (§280). This central question has been overlooked by most commentators on this text; using it as the point of departure in our inquiry will allow us to illuminate the ambitious purpose of our text, to present an alternative to the vision of Judaism associated with the Babylonian academies.

God's answer to Israel's plight reverses the traditional division between Israel and God as we know it from rabbinic literature. Traditionally, Israel studies the Torah and God miraculously builds the Temple in the Messianic era. In the *Sar ha-Torah* narrative, God plans the reverse: "You busy yourselves with the House of my choice, but Torah will not leave your mouth" (§284). Torah does not leave Israel's mouth, but that is the result of the adjuration of the Prince of Torah, the result of God's action; Israel, on their part, "busy themselves" with the Temple.

The angels' protest, which we cannot discuss here in detail, points precisely to the radical implication of God's solution: this solution subordinates Torah study to the knowledge of Torah, doing away with the culture and life that surround the intensive activity of acquiring that knowledge. The miraculization of the building of the Temple served a culture for which it was first impossible, and later, inconceivable or even undesirable, to rebuild the Temple. It then allowed for a preservation of the Temple's centrality in rabbinic ideology while pushing it far away from the daily life of rabbinic culture. Our text, by proposing a miraculization of Torah study, seems to suggest doing with the Torah what the Torah did with the Temple, namely, leaving it for God.

But what is the reason for this move? What is wrong with Torah study? Our text reveals its specific target in the second part of God's speech to Israel. Ephraim E. Urbach and Joseph Dan have offered opposite interpretations of this passage. Urbach suggested that it is an ironic rehearsal of the values of the "men of Halakhah" and a critique of "their material goals and social achievements."[11] Dan finds no irony in God's words; he argues that the passage presents classical rabbinic desires as legitimate, and if there is any distance expressed in it, this is because the author is describing enviously a world in which he would like to take part but in reality does not.[12] Both positions are correct and both positions miss something. These passages include *two* lists: the first (on the left side) is a parody of rabbinic ambition, in which God describes what Israel *wants*; the second (on the right) is a list in which God describes what Israel *gets*.

---

11 Urbach, "Traditions," 23–24.

12 Joseph Dan, "The Theophany of the Prince of the Torah" (Heb.), *Jerusalem Studies in Jewish Folklore* 13–14 (1992), 127–58 (139–41). Swartz, *Scholastic Magic*, 221–22, and Halperin, *Faces*, 464–66, seem to understand this passage in a way similar to Dan.

§ 287

I know what you are asking for, and my
heart recognizes what you are longing for.
Much Torah is what you are asking for,
and vast talmud,
and numerous traditions
to inquire after the laws
is what you are looking forward to.
You desire much *ribbui*,
to mount up mountains and mountains of
testimony,
to pile up hills and hills of difficult
wisdom,
to increase talmud in the squares
and pilpul in the streets,
to multiply halakhot like the sand of the
sea,
and rabbis like the dusts of the world,

§ 288a

to seat academies in the entrances of tents,
to expound in them prohibition and
permission,
to declare the impure, impure, and the
pure, pure, and to declare the fit, fit, and
the unfit, unfit,
to understand in them the bloods
to instruct the menstruating women,
to tie crowns to your heads,
and circlets of royalty to your sons' heads,
to compel kings to bow to you,
and obligate nobles to prostrate before
you,
to spread your name on every shore,
and your memory in great cities overseas,
to enlighten your faces with the radiance
of the day, between your eyes like the
planet Venus.

§ 288b

If you merit this seal, to make use of my
crown,
no ignorant person shall ever be found
and there shall not be a fool or simpleton
among you.

§ 289

You are glad and my servants are sad,
that this mystery, unique among my
mysteries, is going forth from my storehouse. The voice of your academies will be
like fatted calves with it [i.e., this magic],
not through toil and not through weari-
ness—only with this seal,
and by remembering the awesome crown;
there will be astonishment at you,
and sickness over you,
many will die from sighing,
and their souls will expire upon hearing of
your glory;
riches and wealth will accumulate for you;
important people surround you;
the family into which you marry
will be surrounded by pedigree and power
on all sides;
whoever is blessed by you will be blessed,
and whoever is praised by you will be
praised;
you will be called "those who justify the
many,"
they will call you "those who justify
mankind";
the determining of the month will go forth
from you,
and the intercalation of the year from the
cunning nature of your wisdom,
by your agency residents will be anointed,
according to you court chairs will stand;
you will raise exilarchs to office,
town judges on your authority.
A permanent decree will go forth from
you,
no one will take issue with it.

The distinction between the lists is indicated in several ways. First, God introduces each of the lists differently: the list of what Israel wants he introduces by saying, "I know what you are asking for"; the list of what Israel gets he introduces by saying, "if you merit this seal, to make use of my crown." The items in each of the lists are grammatically different: in the "wish list," the items are preceded by verbs of want, and the other verbs are in the infinitive form (you want to increase *talmud*, to seat academies, etc.); in the "reward list," the verbs are in the indicative form (this is what will happen, if . . .).

The separation of the two lists allows us to observe what the author "abandons" and what he "embraces." The first list, of what Israel wants, is an ironic take on the ethos of the Babylonian academies. This ethos comes to expression most obviously in terms that are hallmarks of the study associated with the academy: *pilpul*, *talmud*, and, of course, academies (*yeshivot*); the Midrashic measure of *ribbui*, sometimes associated with *pilpul*, is also mentioned.[13] This ethos is also evident in the way Israel's desired Torah is characterized not only with nouns of large quantity (many, mountains, numerous, vast) but also with verbs of growth and accumulation (to increase, to pile up, to multiply)—an allusion to the creative aspect of Torah study that is implied in the term *pilpul*.[14] Later in this list, this vast knowledge of Torah is applied to the instruction of the law, which, as we have seen, was perceived by the Talmudists as that which differentiated them from *tanna'im*.

Almost none of these "rabbinic goods" are found in the second list, in which God describes the rewards that will await Israel should he grant them the ability to adjure the Prince of Torah. This list includes mostly general, non-academic kinds of prominence: the authority to distinguish the pure from the impure or the permitted from the prohibited, desired by Israel, is replaced by political authority that does not require special academic knowledge, like the authority to elect judges and exilarchs. The academies do appear, but as I hope to show in the following section, the emphasis in the second list on the *voice* of these academies implies a completely different kind of study from the creative study imagined in the first list.

---

13 Following here Ms. Munich 22, which has המון ריבוי where the rest of the manuscripts in the *Synopse* have המון רזי. The originality of the version in Ms. Munich 22 is supported not just by its uniqueness, and because it is more in line with the other attributes of Torah study in the list, but also with a parallel in T-S. K 21.95 G, a text related to Sar ha-Torah traditions, which among the *ba'ale mishnah* and *ba'ale talmud* mentions *ba'ale ribbui*. See more on this fragment later in this chapter.

14 For this term and its application in Babylonian *sugyot*, see Jeffrey Rubenstein, *The Culture of the Babylonian Talmud* (Baltimore: Johns Hopkins University Press, 2003), 48–51, and the literature cited there.

More important, the magical ritual that Israel receives is associated with the conservative aspects of Torah study: the adjuration of the Prince of Torah allows its users to retain what they had studied and to recite it without effort. It ensures, as God says, that "no ignorant person shall be found . . . among you"; and when the angels object, they focus on the fact that, if Israel receives the magical ritual, they will no longer forget. Adjuring the Prince of Torah cannot help Israel increase *talmud*, build up *halakhot*, accumulate more traditions; rather, it allows them only to retain what they have studied. The subordination of Torah study to the knowledge of Torah, which is implied in the general move of miraculizing the Torah, is a response to the ethos of the Babylonian academy. My suggestion, then, is that Dan's reading misses the text's critique of the academies, while Urbach's account mischaracterizes that critique: our author is not hostile to knowledge of *halakhah* in itself or to its material rewards[15]—both, after all, are given to Israel by God; he is critical of the academies' particular mode of study.

Reading this text in this context illuminates God's answer to the angels. The primary purpose of this passage is to explain why God is inclined to reward Israel. Continuing a line of reasoning expressed earlier in the text (§283), God explains that now, after the harsh punishment of exile, is the time to show kindness to his people. But a closer reading of the answer in light of the analysis above reveals that it, too, contains a critique of the Babylonian academies:

> No, my attendants; no, my servants! Do not trouble me with this matter. . . .
>
> [This magic] was reserved for this generation, so that they could make use of it to the end of all generations. For they went out from evil to evil, and did not know me; for their hearts were stupefied by the exile, and the words of Torah have been as hard in their ears as brass and iron. It is fitting for them to make use of it, to let Torah enter into them like water, like oil into their bones. (§293)

This passage poses an incongruity between Torah study and the exile or diaspora from which Israel has just returned: their hearts were "stupefied," Torah is hard for them, and therefore they need the magic that will facilitate Torah study. A similar incongruity is described earlier, in §283, when God says to Israel, "because you had great idleness [*batala*][16] in the

---

15   Both identified as the target of critique by Urbach, "Traditions," 24–25.

16   Most manuscripts read *batala* (idleness), but Mss. N8128 and M40 read ביטול, clearly referring to *biṭul torah*, the rabbinic term for lacking in or actively diminishing the study of Torah.

exile, I was longing, 'When will I hear Torah from their mouths?' "[17] The idea that the diaspora brings about *bitul torah*, a diminishing in Torah, is expressed in the monument of diasporan Torah study itself (see *b. Hag.* 5b). But the sharp contrast our text draws between Torah study and the Babylonian exile must have been striking to its readers. First, by that time Babylonia had become the undisputed center of Torah learning. Second, that center of Torah learning traced its roots precisely to the historical period in which our narrative is set. We have already seen one example of that claim in the story about Ezra teaching Baruch the Torah before coming up to Palestine (*b. Meg.* 16b).

The two particular images invoked in the last lines cited from God's answer are an attack not on the existence of Torah study in Babylonia, but on the particular Babylonian *form* of Torah study. The first image presents the Torah as hard as "brass and iron" in the ears of the returnees from the diaspora. The use of these two metals to illustrate general hardness is not in itself unusual (see, e.g., Isa. 48:4). But I think its use here to describe the status of Torah in the diaspora is pointed and specific: the passage alludes to a *derashah* that the Babylonian rabbis themselves used as proof of their antiquity.

In 2 Kings 24:16, we read of the first exile from Judea that Nebuchadnezzar "brought captive to Babylon all the men of valor, seven thousand, the artisan and the welder, one thousand, all of them mighty and wagers of war." A *derashah* that appears in *Sifre Deuteronomy* (§321) and the Babylonian Talmud (*b. Git.* 88a) identifies these figures as formidable sages.[18] The potential of this *derashah* to demonstrate the ancient greatness of Babylonian Torah study is readily apparent in the fact that the Yerushalmi rejects it, without even fully quoting it, in a *sugya* that confronts the Babylonian claim to Torah authority.

The passage comes right after the story about the dispute between the two communities concerning the intercalation of the calendar, one of the most famous accounts of the confrontation between these centers, which also includes the famous pro-Babylonian paraphrase of Isa. 2:3, "For out

---

17   One of the manuscripts, while presenting an unlikely version, catches the spirit, when it refers to the "contempt of exiles," בח הגליות (Ms. M40, §293).

18   "'All of them mighty and wagers of war': what might is there for people who are going into exile? And what war can people who are fettered in shackles and bound by chains wage? Rather, 'mighty'—those who are mighty in Torah . . . 'wagers of war'—who engage in the give and take in the war of Torah . . . 'the artisan and the smith, one thousand': 'artisan' [ḥarash—also Heb. root for "silent"]: one speaks and everyone is silent; 'smith' [masger—from the same root as "close"]: everyone sits before him and learns from him, one opens and one closes" (*Sifre Deut* §321, ed. Finkelstein, 370; cf. *b. Git.* 88a, which makes these sages even greater).

of Babylonia shall go forth Torah and the word of the Lord from Nehar Peqod." Shortly after that astounding assertion, we find the following discussion:

> It is written, "and to the rest, the elders of the exile" (Jer. 29:1). Said the Holy One, blessed be he, the elders of the exile are dear to me, but a small group in Palestine is more dear to me than a great *sanhedrin* abroad. It is written, "the artisan and the welder, one thousand," and you say this?! [A dispute between] Rabbi Berekhiah in the name of Rabbi Helbo and our Rabbis: . . . Rabbi Berekhiah in the name of Rabbi [Helbo]—these are *haverim* [i.e., sages], and our Rabbis say—these are councilmen. (*y. San.* 1:2 19a)

The Talmud of the Land of Israel combats the very association of these artisans with Torah study by making it a minority opinion. The majority of sages, according to the Yerushalmi, believe the artisans and welders were "councilmen," which subsequently supports the assertion that even a small group in Palestine is dearer to God than a great *sanhedrin* abroad. While this *derashah* appears in other contexts as well, the fact that it is used by the Yerushalmi here in the context of the competition between the two centers implies it was perceived as part of the Babylonian claim to authority.[19]

Our passage in *Sar ha-Torah*, I would argue, alludes to this understanding of "the artisan and the welder" as the founding fathers of Babylonian Torah when it says that Torah was hard for Israel like "brass and iron." One of the most common kinds of artisan, or *harash*, in Hebrew literature is *harash ha-nehoshet*, the artisan of brass; the connection between welders and iron is self-evident; and, finally, both this interpretation of 2 Kings 24:16 and the *Sar ha-Torah* narrative concern Torah study in the early history of the Babylonian exile. Our passage may thus use the Babylonian rabbinic claim to antiquity in order to subvert it.

If this is correct, our author, in contrast with the Yerushalmi, accepts the identification of these artisans as Torah scholars. But he builds on this identification to mock the "iron-y," "brassy" way in which Babylonians were known to teach and study. The Talmud itself employs the same metallic image to praise this kind of Torah study: "Rav Ashi said: Any scholar who is not stiff as iron is not a scholar for it was said [*Is not my word . . . says the Lord,*] *like a hammer that breaks a rock in pieces* (Jer. 23:29)?" (*b. Ta'an.* 4a). Later, in the same tractate, we read: "Said R. Hama b. R. Hanina, what is [the meaning of] the verse, *Iron in iron together* (Prov.

---

19 On the *derashah* itself in all its appearances and textual variations, see Daniel Sperber, "Qetef melilot," in *Mehkarim ba-sifrut ha-talmudit* (Jerusalem: Israel Academy of Sciences and Humanities, 1983), 193–99 (195–99).

27:17)? It [comes] to tell you that just as one [piece of] iron sharpens the other, so do two scholars sharpen each other in *halakhah*" (*b. Ta'an.* 7a). R. Hama's teaching is particularly illuminating of our passage in *Sar ha-Torah*, because it associates the metal nature of Babylonian Torah study with its admiration for the dialectic process (the two scholars "sharpen" one another), the same dialectic of *pilpul* that we have seen in Israel's "wish list." The Talmud itself identifies this manner of study as uniquely Babylonian:

> Said R. Hoshaya, what is [the meaning] of that which is written, *I took two staffs; one I named Pleasance, the other I named Bonds* [also, "Injurers"]? "Pleasance," these are the scholars in Palestine, who are pleasant to one another in *halakhah*. "Injurers," these are the scholars in Babylonia, who injure each other in *halakhah*. These are the anointed ones [also, "sons of clear oil," Heb. *yitshar*; Zech. 4:14]; And by it there are two olives (Zech. 4:3). "Sons of clear oil"—R. Yitshak said, these are scholars in Palestine, who are as smooth to each other in *halakhah* as olive oil; "Two olives"—these are scholars in Babylonia who are bitter as olive to one another in *halakhah*. (*b. San.* 24a)

The imagery in this passage brings us back to our passage in *Sar ha-Torah* (though the passages are not close enough to posit a direct relationship between them): here the sharp Babylonian style, which we have seen associated with the metaphor of iron, is contrasted with the smooth, oil-like Palestinian style; in our passage in *Sar ha-Torah*, God says that he will ameliorate the situation in which Torah is as hard as iron for those who return from the diaspora by injecting it "like oil into their bones."

While we cannot rule out the possibility that *Sar ha-Torah* was written in Palestine,[20] we have seen that it uses several terms in their Babylonian sense. Even if this text is Palestinian, it differs from other Palestinian sources in that its claim against Babylonia is not based on the superiority of the Land of Israel over the diaspora. If that were our author's intention, we would have expected him to say something about the Land of Israel or its superior status, especially given the rich rabbinic Palestinian tradition that does just that.[21] Our narrative is more interested in contrasting *pilpul* with knowledge of the Torah, in mocking the ambition for vast *talmud*, and in ridiculing the dialectical roughness of Babylonian study, than in the Palestine/Babylonia dichotomy per se.

---

20 This was suggested by Joseph Dan, *Ancient Jewish Mysticism* (Heb.; Tel Aviv: Ministry of Defense, 1989), 119.

21 See Isaiah Gafni, *Land, Center and Diaspora* (Sheffield: Sheffield Academic Press, 1997), 96–117.

Our text begins by setting Temple vs. Torah to make a point about cultural priorities, then marginalizes the study of Torah as the organizing principle of Jewish life by miraculizing it and reducing the activity to its result—knowledge of Torah. This move is coupled with an attack on the Babylonian form of Torah study, with its focus on innovation for innovation's sake and reliance on brutal dialectical procedure. The second move complements the first: because our values are different from the Babylonian ones, because we are not interested in study for its own sake, the only desideratum of Torah study is the memorization of Scripture and tradition, something that is made instantly possible by the adjuration of the Prince of Torah.

If we have thus far focused on the world the narrative rejects, the final parts of the text will allow us to focus on the new era it promises:

> Our fathers did not accept upon themselves to put a single stone on another until they compelled the King of the World and his servants. They compelled him and he revealed to them the Prince of Torah, how to perform it and how to use it. Immediately, the Holy Spirit appeared from the third entrance to the House of the Lord. . . . [22] When our fathers saw the throne of glory that was elevated inside it, hovering between the hall and the altar, and the King of the universe on it, they immediately fell to their faces. And at that moment he said: "*Greater will be the glory of the latter House over that of the former one* (Hag. 2:9). For in the First Temple I was not bound to my children, except by a voice, [but] this [Temple] is for me, my throne and my servants.[23] O, my sons, why do you prostrate yourselves and fall to your faces? Get up and be seated before my throne, the way you sit in the academy." (§297–98)

As Dan has shown in detail, this passage deliberately alludes to, and tries to surpass, the biblical account of the giving of the Torah at Sinai.[24] The purpose of our author seems to be to portray the revelation of the *Sar ha-*

---

22 I omit here a gloss of uncertain origin. Cf. Swartz, *Scholastic Magic*, 106.

23 Most manuscripts here read שבמקדש ראשון לא נזקקתי לבניי אלא בקול זה לי ולכסאי ולכל משרתיי, which seems difficult. Swartz's solution is simply to omit לי ולכסאי ולכל משרתי without even mentioning the omission. Ms. N8128 presents a version that is grammatically easier, "That in the First Temple, I was not bound to my sons. But in this voice you have atoned for me, my throne, and my servants" (שבמקדש ראשון לא נזקקתי לבני; אלא בקול זה כפרתם לי; ולכסאי ולכל משרתי). But the atonement that it refers to is not alluded to elsewhere in the text. I follow here David Halperin's translation, which takes זה in the majority version not as referring to קול but as going back all the way to מקדש; perhaps the word מקדש did appear here, for a second time, but was omitted.

24 Dan, "Theophany," 149–51, which the analysis *here* follows. See also Schäfer, *Hekhalot-Studien*, 271–72, who also shows that our text—albeit in another passage—seeks to supersede Sinai.

Torah as more intimate and God more immanent than in its Sinaitic pre-
decessor. A case in question is God's explanation of the superiority of the
Latter House expressed in Hag. 2:9. God explains that in the First Temple
(and thus, in the age of the first Torah), he was bound[25] to his children
"only by his voice." The biblical account of Mount Sinai is indeed replete
with references to God's voice. For example, Exod. 19:19 describes how
the dialogue between God and Moses was conducted: "As the blast of the
trumpet grew louder and louder, Moses would speak and God would answer him with a voice." Still more interesting is the comparison with the
famous synesthetic expression in Exod. 20:14: "and all the people see the
voices." At Sinai, the people's only access to God was through his voice,
and all they saw were voices; in the new revelation of the new House, the
people behold God seated on his throne.[26]

God's invitation to Israel to sit with him the way they sit in the academy[27] is the moment in which the old Torah, typified by the academy, is
literally replaced by the Latter House. This study session is markedly different; it opens with God's words:

> "Sit ... and seize the crown and accept the seal and study this order of the
> Prince of Torah,[28] how you shall perform it, how you shall expound it, how
> you shall use it, how you shall raise the paths of your hearts, how your
> hearts shall gaze into Torah!" At once Zerubbabel the son of Shaltiel stood
> up before him like a meturgeman and explained the names of the Prince of
> Torah, one by one, with his name, the name of his crown and the name of
> his seal. (§298)

The use of the word "order" (*seder*) is another allusion to the classical
rabbinic curriculum; here again Israel sits as they do in the academy and
studies an order, but their study companion is God and the order is an
adjuration of an angel. The choice of Zerubbabel is instructive for our
purposes here because of the figure not chosen. We might have expected
this new age of Torah to be inaugurated by Ezra, the great scribe and also
a favorite icon of Babylonian Torah study.[29] But our text chooses Zerub-

---

25 נזקקתי. On this term, see Schäfer, *Hekhalot-Studien*, 259.

26 Azzan Yadin-Israel pointed out to me that while Dan is correct that the narrative
here contrasts with Exod. 19–20, it does recall the vision of and intimacy with God described in Exod. 24:9–11.

27 במידה שאתם יושבין בישיבה. Swartz translates *yeshiva* as "council"; I follow the German, which supplies *Lehrhaus*.

28 Following, with the German translation ("Ordnung des Fürsten der Torah"), Mss.
Oxford 1531 and Vatican 228. Other Mss: ולמדו שר סדר של תורה (NY 8128), ולמדו כתר התורה
(Munich 40); סדר ספר תורה (Munich 22); סתר התורה (Dropsie 436, which Swartz follows); סדר
סוד התורה (Budapest 238).

29 See Richard Kalmin, *The Sage in Jewish Society of Late Antiquity* (New York: Routledge, 1999), 15–17.

babel who is associated not with Torah but with Davidic lineage and the building of the Temple (see Hag. 2:20–23 and Zech. 6:9–15).

More important, this passage reveals an aspect of Israel's relation with the Torah that we did not hear of before. Like its new relationship with God, this relation is now also visual: their hearts may "gaze into Torah." The following section of this chapter is dedicated to the elucidation of this idea.

VISION AND MEMORY IN HEKHALOT LITERATURE

Visions into Torah are recorded in several other Hekhalot traditions, some relating to Sar ha-Torah. In the Ozhaya fragment, R. Ishmael tells us, "I testify this to the generations [to come], that since I called the name of this Prince . . . I immediately sat and observed and gazed into *midrash* and *halakhot* and *shemu'a.*"[30] A more detailed account of this kind of vision and its context is preserved in a Sar ha-Torah tradition known as The Chapter of Rabbi Nehuniah:

> R. Ishmael said: When I was thirteen years old Rabbi Nehuniah saw me in great trouble, affliction and great danger. A scriptural passage that I was reading one day I would forget the next, and an oral tradition that I was reciting one day I would forget the next. . . . [31] Immediately Rabbi Nehuniah my teacher seized me and took me from my father's house and brought me into the Chamber of Hewn Stone and made me swear by the Great Seal, by the Great Oath that is for Zekhuriel YYY, God of Israel . . . and revealed to me the praxis of the secret of Torah. Then immediately my heart was enlightened like the gates of the east, and my eyes gazed into the depths and paths of Torah, and never again did I forget anything my ears heard from my teacher, nor would I ever forget anything of the paths of Torah in which I engaged for their truths. (§308–9)[32]

This passage furthers our knowledge of the vision associated with Sar ha-Torah in two ways. First, it tells us about what one sees—the "depths and paths" of Torah. More important, it ties the vision more clearly with the

---

30 T.-S. K21.95C (= G8), 2b.36, see Peter Schäfer (ed.), *Geniza-Fragmente zur Hekhalot-Literatur* (Tübingen: Mohr Siebeck, 1984), 105. See more on this fragment later in the chapter.

31 I omit here the ascetic restrictions R. Ishmael takes upon himself, as they are not immediately relevant to the discussion here.

32 Translation from Swartz, *Scholastic Magic*, 63. On this story and its different versions in the Hekhalot corpus, see ibid., 62–81.

memorization effect of the adjuration: the vision is a solution to the problem of forgetting Torah, and the result of the vision is that R. Ishmael
never again forgets Scripture or oral tradition. The last detail is worth
emphasizing: these visions of Torah explicitly include Oral Torah, even,
in the case of our last text, anything Rabbi Ishmael heard from his rabbi.
But how can one gaze into oral traditions?

In what follows, I explore the possibility that these and other Hekhalot
texts partake in the visual, locational, and architectural construction of
memory that was prevalent in the ancient and medieval discourse of
memorization. The nature and formulation of this art of memory vary
across authors and periods. In most sources, this art consists of forming
mental images of the knowledge one wishes to remember and storing
these images in a structured array of distinct places in the mind.[33] Until
recently, it was thought that rabbinic culture lacked this art of memory,
that this culture was too "auditory" to think of knowledge as images or as
placed within architectural structures.[34] Shlomo Na'eh's recent work on
memory argues against this view, showing that an understanding of
memory in visual and spatial terms underlies a significant number of rabbinic sources.[35]

In the classical formulation in Cicero's De oratore, this art of memory is
premised on the superiority of the sense of sight to other senses. Even
items of knowledge acquired "by the ears or by reflexion can be most easily retained in the mind if they are also conveyed to our minds by the
mediation of the eyes, with the result that things not seen and not lying
in the field of visual discernment are earmarked by a sort of outline and
image and shape so that we keep hold of as it were by an act of sight
things that we can scarcely embrace by an act of thought."[36]

Rabbi Tanhum's statement in y. Ber. 5:1 9a, הסובר תלמודו לא במהרה הוא
משכח, advocates, according to Na'eh, precisely the same sort of visualization of knowledge. Interpretations of this statement usually take the word

33   For description of the various forms and developments of this location view of
memory, see Mary Carruthers, The Book of Memory: A Study of Memory in Medieval Culture
[2nd ed.] (Cambridge: Cambridge University Press, 2008); idem, The Craft of Thought:
Meditation, Rhetoric and the Making of Images, 400–1200 (Cambridge: Cambridge University Press, 1998); Frances Yates, The Art of Memory (London: Routledge, 1966), especially
the useful account of the Latin sources, 1–26. Jocelyn Penny Small, Wax Tablets of the
Mind: Cognitive Studies of Memory and Literacy in Classical Antiquity (London: Routledge,
1997), 81–116.

34   José Faur, Golden Doves with Silver Dots: Semiotics and Textuality in Rabbinic Tradition (Bloomington: Indiana University Press, 1986), 32–37.

35   Shlomo Na'eh, "Omanut ha-zikaron, mivnim shel zikaron ve-tavniot shel teqst
be-sifrut ḥazal," in Talmudic Studies III (ed. Y. Sussmann and D. Rosenthal; Jerusalem:
Magnes, 2005), 543–89.

36   Cicero, De oratore, 2.87.357, trans. E. W. Sutton and H. Rackham, LCL.

sover to refer to *sevara* or the "reasons" behind Talmudic teachings; the statement then makes the plausible argument that, if one makes sure to understand the reasons behind certain teachings, one will not forget them.[37] But based on the context of this teaching and its prooftext ("lest you forget what your eyes saw," Deut. 4:9), as well as on a lexical investigation into the word *sover*, Na'eh reinterprets the statement to mean, "one who visualizes his study will not be quick to forget it."[38] Similar are the instances in which rabbis are said to "pass their eyes over," that is, scan with the "mind's eye,"[39] material they have studied—in one case the Aggadah on Psalms and in another the entire Torah.[40]

The vision in our Sar ha-Torah texts is the same vision of memory. That is why the subject of this vision is Torah rather than God; that is why the vision in the *Sar ha-Torah* narrative it is the heart that is gazing into Torah; and that is why this vision solves Rabbi Ishmael's problem of forgetting. Note that, just like in Cicero's explanation of the *ars memoriae* and Rabbi Tanhum's exhortation, *Merkavah Rabbah* contrasts the forgetting of oral instruction with the durable and accessible visual memory: "my eyes gazed into the depths and paths of Torah, and never again did I forget anything my ears heard from my teacher" (§678). The use of spatial terms such as "depths" and "paths" might also refer to the architectural construction of memory; "paths" is especially interesting, given the importance in classical memory constructions of the routes that led from one "place" to another.[41]

An element of this architectural discourse that is particularly interesting in the context of Hekhalot literature is the discussion of memory as a treasury or house with many rooms.[42] Na'eh argues that this image underlies R. Eleazar's famous exhortation, "make for yourself a heart of many chambers [*hadre hadarim*] and place therein the words" (*t. Sot.* 7:12 and parallels), which instructs the student to organize his vast knowledge into different spaces so that different dicta could be retained

37 We will see in the following section that at least some sources argued precisely for the opposite position.

38 Na'eh, "Memory," 559–62.

39 The phrase is common in Greek and Roman discussions of memory; see already Aristotle, *Topics*, 8.13; Quintillian, *Institutes*, 11.2.32.

40 Na'eh, "Memory," 555–56

41 See, e.g., Carruthers, *Craft of Thought*, 60–62, and passim; see also the modern study of the mnemonist who organized his remembered items along a street: Small, *Wax Tablets*, 101–2.

42 According to Small, *Wax Tablets*, 95–98, this is a particularly Roman development that would have been unthinkable to the Greeks. For a discussion of the architectural paradigm, see Carruthers, *Book of Memory*, 89–98, and Yates, *Art of Memory*.

together but distinguished from one another. The desired item could thus be retrieved on demand.[43]

The expression "chambers of the Torah" in Hekhalot texts may likewise refer to this architectural division of textual knowledge. While this expression appears elsewhere in rabbinic literature, in the Hekhalot texts it gains both a visual dimension and a connection with memory.[44] R. Nehunia's prayer in *Ma'aseh Merkavah* includes several requests for knowledge, all using spatial terms:

> and may I discourse in the gates of wisdom,
> and may I examine the ways of understanding,
> and may I gaze into the chambers of Torah,
> and may I discourse in the storehouses of blessing. (§569)[45]

The gazing into the chambers of Torah seems to be linked explicitly to memory in another passage from the same macroform. This other passage also, significantly, links these chambers with another kind of chamber that is pervasive in Hekhalot literature, the chambers of the heavenly palaces after which this literature is known:

> Rabbi Ishmael said: when Rabbi Nehuniah my teacher told me the secret of the chambers of the *hekhal* and of the *merkavah* and also of the Torah[46]—I shall not forget a single chamber of these[47]—I saw the King of the Universe sitting on a throne high and exalted, and all the angels of the holiness of his name and his power were sanctifying his name in his praise. (§556)[48]

Rabbi Ishmael tells us that he will not forget a single chamber of the chambers to which he was given access through his master's instruction. It is possible that this memory refers to the vision of the heavenly chambers or to the secret that Rabbi Nehuniah tells Rabbi Ishmael. But the verb "forget," in the majority of the instances recorded in Schäfer's *Kon-*

---

43 Na'eh, "Memory," 574–76 (see 576–79 for similar texts).

44 See *t. Ket.* 5:1 and parallels, but see also note 51 below on *Tanna de-bei Eliyyahu*.

45 Translation from Michael Swartz, *Mystical Prayer in Ancient Judaism* (Tübingen: Mohr Siebeck, 1992), 240.

46 וגם תורה, following Mss. New York, Munich 40, Dropsie; Ms. Oxford has וגב תורה, and Ms. Munich 22 has וגבורת תורה.

47 לא אשכח חדר מהם; Swartz's translation skips the mention of Torah and this clause ("and also of Torah, I shall not forget a single room of these"), marking it as difficult (*Mystical Prayer*, 240 n. 35); the German translation is "das Geheimnis der Gemächter des Palastes der Merkava, und (auch) die Torah—keines der Gemächter will ich vergessen" (Schäfer, *Übersetzung*, 3.261).

48 Translation from Swartz, *Mystical Prayer*, 233, but see previous note.

kordanz, refers to Torah knowledge, and it never refers to visions.[49] And if Rabbi Ishmael wanted to tell us he will not forget any of the secrets he was told, he would have said "not a single secret." The conjunction between the image of Torah chambers[50] and Rabbi Ishmael's emphasis on his durable memory makes it likely that, in addition to the reference to the vision of the heavenly chambers, this passage alludes to images of structured and visualized knowledge of Torah. This juxtaposition of the vision of the throne with the vision of Torah brings us back to the conclusion of the *Sar ha-Torah* narrative in *Hekhalot Rabbati,* which has Israel first gazing into the Torah while seeing God on his throne.[51]

Recognizing the visuality of memorization and its architectural elements thus allows us to understand one way in which the transmitters of Hekhalot literature bridged what often seem to be the two poles of the corpus—the heavenly ascents and visions, on the one hand, and the adjuration of angels such as Sar ha-Torah, on the other.[52] The passage in *Ma'aseh Merkavah* in particular might allow us a glimpse into the way in which Hekhalot traditions were developed by individuals or groups with

---

49   The instances in which forms of שכח relate to Torah (inclusive of parallels): §77, §292, §309, §330, §336, §340 ("anything I hear, whether words of Torah or anything else"), §388, §574, §677, §678, §705, §706 ("let Torah be retained in my body and let nothing be forgotten from my mouth from this day on"—this prayer parallels §705, which only mentions Torah); §831 (this is a *petihat lev,* and while the text is fragmentary and so might refer to forgetting things more generally, the instance of שכח immediately follows the request, "God, teach me your laws"). It relates to divine names in §564 and §165 and to secrets in §563 and §504, and is said of God in §378. Again, none of these refer to visions of the heavenly palaces. See Peter Schäfer (ed.), *Konkordanz zur Hekhalot-Literatur* (Tübingen: Mohr Siebeck, 1986-88), 2.650.

50   Here reading "Torah" as connected to "chambers"; it is possible to connect it with "secrets" ("my teacher told me the secret . . . of Torah"), but the following reference to the chambers makes the reading suggested *infra* more likely.

51   A strikingly similar move is found in the *Tanna de-bei Eliyyahu.* In its interpretation of Song 1:6, "the king has brought me into his chambers," it says that God brought Israel into his innermost chambers, but while it mentions in the same chapter the heavenly liturgy, it also identifies these chambers as "the chambers of Torah," a shared property of both God's Torah and the sages: "just like God has a chamber within chambers of chambers in his Torah, so for the sages each of them has a chamber within chambers of chambers in his Torah" (*Seder Eliyyahu Rabbah,* 7, ed. Friedmann, 32). Jacob Elbaum first directed scholarly attention to these passages as relating to the Hekhalot corpus. He writes that the interpretation of the chambers as referring to Torah constitutes a "dimming of the mystical connotation." The fact that such a move can be found even in Hekhalot literature and that it reflects broader concerns of this literature complicates the assumption behind this statement. See Jacob Elbaum, "Tanna de-be Eliyyahu and the Early Mystical Literature" (Heb.), in *Proceedings of the First International Conference on the History of Jewish Mysticism I: Early Jewish Mysticism* (ed. J. Dan; Jerusalem: Hebrew University, 1987), 139–50 (140).

52   See Peter Schäfer, "The Aim and Purpose of Early Jewish Mysticism," in *Hekhalot-Studien,* 277–95.

different interests. In the narrative preserved in *Hekhalot Rabbati*, both visions, that of God and of the Torah, seem integral and original to the composition. In *Ma'aseh Merkavah*, however, Torah is quite awkwardly strung into the list of secrets and the statement about never forgetting seems to disrupt the structural unity. It seems like the passage originally referred to the chambers of the heavenly palace and the vision of the throne, and then an interpolation was introduced that combined these visions with the allusion to memory and the vision of Torah. The author who introduced this juxtaposition relied on the the common architectural and visionary elements in both strands in order to understand one tradition in terms of another.[53]

TRANSFORMATION, ESOTERICISM, AND THE EMBODIMENT OF TORAH

In the world promised by the *Sar ha-Torah* narrative, this vision of Torah is bound with an embodiment of Torah. Earlier in the narrative God contrasts the current status of Israel, in which Torah is hard in their ears like brass and iron, with his plan to grant them the magical names and "let Torah enter into them like water, like oil into their bones" (§293, offering a positive paraphrase of Ps. 109:18). This embodiment is expressed in the recitation of Torah, which is referred to in God's promise that Torah will not leave Israel's mouth (§284), as well as in the promise that the "voice of your academies will be like [that of] fatted calves" (§289). Torah is no longer something external to be heard, analyzed, or increased by way of dialectic; rather, it goes into the bones of the sage and naturally, automatically comes out of his mouth.

The ideal of embodying the Torah is expressed already in some of the earliest rabbinic texts.[54] In the *Mekhilta de-Rabbi Ishmael*, God explains that he is leading Israel for forty years in the desert "so they will eat the manna and drink from the well and Torah will be mixed into their body" (*Mek. be-shalah*, ed. Horovitz-Rabin 76). A story in the Bavli links this

---

53   Klaus Hermann has observed a similar, and possibly contemporary process of uniting different strands of Hekhalot traditions in his study of Jewish mysticism in the Geonic period. See Klaus Herrmann, "Jewish Mysticism in the Geonic Period: The Prayer of Rav Hamnuna Sava," in *Jewish Studies between the Disciplines: Papers in Honor of Peter Schäfer on the Occasion of his 60th Birthday* (ed. K. Herrmann, M. Schlüter, and G. Veltri; Leiden: Brill, 2003), 180–217 (especially 215–17).

54   See the discussion in Martin Jaffee, "Oral Transmission of Knowledge as Rabbinic Sacrament: An Overlooked Aspect of Discipleship in Oral Torah," in *Study and Knowledge in Jewish Thought* (ed. H. Kreisel; Beer Sheva: Ben Gurion University of the Negev Press, 2006), 65–79 (72–78); Na'eh, "Memory," 586–89.

embodiment with recitation and memorization. Beruria finds a student whispering, rather than loudly reciting, the teachings he is studying. She kicks him and, expounding on 2 Sam. 23:5, says, "if [Torah] is arranged in 248 organs it is retained [*mishtameret*] in the heart, if not, it is not retained in the heart"[55] (*b. 'Eruv.* 53b–54a).

In addition to the *Sar ha-Torah* passage quoted above, this image of embodied Torah appears in several other Hekhalot traditions related to memorization. One prayer in *Merkavah Rabbah* asks, "let my study [*torah*] be retained [*shemurah*] in my body, and let me forget nothing" (§706). As in the story about Beruria in the Bavli, so, too, in the Hekhalot corpus this embodiment is achieved through recitation. Thus a passage in *Ma'aseh Merkavah* instructs that "he must stand and recite a name and give praise so that [the name] be engraved on all his limbs and wisdom and the search for understanding be in his heart" (§562).[56] Similarly, forgetting means the destruction of the body, "for if he forgets, all his limbs are destroyed" (§563).[57]

The famous opening passage of *Hekhalot Zutarti* is particularly instructive about this process of the internalization of tradition through recitation and how it relates to other Hekhalot traditions.

If you wish to single yourself out in the world, so that the mystery of the world and the secrets of wisdom are revealed to you, recite[58] this tradition [*mishnah*] and be careful with it until the day of your passing. Do not seek to comprehend what is after you and do not examine the sayings of your lips. Seek to comprehend what is in your heart and keep silent so that you will be worthy of the beauty of the *merkavah*. (§335)

This passage offers instructions to the person who wants to become worthy of the beauty of the *merkavah*. At the heart of these instructions is a recitation of a certain *mishnah* or tradition—presumably a Hekhalot text of some sort, maybe even *Hekhalot Zutarti* itself.[59] Several scholars have shown that

---

55   Printed editions omit both instances of "in the heart," which appear in all manuscripts.

56   Translation from Swartz, *Mystical Prayer*, 236–37.

57   Reading with Mss. New York (שאם שכח כל אבריו בהשחת) and Munich 22 (שאם ישכח ממנו דבר אחד אבריו בהשחת), which explicitly connect the state of memory and the state of the body. Swartz's translation (*Mystical Prayer*, 237), "so that nothing of it be forgotten; all his limbs are [in danger of] being destroyed," follows other manuscripts, in which the two clauses are unrelated (e.g., Ms. Munich 40: שלא ישכח ממנו דבר אחד כל איבריו בהשחתה), but it seems to me that in light of the preceding passage this connection can be made safely.

58   שונה. This verb is often rendered "study" (see, e.g., Schäfer, *Übersetzung*, 3.1: "lerne"), but to the extent that "recite" and "study" can be differentiated, the latter seems to be preferable—see *infra*.

59   For a discussion of the identity of the text to which the passage refers, see Annelies Kuyt, *The "Descent" to the Chariot* (Tübingen: Mohr Siebeck, 1995), 206–9. To me,

this passage reworks *m. Hag.* 2:1 and other rabbinic sources about engagement with knowledge that is constructed as esoteric. Schäfer suggests that the "singling out" this text promised to the one who will follow its instructions alludes to the "single" sage who is according to *m. Hag* worthy of expounding the *merkavah*.[60] The injunction, "do not seek to comprehend what is after you,"[61] clearly alludes to the same *mishnah*, which chastises anyone who looks into the spatial or temporal "beyond": "that which is above, that which is below, that which is before, and that which is after" (*m. Hag.* 2:1). The following instruction, "do seek to comprehend what is in your heart," seems to paraphrase the Yerushalmi's comment that in esoteric matters one must expound in the heart—that is, silently and privately: "[when investigating what happened] before the world was created—you inquire and your heart contemplates; [but investigating what happened] since the world was created, you proceed and your voice proceeds from one end of the world to another" (*y. Hag. 2:1* 77c).[62]

The inclusion of these sources in our passage, their juxtaposition with one another, and the particular formulation in which they appear here all give them a new meaning, though it is not immediately clear what that meaning is. The passage raises an important question: what can the Mishnah's warning against engagement with speculative knowledge mean in a passage that promises the sage who will follow its instructions mysteries and secrets and the beauty of the *merkavah*? The new context also changes the meaning of the comment from Yerushalmi: in its original context, the comment about studying silently and in the heart is meant to distinguish between private and public exposition. But here it appears after two prohibitions that do not make such a distinction, warnings against processes of inquiry that seem just as private as the one discussed in the Yerushalmi. The primary original sense of this source is thus lost. More important, the juxtaposition of the Yerushalmi's comment with the Mishnah's prohibition creates a tension between an understanding that is prohibited and an understanding that is required—a tension that is emphasized rather than harmonized by the particular form the sources are given here: first, "Do not try comprehend . . . do not examine . . ."; but then: "Seek to

---

it seems likely that at least in its current context at the head of *Hekhalot Zutarti*, our text refers to the macroform as a whole.

60   Schäfer, *Origins*, 284.

61   In all manuscripts but Ms. New York, which reads: אל תבין בה מה שלא הורוך.

62   עד שלא נברא העולם את דורש וליבך מסכים. משנברא העולם את הולך וקולך הולך מסוף העולם ועד סופו. This comment comes at the end of a Tannaitic source, a series of exegetical remarks all prohibiting any investigation about the time before the creation of the world. As both David Halperin (*The Merkavah in Rabbinic Literature* [New Haven: American Oriental Society, 1980], 103) and Schäfer (*Origins*, 209 n. 167) write, it must be a gloss added to the Tannaitic source (either by the Yerushalmi itself or perhaps earlier, even by a Tannaitic transmitter).

comprehend . . ." What is the difference between the prohibited comprehension and the required one?

Rachel Elior suggests that what we see here is a "surrender of rational autonomous thought," that our passage tells the observer to "relinquish any attempt to judge the vision according to rational criteria."[63] Similarly Vita Daphna Arbel writes that "the 'understanding of the heart' appears to be associated with a more than logical investigation and intellectual comprehension," that it refers to "spiritual awareness, insight, and inner understanding."[64] But there is no reason to assume that the understanding prohibited is particularly "rational" while the understanding recommended in the last instruction is "spiritual." Moshe Halbertal suggests that the *mishnah* that the passage requires to recite "is not destined for those individuals who understand their own knowledge. The opposite is the case—it is the constant repetition of the Mishna that transforms the reader into an exceptional individual."[65] The solution that will be proposed here follows Halbertal's suggestion; but this suggestion must be modified since the text immediately proceeds with the instruction: "seek to comprehend what is in your heart." Understanding is, in fact, required and desired.

The key to this passage, I suggest, is the one element in the list of instructions that does not paraphrase earlier rabbinic sources on esotericism: the instruction, "do not examine the sayings on your lips." By placing this instruction here, the passage equates the esoteric knowledge against which *m. Hag.* 2:1 warns with the meaning of the *mishnah* it requires the sage to recite—both are things with which one should not engage. It thus focuses the warning from the Mishnah on the practice of recitation, rather than on a general engagement with esoteric knowledge. The message is that the recitation required here should not include an understanding of the recited text. Again, because the passage proceeds to instruct the sage to understand what is in his heart, it rules out an interpretation of the initial prohibition as relating to the content of the teaching or to the sage's general ability, obligation, or interest to understand the material.

The contrast between the prohibited and required understandings should be interpreted precisely as it is marked by our passage, a contrast between understanding what is "on the lips" and understanding what is

63   Rachel Elior, "The Concept of God in Hekhalot Literature," *Binah: Studies in Jewish Thought* 2 (1989), 79–129 (113).

64   Vita Daphna Arbel, *Beholders of Divine Secrets: Mysticism and Myth in the Hekhalot and Merkavah Literature* (Albany: State University of New York Press, 2003), 29.

65   Moshe Halbertal, *Concealment and Revelation: Esotericism in Jewish Thought and its Philosophical Implications* (trans. J. Feldman; Princeton, NJ: Princeton University Press, 2007), 27.

"in the heart." The first clearly refers to what is being recited. As for the second, we have already seen the heart designated as the location of memory in Hekhalot literature and other Jewish texts; in fact, immediately after our passage, *Hekhalot Zutarti* itself refers twice to the heart in the context of forgetting and remembering.[66] Thus I think our passage refers to the process of memorization: the recitation on the lips leads to the retention in the heart, like in the Beruria story from the Bavli cited above.

If that is correct, the distinction between a recitation without understanding and an inquiry into what is in the heart may reflect a well-known rabbinic rule about memorization: the oral repetition of traditions should precede an inquiry into their meanings. This rule appears several times in classical rabbinic literature (famously, in *b. Shabb.* 63b, but also many other places).[67] Shlomo Goitein showed that it is frequently reflected in Geonic sources.[68] Shmuel ben Hofni Ga'on, for example, writes that "one must recite from the Mishnah and the Talmud and only then reason and examine." Some of the terms employed by the Ga'on are identical to those used in our passage: first recitation (*heve shone* in our passage, *lishnot* in the Ga'on's letter), then examination (*al taḥqor* in our passage; *we-aḥare khen . . . laḥqor* in the letter).[69]

Our passage insists that at first the sage should not preoccupy himself with the meaning of the text recited not because this text is beyond rationality or because the sage is uninterested in or incapable of understanding the text, but because our passage insists on the importance of ritual recitation, divorced from the study of meaning, as a way to memorize, that is, internalize the *mishnah*. This internalization modifies the body of the sage—he now has the *mishnah* "in his heart," "inside his body," as we have seen. And like other bodily transformations we know from the Hek-

---

66 "When Moses ascended to God, the Holy One, blessed be he, taught him: anyone whose heart errs (שיהא לבו שוגה), mention these names about him . . . so that anything I hear be captured in my heart, Scripture and Mishnah and Talmud, Halakhot and Aggadot, let me never forget, neither in this world nor in the world to come" (§336). The version in some of the manuscripts, שיהא לבו שונה, seems to me influenced by the recitation in §335, but for our purposes here this variation is inconsequential since it still refers to the heart as the location of memory.

67 See the references in Yaacov Sussmann, "Torah shebe-'al peh—peshuṭah ke-mashma'ah," in *Talmudic Studies III* (2 vols.; ed. Y. Sussmann and D. Rosenthal; Jerusalem: Magnes, 2005), 209–384, (251 and n. 29).

68 See Shelomo Goitein, *Jewish Education in Muslim Countries* (Heb.; Jerusalem: Ben-Tsevi Institute, 1962), 160–61, and see the references there to other parts of the book.

69 Goitein, *Jewish Education*, 160–61, cites the passage from Mann's Texts and refers to the Genizah fragment as T.-S. Loan 4; it is now marked as T.-S. Misc 35.4. Note that while this letter is speaking about the general progression of studying Torah, the rule is also applied to the more relevant context, for our purposes, of studying a single text.

halot corpus,[70] this transformation is what makes him worthy of the "beauty of the *merkavah*."

If in the previous section we saw how the visionary aspects of Hekhalot could be harnessed to represent the art of memory, this passage in *Hekhalot Zutarti* shows us how traditions about esotericism and ideas about transformation can be employed in discussions of recitation and memorization. To be sure, even if we limit ourselves to this passage in *Hekhalot Zutarti*, a theme as rich as esoteric knowledge cannot be reduced to a single sense; this is evident from the rest of the paragraph, which is concerned with the honor of God (though the text does immediately return to the topic of memory in §336). What I would claim, however, is that the transmitters of these texts, through a series of literary maneuvers, such as glosses, recontextualizations, and reformulations, anchored a multivalent network of traditions in a new and particular field of meaning.

The Hekhalot texts we have investigated in this section allude to approaches to textuality that were common in rabbinic culture, but they amplify them, reimagine them, invest them with more power, and crown them with the revelation of the heavenly palaces themselves. While the visualization of memory may be found in classical rabbinic literature, this theme is here equated with the vision of God. Repeated recitation may appear in rabbinic sources as an aid to study, but here it is constructed as transformative ritual that makes the sage worthy of the most precious form of knowledge.

The recruiting of visions, palaces, and mysteries for these approaches to Torah gains a special significance if the texts we have examined were formed in a polemical environment of the sort we posited for the *Sar ha-Torah* narrative. Consider Rav Nahman's statements we have examined earlier in this book: our texts not only provide a positive ideological framework for becoming a "basket full of books" or for recitation without understanding, but argue that this internalization of Torah in the body and this ritual recitation are gateways to singular greatness. Placed in this polemical context, the vision of Torah we see here emerges as a reassertion of traditional rabbinic values, coupled with a radical claim to divine knowledge and power, against Babylonian Talmudic culture.

A RECITATION AT THE THRONE OF GLORY

This chapter's proposal, that the recitation of the *tanna'im* served as a context for Hekhalot composition, may shed light on a mysterious seg-

70 See Arbel, *Beholders*, 37–47.

ment in one of the Hekhalot Genizah fragments, T.-S. K 21.95g, first published by Ithamar Gruenwald[71] and then in Schäfer's *Geniza-Fragmente*.[72] This text, I argue, is striking in the way it describes recitation as well as the kind of recitation it describes. It assimilates the recitation of rabbinic tradition to the angelic liturgy, offering us a fantastically ritualistic interpretation of this recitation; and the recitation it describes seems to be not that of Hekhalot traditions but of the standard, *halakhic*, repertoire of the *tanna'im*.

The verso of the fragment seems to describe a group that is shown to R. Ishmael by an angel (1b.8), a group that is said to have enormous power (1b.9–11). It is not clear whether this group is of angels or humans, or whether the text deliberately blurs the distinction between these categories for some purpose. They are identified as *ahronim* (1b.8), "the latter ones," which is a common term in rabbinic literature for later (or even contemporary) generations of sages,[73] but is possibly used in some Hekhalot texts to refer to a group of angels.[74] The text also identifies them as *yesharim* (1b.9), which commonly means "righteous people,"[75] though at least in *Seder Rabbah di-Vreshit* the *yesharim* of Ps. 49:14 and Ps. 140:14 are identified as the ministering angels (§449).[76]

This ambiguity between exceptional people and angels is clearest in a clause that creates an identity between titles that are otherwise unambiguously connected with either humans or angels: "for they are *ba'ale mishnah, ba'ale talm[ud, ba]'ale ribbui*, and they are in fact [*we-hen hen*] princes of prophecy at the throne of my glory" (1b.11–12). We have met the first two, *ba'ale mishnah* and *ba'ale talmud*, as the two groups of sages specializing in recitation and dialectic respectively; this is the only instance I can find of *ba'ale ribbui*, but it seems plausible that this term similarly describes some kind of scholarly specialty (perhaps relating to Midrashic exegesis).[77] "Princes of prophecy" is also attested only here, but "princes" is of course the common term in Hekhalot literature for angels. It is possible that the particular formulation of this identification, the emphatic *we-hen hen*, is supposed to call attention to this difference between the groups of scholars and the angelic title. In the recto of our frag-

---

71   Ithamar Gruenwald, "New Passages from *Hekhalot* Literature" (Heb.), *Tarbiz* 38 (1969), 354–72 (368–72).

72   Schäfer, *Geniza-Fragmente*, 183–89.

73   See, e.g., *b. Yoma* 9b.

74   See, e.g. §274, though that text can also be interpreted as referring to humans.

75   Even in Hekhalot traditions; see, e.g., §92, §426, as well as in the Ozhaya fragment (= G8) 2a.2 (this is particularly important since this fragment might be related to fragment discussed here).

76   Cf. Sifre Deuteronomy §10 (ed. Finkelstein p. 18) and parallels noted there.

77   Gruenwald, "New Passages," 371 n. 12, already noted the Midrashic method *ribbui* in this context. See also the reference to it in the *Sar ha-Torah* narrative, n. 13 above.

ment, however, the same formulation is used simply to identify named angels as "the princes of Torah."[78]

This ambiguity goes beyond the titles that are applied to these protagonists. On the one hand, they are based at the throne of glory, where they are said to be "circling and standing" (1b.12), and we also hear of the turning of faces and vertical arrangement (1b.17), all details that resemble the choreography of the angelic liturgy in heaven. On the other hand, the protagonists are praised for their memory (1b.13). They engage, I argue in this section, in an activity we usually associate with human beings: the memorization, recitation, and processing of Tannaitic traditions. Even though they are described not just as *ba'ale mishnah* but also as *ba'ale talmud*, our text focuses on activities that seem much more appropriate to the former than the latter.

The passage that will concern us here, which begins in line 1b.13, was deemed by both scholars who published the fragment as incomprehensible, and both left it without much comment except that it somehow relates to Sar ha-Torah traditions.[79] The fragmentary, and possibly corrupt, nature of the text prohibits an interpretation of all its details, at least at this stage. Nevertheless, I think placing the passage in a hypothesized context of the recitation of Tannaitic tradition can shed considerable light on it.

The first two legible words of line 1b.13 are כאוצר בלוס. The expression אוצר בלום or אוצר בלום or אוצר בלוס is a difficult one, but at least in one other context, in *Avot de-Rabbi Nathan*, it is used to praise Rabbi Akiva's ability to process, memorize, and sift traditions.[80] Na'eh suggested tentatively, but convincingly, that the image is of a partitioned treasure box, close to the images related to the spatialized construction of memory discussed above.[81] Here, presumably, this phrase serves a similar function of praising the structured memory of "the latter ones." Both editions read the next word מע[..]ה and mark the ע as dubious since there is hole in the middle of the word. I propose to read this second letter as ש with the left side missing, and fill the lacuna to read משנה, best rendered here as "oral tradition" generally rather than the Mishnah. The clause would thus read: משנה מפיהם אין לה הפסק, "*mishnah* does not cease from their mouth." This line then praises the members of this group for their structured memory and for their ceaseless recitation of a large number of Tannaitic traditions (*rov mishnayot*).

---

78 ומרגיואל והדרוילייי כי הן הן שרי תורה in 1a.37.

79 See Grünwald, "New Passages," 371, and Schäfer, *Geniza-Fragmente*, 188.

80 למה היה רבי עקיבא דומה? לפועל שנוטל קופתו ויצא לשדה. מצא חטים, נתן בה; שעורים נותן בה . . . כך היה ר' עקיבא עושה כל התורה מטביעות מטביעות. *Abot de-Rabbi Nathan* A, 18.

81 Na'eh, "Memory," 566–68.

The next couple of lines are very intriguing and, if the reconstruction here is correct, they offer us a rare glimpse into the way scholars transmitted Jewish oral traditions in the early medieval period. Lines 1b.14–15 read: שהיא מושכת מ[ן] התוספות, שראשה שלה סותר אחריתה. The term *tosafot* ("additions") is a common term for collections of Tannaitic traditions that circulated in the Amoraic and Geonic periods;[82] in a responsum to which we shall return later, Rav Natronai Ga'on numbers the *tosafot* among things with which the *tanna'im* are occupied after prayer. Our text is referring to something that is "drawn[83] from" the *tosafot*, presumably a tradition (a *mishnah* or *baraita* or *halakhah*). The text also tells us that the beginning of this tradition contradicts the end of the tradition. The phenomenon described by our text, that is, a Tannaitic tradition in which the beginning contradicts the end, is often noticed by the Bavli, and in one place the formulation of that possibility (though it is rejected) uses the Aramaic equivalents of the terms in our text: ותני סיפא מלתא דסתרא ליה לרישא, "He recites an ending of a teaching that contradicts its beginning?!" (*b. Qidd.* 5b).[84]

The next line, 1b.15, reads, with my reconstruction: אמ[צעי]תה] ומשווין לראשיהן ומתוך השואה חזרת וסותרת זו את. The only fully legible letters of the first word are עצ, but what is legible from the other letters seems not to exclude the reconstruction proposed here. This reconstruction, אמצעיתה, "its middle," assumes that the text continues to refer to the same tradition from the *tosafot*, and that the problem is not only in the beginning and end of the tradition, but also in its middle. Again, the Bavli supplies a good parallel—see, for example, the discussion in *b. Ket.* 23b of the different contradictions between the beginning, middle (מציעתא), and end of a Tannaitic tradition (similar discussions are in *b. Git.* 17a and *b. 'Eruv.* 69b).

The text goes on to say that "they," presumably the "latter ones," seek to solve the problem by imposing coherence on the text. The verb employed here in two forms, משווין and השואה, is used in several Tannaitic sources that relate that R. Eliezer made his teaching corpus coherent, that is, that he ensured his rulings were consistent with one another. Thus, in *m. Sheqal.* 4:7, Rabbi Akiva prefers R. Eliezer's ruling because "he has made the totality of his teachings equal," while in *t. Yevam.* 13:2 it is R. Ishmael who prefers R. Eliezer's ruling for the same reason.

This harmonization seems to fail, since on account of it the tradition "again contradicts" another tradition (or perhaps, a part of this tradition

---

82 See Chanoch Albeck, *Studies in the Baraita and Tosefta* (Heb.; Jerusalem: Mosad Ha-Rav, 1954), 60–65.

83 Though grammatically the verb here is in the active form, מושכת, "draws."

84 For a use in rabbinic Hebrew of סותר in the sense of "contradict," see, e.g., *b. Shab.* 30a.

now contradicts another part—the crucial words are missing). It is possible that this failure to process properly the tradition from the *tosafot* is what leads to the "darkness and gloom" (כחשכה וכאפלה) mentioned in the following line (1b.16). The language of darkness is used several times in rabbinic literature to denote problems in study (see, e.g., the traditions about Babylonia in *b. Pes.* 34a and *b. San.* 24a). More important, the rhetoric of light or enlightening is applied in several sources to learning, and in particular to instruction in *mishnah*. Thus, as we have seen in Chapter 4, R. Yose refers to a master who enlightens his student's eyes in *mishnah* (*t. B. M.* 2:13). A similar expression occurs in another passage in our fragment, which promises its reader that he can use certain names "to open your eyes, which are as good as blind with respect to *mishnah*, and to enlighten your kidneys, which are like an opaque bottle." It is not clear how the problem indicated by this darkness is solved, but a few lines later we hear of the daily recitation of a fantastic number of collections of oral traditions (*sidre mishnayot*, 1b.20; cf. also 1b.18: "he recites fifty thousand and sixty others by heart"). The "latter ones," if we can assume they are still the subject of the passage, are gazing into these traditions every day (1b.21)—a reference to the visualization of oral tradition explored above.

If this reconstruction of lines 13–15 is correct, what is striking about this passage is that the recitation it describes is not a recitation of Hekhalot material or magic formulas but rather of the more conventional Tannaitic corpus with its typical *halakhic* detail. To be sure, the term *mishnah*, as we have seen, can certainly refer to Hekhalot narrative traditions or collections of divine names. The same might even be true for the *tosafot* mentioned here, though I have found no instance of such use of this term.[85] But it is hard to see how the attempt at harmonization described in lines 14–15 could apply to that kind of material: not only is the terminology in these lines familiar to us from *halakhic* contexts, but the attempt is premised on a striving for consistency that seems to fit a *halakhic* context much better.

Our passage places this scholarly recitation at the throne of glory; it describes whoever is performing it in terms that are elsewhere employed exclusively to describe angels;[86] and, as the description progresses, even

---

85   The term *tosafot* appears in one other tradition in the Hekhalot corpus (§77, §388, in a variation of the common curricular list: "Torah . . . *halakhot . . . shemu'ot . . . haggadot . . . tosafot. . . .*" The fact that this text alludes to the "seventy faces" of each of these bodies of tradition, which could be a reference to their hidden meanings, strengthens rather than weakens the reading of *tosafot* here in its conventional sense.

86   It is possible that the problem of identification can be solved by positing that the passage is describing some kind of transformation that occurs at some point after the darkness of line 16. Before that point, the protagonists are described as having great

the recitation itself seems to sound like the heavenly liturgy with its fantastic numbers and its ceaselessness. The text is too fragmentary to say much more about its message or context, but since the activities it describes were associated first and foremost with the *tanna'im*, it seems plausible to posit that it was composed by reciters who imagined their craft in the loftiest of terms. Another possibility that does not necessarily exclude this interpretation is that our text reflects the increasing role of Tannaitic materials in the liturgy of the Geonic period.[87] Be that as it may, our text equates, at least in some sense, the transmission of Tannaitic traditions with the highest form of worship, the angelic liturgy, assimilating an activity that we have not before associated with the Hekhalot tradition to the liturgy that stands at the very heart of that tradition.

BACK TO THE *TANNA'IM*

The centrality of memorization and recitation to these Hekhalot texts does not necessarily suggest any particular group of authors. These texts could have been composed by a wide range of sages. As we have seen, the Bavli's warning against sages associating with reciters should make us suspicious of attributing the values of memorization and recitation to that group alone, and it is possible that sages who had a different view than the Bavli would have wanted to emphasize these values to contest the dichotomy between scholarship and recitation. But when the centrality of these themes in Hekhalot literature is joined with other pieces of evidence about Hekhalot literature and the Babylonian reciters, it suggests that the latter had some role in shaping the former.

---

memory and ability to recite many traditions, but they also run into problems. After that point, they recite a number of traditions that far exceeds human capacity, and they can also view them. It is possible then, that the passage describes a transformation of reciters into reciting angels, that it tells us how the *ba'ale mishnah* and *ba'ale talmud* became the princes of prophecy at the throne of glory.

87   See the treatment in Adiel Kadari, "Between Scholars and the General Public in the Synagogue during the Gaonic Period: On the Historical Development of Torah Reading and Scholarly Customs Associated with Public Prayer" (Heb.), *Sidra* 19 (2004), 135–58, and the references to earlier literature there. Even if our text indeed reflects the recitation of Tannaitic materials in the synagogue, it does not seem to reflect the straightforward, uniform recitation (which Kadari terms "ritual") but rather the free-form liturgical study session; the one description of the *tanna'im*'s recitation in the synagogue indicates that it took the latter form rather than the more ritual form—it says they "engage [עוסקים] in *mishnah* for four hours" (Kadari, ibid., 150, implies that this engagement belongs in the "scholarly" category). For the source itself, see the following section.

We have already seen Rav Hayya's testimony that it is through the *tanna'im* that we know *Hekhalot Rabbati* and *Hekhalot Zutarti*. In another responsum, Rav Hayya numbers several Hekhalot texts as *mishnayot*,[88] "recited," or "Tannaitic" traditions. This conforms to those Hekhalot texts that identify themselves or other Hekhalot traditions as *mishnah* and instruct their readers to recite them.[89]

In fact, even if we did not have Rav Hayya's statement, it would stand to reason that Hekhalot texts were transmitted by the *tanna'im*. The repertoire of these reciters included all Tannaitic traditions, and since Hekhalot texts were attributed to Tannaitic sages such as Rabbi Akiva and Rabbi Ishmael, and since Geonic authors generally did not contest this attribution (to the best of my knowledge), there is no reason to think that this corpus would be an exception.[90] The consistent attribution of Hekhalot traditions to these Tannaitic sages gains further significance by the suggestion that these traditions were transmitted by *tanna'im*: on the one hand, Geonic-era *tanna'im* are never identified, nor do they ever identify, by name;[91] on the other hand, as those entrusted with the traditions of Tannaitic-period sages such as Rabbi Ishmael and Rabbi Akiva, we might understand why they would conceive their own creation as the development of the Torah of these sages.

Another source that is instructive for our purposes is a version of a Talmudic anecdote preserved in *Midrash ha-Gadol*. The anecdote comes in the middle of the famous Messianic discussion in *b. San.* 97a, and it

---

88   See Simcha Emanuel, *Newly Discovered Geonic Responsa* (Heb.; Jerusalem and Cleveland: Ofeq Institute, 1995), 132 (§115). This reference might be talking about written texts (Rav Hayya says that anyone who sees these compositions becomes afraid), but the term *mishnayot* still indicates that they were transmitted and recited by *tanna'im*; compare the Mishnah, which was by Rav Hayya's time certainly written in copies of the Talmud, and yet was still transmitted by *tanna'im*. The earliest reference to something like our Hekhalot texts does seem to refer to writing. Rav Natornai Ga'on refers to "letters written in *ma'aseh merkavah* in couplets" (Robert Brody, *Teshuvot rav natronai bar hilai* [2nd ed.] (Jerusalem and Cleveland: Ofeq Institute, 2011), §516, 626). This has often been identified with a passage in *Hekhalot Rabbati* (§276)—see, e.g., Lawrence H. Schiffman and Michael D. Swartz, *Hebrew and Aramaic Incantation Texts from the Cairo Genizah* (Sheffield: Sheffield Academic, 1991), 141. Since, however, Natronai's discussion comes in the context of the Talmud's discussion of amulets (גלוטרין, *ligaturae*, thus Sokoloff, *JBA*) in *b. Shab.* 103b, his statement may also refer to amulets (but see Brody's reservations in *Teshuvot rav natronai*, 626 n. 4).

89   See Schäfer, *Synopse*, §419, §421, §424, §300, §311, §§705–6, §952.

90   See Brody, *Geonim*, 170, and the exception noted there, n. 55. Rav Hayya comes close to implying that they are not really Tannaitic when he claims neutrality on the question of whether Hekhalot-related passages in the Talmud (and, by implication, the Hekhalot texts he mentions) are reliable traditions (*halakhah*) or not. See Lewin, *Otzar*, Ḥag., Resp. 14.

91   Simcha Emanuel, "New Responsa of R. Hai Ga'on" (Heb.), *Tarbiẓ* 69 (2000), 105–26 (117).

tells us, in the common version, that R. Ze'ira saw "rabbis who occupied themselves with him [i.e., the Messiah]. He told them, 'Please, I beg you, do not drive it [i.e., redemption] away. For it was taught: Three come unawares: the Messiah, a found article, and a scorpion.'" The version preserved in *Midrash ha-Gadol* is different in three ways: first, it identifies those whom R. Ze'ira sees not as rabbis but as "those reciters" (*hanne tanna'e*); second, it identifies the subject of their activity not as the Messiah himself but as "the chapter of Messiah," that is, a certain text concerning the Messiah (this variant also correlates with a Yemenite manuscript of the Bavli); third, R. Ze'ira says, "do not raise him up, so he [or his time] would not be pushed away."[92]

Given the subject matter and R. Ze'ira's response, one intriguing possibility is that the activity referred to here is magical, and that the *tanna'im* are trying to "adjure" the Messiah by reciting the "Chapter of the Messiah" (which might refer to the *baraita* cited on that folio in the Bavli). This also coheres with the list R. Ze'ira uses: just as you do not find a lost article or encounter a scorpion when you are actively looking for them, the Messiah does not come when you are actively seeking him.

It is possible that the first variation of the version recorded by *Midrash ha-Gadol* is apologetic, that it only replaces "rabbis" with "reciters" in order to distance "real rabbis" from a controversial practice; it is difficult, however, to understand why a scribe would replace the generic "it" with a specific "Chapter of the Messiah" or why such a scribe would introduce the enigmatic element about raising up the Messiah. Be that as it may, this version need not be original for it to reflect the way that the *tanna'im* were perceived by whoever produced it. For our purposes here, what is crucial is that the text raises the possibility that the *tanna'im* had their own interests—in matters not too far from Hekhalot literature, however we may interpret the anecdote—which they pursued through the texts that they were reciting.

A most intriguing link between the Babylonian *tanna'im* and Hekhalot literature may also be suggested by the Ozhaya fragment. This fragment weaves together several Hekhalot traditions, including Sar ha-Torah traditions and an ascent account, into a narrative in which the angel Ozhaya plays an instructive role.[93] One of the difficult passages in the fragment

---

92   Mordechai Margulies, *Midrash Haggadol on the Pentateuch: Genesis* (Heb.; Jerusalem: Mosad Ha-Rav, 1947), 2.688. On this version as well as on Ms. Yemenite, see Mordechai Sabato, *A Yemenite Manuscript of Tractate Sanhedrin and its Place in the Text Tradition* (Heb.; Jerusalem: Yad Ben Zvi; Hebrew University, Department of Talmud, 1998), 32 and n. 35.

93   The fragment is catalogued as T.-S. K 21.95.C in the Cambridge catalogue. See Schäfer, *Geniza-Fragmente*, 97–111, marked there G8. For the first edition and commentary, see Gruenwald, "New Passages," 354–72; see also idem, *Apocalyptic Literature and*

concerns the identity of the receiver of a name which, like the name in
the *Sar ha-Torah* narrative, was hidden, only to be revealed in a certain
generation. This name, however, is much more exclusive and is revealed
not to any of the angels,

> but to another sage who is destined to be in the later years in *bet ha-rav*
> which is destined to be appointed before me in Babylonia, and by that house
> [*bayit*] Babylonia is destined to tie both crowns, the one from the six days of
> creation and the other from the later years, when I give this name to that
> sage who is destined to be appointed before me in Babylonia in *bet ha-
> rav. . . .* [94] (G8 2a 13–16)

The references in this passage to the sage and to *bet ha-rav* (Halperin
translates this expression as "the master's house";[95] Swartz renders it
"house of the rabbi";[96] Davila, "great house"[97]) are enigmatic. Gruenwald
suggests that it refers to the house of a head of an academy in Babylonia,
a house in which mystical speculation took place.[98] But since *bet ha-rav*
here seems to precede the sage that is destined to be in it, and thus cannot be that sage's house, and since it is improbable that the text speaks of
the appearance of the sage in some other sage's house, *bet ha-rav* here is
most likely an institution (this is also apparent in the expression "appointed in"; see more below).

I suggest we reconsider a possibility that Gruenwald raises and
rejects:[99] that *bet ha-rav be-bavel* here is *bet rabbenu shebe-bavel*, the synagogue associated with the Sura academy that was an important institution in Babylonia in the Geonic period. It is first mentioned in the Bavli,
where it appears once (*b. Meg.* 29b), but is also mentioned frequently in
connection with liturgy and synagogue customs in Geonic literature.[100]
The difference in the form of the name itself is inconsequential, and at

---

Merkavah Mysticism (Leiden: Brill, 1980), 188–90; Halperin, *Faces*, 369–71; Martha Himmelfarb, "Heavenly Ascent and the Relationship of the Apocalypses and the *Hekhalot*
Literature," *HUCA* 59 (1988), 73–100 (78–88).

94   Supplying three letters for a lacuna in the fragment, which reads: בבבל [ ] ת הרב.

95   Halperin, *Faces*, 390.

96   Swartz, *Scholastic Magic*, 213.

97   Davila, *Descenders*, 285.

98   Gruenwald, "New Passages," 355; see also Boustan, *From Martyr to Mystic*, 277–
88, "a circle or a school located in Babylonia in which esoteric knowledge and practice
are apparently taught."

99   Gruenwald, "New Passages," 355 n. 7. Gruenwald does not give any specific reason for his preference for the explanation cited in his name *infra*.

100 For a survey of this institution and a mention in Geonic literature, see Louis
Ginzberg, *Geonica I* (New York: Jewish Theological Seminary, 1909), 41–43.

least one text refers to the synagogue as *be rav*.[101] The identification is possible, even likely, because of the prominence of the institution: it seems to have been known throughout the Jewish world.[102] The fact that it is a synagogue makes it an even likelier context for the sort of traditions included in this fragment.

In a letter to the community in Fustat, Rav Sa'adyah Ga'on includes, among other greetings from elements in the Baghdad academic community, a greeting from "the reciters appointed in *bet rabbenu*."[103] Sa'adyah's description of the reciters as "appointed" (*qevu'im*) in the synagogue is interesting not just because it implies a permanent, institutional connection between *bet rabbenu* and the *tanna'im*,[104] but also because it is precisely the same term that the Ozhaya fragment uses when it describes the sage who is "destined to be appointed [*lehiqava*] ... in Babylonia in *bet ha-rav*." To be sure, this resemblance in itself is not sufficient to identify the sage from the fragment with one of the appointed *tanna'im* to which Rav Sa'adyah refers—though I know of no other instance of individuals described as appointed in this synagogue—but the possibility is certainly intriguing. At the very least, the similarity between the formulations adds to the similarity between *bet ha-rav* in the Hekhalot fragment and the *bet rabbenu* we know from Geonic responsa.

These *tanna'im* appointed in *bet rabbenu* are described in a responsum from Rav Natronai Ga'on as follows:

> This is the custom in *bet rabbenu shebe-bavel*: after they say all the prayer and complete it and stop, *tanna'im* engage in Mishnah, *midrash* and *tosafot* up to four hours, and after four hours they say "[The Lord] answer you [in the day of trouble, the name of the God of Jacob will protect you [*yesagevkha*]" (Ps. 20:2), and complete it, and then they say "And one called to another and said ['Holy, holy, holy is the Lord of hosts; the whole earth is full of his glory' "] (Isa. 6:3), and they complete these two verses and they sanctify and leave to their houses.[105]

This report on the practice of the *tanna'im* in *bet rabbenu* is suggestive for our purposes in several ways. First, it considerably strengthens the association between this institution and the *tanna'im*, informing us that their recitation was an important feature of the ritual in *bet rabbenu* that

101   See Benjamin M. Lewin, *Ginze Qedem II* (Heb.; Haifa, 1922), 34 n. 8.

102   In addition to the number and diversity of references cited by Ginzberg, let me also note that the source in Lewin, *Ginze Qedem II*, 34 n. 8, is R. Shmuel ha-Nagid.

103   Lewin, *Ginze Qedem II*, 34 line 17.

104   See also Brody, *Geonim*, 42.

105   Brody, *Natronai*, 147. On the different versions of this responsum and their implications, see Emmanuel, "Hai Ga'on," 110–11.

occupied a significant amount of time of the liturgy.[106] This supports the
possibility that the sage "to be appointed in *bet ha-rav*" from the Ozhaya
fragment is indeed one of these *tanna'im* who played such a visible role in
the life of *bet rabbenu*.

Second, the Ga'on's report shows us how the engagement of the
tanna'im with Tannaitic traditions might not be just an auxiliary and inferior part of the study session, as we know it from Talmudic sources, but
rather have its own importance as a part of the liturgy. It is also suggestive that the particular liturgical context in which it is deployed also includes the verse most associated with the heavenly liturgy, Isa. 6:3
(though, it seems, not Ezek. 3:12 or other verses from the *qedushah*), and
another verse that could easily have associations with magical practice or
even ascent.

If we trust Rav Hayya's testimony that the repertoire of the *tanna'im*
included the recitation of Hekhalot traditions, there is good reason to
think that the daily recitation after the prayer in *bet rabbenu* included
such traditions. This coheres with the way recitation is prescribed in the
Hekhalot texts themselves: a passage in *Hekhalot Zutarti* urges its audience to "recite this *mishnah* every day after the prayer" (§419); a tradition in *Shi'ur Qomah* says that "whoever recites this great secret, recites
this *mishnah* every day after his prayer, let him say it in purity either at
home or in the synagogue" (§706);[107] and the *Sar ha-Torah* section of *Hekhalot Rabbati* instructs the sage to "set this *midrash* of Sar ha-Torah in his
prayer three times each day after the prayer that he prays from beginning
to end, and then let him sit and recite [*yishneh*] it in his recitation [*be-
mishnah*] ..." (§300).[108] To be sure, even here the connection is not necessary, and we certainly know of recitations of *mishnayot* and *baraitot*
after prayer that seem to involve neither *tanna'im* nor Hekhalot texts. At
the very least, however, the fact that both the recitation of Hekhalot material and the recitation of Tannaitic materials occur after the prayer indicates that both kinds of traditions belong to the same liturgical "syn-
tax." Indeed, it seems likely that if the *tanna'im* transmitted such texts as
Hekhalot Zutarti or the *Sar ha-Torah* section, which instruct their users to

---

106 See also the reference in *b. Naz.* 4a, "As is recited by *beit rabbenu*," where we
would expect *bei rav* if the reference is to Rav's students; this unique formulation (which
is perhaps connected with the linguistic uniqueness of the tractate) might therefore quote
a tradition as it was recited by *tanna'im* appointed in the synagogue.

107 Reading with Mss. M40 and O1531; N8128 reads: "whoever recites this great
secret, shall pray after it eight blessings." The version in Ms. New York is of course much
easier, but it is difficult to see how, if it is the original, the other version emerged (perhaps it is a transfer from elsewhere?).

108 See textual variants in the *Synopse*.

recite them every day after the prayer, they would do so in contexts like the one described by Rav Natronai.

The Ozhaya fragment discusses a sage, destined to be appointed in *bet ha-rav* in Babylonia, for whom a name is kept that will allow Babylonia to "tie two crowns." I have suggested that this *bet ha-rav be-bavel* is *bet rabbenu shebe-bavel*, the synagogue known chiefly from Geonic sources, and that the sage referred to in the fragment might be one of the *tanna'im* permanently and visibly associated with that synagogue.

This suggestion can be extended by raising the possibility that the Ozhaya fragment and Rav Natornai's report are connected with the recitation fragment discussed in the previous section (T-.S. K 21.95g). Schäfer observed that the handwriting of both fragments, as well as of a fragment of *Shi'ur Qomah* (Heb. c.65), is so strikingly similar that the three could be ascribed to a single scribe if not a single codex;[109] but, as Gruenwald wrote, the precise connection between the contents of these fragments is unclear.[110] If *bet ha-rav* in the Ozhaya fragment is indeed *bet rabbenu*, the two fragments may also be connected in content.

The Ozhaya fragment tells us that the sage for whom the name was kept will be appointed in "the latter years" (*aharit ha-shanim*; from Ezek. 38:8). The protagonists of the recitation fragment are identified as "the latter ones" (*ahronim*). The same fragment describes a recitation of Tannaitic texts that is both liturgical and scholarly, much like the recitation in *bet rabbenu*, while the sage of the other fragment is appointed in *bet ha-rav*. It is possible, therefore, that the sage of the "latter years" is connected with the "latter ones" of the recitation fragment, and that the recitation described in that fragment is the recitation in *bet rabbenu*.

What precisely these fragments tell us is again very difficult to say. But if the reconstruction here is correct, they seem to provide a narrative framework for the work of the *tanna'im* of that synagogue, a narrative that will imply that one of them was meant for greatness, that Babylonia is crowned on their account, and that through their engagement with Tannaitic sources they participate in a heavenly liturgy that consists of the same recitation.

CONCLUSION

This chapter has offered a particular historical context for a stage in the formation of Hekhalot literature. It explored the possibility that parts of this literature were shaped by a debate about the Babylonian ethos of

109   Schäfer, *Geniza-Fragmente*, 183.
110   Gruenwald, "New Passages," 354.

Torah study in the late Talmudic and early Geonic periods, that the *tanna'im* of that time contributed to this literature's development, and that the passages studied here give us a glimpse into what the Hekhalot tradition in general might have meant to those who transmitted it in this particular time and place.

The investigation undertaken here of memorization and recitation in Hekhalot texts contributes to our understanding of this corpus whether one accepts or rejects this hypothesis about its historical context. The focus on these topics allows us to uncover the locational construction of memory behind a significant number of Hekhalot passages, the transformative performance of recitation central to the self-conception of some Hekhalot works, and the interest in a particular configuration of Torah study that drives the *Sar ha-Torah* narrative. These features are important enough to the texts in which they appear that they merit study and emphasis independently of our ability to fix firmly these texts' exact social and institutional context. This chapter also sheds light on the Bavli's opposition between *talmud* and recitation even if our Hekhalot authors did not have the Bavli in mind. Our texts show us what an ideology of rabbinic recitation and memorization could look like, and implicate it with passages that seem to mirror the Bavli's ideology. They thus allow us at least to imagine the other side of the Bavli's polemic.

Still, if this chapter's suggestion about their context is indeed correct, these texts offer us a rare opportunity to hear the opposition to the voice of the Bavli, which is all too often the only voice that survives. The debate that emerges from the juxtaposition of the Talmud with Hekhalot traditions is a debate between two approaches to engagement with tradition—one that stressed internalizing memory and embodying ritual, and another that emphasized externalizing analysis and scholastic innovation. If these texts do indeed oppose the Bavli, they highlight the particularity of the Talmud's position in this debate and indicate that it did not go uncontested.

It is the recognition of this diversity that allows us to locate these Hekhalot traditions close to the heart of the rabbinic enterprise, both in terms of their social location and in terms of their concerns, while seeing in them an opposition to this enterprise's increasingly hegemonic claims to authority. These traditions were recited in the mouths of individuals who worked in the academies, and they participated in conversations on matters that lie at the center of rabbinic academic culture, but they also offered this culture an alternative vision of Torah.

CONCLUSION

This Conclusion aims to recapitulate the central arguments of this book and their implications, as well as to offer some reflections on developments in Jewish history that directed rabbinic culture away from the concerns and contexts studied in this book.

The first part of this book argues that it is precisely when the Talmud's creators seem most conservative—when they preserve traditions rather than reject or revise them—that we find their most profound break with tradition. It is through the embedding of fixed and authoritative traditions in discursive frameworks that are stylistically and substantially differentiated from them and through the presentation of traditions as products of certain historical moments that these scholars created their past and separated it from their present. It is in this process of past-making that the creators of the Talmud emerge most clearly as the authors of a text that is sometimes seen as lacking authorship. The focus on this process offers us a new perspective about some of the most pervasive and characteristic literary strategies of the Talmud.

Previous scholars have focused on passages that present opposite processes: passages in which the Talmud's creators rephrase traditions in their own words to fit new textual and cultural contexts, passages in which they create a system that homogenizes and harmonizes the traditions they had received, and passages in which they justify these traditions by reading back their own reasoning into them. As we have seen in the Introduction, scholars have explained such passages by appealing to supposedly omnipresent features of rabbinic, pre-modern, or oral discourse. The passages discussed in this book warn us against such explanations by showing us that the Talmud can act very differently. It is not the case that oral culture cannot produce a distinction between the transmitters and the transmitted. It is not the case that rabbinic, Jewish, or religious culture by definition requires a specific kind of "deference" toward the past, that it always appeals to the "eternal yesterday" or that it always "merges the horizons."

Still, these chapters aim to do more than show the limits of previous theories or point at exceptions to the rules with which we have been reading the Talmud. They seek to offer a different perspective on these rules and the Talmudic practices and texts from which these rules were derived. The division of materials into distinct layers was not always imposed, as it is in the *Pesahim* passage studied in Chapter 2, on material that did not feature this division. But because the formation of this passage shows us this division as the product of labor and art rather than the inevitable indication of the passage of time, it allows us to focus on the work it does for the creators of the Talmud. It shows us how this division produces a space for the creators' own interpretation, how this space allows them to display their virtuosity, how the division between "ruling" and "dialectic" may have supported an oral performance that won points for the performer-authors in a competitive environment that looked up to tradition but demanded innovation.

Not in every text does the Talmud call attention, as it does in the opening of *Bava Qamma* studied in Chapter 1, to the contrast between its own approach and the approach of the tradition it cites. The conclusion of that passage works so well because it frustrates the audience's expectation that the two approaches will be harmonized, an expectation that is informed by the hundreds of instances in which the Talmud does offer such harmonization. But the contrast that passage in *Bava Qamma* presents between "our" systematic conclusion and "their" tradition expresses an alienation that is present even when it is not advertised. It raises the possibility that even when the creators of the Talmud do justify tradition, that is, when they bridge the gap between their standards and the materials they receive, they do so out of a sense of this gap and through a literary form that maintains it and makes it visible.

The discussion in *Qiddushin*, studied in Chapter 3, depends on some particularities of rabbinic genealogical traditions, and the topic of genealogy offers the Talmud an opportunity to discuss the production and manipulation of traditional knowledge with a special intensity and clarity. But this discussion of genealogy shows how attribution and narratives about sages work to throw a spotlight on the context in which tradition is produced. It is not rare for the Talmud to use these literary devices to situate a tradition in a certain moment and tie it to a personal or collective motive (benevolent or malevolent). To a certain extent, these literary phenomena always historicize the knowledge that they qualify.

Precisely because the argument here is about pervasive literary devices, it concerns an attitude basic to the Talmud's mode of literary production rather than some particularly Talmudic "philosophy of tradition." More than executing some ideological plan for the Talmud's creators, this mode of production balances a reliance on traditional authority with a claim to intellectual virtuosity, preserves a commitment to tradition even as it acknowledges a shift in values or positions, and answers particular challenges of oral textuality. More than imparting a certain propositional statement or message through literary design, these moves shape the Talmud's audience to have a certain disposition of discontinuity (critical or admiring, suspicious or affirming) toward the traditions it presents.

The second part of this book argues that this relation to tradition was important for the self-understanding of the Talmud's creators, and that both this relation and this self-understanding were informed by debates within and outside the Jewish community in Babylonia. When the "masters of *talmud*" thought about what made them "masters of *talmud*," they did so in part by thinking about how they were different from "masters of *mishnah*," or the reciters of tradition. They presented themselves as scholars defined by their ability to analyze tradition and generate new knowledge, and they presented the reciters as mindless assistants whose recitation helps the scholarly enterprise if done properly but it is of little value in itself.

We have seen that this distinction misrepresents the Talmud's opponents. It is not just that the reciters had a more central and more diverse role in the religious and intellectual life of the Babylonian Jewish community; it is that the very distinction between "masters of *talmud*" and "masters of *mishnah*" was overdrawn. Even the most polemical Talmudic text against the latter implies that: the Talmud's objection to reciters who "instruct the law" shows us that at least some reciters issued legal rulings; its warning to its own audience of scholars not to intermingle with reciters would have been needed only if the boundary between scholars and reciters was, at least occasionally, blurred in reality.

We are dealing here not with scholars mocking their mindless assistants but with a debate over the definition of scholarship. The recitation of tradition, it is posited here, was not just an aid to scholarship that then analyzed tradition, as we find it in the Talmud. Rather, it was a ritual in its own right, which allowed agents at various levels of learning to embody tradition. It was an integral part of the kind of scholarship that transmits tradition creatively, and our evidence suggests that reciters were indeed scholars in that sense that does not differentiate transmission and analysis. The last chapter of this book argues that some texts in Hekhalot literature were shaped by those reciters; but even if this was not the case, these Hekhalot texts show us how recitation can be the cornerstone of Jewish intellectual culture rather than a mocked aid to Talmudic-style scholarship.

Taking the Talmud's opponents seriously allows us to imagine what mostly undocumented visions of Jewish culture existed outside the circle of the Talmud's creators. When we consider the Talmud's definition of scholarship not as the necessary result of the development of rabbinic culture but as a position formulated in a debate with other alternatives, we can see more clearly the distinctive features of these alternatives. Since this contrast is between hierarchies of practices—emphasis on analysis and objectification of tradition vs. emphasis on transmission, recitation, and memorization—we can tie this debate to the Talmud's literary practices as well. The differentiation between the citing layer and the cited layer, the critique of tradition through narrative, the contrast between the present "us" and past "them" all cohere with the Talmud's insistence that reciters are distinct from scholars and with its derogatory references to the former.

The focus on recitation as a practice against which the Talmud's creators shape their own literary practice also offers us a way to relate this debate within the Jewish community to its encounter with other religious traditions of late ancient Mesopotamia. Because the Zoroastrian sacred texts had not been committed to writing until relatively late, the recitation of oral tradition was more central to Zoroastrianism than to other cultures that Jews and Christians encountered in late antiquity. The Talmud's unprecedented objection to recitation and the centrality of this objection in its creators' self-definition may have been in part a response to an intensification among Jews of the importance of recitation as a result of the encounter with Zoroastrian culture. Some Syriac texts close to the Talmud in time and place might indicate that the Christian community was engaged in a similar debate.

Even if the Talmud's negotiation of tradition and its ideology of scholarship were born out of a particular historical dynamic, they still belong in the longer intellectual history of Judaism. Certainly the tension between the authority of tradition, Scripture, and logical derivation (*din*) existed already in the earliest rabbinic texts that form the Tannaitic corpus. As is the case with the Talmud, the different approaches to these tensions were often thematized in these texts themselves or even define their very structure.[1] The most significant new solution the Bavli offered to these tensions, it was argued here, were the innovative literary techniques it employed to preserve and commit to tradition on one level, while distancing and undermining it on another. To be sure, some patterns in the Talmud's negotiation of tradition are already present in the

---

1 For recent treatments of differing modes of justification in Tannaitic culture, see Menahem Kahana, "On the Fashioning and Aims of the Mishnaic Controversy" (Heb.), *Tarbiz* 73 (2004), 51–81; Ishay Rosen-Zvi, "Who Will Uncover the Dust from Your Eyes?: Mishnah Sotah 5 and Rabbi Akiva's Midrash" (Heb.), *Tarbiz* 75 (2006), 95–128; Azzan Yadin-Israel, "Rabbi Aqiva: Midrash as a Site of Revelation," in *Revelation, Literature and Community in Late Antiquity* (ed. P. Townsend and M. Vidas; Tübingen: Mohr Siebeck, 2011), 181–221.

earlier Talmud of Palestine. It would be misleading, however, to read that earlier document teleologically, as a "prototype" of the Bavli. The relevant discussions above show how the Palestinian scholars substantially differed from their Babylonian counterparts in both literary practice and self-conception.

The world that was described in this book was gradually replaced by another. At some point early during the Geonic period, *talmud* had become The Talmud—no longer the activity of creative engagement with tradition, but rather a text that was a product of past instances of that activity, transmitted in an increasingly fixed form. This text now formed the basis of legal rulings in the Babylonian academies and stood at the center of these academies' claim to authority, both in their competition with the Palestinian community over leadership of the Jewish world and in their defense of rabbinic tradition against the Karaite challenge.[2] Pirqoy ben Baboy, a ninth-century champion of both campaigns, offers us some indication of the way in which the Talmud functioned in the early Geonic period. He quotes R. Yehudai, an eighth-century Ga'on and, according to Pirqoy, his teacher's teacher, as assuring his readers that he had only issued legal rulings when he had found support for them in the Talmud and when he had a tradition that the law in question should be followed.[3] The fact that tradition is placed here as a control on the Talmudic text shows us that the Talmud has not yet achieved the overwhelming and self-sufficient authority it would acquire later on; but it is an astonishing testament to the new authority of the Talmud that R. Yehudai explicitly says that even when he *did* have a tradition from his

---

2 See Brody, *Geonim*, 161–62. On the problem of treating the Talmud as a *halakhic* document in the Geonic period in particular, see Neil Danzig, *Introduction to Halakhot Pesuqot* (Heb.; New York and Jerusalem: Jewish Theological Seminary, 1999), 133–35; Brody, *Geonim*, 164–65; and on the same problem beyond Geonic sources, see Ephraim E. Urbach, *The Halakhah: Its Sources and Development* (trans. R. Posner; Tel Aviv: Massada, 1986), 345–57. The scholarly consensus on the emergence of the Talmud as a fixed, authoritative source for ruling in the Geonic period was recently challenged by Talya Fishman, *Becoming the People of the Talmud: Oral Torah as Written Tradition in Medieval Jewish Cultures* (Philadelphia: University of Pennsylvania Press, 2011), 20–64. Fishman's arguments about the fluidity of the text are undermined both by the evidence of actual variation and by the way Geonic authors speak about the Talmud's text (see n. 5 below). More important, while her account is correct in emphasizing the importance of the concept of *halakhah le-ma'aseh* (a tradition to be followed in practice; see also Brody, *Geonim*, 171–81), it underestimates the way that the Talmud did become an authoritative source for the Geonim—see also n. 4 below.

3 The most extensive publication from the letter is in Louis Ginzberg, *Geniza Studies II: Geonic and Early Karaitic Halakah* (New York: Jewish Theological Seminary, 1929), 504–73; the passage in question is on pp. 558–59. See Danzig, *Introduction*, 19–22. On Pirqoy, see Brody, *Geonim*, 113–17.

rabbi that a certain law is to be followed, he did not in fact issue a ruling to that effect if it had no support in the Talmud itself.[4]

While the predominantly oral transmission of this Talmud still resulted in considerable fluidity in form, the contents of the text had by then become more or less fixed.[5] Geonic authors could talk about things that are or are not in the Talmud and, in some specific contexts, even about specific formulations: according to Pirqoy, R. Yehudai said that "it is forbidden to recite any benediction that is not found in the Talmud, and it is forbidden to add even one letter."[6] Talmudic *sugyot* were no longer developed dramatically as they were presented in the academy. If the dynamic relationship between tradition and innovation observed in Chapter 2 was driven in part by the fact that *sugyot* were presented by advanced scholars who were expected to re-create them as they were transmitting them, at some point during the Geonic period the presentation of the Talmud was given to junior professional transmitters, who were criticized if they deviated from the text.[7] By the ninth century, the Talmud began circulating in written copies.[8]

---

4   Fishman's translation of this passage (*Becoming*, 46) misrepresents R. Yehudai's point. The translation Fishman offers is, "But any matter for which there is proof in the Talmud, but for which I did not have [testimony] from my teacher or from his teacher, as a *halakhah le-ma'aseh*, I did not say to you." The text actually reads: "But any matter for which there is proof in the Talmud, but which I did not have *halakhah le-ma'aseh* from my teacher, *or which I had halakhah le-ma'aseh from [my] teacher, but for which there is no proof in the Talmud,* I did not say to you." Fishman's translation ignores the words "but for which there is no proof in the Talmud," and this omission allows her to understand the "or" as referring to "his teacher" (which I corrected here to "my teacher," as the structure of the complete sentence implies; see Danzig, *Introduction*, 20). In the footnote to her translation, Fishman writes, "translation from Brody, *Geonim*, 179"—but the translation given in Brody is different and does not omit the second condition. The translation Fishman offers presents R. Yehudai as emphasizing the non-exclusivity of the Talmud, when in fact he emphasizes the importance of both practiced tradition and the Talmud, showing us, strikingly, that by that time the absence of textual Talmudic support had the power to cancel rabbinic tradition.

5   See Brody, *Geonim*, 161, and in much more detail idem, "Sifrut ha-ge'onim veha-teqst ha-talmudi," in *Talmudic Studies I* (ed. Y. Sussmann and D. Rosenthal; Jerusalem: Magnes, 1990), 237–303. On the emergence of Geonic textual criticism in the ninth century, see Uziel Fuchs, "The Role of the Geonim in the Textual Transmission of the Babylonian Talmud" (Heb.; Ph.D. dissertation, Hebrew University, 2003), especially 290 and 297–98.

6   Ginzberg, *Genizah Studies II*, 550.

7   Neil Danzig, "From Oral Talmud to Written Talmud: On the Methods of Transmission of the Babylonian Talmud and its Study in the Middle Ages," *Bar-Ilan* 30–31 (2006), 49–112 (90–102); David Rosenthal, "*Rabbanan de'Siyyum'a* (רבנן דסיומא) and *Bene Siyyume* (בני סיומי)" (Heb.), *Tarbiẓ* 49 (1980), 52–61 (and see ibid., 58, on the similarities of these functionaries to *tanna'im*).

8   Danzig, "From Oral Talmud to Written Talmud," 61–67.

The emergence of the Talmud as a fixed and authoritative text entailed not just a gradual end of the compositional activities described in this book, but also an understanding of the Talmud that weakened some of the effects of these activities. Because the anonymous layer came to lose a great deal of its function—it no longer operated as a dynamic space for the presenters' own *talmud*, but was more or less a fixed narration to be retrieved from memory or books—it also lost much of its identity. The anonymous framework was now almost as stable as the traditions embedded in it, and the relationship between these traditions and their interpretations in the *stam* was cemented.

This process was gradual and hardly uniform. Even in medieval manuscripts of the Talmud, the *stam*, while relatively stable, shows more variation than its sources. Rav Sherira Ga'on's classic letter about the formation of rabbinic literature refers to different versions of the Talmud as resulting from different oral presentations of the material. But R. Sherira does not make a distinction between the layers in this matter. Furthermore, he does not see these variations as intentional innovations; like other Geonic authors he minimizes the importance of variation, arguing that while particular formulations may differ their meaning is nonetheless uniform.[9] Later on, in the twelfth century, R. Jacob b. Meir admonished those who changed the text of the Talmud not just in parts that "seem like an interpretation," but in "the words of the *tanna'im* and *amora'im* themselves."[10] This formulation may indicate that Rabbenu Tam expected, and perhaps even tolerated, changes in the *stam*; but evidently at least some of his contemporaries did not make such a distinction between the layers, and even he himself was only making a tentative and relative distinction between interpretation and sources.

A more important factor in the reception of the layered structure was the authority of the Talmud as a whole. The Geonim treated the anonymous layer as authoritative[11] and read Talmudic traditions through it

9   See especially his discussion in Benjamin M. Lewin, *Iggeret rav sherira ga'on* (Haifa, 1921), 48 and 58. Some of the types of variations Rav Sherira discusses could be related to the *stam*, but he may also refer to alternative formulations of traditions.

10   The translation is according to the emendations suggested, based on manuscript versions, by Schlesinger as cited in Shamma Friedman, *Talmudic Studies: Investigating the Sugya, Variant Readings, and Aggada* (New York and Jerusalem: Jewish Theological Seminary, 2010), 12.

11   This is evident not just from rare programmatic statements in which a Ga'on seems to explicitly include the *stam* in the authority of the Talmud (for which, see Friedman, *Talmudic Studies*, 13), but also, more interestingly, from Geonic rules for *halakhic* decisions. Those include, for example, ruling according to tradition on which the Talmud comments, relying on the Talmud's statement that a certain solution is valid, trusting that the citation by the Talmud of a certain source means that the source is authoritative, and so forth. For examples, see Robert Brody, *Teshuvot rav natronai bar hilai ga'on* [2nd ed.]

rather than in contrast with it. Differences between the *stam* and its sources did not, therefore, play an important role in their engagement with the Talmud.[12] In fact, it is not out of the ordinary for Geonim to attribute to an Amoraic sage a statement that the *stam* offers in that sage's defense.[13] In contrast, the layered structure is present in the commentaries of Rashi and the Tosafists who refer on a significant number of occasions to "the Talmud" or even "the authors of the Talmud" as agents distinct from attributed traditions, but even the latter apply this distinction only in the case of specific interpretive problems.[14] This book argues that the division between the layers was adopted by the creators of the Talmud to distance source from interpretation and tradition from innovation. The way medieval readers transmitted and used the Talmud meant that they had few occasions to pit the anonymous layer against its sources; both were now the authoritative words of the Bavli.

The authoritative Bavli was part of a Geonic understanding of rabbinic tradition that was more conservative than the one we find in the Bavli itself. While the Talmud records a number of perspectives on the relative merits of transmission and innovation, we have seen that its creators clearly identified with the latter. Geonic authors present the opposite preference, both in their construction of the rabbinic past and in their own vision of Torah study. One example of this preference from Rav

---

(Jerusalem and Cleveland: Ofeq Institute, 2011), 82–87; Tsvi Groner, "Rav Hai Gaon: His Halachic Methodology" (Heb.; Ph.D. dissertation, Hebrew University, 1974); Simha Assaf, *Tequfat ha-ge'onim ve-sifrutah* (Jerusalem: Mosad Ha-Rav, 1955), 231. These are in addition, of course, to Geonic acceptance of anonymous rulings in the Bavli.

12   We do find in Geonic literature objections to the authority of certain dialectical components, in particular to the *shinuya*, or "solution for an objection," objections that follow statements found already in the Bavli itself (see, e.g., *b. B. B.* 135a, "should we rely on a [mere] solution?"). But while such components are found mostly in the *stam*, these objections were applied to attributed interpretations as well; and the Geonim (as opposed to North African scholars) only rejected such elements when the law was to be decided against the rabbi in whose defense such "solution" was made, accepting the legal applicability made in other cases. See Yedidya Dinari, "The Attitude to the Talmudic 'shinuya' in the Rabbinical Literature," *Bar Ilan* 12 (1974), 108–17 (108–13); Groner, *Rav Hai*, 69–70, and the examples cited there. The formulation in Friedman, *Talmudic Studies*, 15, is therefore somewhat misleading.

13   See Brody, *Natronai*, 77, on Natronai Ga'on and others, and see especially the examples on p. 450 (and n. 12) and pp. 175–77 (nn. 6, 7, and 10). The latter example, as Brody writes, is important precisely because it shows awareness of the distinction (the Ga'on uses the first-person plural when paraphrasing the anonymous layer, but does not do so for the part of the *stam* that speaks for the *amora*; the use of the first-person plural for the *stam* itself is very interesting, showing a certain degree of identification of the Ga'on as a reader of the Talmud with the Talmud's anonymous voice).

14   Friedman, *Talmudic Studies*, 13–15; Ephraim E. Urbach, *The Tosaphists: Their History, Writings, and Methods* [5th ed.] (Heb.; Jerusalem: Bialik Institute, 1986), 726 and 717–20.

Sherira's letter is particularly instructive for our purposes because it presents a reversal of the passage from tractate *Sotah* studied in Chapter 4. The passage in the Talmud mocks the reciter who "does not know" what he recites, implies that reciters are unable to engage in the innovative study of *talmud*, and culminates with harsh words against reciters who dare to issue legal instructions. The Ga'on, in his discussion of the transmission of Tannaitic sources, acknowledges the importance of penetrating dialectical study for understanding them, but this acknowledgment prompts him to digress from the letter's historical narrative to assert, unambiguously, the preferability of conservation. Even though the memory-inclined scholar "does not know" how to extract logical implications from what he recites, the Ga'on explains, he is preferable to the innovation-inclined scholar because the *former* is more apt to issue legal instructions.[15] It is also telling that toward the conclusion of this digression, R. Sherira quotes approvingly a statement that the Talmud explicitly associates with the Palestinian rabbis about the preferability of the scholar who can retain over the scholar who can innovate.[16]

This ideal also informed the way that the Geonim understood the formation of rabbinic literature in general and the Talmud in particular. Geonic authors emphasize that the rabbis of the Mishnah and the Talmud were transmitters rather than creators. They saw rabbinic biblical exegesis not as the source of new laws but as a way to show connections between Scripture and previously established traditions of the Oral Torah.[17] In a number of passages, R. Sherira mentions intellectual innovation and then reframes it in terms of conservation. In his account of the Talmud's formation, for example, he writes that "the rabbis would add and innovate explications and analytical discussions. And not [in such matters] that were unknown to the earlier rabbis; but rather in what they [the earlier rabbis], left to those after them so that they [the later rabbis] may distinguish themselves with it."[18] The Talmud was thus understood to be not a document of innovative, analytical engagement with the traditions

15 Lewin, *Iggeret*, 44–45.

16 Lewin, *Iggeret*, 46, quoting *b. Hor.* 14a. While we may infer (mostly from other texts) that in the story the Palestinian preference is meant to be opposed to a Babylonian preference, that is not explicit in the story.

17 See David E. Sklare, *Samuel ben Hofni Gaon and his Cultural World* (Leiden: Brill, 1996), 43–46; Jay Harris, *How Do We Know This? Midrash and the Fragmentation of Modern Judaism* (Albany: State University of New York Press, 1995), 73-81. The Geonic understanding of *midrash halakhah* reflects faithfully some constructions of *midrash* in the Tannaitic period itself; but it stands against the Bavli's construction of *midrash* as a creative and constitutive interpretation of Scripture. See Yadin-Israel, "Midrash as the Site of Revelation," for a discussion of the difference between the Tannaitic sources and the Bavli on Aqivan *midrash.*

18 Lewin, *Iggeret*, 67 (cf. *b. Hul.* 7a and parallels; but note that what is applied to

of the past, but rather an elucidation of what was already implied by earlier generations. This representation of the development of rabbinic tradition has, of course, good precedence in rabbinic literature as a whole and even in the Talmud itself.[19] But this emphasis on conservation is tied to an ideal of Torah study that stands against a significant body of *sugyot* that have been identified by scholars as forming the core of Talmudic ideology.[20] In staking these claims, Geonic authors chose certain passages from the Talmud that supported their position, ignored other passages, and on occasion, as we have seen, reversed the tone of certain *sugyot*.[21]

This difference between the Geonim and the Talmud may be connected with a shift in the rabbis' rivals. One of the *sugyot* studied in Chapter 4 called the "masters of *mishnah*" the rabbis' haters and the "masters of Scripture" the rabbis' brethren. By the middle of the Geonic period, the major challenge for the rabbinic establishment was presented precisely by such "masters of Scripture," the Karaites. The Geonim now had to defend *mishnah* or rabbinic tradition and present themselves as the last in a long chain of faithful transmitters. Conservative accounts of rabbinic texts, which ascribed them to an "eternal yesterday" or to divine revelation, may have become more prominent in the Geonic period to fend off Karaite claims.[22] But we can also see Karaite critiques of rabbinic tradition and Geonic anxieties about rabbinic innovation as cognate phenomena reflecting broader intellectual patterns of the time, which were shared by, or perhaps even stemmed from, Islamic culture.[23]

To be sure, rabbinic culture in the Geonic period was itself quite innovative. From the perspective of this book's concerns, it is particularly

---

specific legal rulings in the Bavli becomes a principle through which the entirety of rabbinic literature may be understood). For another example, see also ibid., 52.

19   See the texts and studies quoted in the Introduction.

20   See p. 115 n. 1 above.

21   The account of these matters in Fishman, *Becoming*, 28–32 and 36–44, either assumes or argues for a continuity between the Geonic and Talmudic concepts of tradition. Fishman acknowledges that the Geonic representation of the rabbis as transmitters was "undoubtedly precipitated" by concerns of their own era, but urges her readers to consider that the view of the rabbis as innovators is in fact unduly influenced by the Tosafists (44). Again, while the Geonim certainly are continuous with certain strands of rabbinic literature, Fishman ignores not just passages from the Bavli that celebrate the rabbis as innovators but also recent works that have emphasized the centrality of these passages to the academic culture that created the Bavli. Thus, for example, she sees the Geonic preference of the memorizer over the innovator as representative of late ancient Jewish society as a whole (29).

22   On the Geonic view of *midrash* as a response to the Karaites, see Harris, *Midrash*, 79–80.

23   See especially Sklare, *Samuel ben Hofni*, 159–65; Marina Rustow, *Heresy and the Politics of Community: The Jews of the Fatamid Caliphate* (Ithaca, NY: Cornell University Press, 2008), 24–8.

important to note the rise of individual authorship: for the first time, rabbis began producing single-authored works bearing an author's name.[24] This new mode of writing obviated many of the problems the Talmud solved through the strategies we have examined: the original contribution of a text and its relation to its predecessors were now clear. But if a move toward an authorial voice and a differentiation between tradition and systematization indeed underlie some of the innovations the Bavli introduced to rabbinic writing, as is suggested here, it is possible to see the Talmud as standing on the border between classical and medieval types of rabbinic text production. As it was clinging to the conventions of the former, it also tried to meet some of the expectations of authorial originality and systematic consistency that shaped the latter—and the result was a document that is quite unlike the texts produced in either periods.

The developments surveyed in the last few pages transformed the function of tradition in Jewish culture, the production of Jewish texts, and the way the Talmud's negotiation of tradition was understood. The inquiry undertaken in this book has aimed to reconstruct not just this negotiation, but also the dynamic world of tensions, dispositions, and ambitions of which it was a part: the competitive drive of the Talmud's creators to dazzle their demanding audiences with performances that worked to showcase innovation or outdo previous treatments; the sharpness and humor of the storytellers who exposed the political absurdity behind venerable knowledge; the power with which ritual recitation offered its practitioners to traverse time and embody their sacred texts; the boldness in the Talmud's avoidance of that bridge between past and present and its creation of an ethos of study that thrived over that gap; and the soaring ambition of the Hekhalot authors, who asserted their own vision of tradition with heavenly palaces and princely angels.

24 Brody, *Geonim*, 249–55, and Rina Drory, *The Emergence of Jewish-Arabic Literary Contacts at the Beginning of the Tenth Century* (Heb.; Tel Aviv: Ha-Kibbutz ha-me'uhad, 1988), 171–72.

Acknowledgments

Peter Schäfer directed the Princeton dissertation on which this book is based and taught me how to be a scholar. It is a particular pleasure to thank other members of the Department of Religion—especially Martha Himmelfarb, who has greatly shaped the way I ask questions about ancient Judaism, John Gager, Elaine Pagels, AnneMarie Luijendijk, and Jeffrey Stout—for their mentorship and support both as former teachers and as current colleagues.

The transformation of that dissertation into this book began at the University of California, Davis. David Biale has brought me into that wonderful world and also commented on parts of this book. My chair in Religious Studies Naomi Janowitz, my chair in Jewish Studies Diane Wolf, and Dean Jessie Ann Owens welcomed me warmly to UCD and made sure my research was supported.

Catherine Chin and Daniel Boyarin in particular made my years in California so intellectually invigorating that my thanks to them are owed chiefly for distracting me from this book, giving me energy to work on new projects even while restructuring or fine-tuning parts of this one.

Jeffrey Rubenstein wrote a report on the work that provided a road map for revisions in an early stage. Azzan Yadin-Israel served as one of the readers for the Press, and his detailed comments resulted in numerous improvements, especially to the Conclusion; I am also grateful to the other reader for the Press for another helpful set of comments. Vered Noam offered advice on various aspects of this project, and her teaching has been a resource to me since the earliest days of my undergraduate education. I thank Charlotte Fonrobert for many stimulating conversations and for her support of this project. I learned a lot from Seth Schwartz during my sabbatical at Columbia, and I thank him and Jeremy Dauber for that valuable year. Philip Hollander served as a commentator on the introduction for a workshop organized by the AAJR, and offered the fresh perspective of a scholar outside the field.

For further conversations and comments, I thank Christine Hayes, Talya Fishman, Steven Fraade, Moshe Halbertal, Richard Kalmin, Naphtali Meshel, Hindy Najman, Ishay Rosen-Zvi, Shai Secunda, P. Oktor Skjærvø, David Stern, and Holger Zellentin. I hope to be able to continue to learn from these colleagues for years to come.

Lorraine Fuhrmann, Patricia Bogdziewicz, Kerry Smith, and Mary Kay Bodnar run Princeton's Department of Religion so smoothly that they make working in it a delight. Baru Saul does the same with the Program in Judaic Studies. The Whiting Foundation, the Mellon Foundation, and the American Council of Learned Societies provided financial support at crucial stages of this project.

Princeton University Press has been terrific to work with, from the proposal submission through the production stages—thanks to executive editor Fred Appel, editorial associate Sarah David, production editor Debbie Tegarden, and copyeditor Maria denBoer. I thank Tim DeBold for preparing the indices expertly.

A version of Chapter 3 appeared in a collection edited by Gregg E. Gardner and Kevin L. Osterloh; a version of Chapter 6 appeared in a collection edited by Ra'anan S. Boustan. As editors and colleagues they have had a significant impact on these chapters. I am especially grateful to Ra'anan for his work on Chapter 6. Thanks also to Mohr Siebeck for their permission to reproduce this material here.

The very last round of revisions would not have been possible without three friends—Sarit Kattan-Gribetz, Yaacob Dweck, and Mira Balberg—who were willing, on short notice, to make time for reading and commenting on parts of the book. I thank Yaacob also for making my first year back in Princeton so fantastic; and Mira, for reading every revised line and offering valuable comments until the very last minute, and more generally for a strong friendship that has been the most surprising aspect of a career in Talmudic literature. Yair Lipshitz was spared that last round of revision, but he has accompanied this book for a long time with his characteristically supportive, critical, and witty words.

To Tiki and Avi Vidas, thanks for treat shipments from Tel Aviv to Davis and Princeton and for parental guidance that is felt well into adulthood and even from afar.

It is difficult to imagine this project without Carey Seal's companionship, care, and advice; and so this too, as so much else, has been part of that fortunate *beneficiorum quidem sacratissimum ius, ex quo amicitia oritur.*

Bibliography

Agamben, Giorgio. *The Man Without Content* (trans. G. Albert; Stanford, CA: Stanford University Press, 1999)

Albeck, Chanoch. *Introduction to the Mishna* (Heb.; Jerusalem: Bialik Institute and Tel Aviv: Dvir, 1959)

———. *Introduction to the Talmud, Babli and Yerushalmi* (Heb.; Tel Aviv: Dvir, 1969)

———. *Studies in the Baraita and the Tosefta and their Relationship to the Talmud* [2nd ed.] (Heb.; Jerusalem: Mosad Ha-Rav, 1969), 15–43

Aminoah, Noah. "Qit'ei talmud mi-sidur qadum be-masekhet rosh ha-shanah," in *Studies in Rabbinic Literature, Bible, and Jewish History* (ed. Y. D. Gilat; Ramat Gan: Bar Ilan University Press, 1982), 185–97

———. *The Redaction of the Tractate Qiddushin in the Babylonian Talmud* (Heb.; Tel Aviv: Rosenberg School, 1977)

Amit, Aaron. "The Homilies on Mishnah and Talmud Study at the Close of Bavli Bava' Metsi'a' 2 and Yerushalmi Horayot 3: Their Origin and Development," *JQR* 102 (2012), 163–89

Anklesaria, Tehmuras. *Zand-î Vohûman Yasn and Two Pahlavi Fragments: With Text Transliteration and Translation in English* (Bombay, 1957)

Arbel, Vita Daphna. *Beholders of Divine Secrets: Mysticism and Myth in the Hekhalot and Merkavah Literature* (Albany: State University of New York Press, 2003)

Assaf, Simha. *Gaonic Responsa from Geniza Manuscripts* (Heb.; Jerusalem: Darom, 1928)

———. *Tequfat ha-ge'onim ve-sifrutah* (Jerusalem: Mosad Ha-Rav, 1955)

Atlas, Samuel. "Towards a Development of the *sugya* and the *halakha*" (Heb.), *HUCA* 17 (1942), 1–12

Bacher, Wilhelm. *Die Exegetische Terminologie der Jüdischen Traditionsliteratur* (Leipzig: J. C. Hinrichs, 1905)

Bailey, Harold. *Zoroastrian Problems in the Ninth-Century Books* [2nd ed.] (Oxford: Oxford University Press, 1971)

Bar Asher Siegal, Michal. "Shared Worlds: Rabbinic and Monastic Literature,"
    HTR 105 (2012), 423–56
Baum, Wilhelm, and Dietmar Winkler. *The Church of the East: A Concise History*
    (London: Routledge, 2003)
Becker, Adam. "Beyond the Spatial and Temporal Limes: Questioning the
    'Parting of the Ways' Outside the Roman Empire," in *The Ways That Never
    Parted* (ed. A. Becker and A. Y. Reed; Tübingen: Mohr Siebeck, 2004),
    373–92
——. "The Comparative Study of 'Scholasticism' in Late Antique Mesopota-
    mia: Rabbis and East Syrians," *AJS Review* 34.1 (2010), 91–113
——. *Fear of God and the Beginning of Wisdom* (Philadelphia: University of
    Pennsylvania Press, 2004)
Be'eri, Nurit. *Exploring Ta'aniot: Yerualmi, Tractate Ta'aniot: Forming and Re-
    dacting the Traditions* (Heb.; Ramat Gan: Bar Ilan University Press, 2008)
Benovitz, Moshe. *BT Berakhot: Chapter I* (Heb.; Jerusalem: The Society for the
    Interpretation of the Talmud, 2006)
——. *BT Shevu'ot III: Critical Edition with Comprehensive Commentary* (Heb.;
    Jerusalem: Jewish Theological Seminary, 2003)
Biale, David. *Gershom Scholem: Kabbalah and Counter History* (Cambridge, MA:
    Harvard University Press, 1982)
Boustan, Ra'anan S. "The Emergence of Pseudonymous Attribution in Heikha-
    lot Literature: Empirical Evidence from Jewish 'Magical' Corpora," *JSQ* 14
    (2007), 18–38
——. *From Martyr to Mystic: Rabbinic Martyrology and the Making of Merka-
    vah Mysticism* (Tübingen: Mohr Siebeck, 2004)
Boyarin, Daniel. *Border Lines: The Partition of Judeo-Christianity* (Philadelphia:
    University of Pennsylvania Press, 2004)
——. "Hellenism in Jewish Babylonia," in *The Cambridge Companion to the
    Talmud and Rabbinic Literature* (ed. C. E. Fonrobert and M. S. Jaffee; Cam-
    bridge: Cambridge University Press, 2007), 336–63
——. *Socrates and the Fat Rabbis* (Chicago: University of Chicago Press,
    2009)
Braude, William G., and Israel J. Kapstein. *Tanna debe Eliyyahu: The Lore of the
    School of Elijah* (Philadelphia: Jewish Publication Society, 1981)
Brock, Sebastian. *Isaac of Nineveh: "The Second Part," Chapters IV–XLI* (2 vols.;
    Louvain: Peeters, 1995)
Brodsky, David. *A Bride Without a Blessing: A Study in the Redaction and Content
    of Massekhet Kallah and its Gemara* (Tübingen: Mohr Siebeck, 2006)
Brody, Robert. "The Anonymous Talmud and the Words of the Amoraim"
    (Heb.), in *Iggud: Selected Essays in Jewish Studies: Volume 1* (Heb.; ed. B. J.
    Schwartz, A. Shemesh, and A. Melamed; Jerusalem: Magnes, 2009),
    213–32
——. "The Contribution of the Yerushalmi to the Dating of the Anonymous

Material in the Bavli" (Heb.), in *Melekhet Mahshevet: Studies in the Redaction and Development of Talmudic Literature* (ed. A. Amit and A. Shemesh; Ramat Gan: Bar Ilan University Press, 2011), 27–37

———. *The Geonim of Babylonia and the Shaping of Medieval Jewish Culture* (New Haven: Yale University Press, 1998)

———. "Sifrut ha-ge'onim veha-ṭqsṭ ha-talmudi," in *Talmudic Studies I* (ed. Y. Sussmann and D. Rosenthal; Jerusalem: Magnes, 1990), 237–303

———. *Teshuvot rav natronai bar hilai* [2nd ed.] (Jerusalem and Cleveland: Ofeq Institute, 2011)

Brüll, Nehemia. "Die Entstehungsgeschichte des Babylonischen Talmud als Schriftwerkes," in idem, *Jahrbücher für Jüdische Geschichte und Literatur II* (Frankfurt: W. Erras, 1876), 1–123

Burton-Christie, Douglas. *The Word in the Desert: Scripture and the Quest for Holiness in Early Christian Monasticisms* (Oxford: Oxford University Press, 1993)

Carr, David M. *Writing on the Tablet of the Heart* (Oxford: Oxford University Press, 2005)

Carruthers, Mary. *The Book of Memory: A Study of Memory in Medieval Culture* [2nd ed.] (New York: Cambridge University Press, 2008)

———. *The Craft of Thought: Meditation, Rhetoric and the Making of Images, 400–1200* (Cambridge: Cambridge University Press, 1998)

Cereti, Carlo. *Zand ī Wahman Yasn: A Zoroastrian Apocalypse* (Rome: Instituto Italiano per il medio ed estremo oriente, 1995)

Chabot, Jean-Baptiste. "Histoire de Jésus-Sabran: écrite par Jésus-yab d'adiabène," *Nouvelles archives des missions scientifiques et littéraires* 7 (1897), 485–584

Chaumont, Marie-Louise. "Recherches sur le clergé zoroastrien: Le hērbad," *RHR,* 158 (1960), in two parts: 55–80, 161–79

Dan, Joseph. *Ancient Jewish Mysticism* (Heb.; Tel Aviv: Ministry of Defense, 1989)

———. "The Theophany of the Prince of the Torah" (Heb.), *Jerusalem Studies in Jewish Folklore* 13–14 (1992), 127–58

Danzig, Neil. "From Oral Talmud to Written Talmud: On the Methods of Transmission of the Babylonian Talmud and its Study in the Middle Ages," *Bar Ilan* 30–31 (2006), 49–112

———. *Introduction to Halakhot Pesuqot* (Heb.; New York and Jerusalem: Jewish Theological Seminary, 1999)

Daube, David. "The Civil Law of the Mishnah: The Arrangement of the Three Gates," in *The Collected Works of David Daube I: Talmudic Law* (ed. C. M. Carmichael; Berkeley: University of California Press, 1992), 257–304

Davila, James. *Descenders to the Chariot: The People behind the Hekhalot Literature* (Leiden: Brill, 2001)

Dinari, Yedidya. "The Attitude to the Talmudic 'shinuya' in the Rabbinical Literature" (Heb.), *Bar Ilan* 12 (1974), 108–17

Doniger, Wendy. *The Rig Veda: An Anthology* (Harmondsworth: Penguin, 1981)

Drory, Rina. *The Emergence of Jewish-Arabic Literary Contacts at the Beginning of the Tenth Century* (Heb.; Tel Aviv: Ha-Kibbutz ha-me'uhad, 1988)

Dünner, Joseph Hirsch. *Ḥidushei ha-riṣad* (4 vols.; Jerusalem: Mosad Ha-Rav, 1981–99)

Elbaum, Jacob. "Tanna de-be Eliyyahu and the Early Mystical Literature" (Heb.), *Proceedings of the First International Conference on the History of Jewish Mysticism I: Early Jewish Mysticism* (ed. J. Dan; Jerusalem: Hebrew University, 1987), 139–50

Elior, Rachel. "The Concept of God in Hekhalot Literature," *Binah: Studies in Jewish Thought* 2 (1989), 79–129

Elman, Yaakov. "The Babylonian Yeshivot in the Amoraic and Post-Amoraic Era" (Heb.), in *Yeshivot and Battei Midrash* (Heb.; ed. I. Etkes; Jerusalem: Zalman Shazar Center; Ben Zion Dinur Center, 2006), 31–55

———. "Middle Persian Culture and Babylonian Sages: Accommodation and Resistance in the Shaping of Rabbinic Legal Tradition," in *The Cambridge Companion to the Talmud* (ed. C. E. Fonrobert and M. S. Jaffee; Cambridge: Cambridge University Press, 2007), 165–97

———. "Orality and the Redaction of the Babylonian Talmud," *Oral Tradition* 14.1 (1999), 52–99

Emanuel, Simcha. "New Responsa of R. Hai Ga'on" (Heb.), *Tarbiẓ* 69 (2000), 105–26

———. *Newly Discovered Geonic Responsa* (Heb.; Jerusalem and Cleveland: Ofeq Institute, 1995)

Epstein, Jacob. *Introduction to Amoraitic Literature: Babylonian Talmud and Yerushalmi* (Jerusalem: Magnes, 1962)

———. *Introduction to the Mishnaic Text* [3rd ed.] (Heb.; 2 vols.; Jerusalem: Magnes, 2000)

Ets-Hayim, Yehonatan. *Sugyot muḥlafot be-masekhet neziqin* (Heb.; Lod: Haberman, 2000)

Faur, José. *Golden Doves with Silver Dots: Semiotics and Textuality in Rabbinic Tradition* (Bloomington: Indiana University Press, 1986)

Fishman, Talya. *Becoming the People of the Talmud: Oral Torah as Written Tradition in Medieval Jewish Cultures* (Philadelphia: University of Pennsylvania Press, 2011)

Fraade, Steven. *From Tradition to Commentary: Torah and its Interpretation in the Midrash Sifre to Deuteronomy* (Albany: State University of New York Press, 1991)

Frankel, Zacharais. *Einleitung in den Jerusalemischen Talmud* (Heb.; Breslau, 1870)

Friedman, Shamma. *BT Bava Meẓi'a VI: Critical Edition with Comprehensive Commentary: Commentary* (Heb.; New York and Jerusalem: Jewish Theological Seminary, 1990)

————. *BT Bava Meẓ'ia VI: Critical Edition with Comprehensive Commentary: Text* (Heb.; New York and Jerusalem: Jewish Theological Seminary, 1996)

————. "A Critical Study of Yevamot X with a Methodological Introduction" (Heb.), in *Texts and Studies: Analecta Judaica I* (Heb.; ed. H. Z. Dimitrovsky; New York: Jewish Theological Seminary of America, 1977), 275–441

————. "Ha-baraitot ba-talmud ha-bavli ve-yaḥasan le-maqbiloteihen sheba-tosefta," in *Atara L'haim: Studies in the Talmud and Medieval Rabbinic Literature in Honor of Professor Haim Zalman Dimitrovsky* (Heb.; ed. D. Boyarin et al.; Jerusalem: Magnes, 2000), 163–201

————. "On the Formation of Textual Variation in the Bavli" (Heb.), *Sidra* 7 (1991), 67–102

————. *Talmudic Studies: Investigating the Sugya, Variant Readings, and Aggada* (New York and Jerusalem: Jewish Theological Seminary, 2010)

————. "The Transformations of עולם" (Heb.), in *Sha'arei Lashon: Studies in Hebrew, Aramaic, and Jewish Languages Presented to Moshe Bar-Asher* (Heb.; ed. A. Maman et al.; 3 vols.; Jerusalem: Bialik Institute, 2007), 2.272–85

————. "Uncovering Literary Dependencies in the Talmudic Corpus," in *The Synoptic Problem in Rabbinic Literature* (ed. S. J. D. Cohen; BJS 326; Providence: Brown University Press, 2000), 35–57

Friedmann, Meir. *Pseudo-Seder Eliahu Zuta* (Heb.; Vienna: Ahi'asaf, 1904)

————. *Seder Eliahu Rabba und Seder Eliahu Zuta* (Heb.; Vienna: Ahi'asaf, 1902)

Fuchs, Uziel. "The Role of the Geonim in the Textual Transmission of the Babylonian Talmud" (Heb.; Ph.D. dissertation, Hebrew University, 2003)

Gadamer, Hans-Georg. *Truth and Method* [2nd ed.] (trans. J. Weinsheimer and D. G. Marshall; London: Continuum, 2004)

Gafni, Isaiah. *Babylonian Jewry and its Institutions in the Period of the Talmud* (Heb.; Jerusalem: Historical Society of Israel; Zalman Shazar Centre, 1975)

————. *The Jews of Babylonia in the Talmudic Era* (Heb.; Jerusalem: Zalman Shazar Center, 1990)

————. *Land, Center and Diaspora* (Sheffield: Sheffield Academic Press, 1997)

Gignoux, Philippe. "L'apocalyptique iranienne est-elle vraiment la source d'autres apocalypses?" *Acta Antiqua Academiae Scientiarum Hungaricae* 31 (1988), 67–78

————. "Die Religiöse Administration in Sasanidischer Zeit: Ein Überblick," in *Kunst, Kultur und Geschichte der Achämenidzeit und Ihr Fortleben* (ed. H. Koch and D. N. Mackenzie; Berlin: Dietrich Reimer, 1983), 252–66

————. "Sur l'inexistence d'un Bahman Yasht avestique," *JAAS* 32 (1986), 53–64

Gilat, Yitzhak. "Ben shelosh 'esre le-mitzvot?" in *Talmudic Studies I* (Heb.; ed. Y. Sussmann and D. Rosenthal: Jerusalem: Magnes, 1990), 39–53

————. "The Thirty-Nine Classes of Work Forbidden on the Sabbath" (Heb.), *Tarbiẓ* 33 (1960)

Ginzberg, Louis. *A Commentary on the Palestinian Talmud I* (Heb.; New York: Ktav, 1971)

———. *A Commentary on the Palestinian Talmud IV* (Heb.; arranged and edited posthumously by D. Halivni; New York: Jewish Theological Seminary, 1961)

———. *Geniza Studies II: Geonic and Early Karaitic Halakah* (New York: Jewish Theological Seminary, 1929)

———. *Geonica I* (New York: Jewish Theological Seminary, 1909)

———. *Yerushalmi Fragments from the Genizah* (New York: Jewish Theological Seminary, 1909; repr. Hildesheim: Georg Olms, 1970)

Goitein, Shelomo. *Jewish Education in Muslim Countries* (Heb.; Jerusalem: Ben-Tsevi Institute, 1962)

Goldberg, Abraham. *Tosefta Bava Kamma: A Structural and Analytic Commentary* (Heb.; Jerusalem: Magnes, 2001)

Goldenberg, Robert. "Is 'The Talmud' a Document?" in *The Synoptic Problem in Rabbinic Literature* (ed. S.J.D. Cohen; Providence: Brown Judaic Studies, 2000), 3–12

Goodblatt, David. "The History of the Babylonian Academies," in *The Cambridge History of Judaism IV: The Late Roman-Rabbinic Period* (ed. S. T. Katz; Cambridge: Cambridge University Press, 2006), 821–39

Graham, William A. *Beyond the Written Word: Oral Aspects of Scripture in the History of Religion* (Cambridge: Cambridge University Press, 1987)

Gray, Alyssa. "A Bavli *sugya* and its Two Yerushalmi Parallels: Issues of Literary Relationship and Redaction," in *How Should Rabbinic Literature Be Read in the Modern World?* (ed. M. Kraus; Piscataway, NJ: Gorgias, 2006), 35–77

———. *A Talmud in Exile: The Influence of Yerushalmi Avodah Zarah on the Formation of Bavli Avodah Zarah* (Providence: Brown Judaic Studies, 2005)

Graziosi, Barbara. *Inventing Homer: The Early Reception of Epic* (Cambridge: Cambridge University Press, 2002)

Greenfield, Jonas C. "רטין מגושא" (Eng.), in *Joshua Finkel Festschrift* (ed. S. B. Hoenig and L. D. Stitskin; New York: Yeshiva University Press, 1974), 63–69

Groner, Tsvi. "Rav Hai Gaon: His Halachic Methodology" (Heb.; Ph.D. dissertation, Hebrew University, 1974)

Gruenwald, Ithamar. *Apocalyptic Literature and Merkavah Mysticism* (Leiden: Brill, 1980)

———. "New Passages from *Hekhalot* Literature" (Heb.), *Tarbiẓ* 38 (1969), 354–72

Halbertal, Moshe. *Concealment and Revelation: Esotericism in Jewish Thought and its Philosophical Implications* (trans. J. Feldman; Princeton, NJ: Princeton University Press, 2007)

———. *People of the Book: Canon, Meaning, and Authority* (Cambridge, MA: Harvard University Press, 1997)

————. *Values in Interpretation* (Heb.; Jerusalem: Magnes, 1998)

Halevy, Isaac. *Dorot ha-rishonim* (Frankfurt: Jüdische Literarische Gesellschaft, 1906)

Halivni, David. "Aspects of the Formation of the Talmud" (trans. and ed. J. Rubenstein), in *Creation and Composition* (ed. J. Rubenstein; Tübingen: Mohr Siebeck, 2005), 339–60

————. *Midrash, Mishnah and Gemara: The Jewish Predilection for Justified Law* (Cambridge, MA: Harvard University Press, 1986)

————. *MM BB = Sources and Traditions: A Source Critical Commentary on the Talmud: Tractate Baba Bathra* (Heb.; Jerusalem: Magnes, 2007)

————. *MM BM = Sources and Traditions: A Source Critical Commentary on the Talmud: Tractate Baba Metzia* (Heb.; Jerusalem: Magnes, 2003)

————. *MM BQ = Sources and Traditions: A Source Critical Commentary on the Talmud: Tractate Baba Kama* (Heb.; Jerusalem: Magnes, 1993)

————. *MM 'Er. Pes. = Sources and Traditions: A Source Critical Commentary on the Talmud: Tractates Erubin and Pesahim* (Jerusalem: Jewish Theological Seminary, 1982)

————. *MM Mo'ed. = Sources and Traditions: From Yoma to Hagigah* (Heb.; Jerusalem: Jewish Theological Seminary, 1974)

————. "Reflections on Classical Jewish Hermeneutics," *PAAJR* 62 (1996), 19–127

Halperin, David. *Faces of the Chariot: Early Jewish Responses to Ezekiel's Vision* (Tübingen: Mohr Siebeck, 1988)

————. *The Merkavah in Rabbinic Literature* (New Haven: American Oriental Society, 1980)

Harari, Yuval. "La'asot petiḥat lev: praqiṭqot magiyot li-yedi'ah, le-havanah u-lezkhirah bi-yehadut ha-'et ha-'atiqa uvi-yemei ha-beinayim," in *Shefa Tal: Studies in Jewish Thought and Culture* (Bracha Zack Festschrift; ed. Z. Greis et al.; Beer Sheva: Ben Gurion University of the Negev Press, 2004), 303–47

Harris, Jay. *How Do We Know This? Midrash and the Fragmentation of Modern Judaism* (Albany: State University of New York Press, 1995)

Hauptman, Judith. *Development of the Talmudic Sugya: Relationship Between Tannaitic and Amoraic Sources* (Lanham: University Press of America, 1988)

Hayes, Christine E. "Displaced Self-Perceptions: The Deployment of 'mînîm' and Romans in b. Sanhedrin 90b–91a," in *Religious and Ethnic Communities in Later Roman Palestine* (ed. H. Lapin; Bethesda: University Press of Maryland, 1998), 249–89

————. *Gentile Impurities and Jewish Identities* (Oxford: Oxford University Press, 2002)

Herman, Goeffrey. "Ha-kohanim be-bavel bi-tequfat ha-talmud" (master's thesis, Hebrew University, 1998)

Herrmann, Klaus. "Jewish Mysticism in the Geonic Period: The Prayer of Rav Hamnuna Sava," in *Jewish Studies between the Disciplines: Papers in Honor of*

Peter Schäfer on the Occasion of his 60th Birthday (ed. K. Herrmann, M. Schlüter, and G. Veltri; Leiden: Brill, 2003), 180–217

Higger, Michael. *Masekhtot ze'irot* (New York: Bloch, 1929)

Himmelfarb, Martha. "Heavenly Ascent and the Relationship of the Apocalypses and the *Hekhalot* Literature," *HUCA* 59 (1988), 73–100

———. *A Kingdom of Priests: Ancestry and Merit in Ancient Judaism* (Philadelphia: University of Pennsylvania Press, 2006)

Holdrege, Barbara A. *Veda and Torah: Transcending the Textuality of Scripture* (Albany: State University of New York Press, 1995)

Hultgård, Anders. "*Bahman Yasht*: A Persian Apocalypse," in *Mysteries and Revelations: Apocalyptic Studies since the Uppsala Colloquium* (ed. J. J. Collins and J. H. Charlesworth; Sheffield: JSOT Press, 1991), 114–34

———. "Ritual Community Meals in Ancient Iranian Religion," in *Zoroastrian Rituals in Context* (ed. M. Stausberg; Leiden: Brill, 2004), 367–88

Jaafari-Dehagi, Mamoud. *Dādestān ī Dēnīg: Part I: Transcription, Translation and Commentary* (Paris: Association pour l'avancement des Études Iraniennes, 1998)

Jacobs, Louis. *Studies in Talmudic Logic and Methodology* (London and Portland: Vallentine Mitchell, 2006)

———. "The Talmudic Sugya as a Literary Unit," *JJS* 24 (1974), 119–26

Jaffee, Martin. "Oral Transmission of Knowledge as Rabbinic Sacrament: An Overlooked Aspect of Discipleship in Oral Torah," in *Study and Knowledge in Jewish Thought* (ed. H. Kreisel; Beer Sheva: Ben Gurion University of the Negev Press, 2006), 65–79

———. "Rabbinic Authorship as a Collective Enterprise," in *The Cambridge Companion to the Talmud* (ed. C. E. Fonrobert and M. S. Jaffee; Cambridge: Cambridge University Press, 2007), 17–37

———. *Torah in the Mouth: Writing and Oral Tradition in Palestinian Judaism 200 BCE–400 CE* (Oxford: Oxford University Press, 2001)

———. "What Difference Does the 'Orality' of Rabbinic Writing Make for the Interpretation of Rabbinic Writings?" in *How Should Rabbinic Literature Be Read in the Modern World?* (ed. M. Kraus; Piscataway, NJ: Gorgias, 2006), 11–33

Jong, Albert F. de. "Zoroastrian Religious Polemics and their Contexts," in *Religious Polemics in Context* (ed. T. L. Hettema and A. van der Kooij; Assen: Van Gorcum, 2004), 48–63

Kadari, Adiel. "Between Scholars and the General Public in the Synagogue during the Gaonic Period: On the Historical Development of Torah Reading and Scholarly Customs Associated with Public Prayer" (Heb.), *Sidra* 19 (2004), 135–58

———. " 'Talmud Torah' in Seder Eliyahu: The Ideological Doctrine in its Socio-Historical Context" (Heb.), *Daat* 50–52 (2003), 35–59

Kadushin, Max. *Theology of Seder Eliahu* (New York: Bloch, 1932)

Kahana, Menahem. "On the Fashioning and Aims of the Mishnaic Controversy" (Heb.), *Tarbiẓ* 73 (2004), 51–81

Kalmin, Richard. "The Formation and Character of the Babylonian Talmud,"
in *The Cambridge History of Judaism IV: The Late Roman-Rabbinic Period* (ed.
S. T. Katz; Cambridge: Cambridge University Press, 2006), 840–76

———. "Genealogy and Polemics in Literature of Late Antiquity," *Hebrew
Union College Annual* (1996), 77–94

———. *The Redaction of the Babylonian Talmud: Amoraic or Saboraic?* (Cincinnati: Hebrew Union College Press, 1989)

———. *The Sage in Jewish Society of Late Antiquity* (New York: Routledge,
1999)

Kaplan, Julius. *The Redaction of the Babylonian Talmud* (New York: Bloch,
1933)

Kaster, Robert. "Notes on 'Primary' and 'Secondary' Schools in Late Antiquity," *TAPA* 113 (1983), 32–46

Kennedy, George A. *Progymnasmata: Greek Textbooks of Prose Composition and
Rhetoric* (Leiden: Brill, 2003)

Klein, Hyman. "Gemara and Sebara," *JQR* 38 (1947), 67–91

Kotwal, Firoze M., and Philip G. Kreyenbroek. *The Hērbedestān and
Nērangestān* (4 vols.; Paris: Association pour l'avancement des Études Iraniennes, 1992–2009)

Kraemer, David. "The Intended Reader as a Key to Interpreting the Bavli,"
Prooftexts 13 (1993), 125–40

Kreyenbroek, [Philip] G. "The *Dādestān ī Dēnīg* on Priests," *Indo-Iranian Journal* 30 (1987), 185–208

———. "The Zoroastrian Priesthood after the Fall of the Sasanian Empire," in
Transition Periods in Iranian History (Louvain: Association pour
l'avancement des Études Iraniennes, 1987), 151–66

Kutscher, Eduard. *Hebrew and Aramaic Studies* (ed. Z. Ben-Hayyim et al.; Jerusalem: Magnes, 1977)

———. "Marginal Notes to the Article of Mrs. Japhet," *Leshonenu* 31 (1967),
280–82

Kuyt, Annalies. *The "Descent" to the Chariot* (Tübingen: Mohr Siebeck, 1995)

Labendz, Jenny R. "'Know What to Answer the Epicurean': A Diachronic Study
of the 'Apiqoros in Rabbinic Literature," *HUCA* 74 (2003), 175–214.

Lehmhaus, Lennart. "'Were not understanding and knowledge given to you
from Heaven?': Minimal Judaism and the Unlearned 'Other' in *Seder Eliyahu Zuta*," *JSQ* 19 (2012), 230–58

Lehnardt, Andreas. "The Samaritans (Kutim) in the Talmud Yerushalmi," in
The Talmud Yerushalmi and Graeco-Roman Culture III (ed. P. Schäfer; Tübingen: Mohr Siebeck, 2002) 139–60

Lewin, Benjamin M. *Ginze Qedem* (Heb.; Haifa, 1922)

———. *Iggeret rav sherira ga'on* (Haifa, 1921)

—————. *Otzar ha-Geonim: Thesaurus of the Geonic Responsa and Commentaries* (Heb.; 13 vols.; Jerusalem: Hebrew University Press Association, 1928–43)

Lewy, Israel. *Interpretation des I.–VI. Abschnittes des pälast. Talmud-Traktats Nesikin* (Heb. and Ger.; Breslau, 1895–1914; repr. Jerusalem: Kedem, 1970). In abbreviated references, "Vorwort" refers to the German introduction, *Interpretation* to the Hebrew commentary on *y. Neziqin*.

Lieberman, Saul. *Hayerushalmi Kiphshuto* [2nd ed.] (Heb.; ed. M. Katz; New York and Jerusalem: Jewish Theological Seminary, 2008)

—————. *Tosefta Ki-fshuta* (Heb.; 10 vols.; New York: Jewish Theological Seminary, 1955–88)

—————. *Yemenite Midrashim* (Heb.; Jerusalem: Bamberger and Wahrman, 1940)

Macuch, Maria. "Zoroastrian Principles and the Structure of Kinship in Sasanian Iran," in *Religious Themes and Texts of Pre-Islamic Iran and Central Asia* (ed. C. Cereti et al.; Beiträge zur Iranistik 24; Wiesbaden: Reichet, 2003), 231–46

Mann, Jacob. "Changes in the Divine Service of the Synagogue Due to Religious Persecutions," *HUCA* 4 (1927), 241–310

Margulies, Mordechai. *Midrash Haggadol on the Pentateuch: Genesis* (Heb.; Jerusalem: Mosad Ha-Rav, 1947)

—————. *Midrash Wayyikra Rabbah: A Critical Edition Based on Manuscripts and Genizah Fragments with Variants and Notes* (Heb.; 5 vols.; Jerusalem: Ministry of Education and the Epstein Fund of the American Academy of Jewish Research, 1953–60)

Marrou, Henri-Irénée. *Histoire de l'éducation dans l'antiquité* [6th ed.] (Paris: Éditions du Seuil, 1965)

Meir, Abraham S. *Institutions and Titles in the Talmudic Literature* (Heb.; Jerusalem: Mosad Ha-Rav, 1977)

Merchavia, Chen. *The Church Versus Talmud and Midrashic Literature* (Heb.; Jerusalem: Bialik Institute, 1970)

Miller, Stuart. *Sages and Commoners in Late Antique 'Erez Israel: A Philological Inquiry into Local Traditions in Talmud Yerushalmi* (Tübingen: Mohr Siebeck, 2006)

Mookerji, Radhakumud. *Ancient Indian Education, Brahamical and Buddhist* (London: Macmillan, 1947)

Morony, Michael. *Iraq After the Muslim Conquest* (Princeton: Princeton University Press, 1984)

Moscovitz, Leib. "The Formation and Character of the Jerusalem Talmud," in *The Cambridge History of Judaism IV: The Late Roman-Rabbinic Period* (ed. S. T. Katz; Cambridge: Cambridge University Press, 2006), 66–77

—————. *Talmudic Reasoning: From Casuistics to Conceptualization* (Tübingen: Mohr Siebeck, 2002)

—————. *The Terminology of the Yerushalmi: The Principal Terms* (Heb.; Jerusalem: Magnes, 2009)

Na'eh, Shlomo. "Freedom and Celibacy: A Talmudic Variation on Tales of Temptation and Fall in Genesis and its Syrian Background," in *The Book of Genesis in Jewish and Oriental Christian Interpretation* (ed. J. Frishman and L. van Rompay; Leuven: Peeters, 1997), 73–89

———. "Omanut ha-zikaron, mivnim shel zikaron ve-tavniot shel ṭeqsṭ be-sifrut ḥazal," in *Talmudic Studies III* (2 vols.; ed. Y. Sussmann and D. Rosenthal; Jerusalem: Magnes, 2005), 2.543–89

Neusner, Jacob. *Are the Talmuds Interchangeable?* (Atlanta: Scholars Press, 1995)

———. *The Bavli's One Voice: Types and Forms of Analytical Discourse and their Fixed Order of Appearance* (Atlanta: Scholars Press, 1991)

———. *The Discourse of the Bavli: Language, Literature, Symbolism* (Atlanta: Scholars Press, 1991)

———. *Extra- and Non-Documentary Writing in the Canon of Formative Judaism: Volume 3: Peripatetic Parallels* (Binghamton: Binghamton University Global Publications, 2001)

———. *The Reader's Guide to the Talmud* (Leiden: Brill, 2001)

Neusner, Jacob (ed.). *The Formation of the Babylonian Talmud: Studies in the Achievements of Late Nineteenth and Twentieth Century Historical and Literary-Critical Research* (Leiden: Brill, 1970)

Noam, Vered. "The Later Rabbis Add and Innovate: On the Development of a Talmudic *Sugya*" (Heb.), *Tarbiẓ* 72 (2003), 151–75

Novick, Tzvi. " 'They Come Against Them with the Power of the Torah': Rabbinic Reflections on Legal Fiction and Legal Agency," *Studies in Law, Politics and Society* 50 (2009), 1–17

Ong, Walter. *Orality and Literacy: The Technologizing of the Word* (London and New York: Routledge, 1989)

Oppenheimer, Aharon. *Babylonia Judaica in the Talmudic Period* (Wiesbaden: Ludwig Reichert Verlag, 1983)

———. "Purity of Lineage in Talmudic Babylonia" (Heb.), in *Sexuality and Family in History* (ed. I. Gafni and I. Bartal; Jerusalem: Zalman Shazar Center, 1998), 71–82

Rabbinovicz, Raphael N. N. *Variae lectiones: in Mischnam et in Talmud Babylonicum* (15 vols.; Heb.; Munich, 1867–86; repr. Jerusalem, 1959)

Ratner, Baer. *Ahawath Zion We-Jeruscholaim* (10 vols.; Vilnius: Garber, 1917)

Reines, Isaac Jacob. *Ḥotam Tokhnit* [2nd ed.] (published by A. D. Reines; Jerusalem, 1933–34)

Rosen-Zvi, Ishay. "Who Will Uncover the Dust from Your Eyes?: Mishnah Sotah 5 and Rabbi Akiva's Midrash" (Heb.), *Tarbiẓ* 75 (2006), 95–128

Rosenthal, David. "'Al ha-qitzur ve-hashlamto," in *Meḥqerei Talmud III* (ed. Y. Sussmann and D. Rosenthal; 2 vols.; Jerusalem: Magnes, 2005), 791–863

———. "'Arikhot qedumot ha-meshuqa'ot ba-talmud ha-bavli," in *Talmudic Studies I* (ed. Y. Sussmann and D. Rosenthal; Jerusalem: Magnes, 1990), 155–204

————. "Introduction," in *Babylonian Talmud: Codex Florence* (Jerusalem: Makor, 1972)

————. "*Rabbanan de'Siyum'a* (רבנן דסיומא) and *Bene Siyyume* (בני סיומי)" (Heb.), *Tarbiz* 49 (1980), 52–61

————. "The Transformation of Eretz Israel Traditions in Babylonia" (Heb.), *Cathedra* 92 (1999), 7–48

Rosenthal, Eliezer S. "For the Talmudic Dictionary—Talmudica Iranica" (Heb.), *Irano-Judaica* 1 (1982), 38–134

————. "The History of the Text and Problems of Redaction in the Study of the Babylonian Talmud" (Heb.), *Tarbiz* 57 (1988), 1–36

————. "Le-'arikhat masekhet pesaḥ rishon: bavli" (Ph.D. dissertation, Hebrew University of Jerusalem, 1959)

————. "Rav ben aḥi rabbi ḥiyyah gam ben aḥoto?" in *Henoch Yalon: Jubilee Volume* (Heb.; ed. S. Lieberman et al.; Jerusalem: Kiryat Sepher, 1963), 281–337

Rosenthal Eliezer S., and Saul Lieberman. *Yerushalmi neziqin* (Jerusalem: Israel Academy of Sciences and Humanities, 1983)

Rosenthal, Yoav. "On the Early Form of Bavli *Mo'ed Katan* 7b–8a" (Heb.), *Tarbiz* 71 (2008), 45–69

Rubenstein, Jeffrey. *The Culture of the Babylonian Talmud* (Baltimore: Johns Hopkins University Press, 2003)

————. "On Some Abstract Concepts in Rabbinic Literature," *JSQ* 4 (1997), 33–73

————. "The Rise of the Babylonian Rabbinic Academy: A Reexamination of the Talmudic Evidence," *Jewish Studies: an Internet Journal* 1 (2002), 55–68

————. "Some Structural Patterns of Yerushalmi '*sugyot*,' " in *The Talmud Yerushalmi and Graeco-Roman Culture III* (ed. P. Schäfer; Tübingen: Mohr Siebeck, 2002), 303–13

————. *Talmudic Stories: Narrative Art, Composition and Culture* (Baltimore: Johns Hopkins University Press, 1999)

Rustow, Marina. *Heresy and the Politics of Community: The Jews of the Fatamid Caliphate* (Ithaca, NY: Cornell University Press, 2008)

Sabato, Mordechai. *A Yemenite Manuscript of Tractate Sanhedrin and its Place in the Text Tradition* (Heb.; Jerusalem: Yad Ben Zvi; Hebrew University, Department of Talmud, 1998)

Samely, Alexander. *Forms of Rabbinic Literature and Thought: An Introduction* (Oxford: Oxford University Press, 2007)

Satlow, Michael. *Jewish Marriage in Antiquity* (Princeton, NJ: Princeton University Press, 2001)

SBL Handbook of Style (Peabody, MA: Hendrickson, 1999)

Schäfer, Peter. *Hekhalot-Studien* (Tübingen: Mohr Siebeck, 1988)

————. *Jesus in the Talmud* (Princeton, NJ: Princeton University Press, 2007)

————. *The Origins of Jewish Mysticism* (Tübingen: Mohr Siebeck, 2009)

————. "Research into Rabbinic Literature: An Attempt to Define the *Status Quaestionis*," *JJS* 37 (1986), 139–52

Schäfer, Peter (ed.). *Geniza-Fragmente zur Hekhalot-Literatur* (Tübingen: Mohr Siebeck, 1984)

————. *Konkordanz zur Hekhalot-Literatur* (2 vols.; Tübingen: Mohr Siebeck, 1986–88)

————. *Synopse zur Hekhalot Literatur* (Tübingen: Mohr Siebeck, 1981)

————. *Übersetzung der Hekhalot-Literatur* (4 vols.; Tübingen: Mohr Siebeck, 1987–91)

Schiffman, Lawrence H., and Michael D. Swartz. *Hebrew and Aramaic Incantation Texts from the Cairo Genizah* (Sheffield: Sheffield Academic, 1991)

Scholem, Gershom. *Major Trends in Jewish Mysticism* [2nd ed.] (New York: Schocken, 1946; repr. 1995)

————. "Revelation and Tradition as Religious Categories in Judaism" (trans. H. Schwarzschild and M. A. Meyer), in idem, *The Messianic Idea in Judaism* (New York: Schocken, 1971), 282–303

Schremer, Adiel. *Male and Female He Created Them* (Heb.; Jerusalem: Zalman Shazar Center, 2004)

Schwartz, Seth. "Rabbinization in the Sixth Century," in *The Talmud Yerushalmi and Graeco-Roman Culture III* (ed. P. Schäfer; Tübingen: Mohr Siebeck, 2002), 55–69

Secunda, Shai. "Parva—a Magus," in *Shoshannat Yaaqov: Jewish and Iranian Studies in Honor of Yaakov Elman* (ed. S. Secunda and S. Fine; Leiden: Brill, 2012), 391–402

————. "Reading the Bavli in Iran," *JQR* 100.2 (2010), 310–42

Septimus, Zvi. "Trigger Words and Simultexts: The Experience of Reading the Bavli," in *Wisdom of Bat Sheva: The Dr. Beth Samuels Memorial Volume* (ed. B. S. Wimpfheimer; Jersey City: Ktav, 2009), 163–85

Skjærvø, P. Oktor. "Reflexes of Iranian Oral Traditions in Manichean Literature," in *Literarische Stoffe und ihre Gestaltung in mitteliranischer Zeit* (ed. D. Durkin-Meisterernst et al.; Wiesbaden: Ludwig Reichert, 2009), 269–86

Sklare, David E. *Samuel ben Hofni Gaon and his Cultural World* (Leiden: Brill, 1996)

Shaked, Shaul. *Dualism in Transformation: Varieties of Religion in Sasanian Iran* (London: School of Oriental and African Studies, 1994)

————. "Esoteric Trends in Zoroastrianism," PIASH 3 (1969), 175–221

————. "Popular Religion in Sasanian Babylonia," *Jerusalem Studies in Arabic and Islam*, 21 (1997), 103–17

————. "The Yasna Ritual in Pahlavi Literature," in *Zoroastrian Rituals in Context* (ed. M. Stausberg; Leiden: Brill, 2004), 333–44

Shapira, Dan. "Studies in Zoroastrian Exegesis: Zand" (Ph.D. dissertation, Hebrew University of Jerusalem, 1998)

Sharvit, Shimon. *Language and Style of Tractate Avoth Through the Ages* (Heb.; Beer-Sheva: Ben Gurion University of the Negev Press, 2006)

Sinkewicz, Robert E. *Evagrius of Pontus: The Greek Ascetic Corpus: Translation, Introduction, and Commentary* (Oxford: Oxford University Press, 2003)

Small, Jocelyn Penny. *Wax Tablets of the Mind: Cognitive Studies of Memory and Literacy in Classical Antiquity* (London: Routledge, 1997)

Sperber, Daniel. "Qetef melilot," in *Mehkarim ba-sifrut ha-talmudit* (Jerusalem: Israel Academy of Sciences and Humanities, 1983), 193–99

Stern, Sacha. "Attribution and Authorship in the Babylonian Talmud," *JJS* 45 (1994), 28–51

———. "The Concept of Authorship in the Babylonian Talmud," *JJS* 46 (1995), 183–95

Sussmann, Yaacov. "Manuscripts and Text Traditions of the Mishnah" (Heb.), *Proceedings of the Seventh World Congress of Jewish Studies: Volume 3: Studies in the Talmud, Halacha and Midrash* (Jerusalem: Perry Foundation; World Union of Jewish Studies, 1981), 215–50

———. "Torah shebe-'al peh—peshutah ke-mashma'ah," *Talmudic Studies III* (2 vols.; ed. Y. Sussmann and D. Rosenthal; Jerusalem: Magnes, 2005), 209–384

———. "Ve-shuv li-yerushalmi neziqin," in *Talmudic Studies I* (ed. Y. Sussmann and D. Rosenthal; Jerusalem: Magnes, 1990), 55–134

Swartz, Michael. *Mystical Prayer in Ancient Judaism* (Tübingen: Mohr Siebeck, 1992).

———. *Scholastic Magic: Ritual and Revelation in Ancient Judaism* (Princeton, NJ: Princeton University Press, 1996)

Tenenblatt, Mordechai. *The Formation of the Babylonian Talmud* (Heb.; Tel Aviv: Dvir, 1972)

Urbach, Ephraim E. *The Halakhah: Its Sources and Development* (trans. R. Posner; Tel Aviv: Massada, 1986)

———. "Li-she'elat leshono u-meqorotav shel sefer 'seder eliyahu,' " *Leshonenu* 21 (1957), 183–97

———. *The Sages: Their Concepts and Beliefs* (Heb.; Jerusalem: Magnes Press, 1969)

———. *The Tosaphists: Their History, Writings, and Methods* [5th ed.] (Heb.; Jerusalem: Bialik Institute, 1986)

———. "The Traditions on Merkavah Mysticism in the Tannaitic Period" (Heb.), in *Studies in Mysticism and Religion* (ed. E. E. Urbach, R. J. Weblowsky, and Ch. Wirszubski; Jerusalem: Magnes, 1967), 1–28

Vidas, Moulie. "The Bavli's Genealogy Discussion of Genealogy in Qiddushin IV," in *Antiquity in Antiquity: Jewish and Christian Pasts in the Greco-Roman World* (ed. G. Gardner and K. Osterloh; Tübingen: Mohr Siebeck 2008), 285–326

Wald, Stephen G. *BT Pesahim III: Critical Edition with Comprehensive Commentary* (Heb.; New York and Jerusalem: Jewish Theological Seminary, 2000)

Walker, Joel. *Legend of Mar Qardagh: Narrative and Christian Heroism in Late Antique Iraq* (Berkeley: University of California Press, 2006)

Weber, Max. *Economy and Society: An Outline of Interpretive Sociology* (ed. G. Roth and C. Wittich; 2 vols.; Berkeley: University of California Press, 1968)

———. *From Max Weber: Essays in Sociology* [2nd ed.] (ed. and trans. H. H. Gerth and C. Wright Mills; London: Routledge, 1991)

Weiss, Abraham. *Studies in the Law of the Talmud on Damages* (Heb.; Jerusalem and New York: Philipp Feldheim, 1966)

———. *Studies in the Literature of the Amoraim* (Heb.; New York: Horeb Yeshiva University Press, 1972)

———. *The Talmud in its Development* (Heb.; New York: Feldheim, 1954)

Westreich, Avishalom. "The Crystallization and Development of the Pebbles Ruling in the Words of the Tannaim, in the Words of the Amoraim and in the Talmuds" (Heb.), *Sidra* 19 (2004), 77–100

Wimpfheimer, Barry. *Narrating the Law: A Poetics of Talmudic Legal Stories* (Philadelphia: University of Pennsylvania Press, 2011)

Yadin-Israel, Azzan. "Rabbi Aqiva: Midrash as the Site of Revelation," in *Revelation, Literature and Community in Antiquity* (ed. P. Townsend and M. Vidas; Tübingen: Mohr, 2011), 181–221

Yates, Frances. *The Art of Memory* (London: Routledge, 1966)

Zohar, Noam. "Scripture, Mishnah and Thought: Redaction and Meaning at the Beginning of Tractate Neziqin" (Heb.), in *By the Well: Studies in Jewish Philosophy and Halakhic Thought Presented to Gerald J. Blidstein* (Heb.; ed. U. Ehrlich, H. Kreisel, and D. J. Lasker; Beer Sheva: Ben Gurion University Press, 2008), 195–208

Zunz, Leopold. *Die Gottesdienstlichen Vorträge der Juden Historisch Entwickelt* [2nd ed.] (Heb.; trans. and ed. Ch. Albeck; Jerusalem: Bialik Institute, 1974)

Source Index

Hebrew Bible
Exodus
    19:19 179
    20:14 179
    21–22 26
    21:28 59
    22:30 55n30, 71–74
Leviticus
    4:27–29 125
Deuteronomy
    4:9 182
    14:21 71–73, 73n61
Joshua
    1:8 133n38
2 Samuel
    23:5 186
2 Kings
    24:16 175–76
Nehemiah
    7:61 103n40
Psalms
    109:18 185
    146:8 51
Proverbs
    24 143, 145n64
    24:21 144
    24:21–22 143n60
Song of Songs
    1:3 138
    1:6 184n51
Isaiah
    2:3 175
    6:3 200
    48:4 175
    66:5 159

Ezekiel
    3:12 200
    38:8 201
Haggai
    2:9 179
    2:20–23 180
Zechariah
    6:9–15 180
Malachi
    2:5 51
    3:3 87–88, 90–91

Mishnah
Sheqalim
    4:7 193
Hagigah
    2:1 187–88
Sotah
    3:4 136
Qiddushin
    3:13 83n3
    4:1 82
Bava Qamma
    1:1 26
    1:4 31n18, 37
    2:1 37
Bava Metzi'a
    2:11 118
Avot
    4:13 125
Horayot
    3:8 83n2
Tosefta
Yevamot
    13:2 193

Sotah
  7:12 182
Qiddushin
  5:4 90n21
Bava Qamma
  1:1 40n35
  1:5 38
  2:22–3:24 38
Bava Metziʻa
  2:30 119n5

Halakhic Midrashim
Mekhilta deRabbi Ishmael
  Bo §16 (Horowitz-Rabin
    61–62) 60n38
  Be-shalaḥ petiḥta (Horowitz-Rabin
    76) 185
  Pisḥa §5 (Horowitz-Rabin 15)
    132n37
Sifre Deuteronomy
  §10 (Finkelstein 18) 191n76
  §104 (Finkelstein 163) 71n58
  §321 (Finkelstein 370) 175n18
Sifre to Numbers
  Shalaḥ §112 on Num 15:30 (Kahana
    13–14) 132n37

Palestinian Talmud
  Berakhot
    1:4 (3d) 52–53
    5:1 (9a) 181
  Peʼah
    2:6 (17a) 6
  ʻOrlah
    3:1 (62d) 35, 56n31, 59
  Shabbat
    16:1 (15c) 121n11
    16:1 (16c) 122
  Pesahim
    2:1 (28c) 54–59
  Moʻed Qatan
    3:7 (83b) 119n5
  Hagigah
    2:1 (77c) 187
  Yevamot
    8:3 (8d) 73n61
    8:3 (9d) 86n11, 100n35
  Sotah
    3:4 (19a) 137
  Qiddushin
    4:1 (65c) 85–87, 90n21, 98n34,
      100n35, 107n44

Bava Qamma
  1:1 (2a) 32n21, 33n24
  2:1 (2d) 38
Bava Metziʻa
  2:11 (8d) 119n5
Sanhedrin
  1:2 (19a) 176
  10:1 (27d) 132n36
Horayot
  3:7 (48b) 119n5
  3:8 (48c) 121–22

Babylonian Talmud
  Berakhot
    12a 52–53
    47b 141n55
  Shabbat
    63b 189
    114b 144n63
  ʻEruvin
    53b-54a 186
    69b 193
  Pesahim
    21b 63
    21b-22a 72–72
    21b-23b 62
    49b 129, 129n25
  Taʼanit
    4a 176
    7a 177
  Megillah
    16b 170, 175
    28b 128n23, 139n48, 140
  Hagigah
    5b 175
  Ketubbot
    23b 193
  Sotah
    21b-22a 136–37
    22a 128n23, 140, 142, 144,
      151–52
    22b 143
    28b 144
  Gittin
    17a 193
    88a 175, 175n18
  Qiddushin
    5b 193
    49a-b 128n23
    56b 64n48, 73n62
    70a 101

70b   102n37, 104, 108–9, 135n43
70b-71a   85–86, 89–90, 90n21
71a   96, 98–99
72a   97–98
72b   102n37
73a   107
Bava Qamma
    2a-b   29
    2b   31–32
    2a-3b   26
    3b   33n23, 34–35, 42
    17b   39, 41
    17b-19a   39
    18b   33
    28b   33n23
    41a   64n48, 73n62
    50b   33n23
Bava Metzi‘a
    33a   118–19
    33a-b   118, 123, 159
    33b   124, 126–27
Bava Batra
    130b   145
    133b   162
Sanhedrin
    24a   177
    97a   196–97
    99b   132n37, 133
Hullin
    114b   64n48, 73n62

Other Rabbinic Works
Abot de-Rabbi Nathan, A
    18   192n80
Derek Eretz Zutta
    10:4   128n23
Midrash ha-Gaddol
    Marguiles, Midrash Haggadol
    2.688   197, 197n92
(Pseudo) Seder Eliyahu Zutta
    16 (Friedmann 5)   128–130
    16 (Friedmann 8)   145n64
Seder Eliyahu Rabbah
    6 (Friedmann 37)   138
    7 (Friedmann 32)   184n51
Seder Eliyahu Zutta
    2 (Friedmann 173)   144n62

Hekhalot Literature
Geniza Fragments
    T-S. K 21.95 C (G8)   180n30, 198, 201

T-S. K 21.95 G (G22)   173n13, 191–
    95, 201
Schäfer, Synopse
    §77   194n85
    §281–98   169
    §280   171
    §283   174
    §284   171, 185
    §287   172
    §288a   172
    §288b   172
    §289   172, 185
    §291   169
    §293   174, 185
    §297–98   178
    §298   179
    §300   200
    §308–9   180
    §335   186
    §336   189n66, 190
    §388   194n85
    §419   200
    §449   191
    §556   183
    §562   186
    §563   186
    §569   183
    §678   182
    §706   186, 200

Zoroastrian Sources
Dādestān ī Dēnīg
    40   155–56
    46   153–55
    65   154, 156
Zand ī Wahman Yasn
    4:39–40   158
    4:49–59   159n28

Syriac Christian Sources
Ascetic Homilies of Isaac of Nineveh, Sec-
    ond Part
    10:6   165
    21:1   165
    22:1–3   164
    22:4   165
    29:10   165
    30:4–5   165
Life of Isho‘sabran   162–63

Subject Index

abstraction, legal, 11, 29, 31n16, 33n24, 39, 64n48, 65–67
academy, 15, 18–19, 27, 71, 74, 78, 116–17, 143, 146–48, 166–67, 169, 171–74, 178–79, 185, 198, 202, 207–8
Agamben, Giorgio, 14–15, 19
Amit, Aaron, 121–22
Arbel, Vita Daphna, 188
authority, 7, 74, 77, 79, 82–84, 97, 99–100, 104n41, 110, 116, 134, 138, 173, 202, 204, 206–7, 209–10

Barthes, Roland, 8
Becker, Adam, 163–64
Benjamin, Walter, 14
Benovitz, Moshe, 49, 49n17
Boyarin, Daniel, 5, 25, 46, 110–11
Brody, Robert, 47–49

Chaumont, Marie–Louise, 152
Christian parallels to rabbinic practice, 18, 160–166, 206. *See also* recitation, Christian

damages: attested vs. innocent, 37–39; direct vs. indirect, 39–41; "fathers" and "offspring" of , 26–44
Dan, Joseph, 171, 174, 178
Danzig, Neil, 146

Elior, Rachel, 188
Elman, Yaakov, 62–63n45, 132n65, 134
Epicurean, 132–34

Fishman, Talya, 207n2, 208n4, 212n21
Foucault, Michel, 8

Frankel, Zacharias, 53
Friedman, Shamma, 4–5, 9, 24–25, 45–49, 69–70

Gadamer, Hans–Georg, 7
genealogical status, 15–16, 81–111, 204; in Babylonia vs. Palestine, 84, 92–93, 92n26, 96–97, 106, 106–7n44; role of in eschatological purification, 85–91, 94–95; rabbinic constructions of prior to the Bavli, 83–88, 94–95, 101
Geonim and Geonic period, 3n5, 146, 146n68, 168, 189, 196, 198–202, 207–12; Hayya, 168, 168n5, 196, 196n88, 196n90, 200; Natronai, 193, 196n88, 199, 201, 210n13; Sherira, 209–11, 209n9; Yehudai, 207–8, 208n4
Goitein, Shlomo, 189
Greenfield, Jonas, 152, 160–61
Gruenwald, Ithamar, 198, 201

Halbertal, Moshe, 188
Halivni, David Weiss, 4–5, 10, 23–24, 27–28, 33, 45–46, 49, 69, 72
hāwišt. See Zoroastrian clergy
Hekhalot literature, 19, 167–202, 205
hērbed. See Zoroastrian clergy

identity and self–conception, rabbinic, 16–18, 115–16, 124–31, 136, 140, 147–48, 161, 205–7. See also tanna'im ("reciters") and "masters of mishnah"
Islam and Islamic period, 153, 158–59, 164, 212

Jacob b. Meir (Tam), 209
Jacobs, Louis, 27–28, 36
Jaffee, Martin, 75, 138

Kalmin, Richard, 106n44
Karaites, 207, 212
Kreyenbroek, Philip, 153

layered structure, creation of, 4, 9–10,
14–15, 23, 48, 53–54, 64–66, 69–70,
76–80, 204, 210
literary design: of the Babylonian Talmud, 2–3, 24, 27–28, 35, 45, 54, 69–
70, 79, 81; of the Palestinian Talmud,
59–62. *See also* layered structure, creation of
liturgy, 140, 148, 148n73, 167, 191–92,
195, 198, 200–1. *See also* synagogue

magical practice, 170, 172, 174, 185, 194,
197, 200. See also Sar ha–Torah
narrative
magus. *See* Zoroastrian clergy
mamzerim/–ot. See genealogical status
memorization, 16–17, 19, 70, 75, 78,
115–17, 120–21, 133, 140, 144, 146,
149, 152, 157, 166, 168–70, 181, 184,
186, 189–90, 192, 195, 202, 206, 211.
See also oral performance; oral transmission; recitation; tanna'im ("reciters") and "masters of mishnah"
midrash, 87, 124–25, 129, 173, 180, 199–
200, 211n17, 212n22; midrash halakhah 120, 122, 211n17
mishnah. See tradition, oral

Moscovitz, Leib, 11, 51

Na'eh, Shlomo, 181–82, 192
Neusner, Jacob, 5–6, 12–13

Ong, Walter, 15, 76–77
oral performance, 8, 45, 70–71, 74–78,
204–5. *See also* memorization; recitation; tanna'im ("reciters") and "masters of mishnah"; tradition, oral
oral transmission, 48, 76–79, 116–17,
208. *See also* memorization; recitation;
tanna'im ("reciters") and "masters of
mishnah"; tradition, oral

Palestinian Talmud, parallel *sugyot* with
the Babylonian Talmud, 50–70, 72–73,
84–86, 89–96, 100, 121–24; differences in attribution in, 64–67; different uses of anonymous layer in, 51,
65–70
performance. *See* oral performance
pilpul, 172–73, 177
Pirqoy ben Baboy, 207–8
power, political. *See* authority
prayer, 51–53
prohibition on deriving benefit from prohibited substances, 54–59, 63–64,
71–72
public domain, 38–39, 42–43

Rashi, 97n33, 139, 141, 210
recitation: Christian, 150, 160, 162–66
(*see also* Christian parallels to rabbinic
practice); rabbinic, 17–19, 115–16,
127, 133–34, 137–41, 148–49, 166–
68, 186, 188–92, 194–96, 200–2, 205–
6, 211, 213 (*see also* memorization;
oral performance; oral transmission;
tanna'im ("reciters") and "masters of
mishnah"); Zoroastrian, 18, 140–41,
150–57, 161, 163, 165–66, 206 (*see
also* Zoroastrian clergy)
Reines, Isaac, 29, 36
responsa, 193, 196–97, 199
Rosenthal, Eliezer S., 9, 11
Rubenstein, Jeffrey, 5, 11, 25

Sar ha–Torah narrative, 19, 167, 169–180,
182, 184, 197–98, 200, 202
Satlow, Michael, 95n31
savora'im, 3, 3n5, 24
Schäfer, Peter, 187, 201
Scholem, Gershom, 6–7, 167
Schremer, Adiel, 106
Sussmann, Yaakov, 5, 10, 48
synagogue, 19, 148, 148–49n73, 195n87,
198–201. *See also* liturgy

tanna'im ("reciters") and "masters of *mishnah*", 17–19, 78, 116–17, 128, 130,
131, 140–48, 151–52, 157–58, 160–
62, 167–68, 190–93, 195–201, 205,
211–12. *See also* memorization; recitation, rabbinic

Torah study, 19, 78, 115–17, 120, 125–26, 131, 139, 141, 167, 169–80, 202, 210, 212

Torah, Written vs. Oral, 116, 129, 134, 138, 141. *See also* oral performance; oral transmission;

tradition, oral; writing and written texts

tort law. *See* damages

Tosafists, 210

tradition: conservation and preservation of, 3, 24, 82, 203, 211; continuity with, 1–2, 4–7, 24; distance from and discontinuity with, 2, 13–15, 25, 44, 78–79, 81–82, 111, 205–6, 210; innovation and creativity in, 4–5, 24–25, 35–36, 48–49, 70–79, 82, 100, 115–17, 121, 127, 132–36, 147, 203–4, 207–8, 210–11; oral, 17, 116, 119–22, 140, 148, 181, 192–94, 206 (*see also* oral performance; oral transmission; *tanna'im* ["reciters"] and "masters of *mishnah*"; Zoroastrian clergy); reformulation of, 4–5, 9, 11, 60, 81, 82, 84, 100, 111, 190; transmission of, 2, 5, 17, 19, 45, 48–49, 70–78, 99, 115–17, 136, 139, 141, 147–48, 152, 167–69, 193, 196, 203, 205–8, 210–12 (*see also* oral transmission)

Urbach, Ephraim, 129, 171, 174

Wald, Stephen, 129
Weber, Max, 7
Weiss, Abraham, 30
Westreich, Avishalom, 37n31
Wimpfheimer, Barry, 110–11
writing and written texts: rabbinic, 70, 70nn55–56, 75, 77–78, 140, 147, 196n88, 208, 213; Zoroastrian, 152, 163, 165, 206

Zoroastrian clergy, 18, 139–41, 150–56, 161–65. *See also* recitation, Zoroastrian; *tanna'im* ("reciters") and "masters of *mishnah*"; Zoroastrian parallels to rabbinic practice

Zoroastrian parallels to rabbinic practice, 18, 150–63, 206. *See also* recitation, Zoroastrian,

Zoroastrian clergy